Teach the Children

An Agency Approach to Education

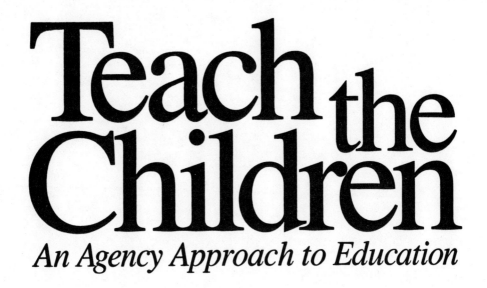

Teach the Children

An Agency Approach to Education

Neil J. Flinders

Book of Mormon Research Foundation
Provo, Utah

What Others Have Said About
Teach the Children

"*Teach the Children* . . . is indeed a rare [and] remarkable compendium of value centered thought on the entire field of education. Without apology and with careful research, Dr. Flinders has brought together eternal concepts of teaching designed equally for professional and lay audiences. It is an education in itself to read this book."

Kay J. Andersen, Former Executive Director, Accrediting Commission for Senior Colleges and Universities Western Association of Schools and Colleges

"Neil J. Flinders, who is no stranger to educational theory, identifies his latest work, *Teach the Children*, as a "non-conventional" approach to education. Unconventional . . . it is, because it is couched in the needs of the learner due to (1) the natural situation of mankind as a result of the fall of Adam, (2) the premises of the gospel of Jesus Christ as providing the needed eternal perspective, and (3) the home and family as a natural unit suited for teaching. [This book] is apparently the most extensive educational plan yet assembled using the revealed facts from the scriptures in determining how people can best be taught."

Robert J. Matthews, Former Dean, Religious Education, Brigham Young University

"False educational ideas are rampant in our day. Unfortunately the victims of these worldwide forces are innocent children, often our own. *Teach the Children* awakens us to the responsibility we have to teach our children in truth and light, in the way of the Lord, according to the Eternal Plan. A courageous author skillfully presents an agency model of education that provides parents, children, and teachers a work that deserves to be carefully pondered (often)—a marvelous resource."

Pamela McCoy, Director, Zion Institute for Children

1

"Teach the Children. . . is a provocative book. It provides a significant alternative to much of what we see in the education of children today. It is thoughtful in that it invites the reader to reason through the issues and concerns of educating our youth. Agency education conveys that the individual is literally the agent in directing his behavior. The content of the book exemplifies eternal principles as the driving force in bringing desired change in a learner's life."

Dan W. Andersen, Dean, College of Education,
Brigham Young University

"For those who believe in divine help in the teaching of children in homes, churches, and schools, this book is a must. It is the most comprehensive statement to date of what scripturally based education really is. . . . Both professional educators and public school watchers will benefit from its historical insights on how and why things have gone wrong. More important, it offers hope and specific advice to individuals in any setting who want education in both sacred and secular subjects to be in the pattern of the nurture and admonition of the Lord. For parents like myself who need the help of heaven to raise righteous children in a difficult world, this statement of Agency Education indeed represents a more excellent way. . . . It also points the way to troubled parents who sense intuitively that something is askew in our education system and that they can and should do something about it."

A. Garr Cranney, Parent and Professor of Education,
Brigham Young University

"Do we have what it takes to make a difference in our children's education? Parents struggling with this question will find encouragement, hope, and ideas which speak with positive familiarity in *Teach the Children.* New insights . . . are brought together in ways that have motivated us and increased our faith in our ability to be teacher-parents. We believe this book has helped us discover capacities in ourselves . . . not always apparent; capacities based on our faith in each other, in our value to our Father, and in the divine nature of our stewardships. . . . With Father's help and our children's agency, all good things are possible. We can make a difference in our childrens' education."

Larrie and Nell Gale, Parents
Professor of Communications and homemaker.

"A book that will surely provoke the reader to ponder the purpose and focus of formal education, . . . [to] reflect upon the past, survey the present, then forge ahead with renewed vigor to be prepared to educate in a better way."

James W. Dunn, Department Chairman of
Elementary Education, Brigham Young University

"It is refreshing for an author to recognize that education . . . has wrongfully abandoned two basic assumptions of American freedom: (1) Individuals have the ability to freely choose and accept the consequences of those choices; and (2) Our institutions presuppose the existence of a Supreme Being. Dr. Flinders unabashedly accepts and builds on these Christian beliefs. . . . His disclosure and clear analysis of modern day assumptions offers a welcome change. Too often, these faulty assumptions go unnoticed and unchallenged. This book offers a 'pair of glasses' through which the reader can better see and understand the complex challenges our legal institutions have imposed on current educational policies and practices."

3

Matthew M. F. Hilton, J. D., Ph. D. , Director,
International Institute for Inalienable Rights

"As an educator and counselor in the public school system, I am always interested in improving the quality of education and the quality of young people. . . . Dr. Flinders' agency approach to learning is both enlightening and exciting. The concept of a student being accountable for his/her learning and behavior is the highest goal, as far as I am concerned, in education and in life. I look forward to having the book printed so I may study it further and develop it in my own work with children."

Mary L. Jones, M. Ed., School Counselor

"Though beneficial to professional teachers, *Teach the Children* is especially valuable to parents and children. We read it with gratitude knowing that its contents would greatly bless our children. It is a book of direction clearly pointing parents to their proper roles as a child's most important teachers. It is a book of hope—our children will be taught correctly by anyone applying the book's contents. Nowhere outside of the scriptures has so much been compiled to help parents correctly direct their children's education."

Perry and Jana Bratt, Parents,
Businessman and Homemaker

"This is a remarkably profound and well documented book which evokes a great deal of soul searching and reflection on the part of the reader. . . .The responsibility to teach more wisely and righteously in harmony with gospel principles is magnified. When prayerful in my preparations, I have found that much of what I have been inspired to do is found in the counsel given in *Teach the Children*. . . .Agency education is indeed the way to prepare us to live as a Zion people."

Sally M. Todd, Educational Psychologist,
Co-author, You and the Gifted Child

"The simple style of this book belies the complexity of the implications it raises for modern education. If we take the ideas of "Agency Education" seriously, much of our current practice must be questioned. For example, consider the idea of believing in a living God who continues to speak to man and who should not be ignored in the process we call education. . . . Should preparing to fulfill one's personal mission actually take precedence over social certification? Could it be permissible to leave lesson plans open-ended and objectives subject to divine redefinition? Is it possible that great teaching cannot be reduced to applied methods or best practices, or measurable outcomes? Neil Flinders is calling for a revolution of the heart."

A. LeGrand Richards, Philosophy Department,
Brigham Young University

4

FOREWORD

This book is about a specific approach to education.

In recognition that an education system is an expression of the history and culture of a people, the author has drawn upon a lifetime of research and study to stimulate the reader with a diversity of material which is organized in three parts to introduce a stimulating approach to education. The approach is based upon sound and enduring principles.

This is not a conventional text. It introduces the dimension of "divine purpose" while examining physical, intellectual, moral, and spiritual lifestyles.

In 1830 Joseph Smith, the Mormon prophet, offered a unique and comprehensive view of education, pointing out that its central mission cannot be divorced from the redemptive power of Jesus Christ. The thread of that unique view is interwoven throughout this book by the author.

Orson F. Whitney records that "Education is creation, but the educator does not create the faculties of the pupil any more than a gardener creates the constituents of a tree. He cannot compel the mind; he can only incite and encourage it, educating or leading out its faculties, thus converting the potential into the actual. This is the highest glory of the educator, it is the acme of his achievement. All development is the result of co-operation between the cultivator and the thing being cultivated" ("The School of Life," *Millennial Star* Vol. 67, p. 499).

The author clearly points out that education in its finest form connects the highest human purpose with proper personal development and that it should promote rather than deny man's divinely bestowed gift of free agency, thus giving credence to the postulate that order and choice are essential ingredients in effective education. The development of personal character is at the very center of the learning enterprise, which, it is pointed out, includes right actions, good thoughts, and correct intentions.

Everyone participates in an educational journey; some journeys are short, some long; some difficult, and some less difficult: Each person is striving for perfection, blinded by the craftiness of men, and/or seeking gratification at each juncture.

The purpose of any education is to make people think. The author—a gentleman, loyal friend, and true servant—has carefully weighed the theories, principles, and practices as he presents relationships of Man to God, Man to Man, and Man to Things. The metaphors are easily understood.

The contents will make the reader think.

I commend this book to parents, teachers, students, and all who are interested in increasing in "wisdom, and stature, and favor with God and man."

J. Elliot Cameron
Former Commissioner, Church Educational System
Past President, BYU—Hawaii

Preface

If I would travel the Holy Land—
   I need not travel far,
For the Kingdom borders near at hand
   Where the feet of the children are.[1]

Companion to the feeling elicited by these words of the poet, is the expression of love in the biblical declaration "I have no greater joy than to hear that my children walk in truth" (3 John 4).

It is sobering to try to say something that may affect the life of a child; I feel the weight of this sacred responsibility. I am acutely aware of Jesus' warning: "Whoso shall offend one of these little ones which believe in me, it were better for him that a millstone were hanged about his neck, and that he were drowned in the depth of the sea" (Matt. 18:6). Knowing this, I have tried, given my limitations, to write the truth. Why take the risk? Because I feel the responsibility to act more than I fear the penalty for honest error.

Children deserve a better choice than the current options of education based on behaviorism or humanism or the various mixtures of the two. Agency education, a restorationist view, is a better alternative for those who believe in it. This book amply contrasts the underlying premises of three major approaches to learning and teaching—behavioristic, humanistic, and agency-oriented education. The territory is familiar, but some of the contrasts become strikingly more vivid when they are laid side by side.

Today's educators, for example, argue for understanding from at least six different positions: (1) *Philosophy*, which summarizes the "isms"—pragmatism, realism, idealism, existentialism, etc. The assumption is that sound education develops from the knowledge and skills of philosophy. (2) *History*, where the focus is on a map of the past. Past records, it is assumed, are an essential source of meaning for present and future education. (3) *Literature*, a forum that displays great minds discoursing on great issues. From this angle people feel the education for the best of us is the best education for all of us. (4) *Sociology*, which dedicates itself to analyzing contemporary issues. Education is considered to be an expression of social forces that need to be understood and directed for the good of society. (5) *Psychology*, holding to the proposition that human nature and its functions can be understood scientifically. In this sector education is viewed as a branch of psychology and it is defined in terms of various theories—psychological theory, learning theory, instructional theory, motivational theory, etc. This position dominates the professional ranks of modern education. (6) *Anti-Intellectualism*, a position held by many who feel that education flows naturally from common sense and personal experience. Disciplines of study, they say, distort the truths of reality by both their methods and their narrow perspective. While recognizing there is value in each of the foregoing areas, the assumption in this book is that the *Gospel of Christ* embraces a better set of premises for understanding and developing effective education. The content that follows describes an approach to education based on assumptions, propositions, and illustrations the writer believes are in harmony with the life and teachings of Jesus of Nazareth.

Agency education, unlike its competition, is not earthbound. Those who favor sheltered places, or fear they cannot change, who look to roads well traveled, may shy away from the challenges of agency education. But those whose restless arms lift upward, who admire peaks and clouds, who dream of flights on eagle's wings, will probably relish the challenges in this book. Each reader is free to choose—to accept or reject.

Modern communities lack a clear vision capable of creating a consensus on basic values and their education suffers from a deficiency in moral order. Where there is agreement it is usually tentative and where there is disagreement it seems to be significant. The common response to problems in contemporary education is to complain about a lack of dollars, materials, and facilities. But the most fundamental issues we face cannot be resolved simply by allocating more money, newer books and technology, and better facilities. The need is evident to free ourselves from following conflicting value structures—believing that right and wrong are different at home, at school, at work, and at play. The current doctrine that all value choices are correct—depending on the period, place, and people—must be replaced with principles of right and wrong that transcend personal desires or social norms. The challenge is to rise above the earthbound educational theory that has dominated the twentieth century.

Those who embrace agency education will need courage, patience, and vision. The learner is given greater opportunity to exercise the powers of responsible choice; encouragement is given to seek and direct the preparation that will enable each individual to better fulfill his or her personal mission in life. Agency education requires lofty expectations, clear standards, an expanded concept of scholarship, a revision of thinking regarding grades, assessment, and evaluation, and a greater role for effective parenting. Practicing a better form of education is not easy, it calls for a commitment that is rooted in faith. The twenty-first century needs a generation whose parents have prepared them to receive their Savior. Latter-day Saints should lead the way.

Many reviewers read this manuscript in its various stages of development, readers from various walks of life and with different points of view. In addition to numerous helpful suggestions, they left the writer with one particularly frustrating conflict—matching the message to a diverse audience. The conflict has not been resolved. Therefore, I introduce this book by explaining my dilemma and requesting the readers' help. I know the rule that a writer should never begin with an apology. At times, however, honesty requires one.

Publishers for the general Church market who reviewed the manuscript were generous in their praise, but concluded the material was too scholarly. Academic critics admired the content and unique perspective, but felt a more precise vocabulary and an expansion of analytical detail was necessary. Some college students found the number of ideas per page too great, while several public school teachers felt the many insights increased the book's usefulness as a reference text. Parents suggested I include more instructions on how to apply the ideas in their homes; readers sensitive to the agency principle wondered if I had become too prescriptive. Professional teachers liked the principles but doubted they would receive administrative support. Nearly every reader said the content was inspiring; some felt it too revealing. "Is the gap between what we recognize as true and where we operate really that wide?" they asked. I could go on, but this illustrates the dilemma.

In response to these conflicting perceptions, I present the material as simply and clearly as I can while supplying details that illustrate the breadth and depth of the message. Readers who prefer a single idea illustrated by several stories will have to stretch a little; those who prefer a very technical treatment with carefully structured proofs will need to exercise forbearance. All readers can profit from the book, I think. Perhaps in time the ideas will be clothed in other wardrobes. I appreciate readers who are willing to look beyond the book's current limitations.

Readers familiar with the scriptural foundations underlying this book may wonder why the temporal economics of agency education were not addressed more directly. The confusion and downward spiral of motives associated with prosperity and security, the unequal distribution of wealth, and the increasing propensity for crime and war is apparent to many. Most individuals recognize that current popular economic orders are driven by greed, power, and pride. Some people are sensitive to the divine alternative to these faulty economic orders. (A recently published study has explored the foundations of these matters in considerable detail.[2]) Important as economic contexts are, however, distinguishing between true and false educational ideas appears more critical. The world's way of doing business is to set our hearts on the things of this earth; education is frequently the tool used to accomplish this purpose. Because individual corrections in education can be implemented more easily than modifying economic systems, the focus in this book is on seeking and establishing moral and intellectual rather than economic order.

The list of those who helped me on this project is longer than my memory—students, colleagues, reviewers, and editors. I appreciate those who generously endorsed this book. I recognize that their witness is to the materials I have used that represent Jesus Christ and his love for us. Without the Spirit, and the loyalty of my parents, wife, children, and grandchildren, this book could not have been written. To all of these people and many others, I express deep and sincere appreciation. Notwithstanding this invaluable assistance, I alone stand responsible for what I have written. I share what I believe without presuming to be a spokesman for any group or organization with which I am affiliated.

NJF

vi

Author's Note:

Gender references in this book follow an alternating pattern. The inclusive "man" and "him" were applied where it was gramatically awkward to refer to both "he/she" or "him/her." Citations in this book from scriptural sources are placed in the text, other references are cited in endnotes at the conclusion of the book. Abbreviations include the following (all published by the Church of Jesus Christ of Latter-day Saints):

CR=*Conference Report* (Published reports of annual and semi-annual conferences of The Church of Jesus Christ of Latter-day Saints).
BM=*The Book of Mormon: Another Testament of Jesus Christ.*
D&C=*The Doctrine and Covenants of the Church of Jesus Christ of Latter-day Saints.*
PGP=*The Pearl of Great Price.*
JD=*Journal of Discourses* (26 volumes of collected discourses).

*This book is dedicated to the youth,
the young people who will rear and educate the next generation;
those individuals who will occupy the twenty-first century.*

Table of Contents

Part I

Agency Education: A Better Way

I

The Scriptures: An Educational Fountain

For a moment reflect: what could have been the purpose of our Father in giving to us a law? Was it that it might be obeyed, or disobeyed? And think further, too, not only of the propriety, but of the importance of attending to His laws in every particular.
—Joseph Smith Jr.

 A one-room school, heated by a coal stove and large enough for 24 armchair desks, was my first assignment as a full-time professional teacher. The school was located in Tabiona, a tiny lumber town, high in the mountains of Eastern Utah. Here, eighty or so twelve- to eighteen-year-old-boys and girls (grades 7-12) received daily released-time religious instruction. At this school, situated on the bend of a scenic river flowing out of snowcapped mountains, I relearned the importance of living waters.

It became obvious in the short but hot summer months why the ranches in the area were all positioned close to the river. Little or no farming—no hay, grain, or gardens—survived if the water from the river could not or did not reach them. In the midst of this arid country, everything within the reach of the river experienced a quality of life that was markedly different than that on the surrounding terrain. To be at its best this land was in constant need of life sustaining water. We are so much like the land—physically and spiritually!

This book is based on information from the Bible, Book of Mormon, Doctrine and Covenants, and Pearl of Great Price (referred to as Standard Works), and on the insights of modern prophets. Why base an education book on scripture? The answer is simple. The scriptures contain our Heavenly Father's instructions to his earthly children—including information about education. Isn't it common sense to seek out and honor counsel from our heavenly parents? Like the land surrounding the river, in the mountains where I taught years ago, our potential shrivels and dies if it is not nourished by living waters. Educators who ignore this principle do so at the peril of both themselves and their pupils.

The scriptures are a reservoir of principles from which parents and teachers can draw correct eductional counsel. These principles are often shaped to match our cultural circumstances. For example, Solomon's counsel to "spare the rod and spoil the child" should be understood in the context of ancient Hebrew life. (Proverbs 13:24). And the resources for these sacred records cannot be exhausted in a book. The spiritual reservoirs are bottomless. Though we can drink deeply, we cannot deplete them. Revealed knowledge also defies packaging; it is defined and illuminated only in the human personality. Only by our living the principles can we give them full expression. Writing about such principles is thus like inviting readers to meet and explore. The quality of the experience resides as much in the reader as in the writer. There is no room in this adventure for a contest between the reader and writer.

An educator who would master any library should master the Standard Works. Consider just a few observations on the family, the child's first school on earth.

The Old Testament

The Old Testament probably contains more references to the family than any great literature we possess. The lives of the patriarchs and the books of the Law and the Prophets are a strong testimony to the family's role in Hebrew communal life. From earliest times, the Hebrews regarded children more highly than did either the Greeks or Romans. The home, presided over by a father who was both a teacher and a priest, was the focal point in the Hebraic society. It was the father's role to teach God's law by example and by precept. This he often accomplished by simple ceremonies designed to draw forth questions from the children (Deut. 6:4-9). These questions, then as now, formed the basis for much of what the child was taught and what he learned.

In the later years of Hebrew history, as their society became more complex, schools were established among the Jewish remnant of the House of Israel. The elementary school was called *Beth Hasepher*, the House of the Book. Here young children were taught the rudiments of education as they learned the law of

Moses. The higher school for teenage children was called *Beth Hamidrash*, the House of Study. It was in such a school in the Temple that Jesus was found conversing with the teachers when he was but twelve years old (Luke 2:42-48). The flavor of education in the ancient Hebrew heritage can be found in the Book of Proverbs. This remarkable treatise was a widely read and generally accepted handbook on secondary education during the centuries immediately preceding the birth of Christ.

A key to the effectiveness of moral education among Old Testament families is the responsibilities placed on the fathers, who in turn transferred these responsibilities to their sons. The apparent harshness of this ancient education mellowed as the children came to realize that in the conduct of life, what was binding on them was equally binding on their parents. This realization made life more sensible, and integrity more desireable and acceptable. What righteous Jewish children lost in breadth of content compared with Greek or Roman children, they gained in moral perceptiveness. This was the education of Jesus in Nazareth and Paul in Tarsus. The central objective can be felt in a Jewish parable: If there are twenty righteous men in the world, my son and I will be among them. If there are ten righteous men in the world, my son and I will be among them. If there are five righteous men in the world, my son and I will be among them. If there are two righteous men in the world, they will be my son and I. If there is one righteous man in the world, I will be that man.

3

The New Testament

The New Testament is famous because it contains the story of the greatest teacher who ever lived. The life and mission of Jesus of Nazareth changed the world. He fulfilled the ancient law by leading the people into a higher order. The same tradition prevailed, but with a new emphasis; the same association between principle and practice, but on a higher level. Those who had ears to hear and eyes to see were edified and lifted.

The life of the Christian community centered in the home. Families were enriched, lifted, and refined by admonitions to turn the other cheek, to go the extra mile, to do good to those that despised them, and to look not with lust on others. Into the midst of cruelty came a preacher of love and patience. His very title, the Son of God, linked the family on earth with the family in heaven.

The witnessed reality of a heavenly family was never more direct than when it was pronounced by God's Only Begotten. "In my Father's house are many mansions . . . . I go to prepare a place for you" (John 14:2). The proof he offered that we will live again is a sobering reminder to mortal parents of a sacred responsibility. Fathers and mothers are engaged in a relationship with each other and their children that transcends our temporal existence. Man's spirit needs schooling. Jesus conducted such schooling throughout his ministry. His brilliant use of parables or earthly stories with heavenly meanings are legendary. His power, sensitivity, and kindness as a teacher of character challenged intellects, melted hearts, and healed spiritual as well as physical deformities. Love was the hallmark of his teaching.

The influence of Jesus' teachings can be seen in Paul's counsel on rearing children. He reminded parents of the reciprocal nature of parent-child relationships: "Children, obey your parents in the Lord, for this is right: honor your father and mother (it is the first command with a promise), that it may be well with you and that you may live long on earth." And to parents he said, "As for you fathers, do not exasperate your children, but bring them up in the discipline and on the admonitions of the Lord." (Ephesians 6:1-4, Moffat translation). The reason Paul gives for kind and considerate treatment of children is that it protects the child against loss of hope and confidence "lest they get dispirited" (Colossians 3:21, Moffat translation).

Christian education is marked by the principle that both parents and teachers are subject to a higher law—above and beyond parental whim. Children are to be obedient to parents, but parents are to employ love, joy, long-suffering, kindness, gentleness, and self-control. They are to avoid unchastity, idolatry, envy, hatred, strife, jealousy, intrigue, and drunkenness. Parents should model the same standards of piety they expect of their children. Divorce is "out"; close eternal bonding of family members is "in." In true Christian families, when the child is subjected to schooling, so are the parents.

The Book of Mormon: Another Testament of Jesus Christ

The Book of Mormon is a family book. It contains intimate disclosures of the impact of parent's decisions on children. This book is a family record from former days intentionally written to families in the latter-days. Perhaps the most remarkable characteristic of this record is its clear and ringing revelation of the role of Christ in the family of man—a message that was intentionally veiled from unrighteous Israel in the writings of Isaiah.

By contrast, Nephi declared in unmistakeable language, "We labor diligently to write, to persuade our children, and also our brethren to believe in Christ, and to be reconciled to God; for we know that it is by grace that we are saved, after all we can do." (2Nephi 25:23) He acknowledged that the Nephites kept the law of Moses, but looked forward with steadfastness to Christ. "We talk of Christ, we rejoice in Christ, we prophesy of Christ, and we write according to our prophecies, that our children may know to what source they may look for a remission of their sins" (2 Nephi 25:26). This was the context for education among the righteous in the Western Hemisphere. In contrast, the wicked chose another pattern and developed schools and curriculum that reflected their choices.

A concerned King Benjamin gathered his people together to give instructions on parental attitudes and the rearing of children. His counsel was direct: Believe in God, repent of your sins, do not have a mind to injure one another, live peaceably, and render to every man his due. Do not suffer your children to go hungry or naked. Teach them to obey the laws of God and not to fight and quarrel with each other. But teach them to walk in soberness, to love one another, and to serve one another (Mosiah 4:9-15).

When Jesus visited these people following his resurrection, he reminded them of that sacred source of knowledge so important to parents. "Whatsoever ye shall ask the Father in my name, which is right, believing that ye shall receive, behold it shall be given unto you."(3 Nephi: 18:20) And the exhortation to fathers was direct: "Pray in your families unto the Father, always in my name, that your wives and children may be blessed" (3 Nephi 18:21). The Book of Mormon is rich and detailed in its instruction to parents and teachers. It is a handbook for people living in today's world.

The family now struggles to survive in the midst of millions of visibly disturbed people. Their frustration is expressed in many ways—from verbal complaint to violent warfare. There is a raging in the hearts of some and a false sense of physical security in the hearts of others. Sin and sinful men and women abound. Only a small proportion of mankind enjoy the peace of a quiet mind and

5

freedom from fear in the heart (2 Nephi 28:19-22). In the midst of this turmoil, the Book of Mormon invites parents and teachers to partake of its practical directions for delivering us from the spiritually damaging influences in which we are enshrouded. It is a marvelous book for conversion, but it can do much more than call men out of the world. It can strengthen men and women and guide them toward spiritual maturity while they live in conditions of perplexing social conflict.

When parents and teachers comply with the teachings of the Book of Mormon, they are entitled to this promise:

> If ye shall do this ye shall always rejoice, and be filled with the love of God, and always retain a remission of your sins; and ye shall grow in the knowledge of the glory of him that created you, or in the knowledge of that which is just and true. (Mosiah 4:12)

6

The contents of the Book of Mormon are so vital and valuable that it is wisdom to seek its spirit and message daily.

For residents on the threshold of the twenty-first century, the Book of Mormon offers some very specific directions. A sample of the significant curricular concerns contained in this book are instructions on how to

a. discern between truth and deception
b. emphasize human dignity
c. eliminate social inequality
d. nurture justice
e. extend personal freedom
f. confront exploitation

Most of the crime, riots, social upheaval, and political controversy we see and read about in the news are linked to one or more of these subjects. How can we place a value on a book that correctly explains how to handle these kinds of challenges?

A powerful message of the Book of Mormon is that all programs on this earth are variations of two basic plans: the one a plan of salvation authored by God and implemented by his son, our Savior, Jesus Christ; the other a plan of destruction conceived by Satan in rebellion and carried out by those who give themselves up to his influences. The writers in the Book of Mormon repeatedly offer assistance on how to discern between these two plans. Their instructional methodology is deliberate and clear. They present historical evidence that demonstrates the consequences of following the plan of salvation versus the plan of destruction. As this evidence is laid out in simple and graphic detail, these teachers adroitly weave in reasons for the failures and successes. These reasons explain how following the one plan will set us free, save us from sin, and exalt us with our heavenly parents, while following the other plan will destroy our freedom, imprison our souls, and leave us stranded in spiritual darkness.

Consider, for example, just one of Mormon's efforts to portray these distinctions and explain their reality. In Helaman 12, Mormon pauses after recounting a long historical narrative to emphasize man's unsteady struggle with physical and spiritual forces. He says:

> And thus we can behold how false, and also the unsteadiness of the hearts of the children of men; yea, we can see that the Lord in his great infinite goodness doth prosper those who put their trust in him. Yea, and we may see at the very time when he doth prosper his people, . . . they do harden their hearts, and do forget the Lord their God. . . ; thus we see that except the Lord doth chasten his people with many afflictions, yea, except he doth visit them with death and with terror, and with famine and with all manner of pestilence, they will not remember him. (Helaman 12:1-3)

7

Mormon follows this observation with a list of items that illustrate man's tendency to frailty. He concludes by explaining how we can escape our weaknesses (vss. 23-26). Then Mormon quotes the great prophecy of Samuel the Lamanite, which includes a description of man's opportunities and responsibilities:

> And now remember, remember, my brethren, that whosoever perisheth, perisheth unto himself; and whosoever doeth iniquity, doeth it unto himself; for behold, ye are free; ye are permitted to act for yourselves; for behold, God hath given unto you a knowledge and he hath made you free. He hath given unto you that ye might know good from evil, and he hath given unto you that you might choose life or death;

and ye can do good and be restored unto that which is good,
or have that which is good restored unto you; or ye can do
evil, and have that which is evil restored unto you. (Helaman
14:30-31)

The Doctrine and Covenants

The stark warning and striking clarity of modern revelation to
parents and teachers are vivid in the Doctrine and Covenants. It
begins in the first section with God's description of our modern
mindset:

> They seek not the Lord to establish his righteousness, but
> every man walketh in his own way, and after the image of his
> own god, whose image is in the likeness of the world, and
> whose substance is that of an idol, which waxeth old and shall
> perish in Babylon, even Babylon the great, which shall fail.
> (vs. 16)

8

In section 29, the Lord reaffirms the ancient doctrine of
parental responsibility—that which is keyed to the father. The Lord
explains that mortal life was divinely designed; individuals were
organized into families, and Satan was prevented from tempting
little children so that parents could prove themselves. Only through
others—primarily parents—does Satan have access to little children
before they reach the age of accountability. All this, he said, was
intentional, so that "great things may be required at the hand of
their fathers" (D&C 29:46-48).

Subsequent instructions clearly inform parents on how to
carry out their responsibilities as the Lord desires. The directives
are straightforward, simple, and brief. Parents are to

   a. teach their children to understand the doctrine of
           repentance and faith in Christ.
   b. see that at eight years of age, they are baptized and
           given the opportunity to receive the Gift of the Holy
           Ghost by those properly authorized.
   c. teach them to pray and to walk uprightly. (While prayer
           is self-explanatory, "walking uprightly" can be
           understood by remembering that animals walk on all
           four. People are not animals. We are to teach our

children the moral order that lifts us above the animal level of existence. Human cleanliness, manners, and consideration for others as well as one's self are essential prerequisites for ultimate spiritual development.)

d. pursue these parental tasks while keeping the Sabbath day holy and while magnifying the callings we receive to serve others. (D&C 68:25-35).

If our family relationships are to endure beyond mortality, we must choose to conform to the requirements that make this possible. The Kingdom of God is a kingdom of order: all covenants, contracts, and vows that are not sealed under his power are null and void after this life (D&C 132:7).

The Pearl of Great Price

Where do we come from? Why are we here? These are questions the Pearl of Great Price answers. The visions given to Moses, the journal writings of Enoch, whose city was translated, the biographical writings of Abraham, a more complete account of the Savior's instructions found in the twenty-fourth chapter of Matthew, the testimony of the prophet Joseph Smith regarding the restoration of the Gospel, and thirteen Articles of Faith all provide a framework of meaning for mortality.

9

In contrast to the history taught by modern man that sheds no light on pre- or post-earth existence, these witnesses offer ample evidence that man is now living in a planned estate. We existed before we came into mortality and are now preparing for an existence yet to be experienced. The drama of life is unfolding; we are actors on an eternal stage. The principal witnesses in this book saw our day; they understood that mortality has its beginning and its end. They freely offer their knowledge to us. One witness, Enoch saw the day of the coming of the Son of Man, in the last days, to dwell on the earth in righteousness for the space of a thousand years; but before that day he saw great tribulations among the wicked; and he also saw the sea, that it was troubled, and men's hearts failing them, looking forth with fear for the judgments of the Almighty God, which should come upon the wicked. And the Lord showed Enoch all things, even unto the end of the world; and he saw the day of the righteous, the hour of their redemption; and received a fulness of joy. . . . And Enoch and all his people walked with God, and he dwelt in the midst of Zion. (Moses 7:65-67)

These insights in the Standard Works should illustrate why I have chosen to write about education from a scriptural point of view. What would make a person want to ignore such information? Would other libraries offer more helpful or useful information to parents and teachers who desired the very best for the children under their care?

2

A Better Way To Educate

Reasoning from doubt rather than faith is a quiet kind of intellectual quicksand; it suffocates our spiritual life.

 True education must be rooted in correct moral principles. Weak standards distort and destroy our efforts to improve ourselves, strengthen our families, build our communities, and secure our peace and happiness. We live in a time that cries out for a spirit of order, sensitivity, and personal responsibility. The twentieth century, in spite of many marvelous and enjoyable material achievements, has been engulfed by a profound confusion and a callous treatment of sacred values. Consequently, the threshold of the twenty-first century is enshrouded by circumstances that invite us to take a hard look at the way we educate ourselves. After all, there is little chance of successful preparation without effective education. More pointedly, our children will rear our posterity, our own flesh and blood, in the century that beckons. They stand in wait of our actions.

It is our opportunity, through the education we provide or do not provide, to increase their strength and fortify their protection, or to weaken and make more vulnerable their character. We should give the best we have to offer. This book explores education in terms of thoughts, feelings, and actions considered to be in harmony with the teachings of Jesus Christ, assuming this is the best we have to offer. Christianity's divinely bestowed moral imperatives are fundamental to a free intellect and the agency that allows a maximum expression of choice.

A Lesson from the Motion Picture Industry

The American motion picture industry is a clear example of what happens when moral principles are exchanged for a license to free expression. In 1929 Martin Quigley, an industry trade journal publisher, observed both a developing trend away from moral standards and the willingness of motion picture executives to correct it—perhaps as a defense against growing public sentiments. He joined with Daniel A. Lord to create "The Production Code." On March 31, 1930 the code was approved by the Motion Picture Association of America. When people read this code today they are often surprised at how much change has occurred in social values since that time.

The 1930 code was composed of (1) three general principles, (2) twelve particular applications, and (3) reasons supporting each particular aspect of the code. The general principles stated:

1. No picture shall be produced which will lower the moral standards of those who see it. Hence the sympathy of the audience shall never be thrown to the side of crime, wrongdoing, evil or sin.

2. Correct standards of life, subject only to the requirements of drama and entertainment, shall be presented.

3. Law—divine, natural or human—shall not be ridiculed, nor shall sympathy be created for its violation.[1]

The twelve areas covered in the particular applications were crime, brutality, sex, vulgarity, obscenity, blasphemy and profanity, costumes, religion, special subjects, national feelings, titles, and cruelty to animals. Under the section on *crime*, for example, one of ten guidelines indicates, "Crime shall never be presented in such a way as to throw sympathy with the crime as against the law and justice, or to inspire others with a desire for imitation." Concerning *brutality*: "Excessive and inhumane acts of cruelty and brutality shall not be presented. This includes all detailed and protracted presentation of physical violence, torture and abuse." Under the topic of *sex*, the preface to eight specific directives reads: "The sanctity of the institution of marriage and the home shall be upheld. No film shall infer that casual or promiscuous sex relationships are the accepted or common thing." Concerning the use of *vulgarity*, producers agreed that "Vulgar expressions and double meanings having the same effect are forbidden. This shall include but not be limited to such words and expressions as . . .[followed by a list of specific terms]".[2]

Brief but comprehensive reasons for supporting the particular aspects of the code included rationale such as

Mankind has always recognized the importance of entertainment and its value in rebuilding the bodies and souls of human beings.

But it has always recognized that entertainment can be of a character either helpful or harmful to the human race, and in consequence has clearly distinguished between:

a. Entertainment which tends to improve the race or at least to recreate and rebuild human beings exhausted with the realities of life; and

b. Entertainment which tends to degrade human beings, or to lower their standards of life and living.

Hence the moral importance of entertainment is something which has been universally recognized. It enters intimately into the lives of men and women and affects them closely; it occupies their minds and affections during leisure hours; and ultimately touches the whole of their lives. A man may be judged by his standards of entertainment as easily as by the standard of his work.

So correct entertainment raises the whole standard of a nation.

Wrong entertainment lowers the whole living conditions and moral ideals of a race.[3]

13

During the late 1950s and early 1960s, some people in the entertainment industry claimed the Production Code was old-fashioned. They argued that the values of the audience and producers were changing and claimed Americans could not compete with foreign producers, who did not have to comply with "artistic" restrictions. In 1968 the industry proposed and implemented a new self-regulatory system that allowed any film to be made, but provided a rating system for classifying these films as G—general audience; M—suggested for mature audience; R—restricted to those over age 16 unless accompanied by an adult; and X—no one under age 16 admitted. This system has subsequently been modified to our present G, PG, PG-13, R, and X.

Under the new system, motion pictures are rated by the Classification and Rating Administration (CARA). This organization is composed of twelve members: four representatives each of the National Association of Theatre Owners (NATO), International Film Importers and Distributors of America (FIDA), and Motion Picture

Association of America, Inc. (MPAA). The criteria now used for determining a film's quality are radically different from those of the Production Code of 1930. The rating guideline provided to the committee of twelve consists of a single sentence: "CARA shall consider as criteria among others as deemed appropriate the treatment of the theme, language, violence, nudity and sex."[4] All industry standards have been removed and the judgment of the product rests with the consensus of the committee.

Prevention vs. Correction

The strategies represented by these two codes are simple, but significant in impact. Under the 1930 Code, questionable pictures were not made. Parents did not have to worry about their children seeing a "questionable" movie. Movies were wholesome and entertaining; they generally stressed justice and morality. The contribution of this code was simple: it *prevented* problems of moral violation from occurring. The 1968 Rating System operates on a different premise, which is to allow any kind of movie to be produced and then seek to treat the problems after they occur by determining who should be allowed to see which films. *Correction* rather than *prevention* may seem exciting and freedom producing, but it can be dangerous and even fatal—spiritually and physically. Is this the price we should pay for technical and artistic excellence—for "reality" in the arts?

We would rebel if the same *correction* strategy were applied to our physical health. Few people argue that any and all forms of epidemics should be allowed, because we can treat the problems *after* they occur. Health professions consistently recommend prevention as the best procedure to follow. The same is true in the food industry or in transportation. In these areas vital to our physical well-being, we demand standards to prevent problems from occurring. We refuse to be content with corrective stategies if prevention is possible. Freedom in the form of unbridled licence is unacceptable. In the moral and spiritual domains, however, we seem to have become more lax. This laxity has had a powerful influence on education and the way our children are taught.

Many consequences of removing standards in the motion picture industry are self-evident, but one impact is evident statistically in the fact that between 1968 and 1982, the percent of "G" compared to "X" and "R" rated movies changed drastically.

14

During this initial period following the adoption of the rating system, the percent "R" and "X" rated movies increased from less than 30% to more than 65%, while "G" rated movies decreased from more than 30% to less than 5%. While researchers may debate the precise impact of these changes on society, individuals such as serial killers Ted Bundy and Gary Bishop offer testimonials on the personal impact of pornographic-like materials on their crimes; the indisputable fact is that endorsed standards can and do make a difference. Education, like entertainment, faces a similar dilemma in identifying and establishing correct standards. The decisions we make will affect the way we go about teaching our children.

The Major Choices in Contemporary Education

An education system is an expression of the history and culture of a people. It is an extension of how a society views life and explains the universe. In colonial America (1600s), for example, it was commonly believed a person had to be a good Christian in order to be a good citizen. The church and state were combined. Dominating colonial schooling, this view was the foundation for the official philosophy of education enforced by the governing powers in the respective communities. For instance, in Massachusetts before 1691 people were not allowed to vote unless they were members of a Puritan congregation.

15

During the 1700s, new liberal ideas growing out of the Enlightenment modified the people's theological views. The American founding fathers were among those influenced by these changing views. They were taught the world operated on fixed laws that were orderly, reasonable, and mechanically constructed. This change in worldview resulted in a movement away from the theological determinism of many early colonists, although morality and religion continued to be endorsed. Thus the founding documents of this nation reflect a view of government that depended on moral and spiritual values. As John Adams phrased it, "Our Constitution was made only for a moral and religious people. It is wholly inadequate to the government of any other."[5] These second generation Americans, however, separated religion and citizenship; the administration of spiritual matters was entrusted to the individual. Freedom of conscience was deemed a personal right to be *protected*, but not *determined* by the government. Early Americans admired rational principles linked to a common morality rooted in personal spiritual resources. Faith in reason was widely promoted; reason became the basis for a new type of public education—a secular and scientific education.

During the pre-Civil War years (early 1800s), a new tax-supported public education was embraced, separate from political partisanship, as religious preference had been separated from government edicts. The new position acknowledged common moral principles, stressed the "three Rs," and enabled educators to convince legislatures to fund schools with public taxes, because schools were politically and religiously "neutral." These schools mushroomed into a massive system of free public education, controlled by parents and envied by the world because of how well it provided for so many.

The turn of the century (1900s) found the new school system driven by the forces of the industrial revolution and the rapid movement of people from the farms into the cities. Curriculum during the 1900s steadily increased its focus on the transmission of knowledge. School primarily became a place to prepare for vocations and professions; developing personal character received diminishing attention. By midcentury, character education was essentially left to the home, church, and other agencies. Science was enthroned as the dominant strategy for managing and directing the educational system in America. This dichotomy of interests set the stage for a conflict between two competing views. John Dewey, the well-known American educator, recognized the contest:

16

> I see at bottom but two alternatives between which education must choose if it is not to drift aimlessly. One of them . . . [is] to return to the intellectual methods and ideals that arose centuries before the scientific method was developed. . . . I believe it is folly to seek salvation in this direction. The other alternative is systematic utilization of the scientific method as the pattern and ideal of intelligent exploration and exploitation of the potentialities inherent in experience.[6]

Robert Mason summarized this controversy in modern education, emphasizing it was a battle between "science and a philosophy based on science, in opposition to the literary humanistic tradition and a philosophy based thereon." He acknowledged the debate has heightened "as people have seen that a scientific, experimental approach to education de-emphasizes, leaves out, or sometimes clashes outright with a poetic, dramatic, imaginative approach to education based on tradition and religion."[7] Parents and teachers faced a difficult question: To which of these traditions should the nation turn: the systematic curriculum structured by modern science favored by men like John Dewey, Edward L. Thorndike, and Emile Durkheim; or the classical "Great Books" literature promoted by people like Mortimer Adler, Robert Hutchins, and Arthur Bestor? This is the conflict that has dominated discussions about education in America for most of this century.

Thirty years before Allen Bloom's bestseller, *The Closing of the American Mind: How Higher Education has Failed Democracy and Impoverished the Souls of Today's Students* (1987), the battle lines were clearly drawn. Scholars of myth, poetry, and religion were aware of the degree to which the scientific movement in educational theory and practice was de-emphasizing literary humanistic studies. They clearly saw the two major poles of the controversy: (1) science and a philosophy and practice of education based on science, and (2) literature, poetry, art, religion, and a philosophy and practice based more on these than on scientific sources.[8] This choice is the fundamental dilemma before parents, educators, and students today. Most educational discussions are some variation of this theme: (1) should the choice be to emphasize science and the comfort of its modern display of precision and prediction, or (2) should it be literary humanism and the stimulating satisfaction of its subjective insights, or (3) shall we turn to the ever popular middleground of noncommitment while we search for a satisfactory mix of the two? This book is written to describe another option—a better way that favors none of the above.

17

A Restorationist View of Education

In 1830 the Mormon prophet Joseph Smith formally offered the modern world a unique and comprehensive view of education. He explained how this view was restored by heavenly messengers with the same insights, principles, and powers that were given by God, the Father of us all, to Adam, Enoch, Noah, Abraham, Moses, and Jesus Christ. Notwithstanding the significance of this announcement, over the succeeding century and a half, the restored view has been less than fully studied, applied, or appreciated. While many individuals have benefitted from the restored knowledge of man's true nature, purposes, and principles of growth and development, many others have ignored it. Too often, those who enjoy full and ready access to this information overlook its value; they choose to spend their time and energy seeking direction and solutions from other libraries. With few exceptions, the professional response to restorationist principles of education during the twentieth century has been to ignore them. Preference in such circles, Latter-day Saints included, has increasingly been given to secular scientific, humanistic, and behavioristic models.

Dozens of prophets and apostles since 1830 have offered inspired insights into the learning/teaching process. Most of these instructions are related to how sacred scriptural writings and the Spirit of God can be used to develop educational effectiveness. Some of these insights have been formally collected and reported along with the rest of their writings. Portions of this commentary on education have received sporadic attention in Church curriculum materials, academic position papers, occasional lectures, and a few religious education booklets with limited and specialized circulation. As of this writing, however, I am unaware of any serious, sustained attempt to collect, analyze, widely distribute, and formally study the words of the prophets, the Teachings of Jesus Christ, on education. The Mormon intellect has yet to plumb the depths of this resource. Meanwhile, thousands of volumes have been written on history, doctrine, and biography. But with the exception of a few private collections and several informally bound volumes of photocopied articles, no library of books from this source is used by educators to write on education. There could be such a library, but most professional educators essentially ignore this literature as a serious resource. One can only imagine where we could be, educationally speaking, if we gave as much attention to sacred sources as we regularly spend on secular ones.

Consequently, Latter-day Saints possess a gold mine of information about education that is largely unworked. The invitation to extract and refine the richest of all ore has been extended repeatedly to the Saints and to others, but there has been little rush to accept this invitation. We stand more or less in the shadows, waiting and wondering, or wandering to and fro, seeking to strike it rich on or near somebody else's claim where the motives as well as the aims are linked to secular positions. We have long been encouraged to change this perspective.

Our challenge is to overcome the darkness that is upon us as a people. More than a century ago President Brigham Young explained,

> As individuals, we enjoy Zion at present, but not as a community; there is so much sin, darkness, and ignorance, and the veil of the covering which is over the nations of the earth is measurably over the Latter-day Saints. The same unrighteous principles, which becloud the minds of men universally, more or less becloud the minds of the Latter-day Saints. Though the veil is partially broken to the Saints, though it becomes thin, as it were, and the twilight appears like the dawning of the day, yet we may travel for many years before the sunshine appears. It does not yet appear to this people, they are merely in the twilight.9

19

And more recently, President Ezra Taft Benson has informed us,

> In section 84 of the Doctrine and Covenants, the Lord declares that the whole Church and all the children of Zion are under condemnation because of the way we have treated the Book of Mormon. (Verses 54-58). This condemnation has not been lifted, nor will it be until we repent. The Lord states that we must not only say but we must do.10

The verses referred to inform us

> And your minds in times past have been darkened because of unbelief, and because you have treated lightly the things you have received—
> Which vanity and unbelief have brought the whole church under condemnation.

>   And this condemnation resteth upon the children of Zion,
> even all.
>
>   And they shall remain under this condemnation until they
> repent and remember the new covenant, even the Book of
> Mormon and the former commandments which I have given
> them, not only to say, but to do according to that which I have
> written. (D&C 84:54-58)

Apparently, we are not totally free from the disposition that affected some of our progenitors. Our condition is reminiscent of an earlier father's observation:

>   He [Heber C. Kimball] said . . . he could look upon his
> family and see the spirit that was in them, and the darkness
> that was in them; and that he conversed with them about the
> Gospel, and what they should do, and they replied, ". . .
> Perhaps it is so, and perhaps it is not," and said that was the
> state of this people, to a great extent, for many are full of
> darkness and will not believe me.[11]

We must hope and pray that we will refrain from harboring the disposition to react to revealed truth with a skeptical "perhaps it is so, and perhaps it is not" attitude. Reasoning from doubt rather than faith is a quiet kind of intellectual quicksand, suffocating to our spiritual life.

The Restoration Accepts both Science and Literature as Tools

Because Latter-day Saints accept the fact that all truth comes from God, they enthusiastically embrace the scientific method and everything it can do to help them gain dominion over this temporal earth and to serve their fellowmen. President Ezra Taft Benson makes this point clear:

>   Our educational system must be based on
> freedom—never force. But we can and should place special
> emphasis on developing in our youth constructive
> incentives—a love of science, engineering, and math, so that
> they will want to take advanced scientific courses and thereby
> help meet the needs of our times. Just as a musician has a love
> of music which drives him to become outstanding in that field,

so we must inculcate in some of our qualified young people such an interest in science that they will turn to it of themselves.[12]

An earlier president of the Church, John Taylor, similarly emphasized acceptance of the opportunity to learn, understand, and appreciate the truths that God gives his children from time to time as expressed in great literature and other art forms, as well as through science:

> We ought to foster education and intelligence of every kind; cultivate literary tastes, and men of literary and scientific talent should improve that talent; and all should magnify the gifts which God has given unto them.[13]

Both of these leaders acknowledge, however, that neither science nor literature and the arts can safely stand on their own. They are simply tools and like all tools they wait upon a craftsman to use them. They are neither pilots nor navigators. They are instruments to be used in the service of predetermined purposes, not as determiners of those purposes. Our quest to fulfill our temporal and spiritual purposes may be limited by the tools we possess, but the tools we possess should not dictate our philosophy or determine our purposes. Hammers can be used to hit things, but this does not mean we should hit everything or any particular thing just because we have a hammer. Neither the scientific or the literary tradition should determine a Latter-day Saint's approach to education. We, like all children of our Father in Heaven, have access to another source that can aid us in discovering and following the charted course.

21

True education for the Saints should be charted and sustained according to principles and practices in harmony with the revealed word of God. We should seek after these gifts before we engage in the act of applying either scientific or literary tools with which to teach the children. It is this disposition that will fulfill the prophecy of President John Taylor when he said,

> You will see the day that Zion will be as far ahead of the outside world in everything pertaining to learning of every

kind as we are today in regard to religious matters. You mark my words, and write them down, and see if they do not come to pass. We are not dependent upon them, but we are upon the Lord. . . . Let us live so that we can keep that up, so that angels can minister to us and the Holy Spirit dwell with us. . . . It is for us now to go on from truth to truth, from intelligence to intelligence and from wisdom to wisdom.[14]

Hopefully, this book will contribute to fulfilling this inspired vision of what will happen as we teach the children of the restoration, an agency approach to education.

Part II

Agency Education: In Theory and Principle

3

Perfect Education in an Imperfect Society

We are not discussing a farfetched, abstract, untried theory. Agency education is not hypothetical speculation; it is real and it is practiced by many ordinary people, but not by most people.

Is Perfection Possible?

Jesus admonished his followers to be perfect.[1] What does it mean to be a perfect teacher? Or perhaps more realistically, how does one approach the challenge of teaching something perfectly? I am not perfect. I am not a perfect teacher. And I am not sure that I ever teach anything perfectly. Then why write of "perfect education"? The answer is simply because some teaching is closer to perfection than other teaching, and we should move in the direction of perfection. If my desire is to teach the children better, I must improve. Improvement, as determined by correct standards, is the path that leads to perfect education. Perfect education is not only a desirable goal, it is a viable option that yields practical and satisfying outcomes. To desire less is to shortchange both ourselves and our children.

We should not deceive ourselves by thinking or feeling that perfection is an impractical goal. Our own personal experience teaches us this is not true. Many of us experience and report to others "perfect" incidents, events, and feelings. Reports of a perfect night's sleep, a perfect evening, a perfect meal, or a perfect day are common. Baseball players have perfect days at the plate, and pitchers become famous when they pitch a perfect game. There are musicians who have perfect pitch, and dancers who dance to perfection. We even have mattress manufacturers and perfume producers who claim perfection for their products. Perfect education is a perfectly worthy goal. It is simply complying with correct standards—doing the right thing, at the right time, in the

25

right way, for the right reason. Our society is imperfect because too many of us fail to choose and implement the right.

As the reader will discover, this book is based on a belief that teaching and learning are independent functions—they are governed by individual choice. Just because I teach does not mean my children or my students will learn what I teach. Generally, they control their learning just as I control my teaching. Some people claim that "If the student hasn't learned, the teacher hasn't taught." I do not believe this statement is a trustworthy guideline. Good teaching, like good water, can exist whether others choose to drink it or not. On the other hand, learning can occur without a teacher. Some learners who have a strong desire to learn often do remarkably well when the teaching is very poor, just as some teachers who desire to teach well do so even if the learners are unresponsive. They do the right thing, at the right time, in the right way, for the right reason—and it is rejected. Nevertheless, learning and teaching are interrelated. If we want to optimize our learning, it is important to have good teaching. And good teaching is an important key to enhancing the desire to learn. Perfection is an ideal goal when it comes to education; anything less is shortsighted.

I Can Become a Better Teacher

I begin this book, therefore, by emphasizing it is possible for parents and teachers to improve their teaching. Regardless of who we are, where we live, what our current circumstances are, what our prior training has been, or what our present vocational interest is, the opportunity to be a better teacher is available. It is not merely wishful thinking or untried theory to suggest that we can enjoy unusual and remarkably effective education. It is already happening here and there, bit by bit, but it is not common; it is uncommon. The argument that certain personal and social barriers make this impossible is invalid. There is too much evidence to the contrary. The real barriers are our own ideas. Too many of us are unnecessarily imprisoned by traditions, practices, and personal experiences that prevent us from becoming better learners and more effective teachers. Although we may have been victims of false educational ideas, we can become the beneficiaries of correct educational ideas. The power is in us to choose for ourselves the kind of learner and teacher we will be. This is a first step toward more successful education, choosing to give personal order to our efforts. I saw this principle demonstrated many years ago by a humble, unpretentious family in Nebraska.

Order and Effective Education

Early in the 1950s I was a guest in the home of a family who lived on a large dryfarm near Scottsbluff, Nebraska. The daily routine of this family was impressive. After the evening meal was over and the dishes were washed and put away, the father and mother gathered their six young children together in a family hour. They discussed the events of that day, made plans for the next day, told stories, read to one another from the scriptures, and knelt in family prayer. By eight o'clock the children were in bed, and by nine o'clock they had all retired for the evening. The next morning, shortly after five, the parents were in the kitchen preparing breakfast. Near six o'clock the entire family was kneeling in prayer around the dining room table. They were well-rested, and the discussion was lively, upbeat, and sprinkled with laughter. This family was a happy family. A special spirit was in the home; it was a good feeling. There was no contention or confusion. Order prevailed, and it was obvious this family was the recipient of blessings that come from following the counsel "retire to thy bed early, that ye may not be weary; arise early, that your bodies and your minds may be invigorated" (D&C 88:124).

27

Over the years, I have often reflected on the education implicit in the order and activities that prevailed in that Nebraska home. The requirements were so simple; nothing the family did required extraordinary talent, training, or resources. It was just a matter of order and choice. Anyone could do what they were doing, regardless of their wealth or station in life. Compared with other family environments I have observed, the differences are remarkable. And the consequences of these differences, I have since learned, shape and direct not only the lives of individuals, but of the society itself.

In many families, young children follow a pattern of staying up late, playing video games, or engaging in other types of independent activity. They may fall asleep near midnight, overtired and irritated. Older children stay out late with friends and often do not return home or go to bed until well past midnight. Parents as well as children in these families often sleep in late, until ten or eleven o'clock, if they do not have to meet a school or work schedule set by others. As a result, their work habits are often poor, and neither their bodies nor their minds are invigorated. Togetherness times are difficult, if not impossible, in homes subjected to these patterns. Meals are seldom family experiences; more often they are grab-and-go events. The feelings in such homes are very different from those I experienced in Nebraska.

It is easy for us to make excuses for not exerting more self-mastery, but they are seldom if ever defensible. We may argue that times have changed, or that our circumstances are unique. But there are many families today, in cities as well as rural locations, who function very similarly to the family in Nebraska. They, too, have the order and the blessings it brings. As adults we can choose to "establish . . . a house of order," not a house of confusion (D&C 88:119). Love, peace, and happiness can rule in our homes rather than contention and disorder (Mosiah 4:14-15). God can and will help us live correct educational principles. The rudiments of successful education can be established in the home. And when this type of order prevails in the home, the lessons taught lay the foundations for a productive and satisfying life. Consequently, all parents are educators; all homes are schools. Order in the home is as vital as order in a formal classroom. Without order we cannot move towards perfect education.

Some Teachers Are Amazing

Good education, according to an American statesman, is "a simple bench, Mark Hopkins on one end and I on the other."[2] More recently the media featured a movie entitled *Stand and Deliver* that tells the inspiring story of Jaime Escalante, a Bolivian immigrant who changed students' lives in a largely Hispanic East Los Angeles high school.[3] Many of us have known teachers who possessed remarkable abilities. Some of these teachers benefit from unusual insights—insights they may have difficulty communicating to others. No one of these teachers may be the perfect teacher, but some of them seem to do some things close to perfection. That is, they are able to relate to others in such a way that, without compulsion, the other person becomes his or her very best self. When this happens, education becomes a positive, uplifting, and edifying experience. Negative side effects disappear; a spirit of satisfaction and fulfillment fills both the learner and the teacher .

28

A Fourth Grade Teacher

This book is not a collection of case studies describing great teachers. It is a book about a specific approach to education. It may be helpful, however, to share a description or two to symbolize one of the extraordinary qualities and insights that sustain the education I am writing about.

Not far from the university in which I teach there is an elementary school located in a small farming community. This school has more than a dozen teachers. One of these teachers is a legend because of his ability to invite students to shoulder the full responsibility of their own learning experiences. He freely admits he is not perfect in his knowledge or skills as a teacher, but those of us who have observed his relationships with students recognize a unique capacity that nears perfection. Here is a living example of doing something in the right way, at the right time, for the right reason.

One morning I visited this school about 8:30. I met with this teacher as 34 fourth-grade students arrived, removed their coats, engaged in conversations, and moved freely in and out of the classroom. Just before the bell sounded to begin the school day, the two of us walked out of the room into a large foyer and stood conversing, perhaps 60 feet from the doorway to his classroom. We could see at an angle into the room, but the students did not have a clear view of us. In fact, they were obviously unconcerned about where their teacher was at the moment. The bell sounded, and in fifteen seconds every student was seated in a chair, preparing to work on some task. There was no conversation between students—none at all. Each child was working from within himself or herself on a task obviously self-defined.

The teacher and I walked farther away from the classroom, around a corner and down a long hall past several other classrooms. As we passed by several doorways, different scenes met our eyes. One teacher was herding students from the hallway into her room. Another teacher was shouting, entreating the students to settle down and get to work because the bell had already rung. In another room I noticed a student standing on top of a desk, entertaining some classmates. Other rooms reflected varying degrees of order, some quite businesslike and others less so. This was school, and school was happening. It was normal to anyone familiar with schools. In fact, most educators would consider the general mood in the building commendable: a cadre of teachers was involving a large number of elementary age students in seemingly meaningful activities. One could sense the teachers' expressions of authority and feel the competition as students in various ways tested the system, its rules, and expectations. Overall, the environment was optimistic, the facilities were clean, and things were happening. This was public school, as most of us have experienced it in a positive sense. However, a story within a story was occurring in this particular school.

After a general orientation to the building, my teacher friend led me back in the direction of his own room. As we turned the corner I glanced into another room full of students intently listening to instructions from a young woman, but my attention was quickly drawn back to his classroom, the one we had left teacherless ten to fifteen minutes earlier. Somewhat astonished, I beheld 34 fourth graders still in their seats, diligently working away. No one was compelling these students to do what they were doing. They were on task and staying on task of their own volition, without direct supervision. This was intriguing.

I sat in a corner toward the back of the room. The teacher walked to the front and asked for the students' attention, explaining that he wanted to go over the day's plan with them. He told the students they would spend the first part of the morning working on math. He identified a project for each of four different groups. The projects varied because each student was pursuing the subject at their own skill level. One group of about twelve students was told to go into the hall and make up a booklet from stacks of mimeographed worksheets which he had placed on a large table. They were then to go down in a basement study room in another part of the building to do their work. Four other students were asked to pick up examinations at the teacher's desk and go into the hall where they would complete their tests. These four students had already finished the fourth grade level math course for the year and were now doing advanced study. The remainder of the students, at two different achievement levels, were instructed to stay in the classroom. Here, the teacher conducted a review and instruction session on decimals before launching these students into new units of work.

The first group put together their booklets, lined up, and moved in single file down the hall toward the basement study hall

30

located at the other end of the building. The advanced students picked up their tests, walked into the hall, and started working. The teacher conducted a fifteen-minute question and answer session with the students who remained in the room. He then asked if I would like to visit the study room in the basement. As we walked out of the room he turned to the four students taking the test and told them that after finishing their exam they could work with students in the room who might need help on their new units. "If not, you are free to work on your own projects," he said. We left the area and headed for the the other end of the building.

By this time the group in the basement had been on their own in another part of the school with no adult supervision for at least twenty minutes. We traveled across the building, down a stairwell, and along an extended hallway, which twisted and turned. Finally we came around a corner and through an open doorway into a comfortable study area. The room contained twenty or more chairs and a wall-hung chalkboard. The austere cement surroundings were well lit. Here we found our dozen students silently studying. They could not have known we were coming; we would have heard any noise or disruptions as we approached the area. The teacher called for their attention, answered questions, and helped them with concerns they expressed. Eventually he asked them to conclude their work on the material they were studying and return with us to the upstairs classroom.

We all moved quickly and silently up the stairs and back to home base. There was no disturbance by anyone as we passed by other classrooms. All of us were quiet; it was like traveling through a well managed library. When we returned to the classroom we found every student busy on his or her own work. Two of the test takers were now quietly working with other students. Two were in their seats reading books. No one was off task.

I spent three or more hours with this teacher and his students on that cold January morning. Not once in that time did any student ever distract other students from doing what they were supposed to be doing. The students were happy, content, energetic, and involved; they showed no evidence of competition between themselves or with the teacher. These students were not fighting a system or each other; they were simply governing themselves and doing it better than most adults. Discipline

31

problems simply did not exist—none whatsoever. I decided to check into this teacher's program more carefully. I wanted to find out what his principal had to say and what other teachers thought.

For the next hour and a half I listened to the principal describe his school in general and the teacher whose class I had visited in particular. I was informed that what I had observed was normal behavior for this teacher's students. Furthermore, the principal acknowledged that when difficult students in the third grade moved to the fourth grade, they were often assigned to this teacher's class. "He just doesn't have discipline problems," said the principal. "But more important, the order in his classroom is not the result of fear or force," he added. The principal explained he had already received requests from the parents of more than fifty third graders asking that their children be assigned to this teacher's class the following year. I also learned that other teachers in the school recognized the difference between this man's program and their own, but for the most part he followed his approach and they continued with theirs. When I returned to the university I questioned professors who had worked with student teachers who were assigned to that school. The reports were consistent. One professor who had been an observer at that elementary school for several years told remarkable stories of this teacher's work. Something very extraordinary was happening here, and it had been going on for many, many years.

A Second Witness

I learned that over the years, dozens of student teachers had worked under this man. Many of these trainees had been highly impressed with this teacher and his way of working with students, but few had been successful in adopting a similar approach. I asked him why. "I'm not sure," he answered, "but they seem to miss the main point. Most student teachers are looking for a *system,* and when they try to do the *things* I do, they don't get the same results. If there is a secret, I believe it is the way I think and feel about education; the things I do are simply extensions of how I think and feel about my students and teaching and learning."

In our conversation, this teacher told me of two student teachers who had been particularly successful in grasping the intangibles. "These students, both young ladies, had different personalities than mine, and their styles were different," he said, "but their results are the same because they do the right things in the right way for them and their students." One of those teachers, I discovered, was teaching in the same school. I wanted to hear her side of this fascinating story.

Several years ago this young woman had been a student teacher at this school. My friend was not her cooperating teacher, but she noticed he had different results with his students than other teachers. She began to ask him questions and carefully study his approach. Eventually, she graduated from college and returned to teach at this same elementary school. The quest to develop her own style continued in the direction she had observed in her chosen mentor. Her success, like his, was now becoming a legend in its own right. She too was doing something in the right way, at the right time, for the right reason. The results were apparent.

When I visited with the principal, he told me about this teacher and her unique impact on the students. Like the first teacher, she never has discipline problems. New students with negative reputations are also assigned to her classes, but in two or three weeks they voluntarily assume the personal responsibility to pursue their education conscientiously without interfering with others. The principal said, "Fifth-grade boys do not like to cry. But last spring when school ended, the boys in her class were a sob mob. They did not want to leave for the summer." When I asked what she attributed her success to, her answer had a familiar ring: "I think it has to do with how you feel about the students you are teaching and how you define your relationship with them. It is important for the student to begin each day with a clean slate. I do not transfer yesterday's negative baggage into a new day. My students know this, and it helps them feel more positive about our experience here at school."

33

What Is the Point?

I realize education is more than discipline-free relationships; it involves many other aspects, such as knowledge of subject matter, individual achievement, a learning/teaching atmosphere, personal experiences with others, and internal satisfaction. I relate the foregoing story about two special teachers to emphasize that real teachers are now doing things near perfection. They are unusual, but they are not rare. They can be found all across the country. Some of these people are professionals who work in public or private schools, others are parents rearing their families, while still others work in the community or church. *The point is this: We are not discussing a farfetched, abstract, untried theory.* Agency education is not hypothetical speculation; it is real. In various ways and in varying degrees, it is practiced by many ordinary people, but not by most people. No one person seems to do it all, but there are individuals who do some aspects of it very, very well. More of us could join them and enjoy similar successes.

As you read this book, keep in mind that somebody, somewhere, is already doing what is being described, and the results are admirable. The challenge is to decide whether or not we want to pay the price to make it happen in our own life. It is true that most people are not doing what is described in this book as *agency education.* They are either satisfied with what they are doing, are unwilling to make the necessary changes to do things differently, or are uninformed about the alternatives. Hopefully, those who desire to change will discover both personal motives and helpful contributions for doing so as they read this material.

34

Perfect Education Described

Education in its finest form connects the highest human purpose with proper personal development. It enables us to discover and learn to fulfill our personal missions in life. The content of this book agrees with Orson F. Whitney's view of perfect education:

> Education, human education, is the leading out and lifting up of the soul into the ripe, full enjoyment of all its powers potential. To educate men and women is to put them in full command of themselves, to completely possess them of their faculties, which are only half possessed until they are educated. Education imparts nothing but discipline and development. It does not increase the number of man's original talents; it adds nothing to the sum of his inherent capabilities; but it improves those talents, it develops and strengthens those capabilities, brightening what is dull, making the crude fine, the clumsy skillful, the small great, and the great still greater. Education supplements creation, and moves next to it in the order of infinite progression.[4]
>
> What is education? . . . It is the expansion of the soul—the body and the spirit—to the fulness of its capacity. It

is the cultivation and the highest possible development of the natural faculties; the bringing forth and perfecting of all the inherent powers of the individual. This is the definition of a perfect education, and it is the limit and index of its capabilities. . . .

Perfect education . . . is the full and uniform development of the mental, the physical, the moral and the spiritual faculties. The cultivation of the intellect, as said, is but one phase of the subject, and not by any means the most important one. Useful and valuable though it [may] be as a branch of education, it is of secondary consideration compared with other departments of that vast system of development by means of which, as an entirety, it is alone possible for the human mind and soul to be perfectly educated. This may not be a popular view, but I am satisfied it is the correct one. Those persons who bestow every care and attention upon their minds, and who seem to have but one thought, How shall I shine in society, or make a financial success in the world? are egregiously in error if they think they are gaining the best part of life's experience, or securing the education of which they have most reason to be proud.

Many of them, if they were wise enough to see it, are not doing justice even to their mental faculties. No one who reads a book simply to be able to chatter about its contents; who witnesses a play, or inspects a work of art, for the mere purpose of saying he has seen it; who journeys to foreign lands with no object in view but to boast of having been there; who lives in fact for show and glitter and not for usefulness and truth, can truly be said to be educated, even intellectually. The magpie and the parrot have an almost equal claim.[5]

35

Parents, teachers, and students are encouraged to create appropriate responses to life's most significant questions; this they can do peacefully and in harmony with correct principles. Individuals do not need to rebel in order to grow and develop, families do not need to be divided by the so-called "generation gap," and classrooms can be orderly if we understand and practice correct principles of true education. Education should promote rather than deny man's divinely bestowed gift of free agency. Individuals, young and old, can be both free and responsible. Theories, principles, and doctrines of education can guide us in organizing the learning/teaching process that facilitates our efforts to learn and develop. These can prepare us to magnify our callings in life.

The Lord explains how we learn:

> For behold, thus saith the Lord God: I will give unto the children of men line upon line, precept upon precept, here a little and there a little; and blessed are those who hearken unto my precepts, and lend an ear unto my counsel, for they shall learn wisdom; for unto him that receiveth I will give more; and from them that shall say, We have enough, from them shall be taken away even that which they have.
>
> Cursed is he that putteth his trust in man, or maketh flesh his arm, or shall hearken unto the precepts of men, save their precepts shall be given by the power of the Holy Ghost. (2 Nephi 28:30-31; see also Isaiah 28:10).

36

This divine educational counsel applies to literacy, art, science, and numbers, as well as to moral and spiritual precepts. The pursuit of true education is dynamic; it is an act of faith for both learner and teacher. We act on the basis of a partial knowledge; we can receive enlightenment by faith and by study; we can learn by our own experience how to develop our God-given faculties. Education begins where creation ends; as creation forms each baby, education forms each man. A powerful organizing force, education shapes the social world we live in.

Each Individual Is Unique

We are each unique. We are also each of infinite worth. Our uniqueness becomes very apparent in education. We must acknowledge this uniqueness in the learning/teaching process. Properly instructed individuals should be encouraged to make their own decisions and learn to be responsible for those decisions according to the level of their maturation. This principle is a valid measure for evaluating the propriety of educational programs. It is consistent with the idea that enriching growth is social. There is harmony, safety, and protection in submission to proper principles and authority. Order is consistent with the idea that human existence is innately free and personal. Next to life itself, volition is God's greatest gift to man. This gift deserves to be revered—especially in the learning/teaching process.

Education in an Imperfect World

A social analysis. As one reads the literature of the twentieth century, a pervasive theme becomes apparent: we are reaching our limits of growth, and this growth is creating a crises for human survival. That is the assertion. Novels, professional journals, daily newspapers, political agendas, and local controversies all reflect a similar message. Overpopulation, agricultural scarcities, natural resource depletion, environmental pollution, and a lack of energy resources to feed our machines are the touchstones that capture the imagination of editors and producers in every field. Tons of typeset have been devoted to these concerns. Problems such as these, we are told, demand that we change our lifestyle. Some people claim the breaking point will be a *resource crises*—the depletion of vital natural resources; others say it will be a *technological crises*—that the machines around which we have built our lives will become dysfunctional or counterproductive; and still others claim our demise is rooted in a *legitimization crises* —psychological confusion, chaos, illness, and suicidal behaviors. The solution to the problem, when one is offered, is nearly always that we must become a more rational people; the answer lies in man's intellect, in human wisdom. We are told that we are our only hope.

37

A century ago in somewhat different circumstances, John Taylor reviewed the social disorder of his day and suggested another source of hope. He noted the futile efforts to substitute man-contrived programs for the divine solutions provided by a benevolent Creator. Citing many contemporary examples, such as the Red Republicans of France, the temperance movements, and the peace societies of his day, he pointed out that "notwithstanding human exertions may have been very necessary in many of these moves to try and better the condition of the world, it must be acknowledged that they have signally failed. . . . In fact it is getting worse and worse, instead of better and better."[6] The solution, he maintained, was to seek answers to our problems by turning to the counsel of God:

> Now, what is it that we want? If we could have it and know how to obtain it, and if there was any way of accomplishing it, we want to get that wisdom which dwells in the bosom of God; that intelligence which governs the

universe, that produces seed-time and harvest, and causes everything to progress in regular order, under the sanction of that care, forethought and comprehension and power that enables the Lord our God to provide for all of his creatures, to supply our wants; and this shows something of that beneficence that dwells in his bosom, that enables him to feel for the wants of his neighbors as for his own, and to seek after common welfare and interest. *If we cannot get God to be interested in our cause, if he won't put his hand to the wheel, we may despair of ever bringing about* [a solution to the problems we face].[7]

In matters of education, most of what we need to improve our circumstances has already been given to us; but we have given little attention to it. Most people prefer to study in another library, to seek solutions from a different order. In this book I suggest we turn to repeatedly revealed and generally ignored premises and principles to establish proper foundations for education. We need the strength of character and the spiritual vigor this type of education fosters. It will provide protection against the relentless tides of telestial turmoil and the incessant waves of debilitating indulgence that seek to wear us away. We need the benefits and the buoyant resilience of an education that is consistent with our eternal nature.

38

The Challenge of Living in a Dividing Society

The final quarter of the twentieth century is an era of subtle but significant social separation. The evidence is pervasive, persistent, and compelling. Society worldwide is now experiencing a monumental change in its moral topography. An ethical earthquake of significant magnitude is rearranging our life-styles. Some people may not be aware of this transformation, but it is occurring nevertheless. As Jose Ortega y Gassett expresses it, "We do not know what is happening to us, and that is precisely what is happening to us—the fact of not knowing what is happening to us."[8] For others the disruption is unmistakably clear, often painfully unavoidable. Whatever the degree of personal awareness, the foundation of our future is being formed as if by the hand of an unseen sculptor.

Out of the social landscape a great divide is emerging. Like a giant mountain range, it is slowly but definitely rising upward, creating an enormous moral watershed. Individuals, families, communities, and nations increasingly experience circumstances and influences that compel them to live on one side of the divide or the other. Much of the turmoil and agitation we feel in our homes or in our jobs is rooted in the moral stress created by this tension toward social separation. Our daily decisions of right and wrong inevitably move us toward or away from that which will bring us satisfaction and peace of mind.

Moral Commotion

A migration is under way from both directions. Inhabitants of the earth appear in a moral commotion. People are running to and fro, looking here and there, climbing up or sliding down the inclines. Look into the faces. See the timid ones—quiet, shy, and unsure of which direction to go; frustration is in their eyes. Observe the content and happy ones, apparently satisfied with their location and pleased with their purposes. Watch the carefree, frivolous, and curious who seek merely a good time: eating, drinking, making merry, and taking little thought for the morrow. Do you see the ones in pain? They suffer anguish, frightened by fears they can't quite identify or control. Look at the lethargic and morose—groping aimlessly, apparently stunned by their experiences. Lastly, there are those full of anger and defiance—who move roughly, pushing and shoving others as they go. Where is safety in this jostling crowd, and with whom should we lock arms?

Educational Confusion

Our efforts to educate the human family in these circumstances are clearly in a state of turmoil. Many studies, hundreds of books, and thousands of speeches record the difficulties now encountered in educating both ourselves and the rising generation. We are past the point where informed people can honestly say, "All is well." But with observable irregularity, life goes on in an environment of social rupture. Throughout the world, the volume of poverty, famine, disease, pollution, crime, and war escalates to new heights—often deceiving the sociologist's fragile statistical instruments. Current changes are not just mildly disruptive, they are increasingly chaotic and violent. To apply a single, mandated programmed solution to educational problems, even with liberal financial support, is both unrealistic and ineffective.

The reported consensus in America, for example, suggests that our educational failures are increasingly rooted in misplaced values, lack of personal discipline, and the inability or failure of individuals to establish specific, personal goals. These problems are clearly manifest by all three elements of the educational equation—parents, teachers, and children. Why? Explanations range from apathy to addiction. Innumerable pages have been and are being written that describe the problem. Defining the problem, however, does not solve it. It only heightens awareness of how serious the problem really is, which is that society is rapidly breeding two cultures of nearly equal numbers: those who can successfully compete in the marketplace and those who cannot. Reports suggest, for example, that roughly fifty percent of America's high school graduates make failing scores on general examinations designed to reflect the skills and values considered necessary to sustain a stable republic. This creates a further subcultural conflict, a conflict that does not lend itself to programmed solutions.

Those people left in the street are perceived as unemployable by the marketplace. Unhappy, increasingly angry, and potentially dangerous, these people are not just the underprivileged or the minorities. Many are the offspring of the employed, who have access to the best education an affluent society can provide. But they are children uninterested in personal preparation. Some may seek part-time jobs, but these are simply to satisfy their immediate desires—popular clothes, prepared food, sensually stimulating entertainment, and material possessions such as cars, stereos, jewelry, gadgets, drugs, and more. Read the magazines and look in the mall shops that are sustained by their purchases. These young people are not inclined toward the submission, self-discipline, and planning that brings success in school. According to a nationally televised documentary on American education: "The alarm has sounded, the clock is ticking, but most of us are still asleep."9

Warnings of the consequences that follow these conditions are numerous. Prophetic leadership has vividly described the conditions that ultimately prevail when moral order evaporates. The desolating destruction that could befall America long after her Civil War has been envisioned:

Do you wish me to describe it? I will do so. It will be a war of neighborhood against neighborhood, city against city, town against town, county against county, state against state, and they will go forth destroying and being destroyed and manufacturing will, in a great measure, cease, for a time, among the American nation. Why? Because in these terrible wars, they will not be privileged to manufacture, there will be too much bloodshed—too much mobocracy—too much going forth in bands and destroying and pillaging the land to suffer people to pursue any local vocation with any degree of safety. What will become of millions of the farmers upon that land? They will leave their farms and they will remain uncultivated, and they will flee before the ravaging. . . . Now these are predictions you may record. You may let them sink down into your hearts . . . . They are not my words, but the words of inspiration . . . of the everlasting God.[10]

A Divergent Society Means Different Approaches to Education   41

This nation is aware, as are other nations, of intense pressures to diversify education. Here again, the numerous reasons are less important than the fact that divisive changes in social values call for different types of educational programs. As public schools in the United States struggle to maintain their enviable record of contribution, established by over a century of success, confidence among the people wanes. In a widespread battle over taxation for education, politicians attempt to determine how this money should be spent. Private schools and schools sponsored by the business sector receive favorable attention and increased support. The scenarios in other countries vary, but the central challenge remains constant. How people pursue education changes when there is a radical diversification of values. In the United States, a voucher system that allows parents to choose from among competing schools is a proposed solution. In other countries, state examinations or parental choice direct children in different directions in their education. A consensus on how we can resolve the educational confusion seems to be disappearing.

It would be naive to suggest that this book will resolve the problems I have described. I do not believe that a single solution to the educational problems of a divergent and dividing society exists. Men are free to choose, and as long as they are free to choose they may choose to follow different paths. Nevertheless, I am firmly convinced that this particular approach is based on sound and enduring principles. For those who desire to pay the price in personal commitment, it does have merit. These principles have worked for me and my family, and for thousands of others. They can work for anyone who has the desire and intent to make the necessary personal commitment. These principles are adaptable, and within reasonable limits can be applied with integrity in both the public and private sector. Agency education is a workable alternative for those who choose to adopt it.

Opposition and Agency

Opposition is a fact of life. A tension exists in all things that makes it possible for man to choose and direct his experience: light and dark, north and south, east and west, high and low, slow and fast, wet and dry, hot and cold. Every condition invites man to exercise his capacity to make choices. Man, as a free agent, exists in a realm that allows him to freely choose for himself—between good and evil, love and hate, kindness and cruelty, righteousness and unrighteousness, happiness and misery, health and sickness, corruption and incorruption. Next to life itself, the most fundamental of all human realities is the capacity to choose. This book explores how parents, teachers, and students might honor that capacity in the process of education.

The Emphasis of Agency Education

The obvious emphasis in this book is threefold. *First*, it is positive and optimistic in the face of much that is negative. For example, many people become discouraged with human nature. Man is frequently described as greedy, selfish, and inconsiderate. The news offers daily illustrations. Man is also perceived by some people as an evolving organism that must be environmentally conditioned in order to prevent cruel and destructive behavior. We all have personal experience that human action can be very negative as well as positive. It is tempting to become cynical instead of compassionate. But compassion, and the character that sustains it, is central to agency education.

After reading the contents of this book, some may decide that it is unrealistic to pursue education from this positive point of view. I am not discouraged, however, by the consequences of human beings who are exercising their free agency. I may be saddened at times, even with myself, but not discouraged. When life is viewed from the eternal perspective of the gospel of Christ, hope—the vital link between faith and charity—springs anew. From the Christian perspective we do not need to embrace philosophies that promote unjust dominion or to adopt ideas that generate despair and hopelessness. We may have to live amidst their influence, but we do not need to make them our beliefs. This book is based on faith in the wisdom of divine governance, on an understanding that reflects ultimate confidence rather than despair for the human condition. "Men are, that they might have joy" (2 Nephi 2:25). Sorrow is born when we fail to choose the path leading to that joy.

Second, the book reflects a fundamental commitment to accepting our time on earth as an opportunity to learn and improve. Mortality is a school. Man can learn from his own experience. The power is in him and the necessary spiritual assistance is available to him. Events in life that block our plans and frustrate our preferred choices can be seen as feedback instead of failure. When used as stepping stones, temporal experiences become means rather than ends. Life was designed to be an invitation, not a sentence. Mortality is a state of probation, not a confinement. The human soul is resilient, not brittle. Man's ultimate nature is the fruit of free agency, not the product of determinism. The limitations of a person's earth life are temporary; personal life itself is eternal. A vision is available that transcends mortal existence; and if followed, this vision will lead man to exaltation and eternal life.

Third, it is imperative that each of us seek to understand what life has to offer. We must then decide what we want out of life, and then act on those desires. Whatever else life may be, it is first and foremost our responsibility. No one else can live our life for us. The responsibility for one's own life is nontransferable. By allowing others to exert influence upon us, we may subject ourselves to their wills, but this is our choice. By divine investiture, it is our inalienable right and duty to decide what we want to do, and what we want to be. True and accurate information is critical to our exercising our power of choice; hence, education is important.

Educational Priorities

Some things have more value than others. Historically, scholarship has pursued three concerns: (a) our relationship to God, (b) our relationship to other people, and (c) our relationship to nature. Of these three, our relationship to God is primary. Like unto it is our relationship with others. These two relationships, as taught by Jesus, constitute the great laws of life. "On these two," he said, "hang all the law and the prophets" (Matt. 22:40). Because God gave us dominion over nature; the world is ours to govern. We do not own it, but we do have stewardship over it. We are obligated to understand, care for, preserve, and utilize nature to sustain the human family. We are inextricably related to nature. From nature we gain food, shelter, clothing, and other amenities that make life joyful. We have learned to use nature to our benefit, but have we learned to properly prioritize our learning?

Contrast and Comparison of Basic Questions

Because there are different approaches, I will attempt to contrast and compare other perceptions with the agency viewpoint of education. My primary purpose is to clarify an agency approach to education, not to fully explain any of the alternatives. To accomplish this purpose, I will note certain basic differences. The intent of comparisons and contrasts is to help the reader see more clearly what agency education is. At times this means understanding what agency education is not. The objective is to highlight the features of the agency approach. Although it is legitimate as a scholarly task to critique other approaches carefully, neither space nor motive permits this in this book. I use contrasting views only to communicate the agency perspective and to emphasize its uniqueness. Anything more will have to wait another time. The reader's acceptance of this deliberate limitation is appreciated.

A Warning to the Reader

This book is a book of directions; it was not written to be a book of answers. That would contradict the very position it seeks to describe. Those who use the material to discover personal questions and answers within themselves will benefit most. The truly important ideas will be those personal introspective thoughts that come to the reader's mind as different issues are considered.

This is the reason for including a review of past as well as present and future considerations related to education. We become what we believe and practice. Our subject deserves careful, honest, serious, and prayerful consideration. Many things that are not in the book can be learned from reading this book, if the search focuses on discovering personal directions rather than looking for quick-fix solutions.

Overview of Part Two: Theory and Principles

Part Two explores basic assumptions related to the theory and principles of agency education. It emphasizes relationships that connect principles and practice. Various educational premises that parents, teachers, and students use are described; those in harmony with an agency view to learning/teaching are indicated. For example, the assumption that the world and its people consist only of physical matter—without spirit matter—is discussed. The methods used by people who believe in a supernatural world to resolve their dilemma of living among those who accept only a naturalistic universe is also treated. A review of how these strategies affect one's definition of excellence follows. Like reflections in a mirror, this review can be personally unsettling.

45

The earthly origins of education are briefly examined. A summary of what the most ancient written records tell us about the human family is included. The purpose and nature of the earliest schools are noted, as well as the response of ancient cultures to these teachings. Six key questions focusing on the nature and purpose of education are presented; agency oriented answers to these questions are introduced throughout the book. Where appropriate, these answers are compared and contrasted with popular alternatives that currently influence western culture. Directly and indirectly you will be challenged to review your personal answers to these key questions:

1. What is my origin, nature, and destiny?
2. What do I consider education to be?
3. How do I explain learning?
4. What is teaching?
5. What should I learn and teach others?
6. What role does God play in the teaching/learning process?

Hebrew, Greek, and modern influences on the world are explained in terms of how these shape and prioritize education. The most popular contemporary approaches to education are described; this will allow parents, teachers, and students to recognize how these approaches influence their own thoughts, feelings, and experience with education. Attention is given to the idea that man is a free agent—a view often denied by popular educational practices.

A Hebrew psychology consistent with an agency approach to education is described. This particular psychology views people using four aspects of the human soul: heart, mind, might, and strength. Contrasts are drawn between this perspective and those of popular modern psychologies. Consistent with ancient Hebrew psychology, ten educational propositions are listed to help parents, teachers, and students better understand the practical implications of this psychology to the learning/teaching process.

46

The question *How does a person learn?* is raised and some of the limitations of research related to learning theory are presented. Unique requirements of a learning theory consistent with the agency approach to education are discussed. The importance of basing education on divine principles, such as "truth manifests itself through personality," are highlighted.[17] The relationships of attention, interest, understanding, and role definition to the process of learning are explored. The relationship of learning for eternity and our knowledge of God is discussed.

Conscience and maturation are related to the principle of agency. Human expression is defined in terms of man's physical, mental, moral, and spiritual capacities. The impact of personal accountability as a capacity and of puberty as a mark of readiness for specific types of learning is related to the educational process. The educational readiness level of young children (before ages 7-9) from those who have passed that age is examined, as is another powerful change that occurs at the time of puberty (ages 11-14). The idea of defining man as an animal is challenged. A proposition suggests that ultimate reality is more accurately seen through morality and religion than it is through science and other intellectual tools we use in the physical world—as vital as the latter are to our temporal welfare and comfort.

The impact of four lifestyles that people adopt (the physical, intellectual, moral, and spiritual) is examined. Developing good dispositions and right actions are related to preparation for learning and teaching. A vital distinction is noted between action and behavior. Decisions differ from choices; this difference is related to how we understand and relate to others. The roles of caring and loving in carrying out the learning/teaching process are described.

Teachers (including parents) are described as artists and as makers of pictures; emphasis is placed on the teachers (or parents) being the quality of person that they want their students (or children) to become. The process of how learners take charge of their learning is described in terms of thoughts and feelings. Desire, disposition, and willpower are defined and then related to how a person makes commitments, creates values, and assumes responsibility. The relationship of knowledge to both tentative and significant thought and action is explored. Motivation and discipline are analyzed in terms of the authority structure that exists between the learner and the teacher.

Illustrations that build upon processes previously described are given to show how these processes function in the dynamics of the learning/teaching relationship. Four requirements for effective teaching are noted. Three conditions in a teacher's performance are compared to three conditions in a learner's performance. Six snapshots of the teacher and four snapshots of the learner are depicted in relation to motivation, discipline, and the agency approach to education. Comments on teaching with one's whole soul—spirit to spirit—and how prayer can be an important tool for both the teacher and the learner are shared.

As a partial answer to the question *What should be taught?* the final chapter in this section reviews five parts of the basic educational curriculum—(1) math, (2) science, (3) social studies, (4) language and the expressive arts, and (5) morality. A primary learning capacity which the individual exercises in mastering these respective areas is identified. The strengths and limitations of each of these ways of understanding and relating to the world in which we live are discussed, as well as disadvantages of failing to develop fully each of these capacities.

Overview of Part Three: Principles to Practice

Part Three of this book probes some of the practical issues related to education. For example, consideration is given to the importance of organizing oneself, preparing a place, and envisioning learning/teaching tasks. The function of the home and the house associated with it, stewardship, leadership, standards of expectation, and relationships between student, peer group, and family are introduced. Suggestions describe how an instructor manages curricular matters, with an emphasis on the importance of the perishable product to successful teaching. In a day when counseling, self-esteem, and creativity are vigorously pushed, the reader is invited to reexamine these ideas from the agency vantage point. Suggestions are given on how to approach personal interviews and enhance the creative potential of each individual.

The dilemma of how to practice agency education in nonagency oriented educational environments or systems is tackled. The American public school system exemplifies the importance of historical and legal contexts in discerning the extent of one's liberty or opportunity. The origin and nature of scholarship is reviewed. Three basic scholarly traditions are identified and described. The way agency oriented educators might view scholarship is examined. Specific examples of this agency view of scholarship in the home, at school, and in the laboratory are presented.

Basic principles to follow in preparing and delivering lessons are outlined for two domains of instruction; (a) the moral and spiritual, and (b) the temporal or physical. There is a brief treatment of the relationship between the strategy of constructing a lesson and the selection and application of methods to improve the effectiveness of instruction. The challenge of evaluation, tests, and giving grades is met head-on. How these practices relate and do not relate to agency education is explained, as well as why they are considered such an integral part of modern educational practice.

The final chapter in the book is a nonconventional description of teacher training. The organization and disorganization of the human family are reviewed. Characteristics of the ideal teacher are identified and related to the design of the patriarchal order of instruction. Double indemnity teaching is proposed as a key to strengthening the foundation of true education. The importance of organizing families and preparing a family curriculum is stressed. A postscript of observations about education within our social systems concludes the book.

4

What Is Agency Education?

Agency education holds that every individual has the inalienable right to choose; every sin is a lie and every lie is an alternative to love; love is appropriately doing for others that which they cannot rightfully do for themselves.

One way to understand agency education is to see it in relationship to other types of education. In the following narrative, distinctions are made between four basic approaches. Two of these approaches accept the reality of both a natural and a supernatural world. We could call these two *agency* and *theological* approaches to education. The other two positions assume that the natural world is all that exists; there is no supernatural world. These approaches can be thought of as *individualist* and *societal* approaches to education. In the agency and the individualist approaches, the focus is on the individual, while in the theological and the societal, the emphasis is on the group. As you read the four accounts, see if you can fit these four titles with the appropriate description.

Education and Values

Imagine two couples, Frank and Ellen, and Harold and Jennifer, conversing after sharing an enjoyable dinner hour together. The food was delicious; they are comfortable and relaxed. They are reflecting on the question *How can we provide our children an education that will enable them to cope successfully with the world we live in?* Clearly, each of the four has come from a background that stressed different values on this subject. As the dialogue develops, each parent describes his or her own education. Let us listen in for a moment. Frank is speaking:

I know my experience with school was very different than Ellen's. Her parents had very strong feelings about letting their kids chart their own course in life. That wasn't the case in my home.

When I was in school both my parents and teachers made it very clear that if I expected to succeed in life, I'd better learn what I was told. Kids are just like other living things. They are going to grow up, and they are a lot better off when somebody makes something worthwhile out of them. People where I lived understood it was the school's job to prepare us to fit into the real world. The teachers knew the rules; they knew what we needed to know, and it was our job to learn what they told us. People generally agreed, I believe, that this was the way to prepare kids for life.

At school my teachers were very definite about things. The objectives were very clear in every course. Due dates on all the assignments were given in advance. Most of my teachers were well prepared; they worked hard to keep us motivated—to make sure we paid attention. They piled on the work, tried to keep the class under control, and the room neat and orderly.

I remember them dividing us into groups according to our abilities. They really did try to make something out of us. I'll never forget the tests. The teachers said they measured how well we achieved the objectives they set for us. I suppose they did, but I always wondered how one point could be the difference between a "B" and a "C." I never felt fully comfortable with the way they compared us against each other and with national standards—probably because I wasn't one of the brains. They told us the grading was fair and accurately reflected our ability, but at the time it didn't always seem that way.

There wasn't a lot of controversy in our school. I remember it was a no-no to talk about religion or church. The teachers always seemed nervous when anyone asked questions about religion. School was school, not something else.

Ellen speaks:

Frank was right when he said things were different at my house. We lived in another part of the country, and I don't believe the public schools were as good as they were in Frank's neighborhood.

Education must have been important to my parents, especially my dad, because when I was very young they enrolled me in a private school. It was a fun place. My teachers always seemed like friends; they were willing to talk about and explain most anything, but they never pushed us into studies we didn't want to do. At times we would sit around for hours, getting very bored doing nothing until some idea or activity would catch our interest. I can't complain about being forced to do things. The only objectives or assignments I can remember originated with me, not my teachers.

It seems like most of us worked on different subjects at different times. I don't remember all of us ever doing the same thing at the same time unless we were involved in doing a play or working on some common project like a musical program; even then different people did different things. Whenever one of us expressed an interest in something, the teachers really became involved. They provided lots of resources, direction, opportunities, and challenges. We were encouraged to explore it all the way. There were times when I would spend days on one subject and get so involved I hardly wanted to play, eat, or do anything else.

51

For example, I remember when I was about thirteen I got interested in geography. For three or four months it seems geography was all I ever studied. My mind became a sponge. I could remember nearly everything I read. I think I knew more about geography at the end of that year than anyone in the school, including my teachers. It was geography that made history and other subjects so interesting to me. I could always connect them to peoples and places I knew about. My father and mother received lots of compliments from my teachers about my work. My parents were very pleased. I'm sure that was the major reason I qualified for a scholarship to attend college when I was sixteen years old.

Independence and self-reliance were stressed. You could believe whatever you wanted, but if you were going to talk about it you needed to be able to defend your point of view. It was sure to be challenged. I can still remember how I felt in those conversations.

Jennifer compares her education with Frank's and Ellen's schooling:

> Well, Howard and I certainly come from the other side of the fence, and yet even our experiences were quite different—in fact, very different in some ways. When I was a child almost everyone in the neighborhood went to parochial school. It was a very religious community in the sense that the Church had a lot to do with most everything—politics, holidays, community standards, etc.
>
> My school experience was something like Frank described—only *everything* began with God. Without God our school wouldn't exist. We wouldn't exist. In fact, nothing would exist. God was in charge of everything—the church, state, family, individual, nature. Our teachers made it very clear that if we wanted to be happy in the next life then certain things were expected of us in this life. Preparing for the next life was most important. Those who fail the big test, we were told, are going to be in serious trouble.
>
> Certainly, there are important things to learn in this life. Our teachers explained how everyone needs food, shelter, and clothing if they are going to be happy. It was clear that we needed to learn how to make a living if we wanted to live comfortable and satisfying lives and be able to help others. They told us if we expected to do this and do it well, it was essential for us to pay attention, do what we were told, and learn the lessons they taught.
>
> We had regular reviews to make sure we knew the right responses to whatever questions were asked. God knew what we should do, and he had put the church in charge of seeing that we did it. Our teachers were well informed and very religious; they were good examples academically and morally. I know they cared about us—sometimes they seemed to care too much. It was hard to get away with anything.
>
> Our teachers made the expectations so clear that we all knew there was no excuse if we messed up. We had time to study and time to meditate on what we studied. We were expected to do our own work, but we also knew it was our duty to assist those needing extra help. We had a kind of family feeling most of the time. There was really no need to fail if a person followed the rules and didn't become rebellious. Life seemed easy as long as we followed the rules and did what we were told.

It was strange to us why people in other areas of the city didn't understand the importance of discipline and the value of following the practices taught by the church.

Howard turns to Jennifer and winks as he reminds her:

Speaking of following the rules, I'm sure Jennifer will never forget the difficulty she had adjusting to my ideas. I grew up believing that parents and the family were primarily responsible for establishing and maintaining personal rules for conduct.

"Howard," she used to say, "Why do you feel that way? Isn't it enough and isn't it easier to just do what we are told and not ask questions? Don't they know what's best?" But that wasn't the way I was reared. I was taught that school rules and church rules wouldn't have much impact unless they first came from the family. Rules had to be family standards before they would work very well at school or church.

I grew up in a little town quite isolated from large cities, big money, or life in the fast lane. Our school seemed like an extension of my home, although we had nearly four hundred students in our high school.

Looking back, I don't think it was the location as much as it was the way the people thought and lived. School for me was something like Ellen described, but it was probably more organized. Teachers didn't make us do things; instead they told us what they were going to do and invited us to join in. We managed to study everything at one time or another. School was seldom boring. It seemed there was always something to touch my curiosity.

Our parents and our teachers were always talking about their mission in life and asking us if we knew what our mission was. We were very much aware that we should be preparing to do something. Like Jennifer's community, the people in my town also looked to God for the basic rules. Scripture study was a part of my life as long as I can remember. We sensed a feeling of partnership with our Heavenly Father. We were on a journey and it was important. Our school helped in some ways and the Church helped in others, but it was the family that seemed to be the main focus.

Jennifer did notice one significant difference: God was not a mystery to my parents or my teachers. They all had a

53

very personal relationship with him. There was a definite feeling that God was leading them along through life. It was all very personal, not distant or formal. People went to Church to get spiritually refueled, to compare notes on how to help people in the community who faced special challenges, and to take turns sharing with each other what they learned from the scriptures. It was something people wanted to do, not something they had to do.

We were never given grades in our school. But we did have lots of interviews with our teachers and our parents on how things were going at school. The interviews at school were something like those we had at home with our parents. A lot of the same kinds of questions were asked. We knew it was our responsibility to compare what we were learning with what we already knew God had said about certain things. This made it fairly easy to decide what was right and wrong as well as what was most important.

In our school everyone was encouraged to succeed in something they felt was important. The teachers went out of their way to help us discover what that could be. We knew we were all different and had different talents and abilities. School was like trying to solve a puzzle.

54

Questions to Consider

As you reflect on the view of education briefly described by Frank, Ellen, Jennifer, and Howard, you might ask the following questions: Which of the four approaches best represents my own experience with education? Which one would I prefer for my child? What happens to a child that goes through each of these types of experiences? Would I want that to happen to my child? What impact do you think each of these approaches has on the society that promotes it? Is that impact important? Why? Why not? Should I worry about this? If I have a preference, is there anything I can do about it? If I do have a preference and choose to do something about it, what will happen? If I have a preference and choose not to do anything, what will happen? Do I really care one way or another? Is it any of my business? So what? Who else cares? Who should care? Education is a different experience when it is *societal* (Frank), *individualist* (Ellen), *theological* (Jennifer), or *agency* (Howard) in its orientation. Our choices do make a difference. (See charts in Appendix A.)

Agency Education Explained

Agency education as described in this book assumes that

(a) man is an eternal personality of divine origin and attributes, composed of both a physical body and a spirit body, *rather than* only a noneternal, mechanistically evolved, biological system;

(b) as man's personal awareness of correct principles increases, he acquires increased ability and should be encouraged to learn by choosing between alternatives with consequences, *rather than* subject himself to systems that indiscriminately enforce conformity or generally promote the unrestricted expression of personal desires;

(c) teaching is a matter of serving others by revealing correct principles through personal example and sharing true information that expands and ensures the availability of richer options, *rather than* the shaping of other people's behavior to match social norms and expectations or simply nurturing natural impulses and capacities for expression;

(d) education should focus on the development of divine character and the pursuit of a personal mission sustained by provident living, *more than* on responding and adapting to social roles that satisfy group needs or simply seeking self-satisfaction and personal fulfillment;

(e) the family unit is designed to provide the most influential and cost effective context for basic life long learning/teaching, *better than* any other external support systems one could create;

(f) the proper development of the individual fosters a yearning for unifying, ministering, compassionate, nourishing, loving brotherhood and a desire to serve, *rather than* nurturing an intensely competitive self-interest or an isolating personal autonomy;

55

(g) emphasis on nonbudgetary resources is more vital to effective learning/teaching,	*than*	a focus on the budgetary resources that normally appear as line items;
(h) the heartfelt moral interests of the individual best serve long-run interests of society,	*rather than*	the popular interests of society should determine the moral interests of the individual;
(i) it is more appropriate to understand education in terms of what it will cause a person to become,	*rather than*	what advantages it will provide to students in the marketplace.

Why Study and Practice Agency Education?

56

As these assumptions indicate, agency education is unique. It is based on a Hebrew worldview. It is a true alternative to the popular views now promoted in our society on how to pursue teaching and learning. People do not have to choose between eductional practice rooted in the naturalistic philosophy of modern science or the relativistic value structure of the humanities. The restoration of the Hebraic perspective provides a way to avoid the consequences of adopting the "irreconcilable contradiction" of modern education. As one critic explains, America's teacher trainers have simultaneously committed themselves to (1) "behavior shaping" and (2) "humanistic education." He continues "The educationists seem oblivious to the contradictions inherent in their two favorite principles. Nor could they abandon either, for in their 'humanism' they can pose as philosophers and priests, and as modifiers of behavior they can claim to be scientists and healers."[1] The statement is cynical, but its point is true. Confusion abounds in education because it is a battleground of opposing premises, and not a field of peace or harmony. Seeking a worthy alternative to this confusion is one good reason to study and practice agency education.

There is another reason to study this book seriously. It provides parents, teachers, and students with a way to understand and teach values more effectively. We have now reached a point at which society endorses compartmentalized value structures within the individual. These personal but independent value structures often contradict each other and lead to hypocritical behavior patterns. For example, individuals may be enticed to use one value system in one setting and a different value structure in another setting. Inconsistency, duplicity, and hypocrisy are natural outcomes; but ironically, so is a sense of comfort. The comfort comes from the positive endorsement provided by our social structure. Conflicting values are often honored because they are both sanctioned. Boyd K. Packer describes the dilemma in these words:

> Something is weakening the moral fiber of the American people. We have always had couples live together without marriage, but we have not honored it as an acceptable life style. We have always had children born out of wedlock, but we have never made it to be respectable. And, we have never before regarded babies, conceived in wedlock or out, to be an inconvenience and destroyed them by the thousands through abortion. . . .We have always had some who followed a life of perversion, but we have never before pushed through legislation to protect that way of life lest we offend the rights of an individual. . . .We have always had those who were guilty of criminal acts, but we have not put the rights of the accused above the rights of the victim. . . .What kind of individual freedom is this, anyway.[2]

57

In the past when a person was taught what was right society usually reinforced that teaching by making clear that its opposite was wrong and why it was wrong. Today this is no longer true. Quite the contrary prevails. Depending on the setting, both "right" and "wrong" are approved. Confusion prevails. The new condition is apparent in government, workplace, schools, churches, neighborhoods, and families.

The presence of two or more conflicting value structures within the same individual creates a new instructional challenge—especially when these value structures are each isolated, insulated, and endorsed by an "acceptable" social group. In order to effectively teach a person to embrace a single value structure that sustains integrity, the parent or teacher must now assume a greater role. In addition to carefully teaching what is right, we must also clearly explain how the opposite of that teaching is wrong and why it is wrong. Then, and only then, can we be confident the individual being instructed has enough information to make an effective choice based on his or her own agency. When this type of confrontive and contrasting instruction is missing, the individual tends simply to compartmentalize contradictory teachings into different value structures. These differing values are then used to cue the person's actions, depending on the setting. The result is we may act according to one set of values in church settings, and according to a contradictory set of values at school or in our profession. Improving our ability to combat this problem is a major focus of agency education.

In addition to these reasons, the agency approach to education offers other features that can make qualitative differences in the lives of individuals, families, and communities. The remainder of this chapter briefly considers some of these qualitative differences. These ideas complement the agency proposal but differ from what is often widely promoted and practiced in education.

58

Three Points of Emphasis in Agency Education

Precepts Precede Methods. First, the agency approach to education emphasizes that what people think, how they feel, and the way they act in relationship to themselves and others is more central to education than what methods, techniques, or organizational strategies are applied. Contrary to the major themes in current educational literature, what matters most for parents, teachers, and students is the quality of our vision of our relationships to God, man, and nature. This vision determines the nature of educational practice. We miss the mark when we focus *primarily* on methods, techniques, and organizational matters. Methodology is important and very popular, but it is secondary in agency education. Too often, we as parents, teachers, and students put the cart before the horse—we seek recipes to guide our practice before we understand and acquire the proper ingredients. We concentrate on the measurable details of information and methods and omit serious consideration of the weightier matters—qualities like purpose, commitment, and integrity.

The true nature of education is determined by the principles inherent in personal vision, not in methods and techniques. The manipulation of methods cannot significantly change true education, appealing as this may be to the practitioner. Methods and techniques may enhance our educational experience, but they cannot change the nature of the process; only principles that govern vision can do this. Regardless of the method or technique one selects to make a meatloaf, it will always be a meatloaf—not a steak or a roast.

Scope Precedes Sequence. Second, the approach to education in this book presumes and depends on an accurate sense of the past, present, and future. When any one of these three elements is missing or distorted, the educational process is weakened. A sense of the past means more than our awareness of history; it is a feeling of our being connected to those who have lived before. To understand the present consists of more than our proficiency in securing a comfortable survival; it is our sense of preparation for and fulfillment of our destiny. Believing in the future means more than anticipating job retention, physical well-being, and financial security; it refers to a vision of how the life I live will connect to those who live with me and after me. The truth of education resides in properly perceiving and carefully honoring the relationships that should exist between what has been, what is now, and what will be. Education that lacks this vision is dangerous; it sows seeds of destruction and causes people to perish. When we learn and how we learn specific lessons in life are secondary to understanding who we are and the purpose of our existence. This is not the pattern in popular education today; its emphasis is just the opposite.

59

Seeking Precedes Finding. Third, the contents of this book are the author's personal examinations of the human journey. It is subject to the writer's limitations and is presented to the reader as an invitation to join in the journey and contribute his or her own experience and insight. There is a theme, a pattern, a story if you will, that pervades human literature. It recurs in nearly every age and every culture. It is a common truth enveloped in the major myths of mankind; the story is simple and always personal. The sequence described in the story applies to man's entire life as well as to any significant part. It is the story of how man lives and how he learns; it is the great human quest. Agency education grows out of this story; it is a personal process, not a prescription to be forced on others. This classic quest portrays man's search to learn the difference between good and evil from his own experience, to prevail, to endure, and to prove himself—to become sanctified and eventually justified in the eyes of the Creator.

Pilgrims or Heroes?

In brief, this is the story that is fostered in human culture: Man is created and nurtured in a safe place—a *home,* meaning his place, his point of origin, his place of departure. Man eventually reaches a point in time when he must leave his home, his safe place, and journey forth into the larger world, or he will cease to develop. The purpose of the journey is to explore the world in search of a gift, find the gift, bring it home, and share it with others. The journey involves risking, encountering the unknown, seeking help, experiencing personal change, acquiring a gift, enduring the return trip, and sharing the gift with someone else. The journey is an adventure, an adventure in learning and refinement. Without the journey, life is unfulfilled, and the person is less than he could be.

The idea of this journey is preserved in the practices of most primitive cultures; it is the focus of the literature and lifestyles of most modern societies. Motives that result in marriage, create parents, move people into vocations, put children into schools, entice athletes onto the playing field, sustain youth on missions, and lure men into space, are modern examples of this age-old urge. The very core of the Christian religion symbolizes this journey. Man leaves a heavenly home, enters a lone and dreary world, exercises faith, seeks a teacher, manifests a changed nature, receives a gift, and strives to endure, so that the gift can be shared with others. It is the story of a plan of salvation, a savior, and a saved people; a process that has been called *Kerygma.*[3]

Two very different views of this story are apparent in Western culture. One view has its origin in the way ancient Greek society viewed man and the universe. Those who describe the journey from this perspective have called it a hero journey.[4] The other view comes from our Hebrew heritage and communicates different values. In the Hebrew view, man is a stranger and pilgrim on the earth, seeking to find the way home. The hero idea is rooted in the images of characters like Promethius and Achilles. In this pattern the journey is characterized by brash courage, cleverness, self-sufficiency, and perhaps even a spirit of defiance. The gods may need to be appeased by outward signs of deference, but the secret of success lies in marshalling and applying the powers of the self. A modern counterpart of the hero-warrior image of antiquity can be seen in our own battles to achieve professional fulfillment in the secular marketplace. The task is to obtain the necessary advantages to overcome those barriers that prevent us from achieving personal power, glory, recognition, and dominion. Success and satisfaction are attributed to generating the same spirit and qualities as those portrayed by Promethius and Achilles.

The Hebrew perspective, in contrast to the Greek, portrays man's journey as a search for and a response to a personal mission of service. The journey of the pilgrim-servant is characterized by the expression of very different qualities than those exhibited by the classic hero. As illustrated by Job and Christ, strength is rooted in a voluntary submission of self to God, a reliance on God's directions, and a focus on service to others. Power, glory, and recognition are transferred to others, rather than embraced by self. There can be joy in the journey, but the ultimate prize is not claimed in this mortal world where man is a stranger. What are considered ends (achievements) worthy of display for Greek heroes are seldom more than means to ends for Hebrew pilgrims. Rendering humble service is of greater value than receiving public recognition. These two different views of the human journey foster different forms of education. They foster different values and create different types of societies.

61

I consider each personal venture, from becoming literate to writing one's memoirs, a mini-journey. There comes a point when our growth is blocked, unless we are willing to venture out, explore new ideas, find something worthwhile, obtain it, and return home to share the gift with others. This is the nature of personal education. If optimum learning is to occur, the student must make the trip and so must the teacher. Likewise, parents must make the trip, and so must children. It is the way of life and the path of learning. The spiritual energy that fuels this form of learning is personal rather than prescriptive; it is natural rather than contrived. The idea of the personal journey is common to human experience, but it is uncommon in formal education. Too often, today's students compete against a system and strive to fulfill goals that have been established by others. Journey learning seeks something worth sharing; it involves believing enough to risk, teaching that touches the chords of change, discovering and obtaining a gift worth giving away, and being willing to share that gift with others.

The human journey can happen in such simple tasks as learning to read, write, or do arithmetic. It can happen at home, at work, and at play; in sickness and in health; in the birthing room and at the cemetery; in war and peace. It all depends on the disposition of the learners and the teachers. It demands a personal faith that enables us to embrace what we learn without requiring us to conclude we know everything because we have learned something. It is important to understand the motive we choose to fuel our quests. Are we striving to be heroes or pilgrim-servants? The qualitative outcome of our journey will not be the same if we strive to become a hero in search of power, glory, and recognition rather than sensing that we are pilgrims striving to become worthy servants of a divine creator.

62

Foundations of Agency Education Defined

The ultimate aim of the education described in this book is something each person must envision. I believe this awareness develops as we learn that every sin is a lie and every lie is an alternative to love. Our understanding increases when we can comfortably define love as appropriately doing for others that which they cannot rightfully do for themselves. Love should be the motive for action in our most sacred relationships. For example, love enables a husband to become a true father, a wife to become a true mother. Since a child cannot conceive or give birth to itself, love is the essential ingredient intended to sustain the miracle of mortality. Procreation was designed to be an act of love; in mortality it is a symbol of the obedient exercise of responsible agency exercised according to divine law. Love brings to pass the mortality and quality of life in man that sustains Deity's divine mission of bringing to pass the immortality and eternal life of man. "Behold, this is your work [and glory], to keep my commandments, yea, with all your might, mind and strength" (D&C 11:20). And "behold, this is my work and my glory—to bring to pass the immortality and eternal life of man" (Moses 1:39).

Agency education endeavors to encourage and assist individuals, without exerting unrighteous dominion, to honor the divine laws and forces necessary to fulfill one's eternal nature. It includes (1) striving to be a personal example of one on the way to the goal; (2) acting as a willing recipient and channel of divine influence; (3) protecting the inherent element of choice that resides in the individual; and (4) complying with legitimate stewardships in directing the individual away from obstructing influences so native endowments and potential are not ruptured, impeded, or encouraged to the point of imbalance.

A Theory Based on Revealed Principles

The contextual explanation of learning/teaching provided in this book constitutes a general theory of education; it is based on clearly stated assumptions and derived from principles that are intended to govern its proper practice. Both the theory and the principles are simple to understand, and their value will be self-evident to those who are willing to examine and use them in the learning/teaching process. The writer is aware that those who do not accept both a natural and a supernatural view of reality will be uncomfortable with this form of education. Likewise, those who feel it is necessary to compartmentalize their views in order to accommodate the exclusively naturalistic view of man and the universe may find it unnerving.

63

Individuals who accept a spiritual reality, however, may find the ideas contained in this book stimulating and helpful, particularly those who are searching for explanations that emphasize personal integrity and responsible liberty in the learning/teaching process. I realize that one person's understanding and experience is not a finished form of education, no more than a single flower makes a bouquet. But what I have written has been helpful and valid in my own life. It may have value for others as well.

Agency Education Can Be Applied Anytime and Anywhere

The reader should be sensitive to the fact that agency education must not be, indeed it cannot be, forced. It must be privately endorsed and personally embraced or it ceases to be agency education. Those who are looking for a program to mandate, one that can be externally imposed as a political panacea will not find it here. The genius of agency education lies deep within the human personality, far beyond the reach of social and political systems. Man is free to act for himself; his innermost being cannot be acted upon unless he chooses to let it be. Contrary forces may circumscribe a full and formal application of an agency approach to education, but unless the person chooses to let them, they cannot eliminate its function within the individual.[5]

Persons who understand agency education will be more free to use it, rather than succumbing to the influences of lesser approaches to learning/teaching. Agency education is not an all or nothing theory; it can be applied by degrees in almost any social, political, or cultural setting. It is consistent with the declaration that "we believe in being subject to kings, presidents, rulers, and magistrates, in obeying, honoring, and sustaining the law" (PGP Articles of Faith, No. 13). Agency education can fill the space of available freedom, whatever the context. Some circumstances may allow full and unrestricted application; others may circumscribe the extent to which individuals are invited to practice its principles. Generally, however, personal choice more than social or physical restraint is the limiting influence; ignorance, false traditions, and willful rebellion are the major enemies of agency education.

64

Current Difficulties that Obstruct the Improvement of Education

The way people think and feel about education determines the nature of education. If we want to change education, it is necessary to change the way we think and feel about education. This is more fundamental than methods or materials. The application of methodology seldom, if ever, corrects wrong thinking, but correct thinking frequently leads to changing incorrect methodology. The story of a people in the South Seas who were influenced by their experiences with the technology of World War II illustrates this point. During the war, a tribe of islanders had a brief experience with military operations. The people saw airplanes land with lots of good material, and they wanted the same thing to happen after the soldiers left the area. So they arranged to make things that looked like runways, put fires along the sides, made a wooden hut for a man to sit in, placed two wooden pieces on his head like headphones, and shoots of bamboo sticking out like antennas—he's the controller. They wait for the airplanes to land. They appear to be doing everything right methodologically. The form appears perfect. But it doesn't work. Something essential is missing. It is flawed by incorrect ideas.[6]

The same principle holds true for education. We must learn to think and feel correctly before we can fully act correctly.

Formal education today is more complex, less effective, and more expensive than it needs to be, because

— Many contemporary educational policies and practices are inconsistent with man's eternal nature.

— The fundamental significance of the parent-child relationship to the educational process is frequently ignored, supplanted, or abused.

— Remedial programs have significantly taken the place of developmental instruction.

— Remedial programs tend to focus more on expansion and self-perpetuation than on reduction.

— There is no clearly articulated, widely received, effectively practiced, and adequate philosophy or model for moral and spiritual instruction.

— Contemporary educational thought is generally preoccupied with budgetary resources; the idea that the primary resources for developing and sustaining correct education are unlimited is largely ignored.

65

— Utility rather than propriety dominates the governance of most modern educational processes: if it works, use it.

— Many current educational policies and practices are contaminated by error, overlap, confusion, and conflict; the essential and the non-essential elements of education need to be disentangled.

These problems are real and they are serious, but they need not be fully resolved in society before individuals can overcome their limitations. The agency approach to education offers parents, teachers, and students a way to address these educational challenges in their personal lives, thereby minimizing or eliminating many of the negative influences. It is unnecessary to wait upon society for their resolution. Each individual can choose a better way, if that way is made known.

In this chapter I have outlined some of the reasons for seriously considering the possibilities and rewards offered in an agency approach to education. Contrasts between this approach and today's popular education have been pointed out. The reader is invited to keep these comparisons in mind as subsequent ideas are explored.

5

First Things First

Man, Earth, and Time are symbols of God, Heaven, and Eternity. [They lift] our thoughts from man to God, from earth to Heaven, from time to eternity.
—Orson F. Whitney

Lessons From A Soap Bubble

Most of us have experienced blowing soap bubbles from a wire or plastic wand dipped into a homemade or commercial liquid. Children are fascinated by these bubbles, made by softly blowing on a thin film of soapy water. A soap bubble can also illustrate an important lesson for teachers, parents, and students. It can help us visualize different ways people define the world, which in turn determines the way they see education and the forces which shape its foundations.

If I suppose that a single soap bubble represents this earth in the universe as it is now understood by modern man—billions of galaxies, each with a huge population of stars—some interesting viewpoints come into focus. Carefully observed, the skin of a soap bubble with its irridescent colors is simply a reflection of whatever surrounds it. If the bubble is in the kitchen, for example, it will reflect the objects in that room. Now, imagine with me at least four views that can be associated with that bubble—one from outside the bubble and three from inside the bubble.

View from Outside. One possible view is to imagine being outside the bubble, seeing it as an object that exists in a particular form for a few moments of time. While the bubble exists in its physical, global, or galactic form, it reflects whatever is beyond it. If I observe carefully, I can see the images. The bubble is real, but it is also temporary; soon it will pop and vanish. The material from which it was originally organized will take on a new form. This view from outside the bubble is one way to view the world (the universe) in which I live. The bubble is real, but temporary, and it simply reflects or symbolizes a more enduring, transcendent reality which exists outside of it.

From this outside vantage point the temporal world is indeed temporary, a reflection of the spiritual reality that transcends the temporal. Joseph F. Smith taught that things on earth are patterned after things in heaven. "Things upon this earth, so far as they have not been perverted by wickedness, are typical of things in heaven. Heaven was the prototype of this beautiful creation when it came from the hand of the Creator."[1] Orson F. Whitney expresses the thought poetically: "Man, Earth and Time are symbols of God, Heaven and Eternity." They lift "our thoughts from man to God, from earth to Heaven, from time to eternity."[2] Those who see the world in this way, from outside the bubble, recognize that reality consists of both a natural and a supernatural domain. I can imagine this is the way God sees earth and its inhabitants. He has said:

> For by the power of my Spirit created I them; yea, all things both spiritual and temporal—
>
> First spiritual, secondly temporal, which is the beginning of my work; and again, first temporal, and secondly spiritual, which is the last of my work—
>
> Speaking unto you that you may naturally understand; but unto myself my works have no end, neither beginning; but it is given unto you that ye may understand, because ye have asked it of me and are agreed.
>
> Wherefore, verily I say unto you that all things unto me are spiritual, and not at any time have I given unto you a law which was temporal; neither any man, nor the children of men; neither Adam, your father, whom I created.
>
> Behold, I gave unto him that he should be an agent unto himself; and I gave unto him commandment, but no temporal commandment gave I him, for my commandments are spiritual; they are not natural nor temporal, neither carnal nor sensual. (D&C 29:31-35)

View from Inside (#1). Another view can be described by imagining one's self inside the bubble while at the same time acknowledging a reality that exists outside the bubble. Some

68

individuals, with divine assistance, have been privileged to penetrate the thin membrane and see that the bubble is only a temporary reflection of that which exists beyond it. These people share in the outside perspective while living inside. They know for themselves that they live in the natural world but, with divine assistance, they also become living witnesses to a greater reality. They know that all things were created spiritually before they were given a natural form within the bubble. Consider the reports of four of these witnesses who have testified of their vision:

Witness #1: *Abraham.*

Thus I, Abraham, talked with the Lord, face to face, as one man talketh with another; and he told me of the works which his hands had made;

And he said unto me: My son, my son (and his hand was stretched out), behold I will show you all these. And he put his hand upon mine eyes, and I saw those things which his hands had made, which were many; and they multiplied before mine eyes, and I could not see the end thereof. (PGP Abraham 3:11-12)

Witness #2: *Moses.*

Moses . . . saw God face to face and he talked with him, and the glory of God was upon Moses; therefore Moses could endure his presence.

And God spake unto Moses saying: Behold, I am the Lord God Almighty . . . .

And, behold, thou art my son; wherefore look, and I will show thee the workmanship of mine hands; but not all, for my works are without end . . .

And now, Moses, my son, I will speak unto thee concerning this earth upon which thou standest; and thou shalt write the things which I shall speak.

And in a day when the children of men shall esteem my words as naught and take many of them from the book which thou shalt write, behold, I will raise up another like unto thee; and they shall be had again among the children of men—among as many as shall believe. . . .

And it came to pass that the Lord spake unto Moses, saying: Behold, I reveal unto you concerning this heaven, and this earth; write the words which I speak. . . .

69

For I, the Lord God, created all things of which I have spoken, spiritually, before they were naturally upon the face of the earth. For I, the Lord God, had not caused it to rain upon the face of the earth. And I, the Lord God, had created all the children of men; and not yet a man to till the ground; for in heaven created I them; and there was not yet flesh upon the earth, neither in the water, neither in the air;

But I, the Lord God, spake, and there went up a mist from the earth, and watered the whole face of the ground.

And I, the Lord God, formed man from the dust of the ground, and breathed into his nostrils the breath of life; and man became a living soul, the first flesh upon the earth, the first man also; nevertheless, all things were before created; but spiritually were they created and made according to my word. (PGP, Moses 1:2-5, 40; 2:1; 3:5-7)

Witnesses #3 and #4: *Joseph Smith and Sidney Rigdon.*

And while we meditated upon these things, the Lord touched the eyes of our understandings and they were opened, and the glory of the Lord shone round about.

And we beheld the glory of the Son, on the right hand of the Father. . . .

And now, after the many testimonies which have been given of him, this is the testimony, last of all, which we give of him: That he lives!

For we saw him even on the right hand of God; and we heard the voice bearing record that he is the Only Begotten of the Father, . . .

And while we were yet in the Spirit, the Lord commanded us that we should write the vision; . . . [and we saw those] whose bodies are celestial, whose glory is that of the sun, even the glory of God. . . .

And again, we saw the terrestrial world, and behold and lo, these are they who are of the terrestrial, whose glory differs from that of the church of the Firstborn who have received the fulness of the Father, even as that of the moon differs from the sun in the firmament. . . .

Behold, and lo, we saw the glory and the inhabitants of the telestial world, that they were as innumerable as the stars in the firmament of heaven, or as the sand upon the sea-shore. . . .

This is the end of the vision which we saw, which we were commanded to write while we were yet in the Spirit. But great and marvelous are the works of the Lord, and the mysteries of his kingdom which he showed unto us, which surpass all understanding in glory, and in might, and in dominion:

Which he commanded us we should not write while we were yet in the Spirit, and are not lawful for man to utter;

Neither is man capable to make them known, for they are only to be seen and understood by the power of the Holy Spirit, which God bestows on those who love him, and purify themselves before him;

To whom he grants this privilege of seeing and knowing for themselves; that through the power and manifestation of the Spirit, while in the flesh, they may be able to bear his presence in the world of glory. (D&C 76:19-20, 22-23, 28, 70-71, 109, 113-118)

View from Inside (#2). A second inside view is held by those persons who, due to limited or undeveloped personal vision, are unable to see beyond the bubble but are willing to believe the reports of those who can. These people live by faith—which is a partial knowledge (John 20:24-29; Romans 1:17; BM, Alma 32:17-22). They know they live in a natural world, but they also believe in a supernatural reality; they act accordingly, on the basis of the testimony of witnesses in whom they have a confidence that is confirmed by the Spirit. Of these Jesus said, "blessed are they that have not seen, and yet have believed." This statement was elicited by his experience with Thomas, one of his disciples.

But Thomas, one of the twelve . . . was not with them when Jesus came.

The other disciples therefore said unto him, We have seen the Lord. But he said unto them, Except I shall see in his hands the print of the nails, . . . and thrust my hand into his side I will not believe.

And after eight days again his disciples were within, and Thomas with them: then came Jesus, the doors being shut, and stood in the midst, and said, Peace be unto you.

Then saith he to Thomas, Reach hither thy finger, and behold my hands; and reach hither thy hand, and thrust it into my side; and be not faithless, but believing.

And Thomas answered and said unto him, My Lord and my God.

Jesus saith unto him, Thomas, because thou hast seen me thou hast believed: blessed are they that have not seen, and yet have believed. (John 20:24-29)

View from Inside (#3). A third inside view is held by those who live within the bubble and then, on the basis of their examination of this physical experience, conclude that the bubble and its contents are real, but there is nothing beyond. For these people the bubble is opaque; they trust only what their physical senses and rational capacities reveal. They believe that what they can see, touch, smell, hear, and taste is real. They do not believe that what their senses reveal to them reflects a reality that exists outside the bubble. Witnesses are ignored who offer contrary testimony that cannot be reduced to a rational, physical demonstration. People who see the world in this way are exclusive naturalists. They believe there is no supernatural world and act accordingly. Yervant H. Krikorian's collection of essays in *Naturalism and the Human Spirit* (1959) is one source of testimonies that maintain this point of view; Peter Angeles *Critiques of God* (1976) is another. Angeles summarizes the message of more than a dozen scholarly essays in the introduction to his book in these words:

> The concept of God as a causal agent has been taken less and less seriously during the past 200 years. The movement of the "heavenly" bodies, diseases, the ebb and flow of the oceans, earthquakes, famines, floods, wars, the origin of the universe and life, the course of history, the subconscious. . . . These and many more natural events have been related at one time or another to the deliberate activity of God. As our knowledge of the universe increases, we recognize that all forms of phenomena can be explained in terms of the interrelatedness of natural processes without reference to a God. . . .Without God, what is left? Man and the Universe. That should be enough. That has to be enough because that is all there is. . . .The ardor man once held for God must be ardor showered upon man and mankind's potential for good and for survival.

72

Setting the Sails

One of the most important educational decisions we make is choosing our position in relation to the bubble—in relation to our definition of reality. This simply means deciding what to believe about ourselves and the world in which we live. At the very heart of this decision is the question: Are we part of *a natural world and a supernatural world,* or is there *only a natural world*? (A few people may suggest a third possibility: there is only a supernatural, all that appears to be natural is an illusion.) The answer to this question sets the sails and influences both the direction and general outcome for human learning and teaching. It is reminiscent of Ella Wheeler Wilcox's poem, *Winds of Fate.*

> One ship drives east and another drives west,
> While the self-same breezes blow;
> It's the set of the sails and not the gales,
> That bids them where to go.
> Like the winds of the seas are the ways of the fates,
> As we voyage along through life;
> Its the set of the soul that decides the goal,
> And not the storms or the strife.

73

If we believe the world is only physical, we will pursue education differently than if we believe the world is both physical and spiritual. In order to explore seriously the challenges associated with learning and teaching, it is necessary to make a conscious and clear choice between these diametrically opposite points of view. The choice is fundamental and exclusive; it determines all the conclusions and consequences which follow. If we do not consciously make this choice, it will be made for us by default. The position a person takes on this basic question significantly shapes the creation of his or her educational theory and practice. It marks the base from which one's integrity is measured.

Vertical vs. Horizontal

This classic tension (perhaps *the* classic tension) in human culture is shadowed in what the Greeks perceived as the *mantic* versus the *sophic* view[3] what has been identified in ancient Judaism as the *vertical* versus the *horizontal* traditions,[4] and what modernists term the *supernatural* versus the *natural*.[5] This ancient problem raises two basic questions: first, in our search for knowledge, are we limited to what we can learn by our explorations inside the bubble, or can knowledge also come to us from outside the bubble? And second, must all explanations of human interest be restricted to discussions of physical evidence, or are there spiritual forces, influences, and powers which operate and should be acknowledged? No parent, teacher, or student can carefully consider the process of education without facing the implications of these questions. There are different responses, but the questions are inherent in the subject and cannot be honestly ignored. To be consistent with their own assumptions, people who believe in a supernatural as well as a natural world must explain and conduct education differently than those who do not. Otherwise there is a breach in integrity; the practice is inconsistent with the belief.

74

The Dilemma in Today's World

The traditional response of the human family to this problem has been to acknowledge the existence of some deity, power, or intelligent force outside the bubble. Most records of ancient societies reflect the idea of a supernatural; it was taken for granted without need for defense. For several millennia, most people apparently accepted on the basis of history and tradition, reason, nature, and divine revelation that there is a God (or gods), the Creator of man and nature, that transcends the bubble. James E. Talmage contends that the conscious subjection to a supreme power appears as an inborn as well as a culturally transmitted attribute of mankind. Until modern times, only incidental attention was given to definitions of existence that denied a spiritual domain.[6] Gabriel Vahanian suggests that "ours is the first attempt in recorded history to build a culture upon the premise that God is dead."[7]

In modern Western culture, the academic power structure that seeks to educate man (that which controls most schools and universities) generally insists on a naturalistic definition of the world. Schools teach that what is in the bubble is all there is; it is foolish to believe in anything more. Everyone, of course, does not agree with this view. In fact, if public opinion polls are correct, the majority may disagree; nevertheless, during the twentieth century the controlling influence in our society has been transferred to those who choose to think, write, and talk as if the supernatural did not exist. The result of this fundamental shift in our schooling is clearly recorded in the accepted public school curriculum of our culture. Mainstream curriculum now presumes the physical world, as discerned through the physical senses and whatever man can create to aid these senses (microscopes, telescopes, radar, etc.), is the world of "truth." No other world is presumed to exist. Contrary beliefs are considered private or irrelevant or both.

In contemporary Western civilization, it is not fashionable in the intellectual power structure to believe in or to act as if a reality beyond the bubble exists. More than fifty years ago Walter Lippmann wrote about this problem. He said that modernists have set aside the idea "that behind the visible world of physical objects and human institutions there is a supernatural kingdom from which ultimately all laws, all judgments, all rewards, all punishments and all compensations are derived."[8] To modern man "the belief in this [supernatural] kingdom . . . is a grandiose fiction projected by human needs and desires."[9]

7 5

Many individuals strive to retain the ancestral view or seek to form some type of compromise between the supernatural and the naturalistic views; generally, however, these people have little or no control over mainstream American education. The educational mindset that governs elementary, secondary, college, and university publications is profoundly secular. Examine how supernatural ideas are treated in professional journals. Contributors to these journals may be given the right to believe what they choose, but legitimacy of the divine is scant. Professional credibility is reserved for those who limit their explanations to the view within the bubble that denies or ignores the reality of a supernatural. God and his influence have been editorially expelled from modern publications and from the modern worldview.

Albert Einstein stated the modern position clearly. He indicated that there is no room in modern thought to believe in anything outside the bubble:

> The more a man is imbued with the ordered regularity of all events the firmer becomes his conviction that there is no room left by the side of this ordered regularity for causes of a

different nature. For him [modern man] neither the rule of human nor the rule of divine will exist as an independent cause of natural events.[10]

It was Einstein's belief that man must give up the idea of a personal God who transcends nature. He wrote, "In their struggle for the ethical good, teachers of religion must have the stature to give up the doctrine of a personal God."[11] Many other modern educators have sought to explain how a correct understanding of nature eliminates the need for man to believe in a divine personality and a supernatural world. John Dewey, the popular American educator, wrote an entire book on the subject entitled *A Common Faith*, in which he described a religion for America that had no need of a divine being that exists outside of nature.

Others, like B. F. Skinner, approach the issue less directly but with equal or greater force. Skinner, a leader among modern behavioristic psychologists, maintains that "there is no place in the scientific position for a self as a true originator or initiator of action."[12] All human behavior, according to Skinner, can potentially be explained by the influence of the "ordered regularity" of the natural environment which Einstein reverenced. For those who take the naturalistic position and assume that nothing exists outside the bubble, this is a perfectly logical and consistent conclusion. It can be presented as both reasonable and workable. A world of this type can be described, embraced, and lived in with apparent convenience, comfort, and social acceptance. Most modern educational theory and practice are based on the assumption that matter acting on matter is the basis for explaining human as well as natural phenomena.

The Foundation of Modern School Curriculum

The most popular view of the general curriculum in our modern schools is structured on the assumption that "progress" is most likely to occur when one presumes psychology can be reduced to biology, biology to chemistry, and chemistry to physics.[13] This assumption has been associated with many developments that have made the physical, and perhaps some aspects of our mental life, more comfortable and enjoyable. In a material sense it is very persuasive. Expressing the confidence of those who embrace modern naturalism, Peter Angeles as noted,

76

said, "The concept of a God as a causal agent has been taken less and less seriously during the past 200 years. . . . .Without God what is left? Man and the universe. That should be enough. That has to be enough because that is all there is."[14] John Dewey explained that nature had endowed man with the capacity to create mental images and to transform these images into action: "It is this active relation between the ideal and the actual to which I would give the name 'God.' [But] I would not insist that the name must be given."[15] This makes man the "god" of modernism. The perceived need for a Divinity, a world outside the bubble, or a reality that transcends our cosmic physical universe, appears very weak in the circles that give public expression to the modern western mindset.[16]

Thousands of those who make up the modern intelligentsia subscribe to the statement: "As non-theists, we begin with humans not God, nature not deity. . . . We can discover no divine purpose or providence for the human species. While there is much that we do not know, humans are responsible for what we are or will become. No deity will save us; we must save ourselves."[17]

Ironically, many people who believe in both a natural and supernatural existence seem to have learned how to live quietly in a society that "conducts its business" generally as if nothing exists beyond the bubble. Their accommodation to this limited perspective seems to be rather complete and satisfying. Day by day, all things considered, life can be lived as if all is well. There is no need to rock the boat; it will only make matters worse. But should believers stand quietly by?

Implications of the Choice

The accepted pattern for action in the modern world is rather clear in practice. Adopt a naturalistic view of the world and answer educational questions *only* within that framework; or act *primarily* within that framework, restricting any exceptions to private experience. The social and legal environment tend to ignore or discourage public expressions in favor of the supernatural worldview. Efforts in its favor are seldom considered significant or important. Lives are lived, goals pursued, vocations chosen, living arrangements accepted and rejected, and wealth accumulated and dispensed quite in harmony with the naturalistic view. If something exists outside the bubble, it is not considered to be professionally or publicly important.

This book rejects the exclusively naturalistic approach to education and chooses instead to accept both a natural and a supernatural dimension to life. I believe the natural can and should be properly influenced by the spiritual. The bubble is temporary; it will pop, and changes will occur. This is not to say that educational theory and practice based on the naturalistic view will not produce results; they can and do, but the focus in that approach leaves much unexplored that is vitally important to those who look beyond the bubble—by faith or by knowledge.

An alternative to naturalism does exist. It is ancient and has many forms; some of these forms may be more appealing, appropriate, and correct than others. Good and bad can be found among those who live within the supernatural tradition, just as there is good and bad among those who hold to the exclusively naturalist position. But history notwithstanding, the supernatural option is a worthy alternative. And this book provides at least one view of that approach to education. This book is directed to parents, teachers, and students who choose to believe there is both a natural and a supernatural world, and that both of these domains can and should influence the structure, function, and outcome of educational endeavors—at home, at work, and at play.

An Important Note About Compartmentalizing Our Values

Another group of parents, teachers, and students may tempt us to join them. These are the parents, teachers, and students who choose to believe in both a natural and supernatural world view, but, because of the world's influence, they think and act as if (1) the supernatural world did not exist, or (2) the supernatural world should not be acknowledged except in special settings. This position leads to compartmentalizing our thoughts and acts. It requires the development of two or more separate value systems. One value system is used in religious settings and another at the workplace, school, or the home. Consequently, such people feel it is possible to seek the acceptance of the world, embrace worldly principles and practices, and still retain a place in the religious community. There is a sense of convenience in this position and many adopt it—some unwittingly and others knowingly.

When this compartmentalized approach is applied in the theory and practice of education as defined in this book, confusion results; inconsistencies become apparent. Children may be disoriented as they view hypocrisy modeled by significant adults in their lives. Under these conditions the development of the children's integrity may be restricted; hypocrisy and guile may be taught. The test seems to be to overcome the temptation to use one set of values in one setting and replace these with a different set of values in another setting. A prominent writer, speaking of Christian schools, has expressed the challenge with this observation:

> Officially, (that is, in their published catalogues and advertisements) they often claim to offer a complete and encompassing Christian education by providing an environment which presents modern ideas and theories in the context and atmosphere of an authentic and profoundly Christian perspective. Indeed, on these campuses, you can often meet teachers and students (as well as administrators) who impressively exemplify such deep-rooted and profound conviction of Christian principles, that a visitor may even become jealous of such belief and sincerity. Even more impressive is to see how they carry such conviction into their daily private lives, where they make vivid what it means to love one's neighbor. But if you attend their classes and critcally analyze what is taught or learned in the formal coursework, the picture often becomes very confusing. The stark contrast is like an ice-cold plunge into secularity.[18]

79

Admittedly, there is a strong temptation in our modern culture to seek the acceptance and admiration of leaders committed to the naturalistic position. Because these people control important reward systems, we are often tempted to hide our allegiance to the supernatural so we won't lose credibility and the rewards they control. It is tempting to do things "their way," and it seems imprudent, pious, or unprofessional to "reveal our beliefs" in the way we speak, act, and write. The fact that this temptation occurs in social, domestic, and business settings as well as in education simply punctuates the need personally to strive for integrity. For those who sincerely believe in God and his transcendent influence, a sobering obligation is in the Savior's statement,

> And in nothing doth man offend God, or against none is his wrath kindled, save those who confess not his hand in all things, and obey not his commandments. Behold this is according to the law and the prophets. (D&C 59:21)

Indeed, the contract made by sincere Christians through the ordinance of baptism includes the promise to

> stand as witnesses of God at all times and in all things, and in all places that ye may be in, even until death, that ye may be redeemed of God, and be numbered with those of the first resurrection, that ye may have eternal life. (BM, Mosiah 18:9)

For those who take this counsel seriously, there is a lot at stake in this matter of integrity. It deserves a careful and periodic self-evaluation.

80

In educational matters, the problem of compartmentalizing our basic values extends even beyond personal valiance; it affects the very tone of the learning/teaching process and conveys a context capable of influencing, positively or negatively, the lives of those being taught. The temptation to compartmentalize our value system is frequently very subtle. It is challenging to be in the bubble and not be limited to the bubble.

Recognizing Differences in Educational Theory and Practice

There is a risk for those who choose to believe in both the natural and supernatural and then borrow and apply educational theories and practices that are the products of exclusively naturalistic assumptions—assumptions that admittedly deny the supernatural. Can the methods be safely separated from the assumptions that generated their development? Can we pick up one end of a stick without picking up the other? The temptation is appealing. These theories and practices not only exist, but they work, and are endorsed and promoted. One may ask: Why not use them? They are convenient, conventional, and often rewarding. Consider the following example.

One prominent educational theorist forthrightly states:

In the traditional view a person responds to the world around him in the sense of acting upon it. . . The opposing view—common, I believe, to all versions of behaviorism—is that the initiating action is taken by the enviroment rather than by the perceiver.[19]

And in another of Skinner's books, *"A person does not act upon the world, the world acts upon him."* [20] As noted, this is a perfectly logical conclusion for the naturalist position. Impressive amounts of factual data have been rigorously contrived and persuasively arranged to support this conclusion. Many educational strategies and techniques are based on this rationale.

But this is not the premise the prophet Lehi taught his sons to use in defining and understanding human nature. Taking the supernatural position, he said,

And the Messiah cometh in the fulness of time, that he may redeem the children of men from the fall. And because that they are redeemed from the fall they have become free forever, knowing good from evil; to act for themselves and not to be acted upon, save it be by the punishment of the law at the great and last day, according to the commandments which God hath given. (BM, 2 Nephi 2:26, emphasis added).

81

Samuel, another prophet, taught, *"Ye are free; ye are permitted to act for yourselves;* for behold God hath given unto you a knowledge and he hath made you free" (BM, Helaman 14:30, emphasis added). This position creates an educational theory and practice very different from that of the naturalist assumption. Care must be exercised by those inclined to pick and choose as they develop their educational position. There may be a useful lesson for educators in the farmer's experience with grafting branches.

Dangers in Borrowing or Grafting

The way we define *excellence* and what we consider *praiseworthy* is determined by the educational assumptions we adopt. It does make a difference whom we choose to be the Master and the servants in our educational vineyards, to borrow a metaphor from Jacob (BM, Jacob 5, 6). One important lesson for agency educators to learn concerns borrowing or grafting. Inevitably, the practice of grafting the branches of knowledge from the exclusively naturalist approach to education leads to (1) the tendency to deemphasize or ignore the spiritual aspects of learning and (2) the teaching of principles and the application of methods that contradict or are less than fully consistent with spiritual premises.

Wild branches can nourish tame roots for a period of time. And wild branches on very strong roots may even bear good fruit for a short season. But eventually the wild branches tend to overrun the tame roots, and then the fruit they produce is not good. It is bitter. Generations have been lost because of this unwise practice. The prophet Ezekiel observed that the "The fathers have eaten a sour grape, and the children's teeth are set on edge" (Jeremiah 31:29). Agency oriented educators should not deceive themselves by thinking they can reap where they have not planted without suffering the consequences. Too often, teachers are willing to accept any methods, whatever their source, so long as they seem to work. When we branch out on somebody else's fruits we should carefully check the rootstock that produced them.

The roots of true education, properly cared for, are capable of bringing forth branches that will bear good fruit. Grafting branches of foreign ideas and methods into our educational tree, however expedient, eventually leads to the production of undesirable fruits—unwise compromise and hypocrisy instead of integrity. There is a better way. If the position held in this book is worthy, it will attract its own light, generate its own plants, and nurture its own fruits. Otherwise, it cannot be true to itself. Agency oriented educators must acquire and use their own principles and practices. It is unsafe to depend on grafted branches to produce the desired fruits.

The Love of Learning Is An Insufficient Goal

Based on its Greek origins, the naturalist position frequently fosters the idea that the highest goal in education is to instill in learners a *love of learning*. Cultivating this attribute is often proposed as the pinnacle of educational achievement. Influenced by the Hebrew heritage, agency educators disagree. It is not the love of *learning*, but the *love of learning the truth and complying with the truth and serving others* that marks the truly educated.

More directly it is the *love of God and complying with his will* that distinguishes the truly educated. The search itself is not sufficient; neither is the finding. Only when man seeks the truth, finds the truth, and obtains the light to act correctly on that truth by using it in the service of God and man is he acquiring a proper education. Searching for truth without seeking the divine light to illuminate that truth is a vain expedition. Learning is a human constant; we are always learning. "Ever learning and never able to come to the knowledge of the truth" disorients the ship of human history (2 Timothy 3:7). Truth is plentiful, even among those who do not search for it. Like rain it falls upon the righteous and the unrighteous. Light, however, is promised only to those who seek it, sacrifice for it, and acknowledge God's hand in giving it (2 Nephi 32:3-6). Agency education requires more than the love of learning.

6

The Earthly Origins of Education

*Human government reveals a pattern. We move from
a kingdom to a republic, from a republic to a republic
in confusion, and from a republic in confusion to
tribal anarchy or mob rule. Education is a window
through which one can observe this process in action.*

Ancient Written Records

According to some scholars, the
oldest written record known to modern
man is recorded on a 3' x 4' black granite
stone. This stone, the Shabako stone, is in
the British museum.[1] The writings on this
stone were copied from a record found in
the cornerstone of an ancient Egyptian
temple. The story on the stone, written 3,000 years before Christ, is
like a play that tells about life, the creation, and plan of salvation
for the human inhabitants of this earth.

The story on the Shabako stone is similar to the one in the
Bible, which also tells about life, creation, and the plan of
salvation. Many other accounts of this story are found in ancient
manuscripts, perhaps a hundred, according to one scholar.[2] Many
of these records have been discovered in the last 200 years. These
ancient records explain the origin of man differently than modern
schoolbooks do. Some of them explain how the first family on
earth, the family of Adam and Eve, divided into two groups and
how the values of these two groups differed. Consider the
following version of that story.

The Divided Family

The first man and woman, Adam and Eve, were created by
God and placed on this earth in a beautiful garden. Because they
disobeyed the instructions given to them by their creator, they had
to leave the garden. After they were driven out of the Garden in
Eden and from the presence of God, they were visited by an angel

of the Lord. The angel explained to them what they needed to know and do in order to return to the presence of their Father in Heaven. The angel further instructed Adam and Eve to teach these things to their children. Adam and Eve did as they were instructed. But Satan, an adversary to the plan, came among the the children of Adam and told them not to believe what their parents taught them regarding the angel's message. And many of the children "believed it not" (PGP, Moses 5:13). They chose to love Satan and his ways more than God and his ways.

Those who rejected the teachings of their parents moved away from the rest of the family. They left the valleys in the mountains and moved down to the plains where they established their own society. They rejected the law and order of God taught by Adam and his righteous posterity (Enoch and Noah). The historian Hugh Nibley reports they built walled cities, organized armies, invented money, established businesses based on greed, worked with metal, created musical instruments, organized brass bands, made covenants with Satan, and wore costly apparel and expensive jewelry. They loved loud music, bright lights, sensuous dancing, did lots of partying, and held wild concerts. The telestial society they established was characterized by cunning, deception, lies, sorcery, fornication, adultery, and all manner of licentious living.

The group who remained on the mountain lived a happy but simple life-style as they tended their herds and crops. They protected a special place called the Mountain of the Cave of Treasures as an important cultural symbol. In this cave on the mountain, these people kept their records, sacred treasures, and most important, a book of remembrance in which was recorded a genealogy of the children of God. This *Book of the Generations of Adam and Eve*, as it was titled, contained an account of Adam's family and many of his teachings, which were passed from generation to generation. According to some accounts, when Adam died he was buried in this cave.

The separation between the two groups continued until the days of Jared, six generations after Adam. Tradition says that those who remained in the high places kept themselves holy. "They were preachers of righteousness" (Moses 6:23), and they prophesied and taught the principle of repentance; they were called the children of God. During the days of Jared, the people on the plains invited the

86

people from the high places to come and join them. Nibley explains that they sent a delegation, dressed up like angels, to meet with Jared to invite him to come down (the name Jared means "going down") and visit in their city below. Jared was curious, so he went down, where he was introduced to all the delights of the big city; he received the "the royal treatment—the real show—with all its conventions, a real orgy with obscene goings on, etc." The people on the plains temporarily won Jared over, but he eventually saw through the scheme after he returned home. He was visited by an angel, who told him, "Look, this is terrible. You've been led astray. Don't let your people do this." Jared was horrified. His hosts had momentarily convinced him with their powerful and effective temptations.[3]

It was not long after Jared's visit that his children started going down to see for themselves. Children have a tendency to imitate the actions of their parents. They knew about the people on the plain. They could hear their loud music and see the lights, dancing, and carousing. This attracted the attention of the young people up on the heights. Warned not to go, they were told that if they went down, they might never get back. At first they didn't know the way down from the mountain, so Satan taught them. They started drifting down in large numbers and joining in the fun. Eventually the group on the mountain was reduced to a small community of righteous and holy ones. Enoch was one of these; the Lord called him to be a missionary and told him to go and reclaim those who had gone astray. (The story should sound very familiar. It has been replicated many, many times. Numerous families in every generation, from Adam's day to the present, could witness to the central theme of this story. Its symbolic reality pierces to the very heart of the human condition.)

The Lord directed Enoch to go up on a high mountain, where he was permitted to see "the world for the space of many generations" (Moses 7:3-4). This vision of the future fueled the efforts of Enoch to seek out all who would listen to his message. Many did listen to Enoch, and they became a people of one heart and one mind. They embraced the message from the mountain. Dwelling in righteousness, they had no poor among them, and their enemies could not prevail against them. These people flourished upon the mountains and in the high places, while the other nations continued their own style of living. The people of these nations relished impulsive responses to their physical appetites; they marvelled at their own ingenuity and cleverness. Eventually, the records show that Enoch and his people were received into the presence of the Lord. Enoch's great-grandson, Noah, was called to carry on the work of Enoch among the people who remained, but they "hearkened not unto his words," and all the inhabitants of the earth were destroyed except Noah, his three sons, and their wives.

The First Schools

Modern man does not have a complete description of the educational programs developed in the Adamic dispensation. The prophet Moses, however, identifies three very crucial elements related to education in Adam's day. First, a book of remembrance—a historical record—was prepared in the language of Adam. Second, those who were righteous became literate and developed their own literature under the spirit of inspiration. Third, using as a curriculum the written materials they prepared, the parents who were literate taught their children to read and write (Moses 6:4-6).

The basic educational program in Adam's day was a priesthood-conceived program. It was home-centered, parent-directed, and priesthood-assisted. Apparently all other education and training, which could have been considerable, was formed around this nucleus. Moses indicates that Adam prophesied, saying, "This same Priesthood, which was in the beginning, shall be in the end of the world also" (Moses 6:7). He also reports a primary application of that generation's educational skills: "A genealogy was kept of the children of God. And this was the book of the generations of Adam" (Moses 6:8).

The Keystone of Ancient Education

In his account, Moses presents the keystone principle underlying the educational program in Adam's day. The idea was simple, but profound: *truth comes from God.* He made the point very clear that man on his own was incapable of guiding himself into lasting happiness. Man needed God's help. He could not find it alone without getting involved in ideas and practices that would jeopardize his future.

The primary instructional procedure, as mentioned, was from parent to child. God made the plan of salvation known unto Adam through three avenues: (1) from "holy angels sent forth from the presence of God," (2) "his own voice," and (3) "the Gift of the Holy Ghost" (Moses 5:58). This knowledge, confirmed to Adam by "an holy ordinance," was to remain in the world until the end. (Moses 5:59). Whatever else man learned about language and government, the mineral, vegetable, and animal kingdoms, or social relationships was balanced and corrected by learning what God taught man about God and man. The importance of understanding the plan of salvation is demonstrated in Moses' accounts of Cain and Seth. When the gospel point of view is lost, man's efforts to learn and progress become confused and unproductive; *even if there is significant literacy and abundant learning pertaining to the things of this world, knowledge tends to become self-destructive.* It is destructive because man's search for knowledge is often misdirected and misapplied when pursued outside the parameters laid down in the plan of salvation. Error creates confusion, even when mixed with truth. Error is the source of both modern and ancient confusion.

The Earliest Schools

When scholars look at available records they learn that "the earliest schools of which we have knowledge were established in ancient Sumer and Egypt. These early schools were always part of a temple complex."[4] Hugh Nibley notes that

> A temple, good or bad, is a scale-model of the universe . . . [It is] a sort of observatory where one gets one's bearings on the universe, . . . [and it represents] the original center of *learning,* beginning with the heavenly instructions received there.[5]

(Interestingly the cathedral of Notre Dame was renamed the Temple of Reason during the French Revolution, signifying the change among those people in where they were looking to "get [their] bearings on the universe.")

A clear connection can be drawn between the way righteous parents in Adam's day were prepared to teach their children and the role of the temple in this preparation process. The temple was the source of their knowledge; this knowledge was confirmed by "an holy ordinance." All other educational efforts were considered complementary and supplemental, extensions to this central purpose. This pattern overlies all that we know about the origins and intents of schooling.

By annotating studies of preclassical antiquity, classical antiquity, the medieval period, the age of the renaissance and reformation, the modern period, and the American experiment itself, the unique nature of modern schooling can be clearly framed.[6] The answer to the question, Why do we send our children to school? has recently changed in Western culture. The traditional answer to this question differs from our modern response. The record shows that schooling began as a temple exercise. Today, because of the prevailing influence of the "exclusively naturalistic" viewpoint, the intents of schooling have become primarily, if not purely, secular.

Western culture, despite its Christian heritage, has essentially moved down from the mountain and out onto the plains in its educational thinking. Its temples of learning have become citadels of secularism. Many of the most highly educated people have been persuaded to think and act as if nothing existed outside the bubble described in Chapter Five. The educational theory and practice in use today reflect this move. As parents, teachers, and students we should ask ourselves, What is the purpose of schooling? Our selection of an *intent for schooling* becomes the tool that we use in sculpting the nature and image of our education.

An Example from the Book of Mormon

Additional testimony to the importance of using correct assumptions and purposes in education is clearly outlined in *The Book of Mormon: Another Testament of Jesus Christ.* This record of God's dealings with some of the ancient inhabitants in the western hemisphere (from 600 B. C to A. D. 400) portrays a pattern of choices similar to those reported in antiquity. The characters change, but the plot remains the same; the scenery is different, but the issues and the consequences are familiar. The account in this record was written to the people of our day. It is a voice of warning. We should learn from the lessons it teaches.

A Divided Family

In the Book of Mormon we read of another divided family. We learn that some of the children in this family also chose to reject the teachings of their parents, who had been instructed by angels and told to teach these things to their children. Many of these children and their posterity, like those in Adam's family, also rejected the plan of salvation. In general, they rejected the instructions that were given by angels and prophets of God who were sent to teach them the truth. In this case, the children who did accept the teachings of their parents had to move away from the rest of the family to preserve their lives. As in Adam's day, the two cultures were not compatible; those who desired to retain a knowledge of God and his ways were ridiculed by those who did not. And physical temptations were invitingly extended by the culture who rejected God's teachings to those who accepted God's teachings, to lure them away from God into the other world; many succumbed to the temptations.

The same spirit that caused the division among Adam's children caused the division of Lehi's family. Again it was brother against brother, the disobedient against the obedient. Nephi, the son who complied with the teachings of his parents, was envied by his brothers Laman and Lemuel, who were not obedient to their parent's teachings. Several incidents clearly exemplify the basic difference between the two factions. One of these incidents involved the children's response to a revelation given to their father about the future of his family.

Lehi was shown by an angel the reactions that members of the human family, including his own children, would have to the plan of salvation. The angel's teachings included symbolic language, such as trees, branches, a river of water, and other things, used to describe social circumstances. When the father shared his experience with the family, it left some questions in the minds of the children. One of the children, Nephi, responded by seeking answers from the Lord in prayer. He asked that he might be instructed more fully concerning his father's experience. Because of his faith he was also visited by an angel, who explained the meaning of the vision given to his father. Nephi's questions were clearly answered.

Laman and Lemuel, two of Nephi's brothers, also had unanswered questions. But they did not seek the Lord's help to understand their father's message. Instead they relied on reason and disputation to try to reach a conclusion. When Nephi asked them if they had "inquired of the Lord" to find a solution, they said they had not: "The Lord maketh no such thing known unto us" (BM, 1 Nephi 15:8-10). Here, as in Adam's day, those who rejected the proper spiritual course chose to pursue life and its questions on their own, in a naturalistic fashion, and subject to the influence of other adverse forces. Both of these alternatives, being on our own or under the influence of the Adversary, lead to error; we are left to suffer the consequences of our own physical and intellectual limitations.

The righteous segment of Lehi's family built a holy temple, kept important family records, taught one another in practical matters, and prospered temporally and spiritually as long as they lived the divine teachings that had been given to them (2 Nephi 5:15-16). The other segment of the family fostered a degenerate society full of idleness, mischief, and a devotion to perpetuating incorrect traditions (2 Nephi 5:24; Alma 3:4-11). In the course of many generations some of the descendents of those who followed Nephi rejected the teachings of their fathers and left their people to settle among those who descended from Laman and Lemuel. Missionaries from the righteous group, like Enoch of old, were called by the Lord to go among those who had rejected the correct teachings of the fathers and invite them to repent. As in Enoch's day some they taught responded and some did not.

Secular Education Instituted

The educational programs that were established among these two divisions of the people reflected competing philosophies and values. These educational programs influenced and were influenced by the social practices, forms of government, and the religious beliefs of the people. Tensions similar to those we experience today were created by the competing ideas taught in the different educational programs. The children in these two societies were brought up under the influence of these differing teachings.

The political and legal background of this educational dichotomy presents an interesting drama. During the two centuries (from 180 B. C. to A. D. 34) prior to the Savior's visit to these people, the government among the righteous part of the family changed from a *kingdom* founded on religious principles to a *republic*. During the early period of the republic, the people used *theistic premises* to establish their laws—including a legally defined separation of church and state. Because of unrighteousness among the people, the republic eventually experienced internal political confusion and *shifted its legal premises from theism to agnosticism, and finally to atheism*. As this shift occurred, the freedoms of expression and action originally granted to the people gradually eroded—especially for the righteous. Those who professed righteous religious commitment were at first persecuted and eventually prosecuted because of their beliefs. The society changed from a condition where the rights of the wicked were protected by the laws of the righteous, to a point where the laws of the wicked denied the rights of the righteous. The change was subtle but definite. (There is a curious similarity between this epoch and America's own history—moving as she has from colonies under a kingdom, to a republic, to confusion, to . . . whatever lies ahead)

It was under these later conditions of corruption that the republic was eventually overthrown and the people subjected to the rule of mobocracy. Civil disorder prevailed and corruption intensified until the righteous lost their freedom to be righteous and were sentenced to death. At first the righteous were persecuted by those who denied God by their theology; they drew near unto God with their lips but their hearts were far from him. Later, it was a secular denial. As wickedness increased, men trusted only in themselves and rejected God altogether. The lesson in this account appears to be this: when the righteous rule, freedom for both the righteous and the wicked is maximized; when the wicked rule, no matter what they profess, freedom for the righteous is minimized. The two cultures ultimately do not mix well. The moods and ideas that sustained these changes as the people shifted from a theistic to an antitheistic based legal system are clearly reflected in the limited description given of the educational enterprises of this period.

Mormon's Account of Two Orders in the Books of Mosiah and Alma

In his abridged account of happenings among Lehi's descendents just before Christ's visit to the Western hemisphere, Mormon reports an ideological conflict between two orders—the

Holy Order of God and an alternative system called the *order of Nehor.* Although Mormon's objective was not to explain the historical details associated with this alternative order, his commentary does provide a general description that includes some names, assumptions, curriculum decisions, teachings, and the type of strategies employed. Those ideas associated with the order of Nehor originated in Mormon's account, from certain advisors who served a king named Noah (ca. 160 B. C., Mosiah 11:1) to the time of a man named Korihor (ca. 75 B. C., Alma 24:28-29; 30:6-12). During this period of nearly a century, the philosophical theories of the order of Nehor seem to have flowered. The impact of the Nehorian philosophy on the society at large was significant.

The storyline of this educational conflict may intrigue and perhaps instruct those of us who live in the twentieth century. It begins with a distant colony (Mosiah 9-22) during the reign of the Kings (Mosiah 7) and ends with its impact on the established republic (Mosiah 29). The account focuses on a king named Noah, who ruled a colony of the descendants from the Nephite side of Lehi's family. The record shows that King Noah "did not keep the commandments of God" but staffed his court with clever, literate advisors who were "lifted up in the pride of their hearts" (Mosiah 11: 2,5). These advisors claimed to teach the morality and laws of Moses but did not live those teachings themselves (Mosiah 12:28-30). One of these advisors, a young man named Alma, was converted by the message of a prophet named Abinadi, who came among the people, warning them to repent and change their lifestyles.

Amulon and the others who sat on King Noah's court with Alma rejected the prophet Abinadi's counsel and removed Alma from the court under threat of death. The colony was later overrun by the Lamanites, who controlled the surrounding territories. These government advisors abandoned their wives and children and fled the colony. While they were fugitives in hiding, these displaced cabinet officers kidnapped twenty-four Lamanite girls (Mosiah 20:1-5), established a community of their own, and lived in relative peace until they were discovered "by the armies of the Lamanites" (Mosiah 23:30-31). When the exiled advisors were discovered, Amulon their leader pled with the Lamanites to spare their lives. He sent forth the Lamanite daughters (now their wives) to plead for the lives of their husbands. The plea was successful (Mosiah

23:33-34). Amulon then pursuaded the Lamanite king, King Laman, to allow him and his associates to establish an educational program among the Lamanite people. This the king did, appointing "teachers of the brethren of Amulon in every land which was possessed by his people" (Mosiah 24:4).

Amulon's Day Schools and Alma's Night Schools

Mormon describes the curriculum of Amulon's educational system as a basic literacy program—secular by design. The people were taught to read and write and engage in commerce. Measured by secular standards, it was very successful. The temporal and economic outcomes of the system were impressive: "The Lamanites began to increase in riches, and began to trade one with another and wax great, and began to be a cunning and wise people, as to the wisdom of the world" (Mosiah 24:5-7). But according to Mormon, the program was flawed. He specifically points out that Amulon's established curriculum in this school system excluded all teachings about God, morality, and the mission of Christ. One would expect this exclusive type of curriculum, given the background of Amulon and his colleagues. Concerning the education of these teachers, the prophet Abinadi at an earlier time observed: "I perceive that ye have studied and taught iniquity the most part of your lives" (Mosiah 13:11).

95

It is interesting to note the contrast Mormon portrays between Amulon's day schools and Alma's night schools. Alma, Abinadi's sole convert from King Noah's court, had fled for his life after defending the prophet Abinadi. While in hiding he made a record of "all the words which Abinadi had spoken" (Mosiah 17:4) and "went about privately among the people, and began to teach the words of Abinadi, . . . and as many as would hear his word did he teach" (Mosiah18: 1, 3). During the day, however, he remained in hiding to preserve his life. As hundreds were instructed, the social order that grew contrasted sharply with that which emerged from the schooling designed by Amulon (see Mosiah 18:18-29 and Mosiah 24:7).

Although Mormon does not *detail* the relationship between Amulon's schools and the rise of Nehor, he does make the connection (Alma 21:4; 24:28-29). It is clear that a professional social order developed from these schools; Mormon identifies it as the *order of Nehor.* It is also apparent that those who fostered and maintained this special society and its unique curriculum were primarily dissidents who left the Nephite communities and went to live among the Lamanites. The professionals who belonged to this order were well educated according to the standards of the school system. They apparently studied a number of disciplines and became influential lawyers, priests, and teachers. Mormon describes the teachers and students in this system as those "who loved the vain things of the world" and sought after "riches and honors" (Alma 1:16). He identifies the basic beliefs, policies, and practices of these professionals; their general strategies are also described in several instances that involved Alma and his associates as they interacted with these people.

Amlici, a prominent member of the order of Nehor, is mentioned by name as "a very cunning man, yea, a wise man as to the wisdom of the world" (Alma 2:1). He had both credentials and professional reputation. When Alma and Amulek were confronted by Zeezrom, also a product of this educational order (a lawyer by specialization), it is apparent that the general society was still conversing in theistic terms. There was a nominal acknowledgement of a "God"—whatever meaning that term might have had for different individuals. (The Lamanites, for example, spoke of a "Great Spirit." And the questions posed by Zeezrom [82 B. C.] were still in the quasi-religious context used by Nehor a decade earlier.) But the growing conflict between the doctrine of the *Holy Order of the Son of God* and the philosophical premises of the *order of Nehor* is evident. There were vital disagreements over the fundamental doctrines of life and salvation. They were different schools with different aims and purposes. They fostered different types of societies.

It is evident by the instructions given Alma by an angel sent from God that the ideological trend took a negative direction in the professional circles of the day. Alma was told to return to Ammonihah—a popular center for those of the order of Nehor—after they had cast him out of their city. The angel told Alma of a project underway among this group that would "destroy the liberty of the people." They were designing a system "which is contrary to the statutes, and judgments, and commandments which" God had given to his people (Alma 8:17). Amulek, Alma's companion, explained these conditions in his testimony to the people in the city of Ammonihah, but they were not interested

(Alma 10:1-32). They preferred the lifestyle, philosophy, and evidence presented by the other school of thought; they later reaped the self-destructive consequences of their choice in a manner reminiscent of those who inhabited Sodom and Gomorrah.

By the time another decade passed (74 B. C.), an educated man named Korihor emerged and flaunted not just distortions of religious doctrines, but gave a full-blown denial of the supernatural world-view (See fig. 6-1). Korihor used a polished rational approach to knowlege, a thoroughly naturalistic argument, as a basis for denying the existence of God and the validity of religious doctrine as taught by the believers. Commitment to such superstitious notions was, he felt, evidence of "frenzied" and "deranged" minds (Alma 30:6-60). He maintained that whatever cannot be demonstrated and confirmed through the physical senses does not exist. Alma challenged Korihor's conclusions by pointing out that they were based on the use of an empirical method in areas where it could not apply. In a different setting with a more open and honest audience, Alma explained an approach to gaining knowledge that went beyond Korihor's limited technique, adding a balance to the learning process that can protect as well as expand man's efforts to understand and grow. Alma's was a faithful approach. He acknowledged both the natural and supernatural paths to learning and used experimentation, reason, and revelation (Alma 32:17-43).

97

Competing Assumptions

Korihor's Arguments	Alma's Teachings
(Compare with the Modern Worldview)	(Compare with the Restored Worldview)
1. Religious doctrines and prophecies are foolish and superstitious traditions created by our unenlightened ancestors. (Alma 30:13-14)	True religious doctrines and prophecies come from God to man through divine revelation.
2. Only evidence that can be confirmed by the physical senses is valid. (Alma 30:15)	Man can learn and know by the spirit as well as by the physical senses.
3. Religious convictions are the result of a frenzied and degranged mind. (Alma 30:16,26)	True religious convictions are the result of revelation to humble and obedient people.
4. God does not intervene in life; we survive only by our own efforts. (Alma 30:17)	God does intervene in our lives; we cannot survive without his intervention.
5. There is no such thing as sin or crime. (Alma 30:17-18)	Transgression of God's law is sin and transgression of civil law is crime.
6. Churches are instruments of bondage, slavery, and oppression. (Alma 30:27)	The true Church has the authority to administer the ordinances that free man from bondage, slavery, and oppression.

Fig. 6-1

These accounts of two families (Adam's and Lehi's) clearly illustrate the consequences of our assumptions to the choices we make. Both the problem and the pattern are apparent in modern society. The education we create for ourselves and our children is determined by the assumptions we embrace and the answers we provide to basic questions about education. We can learn much from these ancient models that have been preserved for our benefit.

98

7

Man is a Free Agent

The belief that man is a free agent, empowered to act for himself and not to be acted upon except by the divine law, requires unique answers to questions about our origin, nature, and destiny. It is in these answers that the foundations for educational thought and practice can be discovered.

Acquiring a Personal Vision of Education

A parent, teacher, or student who desires a correct view of agency education must first formulate a clear understanding of the nature of man,—how we learn, how we should be taught, and what we need to know and do to properly fulfill our lives. Everyone does not respond to these concerns in the same way. The history of education reveals several conflicting responses to these fundamental issues. The most prominent of these views are described in this chapter. Each of us should personally chart our course if we desire to learn and teach the most important lessons in an appropriate way at an opportune time. Developing our personal approach to learning and teaching is somewhat like preparing for a trip. We should have some idea where we are going, how we are going to travel, when we are going to depart, and what we will need to have with us to enjoy the journey and arrive at our destination. If we lack this vision of what we are about, confusion and inconsistency will mark our educational endeavors.

To decide on a destination is only part of the challenge; one must also determine the best means for getting there. That there are different ways to travel is common knowledge. We all know of people who make long journeys flying at supersonic speeds in private planes. We are also aware of dreamers who make long journeys in jalopies that break down, cause extended delays, demand changes in plans, and end up costly indeed. We know of tourists who travel on package deals, with large groups that follow structured tours on strict schedules. And we are aware of curious, independent souls who prefer to go it alone, hiking or biking along the backroads, far from the beaten paths. There are those who favor the cruise, surrounded by conspicuous comfort, varieties of preplanned entertainment, sumptuous meals, and abundant leisure. Some people are forced by economic and other considerations to move from place to place, taking only what they can carry and struggling all the while. Yes, there are a variety of ways that people use to make trips. And embarking on the road to learning is much like embarking on the road of travel. What is seen, felt, and learned is largely determined by the way one chooses to go.

Basic Educational Questions

100

As we explore the nature and purpose of education we are confronted with challenging questions in at least six areas. (1) Questions about the origin, nature and destiny of man: Who am I? What is my purpose and potential? (2) Questions about what constitutes education: How do I prepare? What should I be able to do? What should I become? (3) Questions about learning: How do I discover? What can I know? (4) Questions about teaching: What should I share with others? How should I share it? (5) Questions about what should be taught and learned: What is most important to know? What is most important to do? What will make each of us better? (6) Questions about what God has to do with the learning/teaching process: What does he want of me? Am I in accord with his will? How does he communicate with me?

The way we answer these questions reveals, among other things, our assumptions, preferences, insights, and consistency. Our answers determine the nature of our educational journey—the kind of trip we will have.

Striving to formulate personal answers to such basic questions is one way to better understand and experience the process called education. As indicated in an earlier chapter, people have different answers to questions about God, man, and the universe. These answers provide intellectual, moral, and cultural foundations for the type of education pursued. In other words, our intellectual conclusions become assumptions to shape the content, process, and structure of education. Our moral inquiry leads to assumptions about truthfulness, rightness, goodness, and propriety. And how we combine these assumptions and build upon them forms the culture in which we teach the children.

The primary purpose of this book is to explore answers to the foregoing questions that are consistent with an agency point of view—a view that emphasizes the importance of man's will, volition, and capacity to choose. In this particular chapter the focus is on the first area, viz., man's origin, nature, and destiny.

Viewing man as a free agent, empowered to act for himself and not to be acted upon except by the divine law (BM, 2 Nephi 2:26), requires unique answers to questions about his origin, nature, and destiny. These answers establish the foundation for subsequent educational thought and practice. In providing a description of man that is consistent with the notion of human agency, the agency perspective will be contrasted with other prominent points of view, but will not fully explore or critique these alternatives. The goal is to light a candle for those who would like to explore further.

101

Free Will vs. Determinism

How free is the will of man? This question strikes at one of the oldest and most fundamental issues in education, one of the classic debates in western culture. Theologians, philosophers, and other scholars have argued this question for centuries, and the debate continues today. Three of the more famous contests on this subject are (1) the debate between St. Augustine and the British monk, Pelagius, during the first quarter of the fifth century (A. D. 401-422),[1] (2) a confrontation between Martin Luther and Desiderius Erasmus at the beginning of the sixteenth century (1517-1540),[2] (3) the modern controversy between many behaviorists and romanticists that continues in our own century.[3]

Augustine vs. Pelagius. Augustine believed that man's will after the fall of Adam was inclined toward evil; man could of himself do no good. Pelagius disagreed. He believed that man had free will to do good or evil, but that his will inclined to the good. Pelagius rejected absolutely Augustine's doctrine of "original sin," or "hereditary sin"; he believed that Adam's sin affected only Adam himself and not his posterity. Pelagius maintained that man was created with perfect freedom to choose between good and evil, and that this freedom operates in man at all times. He argued that sin which is necessary, is not sin at all. Man is neither good nor evil because he is free, and without this freedom he could not become good or evil. Pelagius interpreted "grace," not as an irresistible divine force that impelled a certain chosen few to do good acts (as Augustine perceived), but as the aid that God gives to all men to guide them in thinking and choosing rightly. Pelagius taught that man could attain heaven by the use of his native powers alone, since nothing but free will is needed to practice virtue and avoid sin. Men require no special help to repair what Adam is supposed to have lost. Augustine believed man was fallen, evil by nature, and incapable of making good choices of his own volition. He held that man had no direct control over his salvation; otherwise he would compete with and exercise power over God.

102

Pelagius' doctrine was officially condemned on three different occasions (A. D. 416, 418, and 429), and Augustine's doctrine became the policy of the church for succeeding generations. The theories and practices of education that developed from either of these doctrines were not necessarily agency oriented in the sense I use it in this book. Augustine gave man too little influence over his destiny and Pelagius gave him too much—teaching that he could obtain heaven by exercising his native powers alone.

Martin Luther vs. Erasmus. Desiderius Erasmus, a Dutch scholar of the sixteenth century, joined with English scholars from Oxford and Cambridge, England, such as Colet, Grocyn, Linacre, and More; together they promoted the view that man participated in his own salvation by choosing whether or not to accept God's means of salvation. Martin Luther disagreed with this position. His argument was that to follow the free will view of Erasmus was to maintain that man saves himself and does not need God. In our modern era, many people have assumed the position described by Luther.[4] Erasmus did not feel this way, nor did many of those who held this position see the "free will" of man separately from the saving grace of God. Although Erasmus' free-will view of man retained a few pockets of popularity through the Middle-Ages, especially among some scholars in Italy, England, and the European lowlands, traditional determinism dominated education in western culture until the enlightenment.

Behaviorism vs. Romanticism. In our own day the academic debate over free will and determinism continues but is seldom couched in a religious context. Jean Jacques Rousseau argued that man by his nature is intended to be a freely choosing creature; his basic nature was the best guide in these choosing experiences. The ideal is freedom to develop habits that conform to the nature within us. All other educational experience should follow this lead; otherwise harmony becomes impossible.

In contrast, John Watson, an early American psychologist, maintained that all human behavior is a response to external stimuli. Through evolution, the human being has acquired sense organs. The sense organs receive and transfer the environmental stimuli that cause the human organism to respond. This is the source of all action, the mechanism of all choice. Controlling choice is a matter of controlling and manipulating stimuli, which can be reduced to a science by knowledgeable people.

More recently B. F. Skinner has refined the behaviorist argument. In his book *Beyond Freedom and Dignity* (1971), he maintains that it is naive to believe in the free will of man. He says, "Freedom and dignity . . . are the possessions of the autonomous man of traditional theory, and they are essential to practices in which a person is held responsible for his conduct and given credit for his achievements. *A scientific analysis [behaviorism] shifts both the responsibility and the achievement to the environment*" (p. 23, emphasis added). In naturalistic determinism, the environment takes the place of the "grace of God" in determining what will happen to man.

A. S. Neill, a British educator, counters this position with the belief that "we should allow children to be themselves . . . renounce all discipline, all direction, all suggestion, all moral training, all religious instruction . . . . A child is innately wise and realistic. If left to himself he will develop as far as he is capable of developing . . . the function of the child is to live his own life, not the life someone else may choose for him."5 These two extreme positions are the polar points that influence and shape the way modern education is conducted.

Generally speaking, the deterministic assumption, whether in the form of a religious doctrine ("the grace of God") or a scientific doctrine ("environmental cause and effect") has shaped the theory and practice of education in the western world. In developing and

103

implementing educational practices, every parent and every teacher, knowingly or unknowingly, makes a decision about free will or determinism. And every student, wittingly or unwittingly, submits or rebels in some degree to the same issue.

The Origin, Nature, and Destiny of Man—A Hebrew View

Anciently, Hebrews believed man was the literal, spiritual offspring of Deity. God was their Father in Heaven. We were created in the image and likeness of God. We came to earth to obtain a physical body, gain earthly experience with that body, and prepare ourselves to return to our heavenly home. The test of mortality was to see if our spirits could properly manage our mortal bodies with their physical and creative capacities and appetites. These ancient Hebrew beliefs are attested to by modern revelation. The mortal context for this opportunity to prove ourselves was marriage, the family, and the community. Mankind from conception was male and female; in adulthood the two were to be lawfully joined together, learn how to be husband and wife, father and mother, and engage in community interaction. Man, earth, and time were symbolic of God, heaven, and eternity. The design was that men and women were to become like their heavenly parents. The time-frame for this developmental experience covered first a premortal assignment, then a mortal probation, and lastly a period during which the spirit body would be separated from the physical body before its physical resurrection and final assignment of glory.

Our Father in Heaven assigned his Son, Jesus Christ, to provide a place, prepare a way, and instruct us in that way by showing us how to return to our Father. Christ would show us by doing it himself. In order to bring this to pass, it was necessary that we choose to follow the plan provided. Laws of justice and mercy were set in place that provided rewards for compliance and punishments for violations. We were given the capacity and the freedom to choose at every level of experience. Adam and Eve, the first man and woman, made initial choices (as do all those who enter mortality) that led to a separation from the presence of God and the experience of a temporary physical mortality. To overcome this separation, the help of a Savior was needed. The Son of God provided this help. He overcame both the spiritual and physical deaths (separations) associated with this mortal state. His atonement in behalf of man provided the power to overcome physical death and enables us to make choices that will perfect our personal development sufficient to conquer spiritual death. This redemptive process is the means of reuniting us with our Heavenly Parents.[6]

The perfecting process ("be ye therefore perfect . . ." Matt. 5:48; 3 Nephi 12:48), becoming complete, involved our developing the characteristics of our Heavenly Father, who also has a material body of flesh and bone, but who is perfect in all his ways. The primary purpose of all teaching and learning is to sustain and contribute to this fundamental mission—bringing "to pass the immortality and eternal life of man" (PGP, Moses 1:39). True education is, therefore, character education. This is the end; all other learning is simply a supportive means to that end. We entered our mortal experience in a state of innocence (D&C 93:38). We were neither innately evil, nor inevitably good. We were subject to the enticements of both evil and of good; we were free to choose between the two, the one or the other. As we reached the age of accountability (eight years old), we became personally responsible for our choices.

105

Other Views of Man in Western Culture

The Ancient Greek View. The dominant conceptions of God, Man, and Nature held in ancient Greek society differed significantly from the Hebraic view described above. For the Greeks, philosophically speaking, it was the abstract concept of the Cosmos (nature in the sense of the entire universe) that was perfect and eternal—the same yesterday, today, and forever. We were imperfect and so were the mythical gods of Mt. Olympus—Zeus, his wife Hera, and their twelve children. The Greeks held confusing and competing notions about the supernatural. The view that prevailed, however, was the idea that our mind, our rational capacities, our ability to contemplate, connected us to the cosmos. Our mental capacity set us apart from other creatures and enabled us to understand, admire, and revere the pure forms of cosmic nature. Our destiny was linked to our ability to figure things out; we were not dependent on or indebted to a Redeemer. The Greek society was not a redemptive society like that of the Hebrews, who focused on man's need for redemption.

In Greek thought our ability to contemplate is our connection to ultimate freedom. Our individual disengagement from the physical nature of mortality with its imperfections is what makes it possible for us to engage with the perfection of the impersonal cosmic mind. We cease to be "us" and rather become one with "something else." This ultimately nonpersonal view of man makes it more comfortable (perhaps more accurate) to discuss Greek thought in impersonal language. This focus on man as a transient intellect rather than an eternal personality has heavily influenced education in western culture.[7] It is expressed in the word *encyclopedia*, which literally means to put your foot in the center of the universe; embrace all knowledge; comprehend, appreciate, and reverence it; seek to become one with it. This idea of knowing for the sake of knowing continues to shadow much of the theory, practice, and rewards of modern formal education. How much you know, not what you do, is an implicit and pervasive ideal in modern western schooling. Awards are bestowed, scholastic grades are given, and degrees are granted largely on this traditional premise. The condition thrives alongside the competing pragmatism of the marketplace, which strives to honor results, profits, and whatever works.

106

It is important to recognize the Greek's nonredemptive world view. Belief in a redeemer or a physical resurrection was a foreign idea. The idea of *crime* existed in Greek culture, but not *sin*. Ignorance was the path to man's most serious error, which was the shame of intellectual error. Knowledge was the road to man's supreme acquistion—wisdom. In a very humanistic sense, education, not redemption, was the solution to man's most basic problem. Without a fall, no atonement was required. The Hebraic view of man was foreign to Greek culture. The Greek view of the Hebraic beliefs previously described is contained in one word: foolishness (I Cor. 1:19-23). When Paul the Apostle visited Athens, the Athenians clearly expressed this attitude. While visiting with the Stoics and the Epicureans, who were curious about his strange beliefs, Paul explained the Hebraic doctrines of God, man, and nature. Most of his learned listeners mocked him; only a few were interested enough to learn more (Acts 17:22-34). His ways were not their ways.

As a result of the Greek philosophical approach, knowledge becomes the prime value. *Doing*, even doing what God does, *is less important than knowing.* This priority is reflected in the writings of Plato, a Greek philosopher, who acknowledged in *The Republic* three classes of citizens in his ideal society: (1) the artisans, producers, merchants or *makers* of the marketplace; (2) the soldiers or physical *defenders* of the civil order; and (3) the *knowers* or guardians, the philosopher-kings. The last group were the elite, the most highly regarded by the philosophers.

A relationship may be drawn between these three orders of people and three functions of life that characterized Greek society: (1) *'poiesis'* —making, constructing, producing; (2) *'praxis'* — doing, acting, practicing, performing; (3) *'theoria'*—admiring, understanding, knowing, watching, appreciating. Plato's philosopher/kings were of the third order. They were the theorists, the knowers. In our modern society the theorists, the highest order of the ancient Greeks, are likewise the ones held in greatest esteem by the academic community. In the marketplace of modern society, however, *making* rather then *knowing* appears to command the highest value; those who produce, not those who know or those who simply do good things, seem to collect the largest material rewards; this wealth enables the *makers* to rule in society. It is the control inherent in production that appears to dominate the modern western world. The "big money" goes to those who are the makers of touchdowns, homeruns, movies, buildings, products, music, sales, etc.

If we choose to think about and pursue education in the context of traditional Greek assumptions, we should carefully consider these implications. *Knowing, doing,* and *making* are important to every culture. *Which of the three should dominate and in what context should they function?* The premises we select are important. They help form the context that determines the meanings we attach to education. Education built upon a Greek foundation is vastly different than education built upon a Hebraic foundation—whether it is done knowingly or unknowingly. These two philosophies are not the same, and they are not compatible in purpose. The results are inescapably different. The pursuit of knowledge within the context of the fall, atonement, and resurrection is fundamentally different than the pursuit of knowledge within a nonredemptive framework. Mixing the two is like mixing oil and water; the formula is inherently divisive and leads to compartmentalizing the individual's value system. Many modern educators unwittingly suffer from this malady—especially those who belong to churches that teach the need for redemption.

A simple example that illustrates the difference in emphasis between knowing and doing occurred some years ago in connection with the lyrics of a popular song now used in The Church of Jesus Christ of Latter-day Saints. The lyrics and music to the song "I Am a Child of God" were written in 1957. The song was created to complement the theme "Help Me Find the Way—A Child's Plea," which was chosen for the children's organization's presentation at its 51st Annual Conference in Salt Lake City, Utah. Naomi Randall, an officer in the organization, wrote the lyrics. The first verse and chorus read:

> I am a child of God,
>> and He has sent me here,
> Has given me an earthly home
>> with parents kind and dear.
>
> Chorus
>
> Lead me, guide me, walk beside me,
>> help me find the way.
> Teach me all that I must know
>> to live with Him some day.

108

When this inspiring song was presented to Church leaders, the only modification requested was that one word in the chorus be changed. Elder Spencer W. Kimball, a member of the Quorum of the Twelve, strongly urged that the word "know" be changed to "do." "To know," he said, "is not enough."[8] It makes a difference which priority we teach our children.

The Theological View: Another view of man and therefore of education, as Jennifer explained in Chapter Four, also originated under the influence of Greek philosophy. The spirit of this view is captured in the Greek word theology— a rational science or study of God. In its western form, *theology* is a composite of Greek philosophical premises and Judeo-Christian beliefs. A traditional tenet of this view is that we were created by God *ex nihilo*—out of nothing. Man is viewed as a soul or spirit living in a fallen physical body that is by nature evil in its inclinations. If we succumb to our natural desires, we will justly receive the eternal punishment of God; if we are chosen as recipients of God's grace—not for any righteous action, but as a free token of God's mercy—we will receive salvation. We will be granted an immortal life with God. Our primary goal in mortality is to seek God's help in overcoming our natural propensities for evil and accepting a spiritual nature in their place.

Education within this view is to help man overcome the physical world by enabling him to contemplate eternal and spiritual values. The emphasis is on logical reasoning and argument. Knowledge is characterized by learning carefully reasoned positions, such as can be found in the works of St. Augustine and St. Thomas Aquinas, who were famous theologians of medieval Christianity. Rhetorical skill (carefully expressed logical argument) is highly valued. A favored method of schooling is to pose questions to students who recite answers in the manner of a catechism. Content is based on imperatives and absolutes. Great stress is laid on conformance to predetermined objectives established by higher authority. These objectives are founded on specific truths (commandments) which the adherents believe have been revealed to man by God.

109

It was partly in opposition to this theological view of man and learning that many modern educators turned to the secular naturalism that engulfed western culture in the nineteenth and twentieth centuries. The more modern man learned about himself and his world, the less confidence he seemed to place in supernatural influences outside the bubble of his physical universe. Up to this century, however, the theological approach to education was very popular and existed in many forms. Parochial schools have traditionally reflected this type of education, though it is not as popular today as previously. The writings of Socrates, Aristotle, Augustine, Aquinas, Calvin, Luther, and Jonathon Edwards all reflect the theological view of education. An encyclical by Pope Pious XI issued in 1936 is a classic expression of the theological view of education. In part it says,

> Education is essentially a social and not a mere individual activity. Now there are three necessary societies, distinct from one another and yet harmoniously combined by God, into which man is born: two, namely the family and civil society, belong to the natural order; the third, the Church, to

the supernatural order. . . And first of all education belongs preeminently to the Church . . . .

Hence every form of pedagogic naturalism, which in any way excludes or overlooks supernatural Christian formation in the teaching of youth, is false. Every method of education founded wholly or in part, on the denial or forgetfulness of Original Sin and of grace, and relying on the sole powers of human nature, is unsound. Such, generally speaking, are those modern systems bearing various names which appeal to a pretended self-government and unrestrained freedom on the part of the child, and which diminish or even suppress the teacher's authority and acton, attributing to the child an exclusive primacy of initiative, and an activity independent of any higher law, natural or Divine, in the work of his education. . .What is intended by not a few, is the withdrawal of education from every sort of dependence on the Divine Law. . . .

From this it follows that the so-called "neutral" or "lay" [public] school, from which religion is excluded, is contrary to the fundamental principles of education. Such a school moreover cannot exist in practice; it is bound to become irreligious.[9]

The Modern View of Man: As Frank and Ellen noted in Chapter Four, the modern view tends to ignore or reject outright the notion of a supernatural world. Like the Greeks, modern man sees no need for redemption. The idea of a savior and a plan of salvation is irrelevant. Organic evolution, not God, explains the origin of the human species. According to this theory, people evolved over millions of years from lower and less intelligent life forms. We differ from other forms of animal life only in degree and acquired characteristics. Two major views of man and education have been popularized among modern educators. One of these views might be called the individualist and the other the societalist approach to education. (See charts in Appendix A.)

The Individualist View of Education. Some modern educators, like those who taught Ellen, believe humans are born with specific genetic potential, natural drives, and instincts. Based on this assumption, education consists of learning to adjust to and manipulate one's environment while striving to fulfill personal goals. Our destiny is to become a fully mature, actualized, and developed individual. This occurs best when the individual is not imposed upon by unnatural means, but is left free to seek fulfillment according to the forces of natural expression inherent within him. Jean Jacques Rousseau, A. S. Neill, Abraham Maslow, Carl Rogers, Maria Montessori, Jean Piaget, Friedrich Nietzsche, and John Holt have expressed views along these lines.

Jean Jacques Rousseau, a French writer, is well known for his approach to education. Man's learning, he said, comes from three sources; one of these sources, nature, should guide the other two:

> Education comes to us from nature, from men, or from things. The inner growth of our organs and faculties is the education of nature, the use we learn to make of this growth is the education of men, what we gain by our experience of our surroundings is the education of things. Thus, we are each taught by three masters. If their teaching conflicts, the scholar is ill-educated and will never be at peace with himself; if their teaching agrees, he goes straight to his goal, he lives at peace with himself, he is well-educated. Now of these [three] factors in education nature is wholly beyond our control, things are only partly in our power, the education of men is the only one controlled by us; and even here our power is largely illusory, for who can hope to direct every word and deed of all with whom the child has to do. . . . Since all three modes of education must work together, the two that we can control [the teachings of men and things] must follow the lead of that which is beyond our control [nature].[10]

111

A. S. Neill, the British educator, attempted to put a version of the individualist approach to education into full practice in his schools. He said,

> The function of the child is to live his own life—not the life that his anxious parents think he should live, nor a life according to the purpose of the educator who thinks he knows best. All this interference and guidance on the part of adults only produces a generation of robots.[11]

The Societal Approach to Education. Other modern educators, like those who taught Frank, believe not only that man evolved from lower life forms, having individual drives and instincts, but he is also shaped by his culture. Man is born into social relationships; it therefore becomes vital to find some way to introduce people to the goals of the society into which they are born. In this point of view, man begins as a blank slate upon which society writes. The ultimate destiny of an educated person is to become a useful, contributing social role player, relative to the particular society in which the person is reared. The paramount concern is the most efficient way to train the child in societal values.

Modern public or lay school systems, beginning with the earlier Prussian experiments in education which followed the thinking of Robert Owens, have generally embraced this view and have given it professional refinement and definition. Emile Durkheim, Charles Hubbard Judd, Edward L. Thorndike, B. F. Skinner, Mortimer Adler, John Locke, Samuel Bowles, and Herbert Gintis have promoted various versions of this approach to education.

112

Durkheim, for example, explained the general approach to societal education in these words:

> In order that there be education, there must be a generation of adults and one of youth, in interaction, and an influence exercised by the first on the second. . . . We come then to the following formula: Education is the influence exercised by the adult generation on those who are not yet ready for social life. Its object is to arouse and to develop in the child a certain number of physical, intellectual and moral states which are demanded of him by both the political society as a whole and a special milieu [the situation and role] for which he is specifically destined. . . .
>
> In each of us, it may be said there exists two beings . . . . One is made up of all the mental states that apply only to ourselves and to the events of our personal lives: this is what might be called the individual being. The other [being] is a system of ideas, sentiments and practices which express in us, not our personality, but the different groups of which we are a part; these are religious beliefs, moral beliefs and practices, national or professional traditions, collective opinions of every kind. Their totality forms the social being. To constitute this being in each of us is the end of education.[12]

These modern views of man and education, like the ancient Greek view, are by their very nature nonredemptive. There is no place in their theoretical structure to account for the fall, atonement, or resurrection of man. Morality, discerning between right and wrong, is defined as "conforming to the mores" of society.[19] Decisions depend on the people, place, and period in which they occur. The aphorism "When in Rome do as the Romans do" captures a common application of this moral perspective. There is no appeal to a divine or higher law, because such does not exist. Rational analysis, scientific investigation, and social consensus are the standards against which human choice and action are measured. Theories associated with this approach to education do not allow the individual to exercise his or her volition beyond the parameters of the system, parameters primarily designed to serve the group, rather than the individual.

Three Fundamental Options

Because the Hebrew, Greek, and modern traditions are based on differing assumptions and explanations of man, his origin and destiny, they also differ in their approach to education. Examples that illustrate some of these differences have been noted in the foregoing descriptions. Those serious about the power and application of education need to evaluate carefully where they are and where they want to be in relation to these foundational ideas. Each of these three traditions is governed by different values. Attempts to combine the different traditions do not eliminate the problem. Ultimately, any choice we make will be ruled by one of these fundamental assumptions in one way or another. All three traditions value doing, knowing, and making, but each values these processes differently. Our primary value—the one that rules our actions—will set the tone and determine the target of our educational endeavors. (See Fig. 7-1).

113

	GOD	**COSMOS** (Nature)	**MAN**
World View	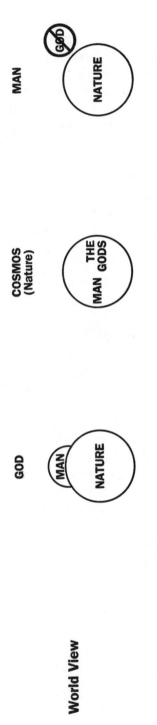		
Prime Value	Becoming like God; doing what God does in order to develop God-like character.	Acquiring knowledge; knowing in order to admire and appreciate the way things are.	Managing phenomena; making and utilizing in order to control and improve the environment.
View of Education	A personal quest for answers to the most basic human concerns in order to develop and perfect one's own character	Comprehending and expressing in order to become more in harmony with nature.	Acquisition of the information, skills, and art that allows one to fill a role, to make a useful contribution toward managing and maintaining nature in the service of man.
Highest Priority	Focus is on choosing and doing what is right rather than wrong.	Focus on increasing awareness and understanding.	Focus on creating and distributing; making and marketing.

It is vitally important that parents, teachers, and students understand which of these traditional value structures they are promoting and experiencing. Dissonance that may lead to hypocrisy and frustration often occurs when people fail to distinguish what they are doing to others and what others are doing to them in educational settings.

The temptation for many people is to make indiscriminate choices in these foundational matters as they relate to education. It seems easier to compartmentalize and make choices simply in terms of whatever works most quickly or whatever is acceptable to others. It is now fashionable to emphasize productivity and results: if it works adopt it, adapt it, and do it. But there is a serious danger in this approach. The simple fact that something works doesn't make it right. For the agency-oriented educator the question *Does it work?* must always be subservient to the question *Is it right?* Pragmatism may be a good copilot, but it is an unsafe and dangerous pilot. Secure movement toward a better and safer future, for those who believe in agency, resides in correctness, not expediency. Agency oriented educators should strive to avoid this subtle trap.

In a similar vein, some who believe in both the supernatural and the natural are tempted to merge carelessly what God has revealed and what man by reason and experiment has concluded. This effort towards reconciliation may cut two ways. First, some people feel great confidence in man's scientific or philosophic explanations of *how* things happen. On the basis of this confidence, they are sometimes compelled to use theoretical explanations that explain how things happen as standards of evaluation, patching in where possible the revelations from God that explain to man *what* has happened. Revelation that does not fit the accepted theories is tacitly, if not explicitly, set aside. This approach seems very inviting, especially when our social and professional world bestows rewards and credibility according to the naturalistic findings of philosophy and science. The history of western culture is the result of a series of these efforts toward intellectual reconciliation. (This pattern of reconciliation is described in a later chapter and illustrated in Appendix B.)

One example of this procedure is apparent in the way modern educators have struggled to explain the origin and nature

115

of man. For the last century many individuals have tried to harmonize various naturalistic theories with more traditional beliefs and doctrines originating from supernatural revelation. The New Haven Scholars of the nineteenth century are one example.[14] These scholars brought a new form of German scholarship to America. They hoped to use it to save Christianity, which was under serious attack by the exclusively naturalistic view of modern man that was emerging at that time. Their efforts were unsuccessful, perhaps counterproductive. But the quest to legitimize religion by methods acceptable to naturalistic scholars continues in nearly every religious subculture.

On the other hand, some individuals attach themselves too rigorously to the language of revelation about *what* God has done and will do. They may deny the legitimate benefits of reasoned experimentation to explain, theoretically, *how* some things do occur. From an agency point of view, we must keep things in perspective. Just and fair men live by faith, a partial knowledge of both the natural and the supernatural (Romans 1:17; Hebrews 11:1; BM, Alma 32:17-21). All things have not yet been revealed. (D&C 101:32-34). But we are capable of discovering new truth. Certainly, no theory that denies the supernatural or seeks to explain man's origin and behavior without allowing for the fall, atonement and resurrection can be ultimately acceptable by Latter-day Saint standards. Such theory provides a sandy foundation. But to deny or discount the usefulness of naturalistic theory to explain, in part and temporarily, naturalistic phenomena is to be closed to new light and knowledge. God does reveal secrets of his handiwork to his children "even by study and also by faith." And because "all have not faith," and because some problems are solved by faith and study, we must "study" (D&C 88:118). What we call science can be a useful tool in learning about the physical world.

Confused over means and ends, we sometimes let that which is less important take precedence over that which is more important. It is well for the educator who favors the agency approach to remember that true revelation about *what* has happened, *what* is happening, and *what* will happen must always take precedence over any philosophic and scientific *theory* of *how* or *why* something might have occurred.[15] It is also important to realize that when one ceases to ask and search appropriately for the *how* and the *why*, he ceases striving for Godlike education. We can be content to be patient if now is not the time or place to know and act on some particular issue, but we cannot be content to be ignorant if now is the time and place to know and act on that matter. Joseph F. Smith gave some wise council on this balance:

> I have always contended that while secular education was laudable, desirable and necessary; that it adds to the sum of human happiness and human enjoyment and usefulness to be acquainted with the arts and sciences, enabling man to cope with the world, and often brings him success in the battle of life, yet it is all of this life, and is not to be compared with the importance of gaining knowledge of God, and of that science which as immortal beings we can take with us beyond the veil.
>
> The knowledge of God, and of his son Jesus Christ . . . is the first and last lesson of life, and this has always been my opinion. It is very desirable to understand the principles of civil government, the sciences and arts, and be filled with the wisdom of men, but after all it is but the tools by which we earn our bread and butter. There is a certain degree of ambition in it, love of power, and opportunity to exert influence and enables us to move in goodly appearance, but when it is all summed up, worldly gain is the incentive.
>
> I greatly commend even this secular education, and the benefits which its right use bestows in the human family, and the delight which a moral and educated people must be to holy beings, but if we learned everything which human knowledge can compass, and it enabled us to grasp the riches of the world we could only embrace their delight, and enjoy their possession for a short time. Then comes death, and we leave the result of the labors of our lives to others, taking nothing with us. If we only have hope in this world, and the things of this world, then, indeed, are we the most miserable of all God's creatures.[16]

117

Karl G. Maeser, an early Mormon educator, emphasized this focus on education when he addressed the first class held at the the Brigham Young Academy on April 24, 1876. "I told the students," said he, that

> Joseph Smith taught his people correct principles and they governed themselves accordingly—[this] is **the leading**

principle of discipline . . . [and] the words of President Brigham Young, that neither the alphabet nor the multiplication table were to be taught without the Spirit of God—[is] **the mainspring of all education.**[17]

According to Maeser, this "was the orientation for the course of the educational system inaugurated by the foundation of the Academy." In his view, "any deviation from [these principles will] lead inevitably to disastrous results.[18]

8

A Psychology for Agency Education

Agency educators describe human nature best in terms of Heart, Mind, Might, and Strength. The heart is the governing center, our mind is a system for attracting knowledge, might is our dominion of resources, and our strength is the attribute of a living temporal body.

What is Psychology?

The word *psychology* has several meanings in modern usage, e.g., the study of mind, the study of behavior, and the study of man interacting with his social and physical environment. These conventional views of psychology do not accommodate an agency approach to education. The popular theories of psychology fail to take into account the full scope of the human being; they do not allow for our spiritual dimensions, powers, and sources of influence. In this book, the term *psychology* refers to our ultimate purpose as well as our specific human functions, such as thinking, feeling, and knowing. The way the term is used here, *psychology is the careful description of man at the fulness of his powers as a choosing, thinking, striving, talking, enculturated being.*[1]

The way we view psychology is important because it influences how we see and explain human experience and behavior. This in turn influences how we act toward other people, especially in the learning/teaching process. The above definition of psychology, when applied to man as decribed in this book, contrasts radically to the popular definitions of psychology used by modern educators. But it fits the ancient Hebraic view of psychology and sustains integrity for those who desire to develop an agency approach to education.

The Merriam Webster's dictionary identifies the term *radical* as "(1) a Latin derivative meaning root or proceeding from the root, (2) marked by a considerable departure from the usual, and (3) an extreme change in existing views." Each of these meanings accurately describes ancient Hebrew psychology when compared to modern psychological theories. It is a radical view, but it is also a comprehensive and sensible view, consistent with Hebraic assumptions regarding man's true nature.

The Hebrew record of origins (Genesis chapters 1 and 2, for example) claims to begin at the very onset of human life on earth. Modern revelation affirms this claim, as chapter two of this book explains. Despite the age of this ancient claim, with its widespread influence in western culture, most histories of psychology ignore this view. Even the more comprehensive ones, such as Brett's *History of Psychology*, simply offer a cursory treatment; the Hebraic contribution to an understanding of man and his origins is considered relatively insignificant, if not primitive.

The Greek connection has had a blinding impact on the modern mind—so powerful among modern intellectuals that it has essentially obliterated the Hebraic influence. When one studies the dominant perspective of the modern western intellect, the premises of the Hebrew worldview are strikingly absent. After careful research, Isaac Newton concluded that even in the arts and sciences, all other ancient peoples were mere imitations of the Hebrews, but this is conveniently ignored in modern thought.[2]

Moses, the author of the best known account of Hebrew origins, describes and explains man "at the fulness of his powers." Moses' assumptions differ from those of popular psychology. That is why most modern psychologies are inconsistent with and sometimes antithetical to the agency approach to education. These psychologies introduce confusion and conflict, because they focus on man exclusively as a physical organism and ignore or deny, or at least minimize, his spiritual dimension. Those who desire to develop an agency approach to education need a different psychology. Naturalistic psychology is insufficient because it denies that man is a spirit being clothed in a temporary mortal body. Studying man without his spirit is like studying fish without acknowledging the existence of water. Yet this is standard today. A more sensible and consistent alternative is available in the ancient Hebraic records.

The fundamental difference between the Hebraic view of man and the modern alternatives is a commitment to the spiritual or supernatural as well as the natural domain. The ancient Hebrews looked outside as well as inside the bubble to establish their premises. Because western thought shifted away from supernatural assumptions to naturalistic assumptions in the late eighteenth century, modern disciplines commonly define their tasks in exclusively naturalistic terms.[3] Psychology is no exception. (Admittedly, recent nonconventional theorists, such as Abraham Maslow, Karl Popper, and John Eccles, have stretched contemporary definitions of reality. But they do not stretch far enough to explain human nature as described in this book.)[4]

Context of Modern Psychology

The question of existence has long fascinated mankind. What exists, why, and for how long? Many of man's greatest concerns cluster around issues related to existence—personal as well as universal. A second fundamental question that has aroused human interest has to do with motion: why do things act the way they do? From these two questions flow many of the queries of man, including those related to space and time. How can I know? What can I know? What is good? What does God want me to do? These are additional questions that have puzzled mankind.

121

In western culture two assumptions contest for the right to answer our basic questions. In the older, traditional view, two basic entities form all existence and all movement—*matter and spirit.* Philosophers have labeled this position *dualism* (meaning two substances). The most popular view today in scientific circles, holds that all existence (and motion) involves a single substance—*physical matter.* Nothing else exists. Philosophers have referred to this position as *monism* (meaning one substance).

The modern approach to understanding the world results in a materialistic explanation for all matter and all motion—including human action. In this approach, everything we do is explained in terms of our physical nature. A dominant explanation of the world from this perspective is known as *reductionism,* the basis for most modern scientific thought. G. R. Taylor explains it this way:

> Scientists . . . like to believe that all phenomena, are in principle, explainable in terms of basic physical laws. Biology can be reduced to chemistry, chemistry to physics. The behaviour of living organisms depends, in the last analysis, on the performance of a large number of chemical reactions.

Chemical reactions depend on the physical properties of molecules and atoms. This belief is known as reductionism. To preserve this reductionist philosophy, it is necessary that all psychology shall reduce to biology. Consequently, if to explain mental activity we have to introduce some new factor, unknown to physics, the whole position crumbles, and the prospect that everything is explainable becomes uncertain.[5]

If one assumes that the only building block in the universe is physical matter, this explanation is clear and probably quite satisfying. It has certainly helped explain many aspects of the natural world, providing increased understanding of our physical bodies and temporal environment. Because it works in the physical domain, it is compelling.

Materialists who believe in the reductionist theory maintain that only one possible relationship can explain action, that is, physical matter influences physical matter. Dualists, those who believe there are two basic building blocks in the universe—matter and mind, or matter and spirit—face a more complex view of the world. They see four possible relationships to account for action: (1) matter influencing matter, (2) matter influencing mind (spirit), (3) mind (spirit) influencing matter, and (4) mind (spirit) influencing mind (spirit). The mind-body controversy associated with contemporary brain research hints at the difference in these opposing views.[6] The central question in this discussion is whether the mind has an existence of its own separate from the physical body and the brain, and if so, how it affects the physical body.

Major Divisions of Modern Psychology Agree

Even *nonconventional psychologists* who wish to free themselves from the restrictions of reductionist thinking (that all psychology must be reduced to biology, all biology to chemistry, and all chemistry to physics) use naturalistic assumptions to define formally human nature and action.[7] *Cognitive psychologies*, which emphasize the mental capacities to explain human nature and actions, resist some of the purely reductionist restrictions which *behaviorist psychologies* freely acknowledge. In the final analysis, most modern psychologies tend to retain a naturalistic, temporal perception of the human being. Their theories do not embrace the supernatural.

Consider, for example, A. L. Blumenthal's explanation of the "central control process" in the individual. Blumenthal notes that *cognition*, "the most basic of biological principles," is the capacity man has to make sense out of what he becomes aware of through his senses. As we encounter the "flux of events" in life, we use our mental capacity to transform what we experience through our senses into perception, thought, and memory. This transformation, which he calls *consciousness*, moves us "away from chaos and disorder toward momentary stability and structure." But Blumenthal concludes, "these processes are fundamentally temporal in nature.[8]

Modern psychological theories explain man's nature and behavior as thinking, learning, teaching organisms, in the light of naturalistic assumptions. They ignore and often deny the relevance of the supernatural. For example, Edwin G. Boring, in his classical study *A History of Experimental Psychology* (1929), begins his report with the acknowledgement that experimental psychology grew out of the scientific endeavor: and "the fundamental principle of science [is] that nature can be explained internally without reference to an external agency."[9] No psychology based on that type of premise is sufficient in developing the agency approach to education being described in this book. Hebraic psychology assumes both the physical and the spiritual and attempts to explain the relationship between the two. An agency approach to education based on naturalistic psychologies would be inconsistent and foolish.

123

Ancient Hebrew Psychology

At the beginning of this chapter, psychology was defined as *a careful description and explanation of man at the fulness of his powers as a choosing, thinking, striving, talking, enculturated being*. Ancient Hebraic literature commonly referred to the *Heart, Mind, Might, and Strength* of man. These are terms used in the scripture to explain "man at the fulness of his powers." A computer search shows that these terms occur 3,306 times in the Bible and in modern scripture.[10] A careful study was made of each occurrance of these words. Unsubstantial meanings associated with the use of each word were systematically eliminated. This left a window of possibility (parameters) within which tentative, defensible, and descriptively operational definitions for each of the terms could be established .[11]

The conclusion of this study was that the use of these terms by God and his representatives describes mutually distinct dimensions of human nature; these descriptions were intentionally specific and not merely stylistic. *In other words, human nature can be described in terms of Heart, Mind, Might, and Strength, and these aspects of human nature should be taken into consideration when dealing with human beings.* This premise applies especially to parents, teachers, and students interested in the educational process from an agency point of view. The assumption is that these four terms actually refer to different dimensions of human nature that are fundamental to carrying out the learning/teaching process in the most effective way.

It is important to remember, however, that as long as life is a mystery, man will remain a mystery. We do not understand man in the absolute sense; theories abound, but agreement is sparse. For example, we know a lot about the eye, but we do not fully understand sight; we have learned a great deal about the brain, but we do not agree on how man thinks; we are able to understand much regarding living organisms, but the origin of life and the complete nature of death remain a mystery. There is more to be learned. Man sees through a glass darkly and the just man lives by faith, which is a partial knowledge. The terminology of ancient Hebraic psychology is not clinical; its purpose is to guide a person to make the covenants necessary for repentance. The terms *heart*, *mind*, *might*, and *strength* are not tools to be used in working on others, to do things to others. This would be contrary to agency education. Words are symbols that help us relate to what we cannot understand completely; they are terms like the terms *north*, *south*, *east*, and *west*; they orient us to a correct understanding of man's true nature.

124

Consistency in the scriptural use of the terms *heart, mind, might*, and *strength*, despite the varied applications made, allows a sensible as well as a technically significant rationale. The four terms can be defined as follows:

Heart denotes the character or dispostion—the governing attitude and feeling—of a person.

The heart refers to what man is cumulatively at any given moment. This controlling character or disposition is formed as the individual expresses life in the form of choices. Making choices, in the sense of making commitments, is governed by this disposition. The heart constitutes the significant decision-making center of human personality; it manifests itself as character or disposition—prevailing tendency, dominating mood, or governing inclination. The heart is the core, the innermost aspect of the person—the human being itself. It is subject to growth, development, and change as it is influenced by those choices. The heart is distinct from the mind. The two are different, but intimately interrelated, aspects of human nature. "As he thinketh in his heart so is he" (Proverbs 23:7).

Mind denotes man's sytem of attracting, organizing, and implementing knowledge or information for use by the heart.

125

A second aspect of human nature is the mind. The mind is man's capacity to become aware of things as they are, as they have been, or as they will be. This system for attracting knowledge functions within the spirit body alone, as well as within the spirit and physical bodies when they are combined. The mind is subject to the management and leadership of the heart. An individual may voluntarily choose to relinquish the management and leadership of his or her mind to another personality, but cannot transfer the responsibility for the consequences of that choice. The mind as an instrument of the heart may select, categorize, classify, and store, but it does not choose in the sense that the heart makes choices. It is a collecter but not a commander. "Behold, the Lord requireth the heart and a willing mind;" (D&C 64:34). *D&C 93:24* *Jacob 4:13*

Might refers to the resources—both temporal and spiritual—that are legitimately accessible to a particular person.

A third aspect of human nature is called might. A person's might extends beyond the heart and the mind. Might includes all resources that an individual legitimately commands or controls that may function more or less independently of the physical body. Might is extrapersonal, the lawful extension of the person, such as one's reputation and all other forces or materials that are within a person's rightful dominion and available for use by the individual. Personal wealth, property, and physical objects are examples of his or her might. "Therefore, O ye that embark in the service of God, see that ye serve him with all your heart, might, mind and strength that ye may stand blameless before God at the last day" (D&C 4:2)

Strength denotes the physical properties associated with an individual's body that are instruments of power in a bodily sense.

A person's strength is a fourth aspect of human nature; it is distinct from heart, mind, and might. Strength includes generative powers in the form of muscle, bone, and tissue; regenerative powers in the form of bodily systems such as the circulatory, respiratory, digestive, neural, and glandular, including reproductive powers—the physical capacity and power to procreate. "Wherefore, I give unto them a commandment, saying thus: Thou shalt love the Lord thy God with all thy heart, with all thy might, mind, and strength; and in the name of Jesus Christ thou shalt serve him" D&C 59:5).

These four categories, abundantly referred to in ancient as well as modern scripture, consistently represent mutually distinct components of man. The governing and responsible center designated as the *heart* has a powerful tool at its disposal, a system for attracting knowledge, the *mind*. This mind is in constant need of management and control. Each individual presides over a dominion of resources, called *might*, that are at his or her disposal. *Strength* signifies the temporal components and boundaries of the living, human body. As outlined in Hebrew psychology, these are the human dimensions that must be considered to develop the agency approach to education. The more one learns to think, feel, and act in terms of these precepts, the less one will be attracted to use ideas and techniques that are manipulative.

Educational Propositions Consistent With Hebrew Psychology

After accepting these descriptions of heart, mind, might, and strength as an accurate description of man, one must consider some radical propositions about education—radical when compared with a contemporary psychology of man. For example, the following statements are consistent with a Hebraic conception of psychology.

1. **The primary focus in any educational enterprise should be the heart—the character or disposition of man.** To deny or ignore this inner core of man's being in any theory, principle, or practice is to miss the essential target. To design and deliver instruction that focuses primarily on the mind and its functions ignores the whole person. To fill the mind with information or to exercise the intellect through arranging information, without consideration of the impact on the disposition, is purposeless and possibly harmful instruction. *It is heartless education.* A uniquely physiological approach, in which the person is simply an organism to be conditioned and trained to respond to various stimuli, is also detrimental. This type of training makes the teacher a tyrant and the student a slave. It violates the legitimate bounds of man's agency and infringes on the expression of man's volition. People have inalienable rights and should not be viewed as experimental subjects.

2. **The heart or decisionmaking center is capable of being perfected—developed to a point where its every function will be perfect (complete) according to proper principles.** This statement implies sound educational programs at home, church, and school which implement principles that nurture and sustain the perfecting of the heart. It also means that the heart represents more than transitory emotions or feelings. The heart, in a descriptive sense, reflects the stable state of the personality, our current point of development relative to our ultimate potential. The term *heart* represents man's nucleus. Someone has noted that 80 percent of *learn* is *earn*. In a similar analogy, the ear by which we h[ear] (feel and understand) by the spirit is the h[ear]t. "My brethren . . . open your ears that ye may hear, and your *hearts* that ye may understand, and your minds that the mysteries of God may be unfolded to your view" (Mosiah 2:9).

3. **Some of the influences mentioned in the scriptures that directly affect the heart or disposition are (1) positive example, (2) faith, (3) works based on faith in Christ, (4) the realization that we are children of God, (5) application of God's revealed principles, (6) prayer, or communicating with God, (7) and acceptance of the pure love of Christ.** To be most effective, educational efforts must embrace and make use of these influences. They can have influence in connection with learning language, numbers, art, music, and manners as well as morality.

These motivational influences constitute a knowledge or awareness to which the heart can respond. They touch a person at the spiritual-feeling level in ways that stimulate, nourish, and allow positive desires to grow and develop. These influences will never generate immoral behavior.[12]

4. **The mind is a *means* and not an *end* in the configuration of human nature.** The mind is a capacity that belongs to the person. It is subject to our will (heart). We can understand and use the mind, but we must remember that the mind legitimately belongs to the individual; it should not be possessed or commandeered by some other personality for training or any other purpose. It should not be incarcerated, misdirected, polluted, prostituted, or otherwise abused by others. It should be cared for and protected by its owner.

5. **The mind is a system of attracting knowledge (awareness and comprehension), capable of operating through and within the limitations of the physical body—including the brain—but it is not restricted to these physical limitations.** The mind can and does function within the spirit body without recourse to physical organs, systems, and structures that are extensions of that spirit body in its mortal state.

6. **A careful study of the brain may reveal how the mind operates within its mortal limits, but it is not likely that this information will permit accurate conclusions about the ultimate nature of the mind.** It seems particularly unwise to circumscribe educational thought by limiting one's thinking within parameters based on physiological evidence alone. To deal with man *primarily* as a physical being is to ignore his primary nature and risk inaccurate conclusions.

7. **Man is a spiritual being functioning temporarily in a temporal environment.** Restricting our perception of man solely to the physical dimension—a temporary form—can seriously distort our understanding of important truths. This may also lead to erroneous and destructive conclusions.

8. **The mind functions together with the light of Christ.** This spiritual energy enlightens the mind (provides it with knowledge) and quickens or activates man's understanding (the proper interaction between mind and heart). The mind is capable of enlargement (accessing increased knowledge) through proper use, just as the heart is capable of increasing in understanding or

wisdom (establishing the proper interaction between mind and heart).

9. **From an educational point of view, the *might* and *strength* of an individual are the grounds for initial contact.** These aspects of human nature are the most easily observed and understood by others. The way we look, sound, act, and display our resources provides an initial image that precedes deeper and more intimate insight into an individual's mind and heart. Sensitive teachers will be slow to judge; wise students will be careful not to convey false images. Either action obstructs education. A soldier who dresses in the uniform of the enemy and acts like the enemy will be perceived as the enemy. Consequences during wartime, though innocent, may be fatal. So it is with educational relationships. Opportunities to learn and to teach are subject to death. Teachers may misperceive students who convey the wrong image by clothes or actions. Students may misperceive teachers in the same way. Our might and strength constitute the outer boundaries of initial contact with others. Care must be exercised lest we convey false impressions. Likewise, we must guard against drawing inaccurate and premature conclusions about others. Useful as these peripheral aspects might be, they are not the person; they are only extensions. Cues are provided, however, within the framework of might and strength to guide interpersonal interaction toward encounters with the mind and heart.

129

10. **The proper use and expansion of one's might and strength are reflected by true education.** It is with the heart and mind that we add to or subtract from our might and strength. Our strength and might are extensions of a functioning mind and heart. When properly educated, individuals reflect this education through their might and strength. It is this outward reflection of internal understanding that constitutes the power of example. The kind of person we are is revealed in the way we use what we possess.

Implications for Educators

As indicated, this view of man is a radical departure from the prominent notions in twentieth century western culture. In America, for example, two psychologies of man dominate—one outside of academic circles and the other within those circles. The *Freudian* view of man emphasizes processes buried in the unconscious and made manifest in the competing interests of the id, ego, and super ego. Pervasively obvious in American culture, Freud's explanation of man's basic nature is portrayed daily—in everyday conversation, entertainment, literature, business, advertising, music, movies, and marketing. This is why we see bikini-clad women on ads designed to sell machinery. People are expected to respond to the powers of suggestion and association keyed to their physical appetites.

Within the academic world the *behaviorist/cognitive* view of man dominates. Administrative policy, instruction, and learning are all submerged in the assumptions of behavioristic pychology. Performance in terms of behavior is the focus; reinforcement occurs in the form of reward and punishment reduced to a methodology. Schooling as a national enterprise seems especially committed to manipulating mental and physical environments to control and direct human affairs. Causation and motivation are explained almost exclusively from naturalistic theories of human nature. The presumption "control the external environment and that controls internal learning" governs everything from classroom management to curriculum development. Student grades, teacher wages, benefits, class loads, school, and district policies are target areas for applying this philosophy at school. Allowances, use of the family car, freedom to go out with friends, and other such perks are typical targets in the home.

Alternative pychologies of man vie for recognition and acceptance, but they have considerably less influence. *Humanistic psychology*, with its emphasis on man's potential, his inherent goodness and self-actualization, is widely promoted, but its practical impact is both recent and restricted. Various forms of *transpersonal psychology* stress nonconventional, transcendent, extrasensory, and altered states of consciousness as governing influences in the human being. Associated with unexplored forces or energy believed to be available to us, these realms are not as yet fully understood or subject to our control. This form of psychology, like humanistic psychology, is a partially developed description of man, not widely accepted. Although these ideas fill dozens of paperback books on shelves across the country, they have had only marginal impact on educational design.

Hebrew Psychology Is Unique

Despite the range of these modern explanations of man, none of them concede the assumptions of Hebrew psychology. No modern psychology explains the "here and now" of man's being with the use of revealed knowledge that originated with the Deity who governs this world, who is responsible for man's origin and intimately involved in his destiny. Conceptions of modern psychologies all derive from rational or transrational observations originating with man in this physical realm and then, rarely, extend into some transcendent domain. Sharing the same naturalistic premise, none can suffice as a suitable foundation for our agency approach to education.

The Hebrew foundation of psychology is different. While acknowledging the realms of physical and rational exploration and confirmation, it also extends beyond these academic processes. Hebrew psychology includes an added dimension that makes it possible for man to acquire knowledge unattainable from purely physical and rational modes of exploration. Man is more than a physical creature and more than a temporal being in search of a spiritual experience; man is a spiritual being briefly experiencing a temporal existence. This realization can change our thoughts about education. Anciently, it was acceptable to combine spiritual and natural methods of learning; today academicians frown on this combination.

131

For some people, accepting a Hebrew psychology has radical implications. It will probably require considerable professional reorientation, even for those individuals who have inclinations toward and experiences with religious education. And for those who have worked exclusively in a secular environment, who have been deeply conditioned by the modern context, the challenge may be doubly difficult . Not only do they face the task of admitting the limitations of the naturalistic approach to education (when viewed within this new and larger context), but they must accept and apply new knowledge derived from sources academia generally considers unacceptable. This is not an easy adjustment for those of us with long histories of doing and thinking in ways that the Hebrew perspective finds either inadequate or unacceptable. But it can be done. We are free to choose the agency alternative. The haunting question, especially for professionals, seems to be: But what will become of me if I do?

9

The Nature of Learning

Learning is becoming aware and then choosing to act on the basis of that awareness. True education for the agency oriented person entails more than gaining knowledge; one must acquire the wisdom (light) to use the knowledge correctly according to the measure of divine standards.

Popular Ideas About Learning

Before we explore the idea of learning from an agency perspective, it may help to review several popular ideas about learning. In the social sciences it is common to define learning as a change in behavior that results from prior experience, not rooted in bodily variations such as sleep, growth, fatigue, and so forth. In other words, learning is experiencing change other than regular physiological responses. Beyond this point definitions and explanations of learning are varied and sometimes in conflict.

133

Many theories attempt to explain how learning occurs in human beings. Some of the most popular theories were developed by studying how animals learn and then applying those explanations to human action by testing the theories on human subjects. This research contributed to the development of what has been called *behavioral psychology.* The work of the Russian scientist Ivan Pavlov and American psychologists B. F. Skinner and Albert Bandura are examples of people who explain learning from a behavioral point of view. This approach to learning limits itself to what is called *observable behavior.* John B. Watson, whom some call the father of behaviorism, insisted it was much more scientific to study observable behavior. Others who have studied human learning do not agree. They "are convinced that it is possible to study nonobservable behavior—such as thoughts—in a scientific manner."[1]

Cognitive psychologists believe learning can be researched by studying what goes on inside the person. "They concentrate on analyzing mental processes, the various sets of principles and conclusions that they have proposed are referred to as *cognitive theories*."[2] Learning focuses on how a person processes the information that comes through his senses to his brain and how that information gets used. These people explain how sensory input is transformed, reduced, elaborated, stored, recovered, and used. Their theories are often very abstract; they rely on explanations called paradigms (mental maps) which often seem disconnected from personal experience—nice in theory but to some people impractical. This is understandable, because the idea of "learning" is a symbol, not a tangible object. A simple but comprehensive definition or description is difficult to create and communicate.

Another, somewhat less popular, approach to understanding learning has been to focus on human feelings or *affective* learning. Those who emphasize learning through the emotions distinguish between the mental and emotional processes. Perhaps the most famous modern example of this distinction is in the work of Benjamin S. Bloom and other educators who developed a system to classify objectives in three domains.[3] Roughly categorized into three types, learning occurs through the physical body (psychomotor), through the mind (cognitive), and through the feelings (affective).

Bernard Berelson and George Steiner, summarizing the scholarly studies on learning, concluded that by and large learning research is still in the hypothetical stage as far as humans are concerned. Many practical generalizations seem effective in given situations, but as yet these do not seem to tie situations together in a meaningful way.[4] Current textbooks on educational pyschology reflect this same conclusion. They describe a variety of learning theories, but there is no single, unifying explanation.

What the research does show, however, is that certain principles seem to work at various levels of learning. Research into the physiological realm of learning has generated some principles that seem fairly reliable. The cognitive realm provides another set of hypotheses that seem quite useful; the affective domain offers another set of helpful insights. This pattern may imply that each domain is governed by forces that operate somewhat

134

independently in that particular sphere (D&C 93:30). Nevertheless, a simple explanation of learning that integrates the parts into a coherent whole is missing. And the danger for parents, teachers, and students lies in selecting one of the fragments (and perhaps the assumptions from which it developed) as the way *all* learning occurs. A precise explanation has little value if it's wrong.

An Agency Definition of Learning

The intent of this chapter is to explore the idea of learning in a way that is consistent with personal agency. A simple definition for learning fits this objective: *Learning is becoming aware and then choosing to act on the basis of that awareness*. From this point of view, learning is a three-part process: (a) becoming aware of something, of anything; (b) making a decision on the basis of that awareness; and (c) acting on the basis of that decision—expressing the decision as a choice. Learning may lead to truth or error. We can attract knowledge (become aware) and respond to that awareness incorrectly as well as correctly. Hence, the great challenge in life is to choose between right and wrong as we act upon our awareness. For example, I may become aware of the element of water. This awareness makes it possible for me to decide what to do in relationship to the water and to act on the basis of my decision. I may choose to drink the water, bathe in it, ignore it, or respond in some other way. Whatever my choice, I engage in the learning process. Depending on the circumstances, my actions may lead to correct or incorrect, useful or not useful, good or bad consequences. What I retain from my experience with the water can be called learning, and this learning may be used to guide my actions in subsequent encounters with water-related experience. The foregoing process applies to all forms of learning in our lives. The challenge is to use the process of learning for beneficial rather than detrimental purposes.

135

Beginning with Revealed Principles

One might accept the idea that education is a matter of learning, and that learning is a matter of acquiring knowledge. For example, we go to school to learn, and in school it is evident that learning is a matter of gaining knowledge—first, knowledge about the alphabet, then numbers, people, places, and things. Theorists recognize this simple idea—whether they prefer a stimulus-response or a mental-map approach. But *true learning,* education for the agency oriented person, *entails more than gaining knowledge; one must acquire the wisdom to use knowledge correctly according to the measure of divine standards.* Defining learning in this way goes beyond what is commonly taught in our textbooks or measured in experimental research.

Wisdom, a human capacity, may be referred to as intelligence. Intelligence, in this sense, is the result of properly combining light and truth. Intelligence is not truth alone; it is truth plus the light God gives to make it possible for man to understand and apply truth properly A person may obtain a knowledge of truth and not be intelligent. In other words, one may discover some truth and not possess sufficient light to properly use that truth. For example, I have sufficient knowledge to operate an automobile, but if I lacked the light and did not understand how to apply that knowledge properly, I could destroy the vehicle, myself, and others. "Intelligence . . . [is] light and truth (D&C 93:36)." When we have truth, plus the light and disposition or heart to use that truth properly, we have true understanding or wisdom. This is the kind of learning that fits the agency approach to education.

136

The Key of Knowledge

Light and truth, though companions, are not synonyms. The pursuit of one without the other is dangerous and is not the aim of the agency approach to education (BM, Jacob 4:14). Separating light from truth is an old problem. Jesus taught that the lawyers (the learned) of his day had forsaken what he called the "key of knowledge" and persecuted those who sought intelligence through that key (Luke 11:52). These lawyers and teachers had rejected "the fulness of the scriptures" or light of the gospel. Without this light, the truth soon became perverted or was lost to them.[5] Human reason without divine light is a dangerous guide. A search for truth without a search for light is a vain expedition, regardless of how useful, popular or convenient it seems at the moment. It leads to pride, vanity, and error.

Parents, teachers, and students should seek both light and truth. The latter-day prophet Joseph Smith spoke plainly on this point: Men will be judged by the light they receive, not by the volume of truth that surrounds them. "God judges men according to the light he gives them,"[6] he said. And "he that will not receive the greater light, must have taken away from him all the light which he hath; and if the light which is in you becomes darkness, behold how great is that darkness."[7] In such is "fulfilled the prophecy of Esaias, which saith, By hearing ye shall hear, and shall not understand; and seeing ye shall see, and shall not perceive (Matt. 13:14)." The key to knowledge, therefore, is light—divine light that enables one to see the truth and understand how to properly act upon it—"For the Lord God giveth light unto the understanding" (BM, 2 Nephi 31:3).

A Burden of Worldly Men

In the context of agency education, then, to seek the truth is folly if we do not also seek the light to guide the truth when we obtain it. This is a burden, if not a curse, men have brought upon themselves from the earliest ages.[8] The misapplication of knowledge has caused much pain and sorrow in the human family. It has long been observed that a little learning can be a dangerous thing. A lot of learning may be even more dangerous, unless it is accompanied by the understanding and wisdom that ensure spiritual as well as physical safety. A sober warning has been given to those who glory in their own learning.

137

> When they are learned they think they are wise, and they hearken not unto the counsel of God, for they set it aside, supposing they know of themselves, wherefore, their wisdom is foolishness and it profiteth them not. And they shall perish. (BM, 2 Nephi 9:28)

This is the type of learning or knowledge that is devoid of light.

From an agency perspective, man's spiritual, as well as his physical, welfare is of great concern. To know but not really understand is hardly better than not knowing at all. The prophet Jacob reminded us that those who "consider themselves fools before God, and come down in the depths of humility" are the ones who will receive the light in addition to their learning (BM, 2 Nephi 9:42-43). Students engaged in the search for knowledge need to be taught this principle if they are to retain balance and propriety in their learning.

The Message of the Restoration

In our dispensation, God has given truth in great abundance. Truth is plentiful, even among those who are not searching. But the light or intelligence to use that truth properly, in an eternal sense, is promised only to those who seek intelligence, sacrifice for it, and acknowledge God as the source of truth. The message of the restoration of the gospel of Jesus Christ in these latter days is that the key of knowledge has been restored. We no longer need to remain in darkness. Our responsibility is to use this key, the light of the gospel, the fulness of the scriptures, and not cast it aside; nor should we prevent others from using it. Agency education is complete only when it embraces the key of knowledge, the fulness of light.

Historically, there has been a pattern among those who reject the key of knowledge to criticize and persecute those who have it and desire to use it. This has happened in homes and classrooms as well as in communities. As inhabitants within western culture, we are encompassed by an intellectual environment that has consciously rejected the requisites to obtaining the key of knowledge. Contemporary society is by choice a secular society in its public stance. It ignores or denies that which is sacred in its educational and governmental functions. John Taylor observed more than a century ago that

138

> One great reason why men have stumbled so frequently in many of their researches after philosophical truth is that they have sought them with their own wisdom, and gloried in their own intelligence, and have not sought unto God for that wisdom that fills and governs the universe and regulates all things. That is one great difficulty with the philosophers of the world, as it now exists, that man claims to himself to be the inventor of everything he discovers. Any law and principle which he happens to discover he claims to himself instead of giving glory to God.[9]

It is not easy to credit God in a society that "unofficially" avoids, ignores, or denies him in most of its professional endeavors. But the responsibility to acknowledge God remains—whether it is easy or not.

Truth Is Manifest Through Personality

To obtain wisdom, understanding, or intelligence, a person must have light as well as truth; in addition, it is important to realize all truth is manifest through personality. Eliminate personality, and there is no way to make truth known. David O. McKay said, "Truth manifests itself through personality. Though ever-existent, it is recognized only as it manifests itself through intelligent entities."[10] Truth is simply knowledge—"a knowledge of things as they are, and as they were, and as they are to come" (D&C 93:24). Obtaining truth is recognizing what is, has been, or must be. As food of the soul, truth is manifest as a person thinks, feels, and acts in harmony with Right. We become acquainted with the truth in two ways: (1) by personal experience, and (2) by observing its manifestations in the lives of others.

If we want to possess the truth, we must seek it from ourselves, others, and from God, through whom all truth is manifest. That is why we are instructed to "love the Lord thy God with all thy heart, might, mind and strength" and "thy neighbor as thyself" (D&C 59:5-6; see Matt. 22:37-39). This is an important insight into the agency approach to education. *Our fellow beings are important; they are potential fountains of truth from which we nourish our very being.* Individuals have inherent value. You are important; you too can manifest truth to others. Jesus taught, "Therefore let your light so shine before this people, that they may see your good works [truth] and glorify your Father who is in heaven" (BM, 3 Nephi 12:16; Matt. 5:16). He also warned that "light and truth forsake that evil one . . . [who] cometh and taketh away light and truth, through disobedience, from the children of men, and because of the tradition of their fathers" (D&C 93:37-39).

139

A Standard to Measure Our Choices

It has always been a challenge for man to be valiant in the truth. Jeremiah the prophet lamented that the people of his day had been given much truth, "but they are not valiant for the truth upon the earth; for they proceed from evil to evil, and they know not me, saith the Lord" (Jeremiah 9:3). How, then, can we as parents, teachers, and students stay in the path that leads our educational decisions in the right way? Orson F. Whitney said that educational balance is a matter of selecting the proper standard by which to measure what we accept and what we reject:

We cannot safely substitute anything for the Gospel. We have no right to take the theories of men, however scholarly, however learned, and set them up as a standard, and try to make the Gospel bow down to them; making of them an iron bedstead upon which God's truth, if not long enough, must be stretched out, or if too long, must be chopped off—anything to make it fit into the system of men's thoughts and theories! On the contrary, we should hold up the Gospel as the standard of truth, and measure thereby the theories and opinions of men. What God has revealed, what the prophets have spoken, what the servants of the Lord proclaim when inspired by the Holy Ghost, can be depended upon, for these are the utterances of a spirit that cannot lie and does not make mistakes; while the teachings of men are often based upon sophistry and founded upon false reasoning. Uninspired men are prone to judge by outward appearances, and to allow prejudice and plausibilities to usurp the place of divine truth as God has made it known.[11]

140

If this counsel is accepted, educational theory and practice must be based on the information provided through revelatory sources. This means we should not follow someone else's lead whose assumptions are not in harmony with those provided by revelation. Textbooks, curriculum, and methodology based on incorrect assumptions will not suffice. As we pursue agency education we should not be content to work as gleaners in the intellectual wheatfields of the world. It will not suffice to piggy-back on the efforts and theories of worldly scholars, picking up a kernel here and there, while leaving unused the key that could unlock treasures of knowledge. Only *after* thoughtfully forming personal foundations of education is it safe to pick and choose methods, materials, and procedures developed and used by others.

The challenge is to our personal integrity. Apparently it is difficult for some individuals to accept in practice the premises of agency education. We may say we believe such and such and perhaps have positive feelings in that direction. But when it comes to acting in harmony with these professed positions, we fall short. The cultural environment often reinforces this gap; more often than not, the assistance we may receive is based on contrary assumptions.

Learning Theory: The Basic Premise

A major barrier to those who desire to become agency oriented is developing the confidence and trust to honor the agency of others—treating them as if they were spiritual beings. This may be difficult for us to do because it emphasizes a higher level of personal responsibility. People may say they believe man has a body and a spirit, then relate to them as if this were not true. The influence of teachings by those who believe man is only a physical organism are very powerful in our day and age. Consequently, many people do not actually develop relationships that are consistent with what they say they believe. Otherwise they would not embrace ideas and indulge in practices that are inconsistent with their stated beliefs.

A *Time* magazine essay illustrates modern man's commitment to probing the physical world in order to solve his problems. The writer of the essay indicates that in our age of scientific miracles, every field of human endeavor seems to look to science for the "silver bullet to pierce the heart of the problem." In the famous case of Albert Einstein, "Slices of his brain were recently pored over by a pair of California neuroscientists" in an attempt to discover the source of his genius—as if the question could be settled on the basis of physical evidence alone. The pattern is worldwide. The idea that the spirit of man is man is no longer academically popular. The essay cites a second example.

141

> In 1925 the Soviets, applying a socialist definition of genius, entrusted his brain [Lenin's] to a German neurologist, Oskar Vogt. The idea, explains psychiatrist Walter Reich, was to "establish an institute in Moscow entirely devoted to the purpose of discovering the [physical] basis for Lenin's political and philosophical genius." Two years and 34,000 slices later, Vogt found, and the *Journal of the American Medical Association* reported, a "large number of paths proceeding from the pyramidal cells [triangular nerve cells in the cerebral cortex]." These were taken to explain "the wide range and multiplicity of ideas that developed in the brain of Lenin and, particularly, his capacity for quickly getting his bearings when confronted with the most complex situations and problems . . ." Conclusion? The key to a materialistic view of Lenin's genius has been found.[12]

The agency-oriented teacher looks beyond the physical to establish a primary frame of reference in dealing with people and explaining their actions. Not that the physical is unimportant—quite to the contrary. The physical body is linked to the spirit person and is essential for personal growth; the physical environment is essential to personal well-being. Because the physical body circumscribes the function of the spirit personality in its mortal state, in very real ways it should not be ignored. The important point is that in order to be consistent with the agency position, the spirit person—not the physical body—must occupy the *primary* place in our perception of the educational task.

Orson Pratt stressed this point when he emphasized that

142

> It is the spirit of man, and not the mortal tabernacle, that enjoys, that suffers, that has pleasure and pain. But the mortal tabernacle is so closely connected with the spirit of man, and we have so long been in the habit of associating the pains and pleasures of the spirit with what is termed the pains and pleasures of the body, that *we have almost worked ourselves into the belief that it is actually the body that suffers pain, and enjoys pleasure; but this is not the case;* the body, so far as we know, is incapable of feeling; it is naturally incapable of it; it is only the spirit, that dwells within the body, that feels. However severely the body may be injured, it is not the body that discerns the injury, but the spirit within the body that discerns it. . . . When the spirit has left it [the body], it is incapable of any sensation whatever; it does not form any portion of that identity that belongs to ourselves as spirits; we are not aware of its pleasures or its pains; for it has neither; but we are aware that if our mortal tabernacle is injured or infringed upon, the spirit within is troubled and pained; but we have become habituated to call this the pain of the body.
>
> I make these remarks in order to extend our ideas beyond this state of existence.[13]

This point of view is very difficult for contemporary scholars to adopt. This is one reason the development of theory and practice in educational matters consistent with agency assumptions receives so little emphasis. We are so influenced by the modern world view with its exclusive emphasis on the physical that even when we believe in the physical and the spiritual, we think and act as if the spirit were secondary or irrelevant. We feel constrained by our society and our profession not to acknowledge what we know to be true. Nevertheless, Brigham Young reminds us,

> It is not the optic nerve alone that gives the knowledge of surrounding objects to the mind, but it is that which God has placed in man—a system of intelligence that attracts knowledge, as light cleaves to light, intelligence to intelligence, and truth to truth. *It is this which lays in man a proper foundation for education.*[14]

Agency-oriented educators who are to achieve their potential must look beyond the prisons of popular paradigms. Otherwise they will never obtain the vision that produces the fruits to bring the world to their doors.[15] Spencer W. Kimball expressed the challenge to educators in these words:

143

> This means concern—curricular and behavioral—for not only the "whole man" but for the "eternal man". . . . The Lord seems never to have placed a premium on ignorance and yet *He has, in many cases, found His better trained people unresponsive to the spiritual,* and has had to use spiritual giants with less training to carry on his work.[16]

The Learner is in Charge of Learning

Learning from an agency point of view is like a three-link chain; first, we become aware, then we choose, and last, we act. It is the individual who becomes aware, chooses, and acts. All these functions reside in and are legitimately controlled by the individual. This puts us in control of learning. By the very nature of our being, we as learners are in charge of our own learning. All other influences related to learning are secondary—materials, strategies, facilities, and other people. The primary forces of learning begin within the person and extend into the world of secondary influences. It is incorrect and ineffective to practice education by reversing this order; it violates the principles of agency education. Boyd K. Packer emphasized the application of this principle in these words:

I have a message for parents about the education of your children. . .We develop *control* by teaching *freedom*. . . .When one understands the gospel, it becomes very clear that the best control is self-control.

It may seem unusual at first to foster *self-control* by centering on *freedom of choice*, but it is a very sound doctrinal approach.

While either subject may be taught separately, and though they may appear at first to be opposites, they are in fact of the same subject.

Some who do not understand the doctrinal part do not readily see the relationship between obedience and agency. And they miss one vital connection and see obedience only as restraint. They then resist the very thing that will give them true freedom. There is no true freedom without responsibility, and there is no enduring freedom without a knowledge of the truth. . . .

Latter-day Saints are not obedient because they are compelled to be obedient. They are obedient because they know certain spiritual truths and have decided, as an expression of their own individual agency, to obey the commandments of God. . . .Those who talk of blind obedience may appear to know many things, but they do not understand the doctrines of the gospel. There is an obedience that comes from a knowledge of the truth that transcends any external form of control. We are not obedient because we are blind, we are obedient because we can see. The best control, I repeat, is self-control . . .Responsibility for teaching the doctrines rests upon parents.[17]

144

Awareness is requisite to learning. Becoming aware is what makes choice possible. The act of choosing initiates action for learning. Choosing entails what, how, where, when, and why we do something. Each of these manifestations can be affected by outside influences. That is why our learning is susceptible to the teachings of others. The spirit person within the physical body becomes aware within the limits imposed by his or her prior development and present readiness. The mind attracts whatever knowledge it can access and makes it available to the person—*this is awareness.* The individual then acts upon this awarenss—*this is choosing.* Choosing creates an intentional learning experience —*this is consequence.*

Personal learning is the outcome of personal experience —becoming aware, choosing, and experiencing the consequence. For example, I can be aware that an apple and a pear are before me on the table. Because I am aware they are there, the possibility exists to choose which of the two I would like to eat. I choose the pear to eat and in eating the pear I learn what a pear tastes like. Or I am told that the mother in the family next door is ill. My wife suggests we prepare and provide them with a meal. I choose to join in the experience. I learn about feelings that are generated by sharing with others. In school my son hears his geography teacher refer to Burma. He observes the teacher point to a designated location on a large map near India and China and say, "This is the country called Burma." He chooses to remember that Burma is a place near India and China. Consequently, when he looks on a map to find Burma, it is possible for him to look near India and China to find Burma.

Attention, Interest, and Understanding

145

A practical view of learning requires more than consideration of abstract theoretical propositions. Boyd K. Packer illustrates this by giving examples related to such learning principles as "Readiness to be taught," "Too much too soon," "The time is now—right now," "Let them help," and "Feed them when they are hungry."[18] Making abstract ideas come alive in concrete illustrations is one avenue that leads to and demonstrates learning. Transforming ideas into illustrations is another way to teach—to organize influences that affect learning. In order to emphasize this principle, it may be helpful to review three very common capacities that direct, sustain, and contribute to our learning: *attention, interest,* and *understanding.* Everyone is familiar with these; we all use them daily.

What is attention? Attention is the application of the mind's powers in a given direction. This is the way a person becomes aware of something. When we give heed to, or consider, a specific idea, object, or incident, we give it our attention. When we say to a child, "Now pay attention to me," we are requesting the child to aim and focus mental powers in our direction. Each individual may intentionally direct his or her attention to other people or objects that solicit attention. The ability and power to focus is a gateway to learning. We must become aware, and to become aware, we must focus our attention.

What draws attention? Conscious attention is attracted to situations involving intensity, relevance, repetition, definite form, and striking quality. When these characteristics prevail or are introduced, people "pay attention." A situation that invokes *intense feeling*, such as strong emotional exchanges between people—an angry argument, a burst of laughter, or a quiet but tearful expression—calls for our attention. Those things that are *relevant* to our desires also draw our attention. Hungry people notice food, just as people who have burning questions are responsive to what they perceive to be answers to those questions. The *repetition* of blinking lights on advertisements attracts attention. The whole principle of camouflage is based on our tendency to direct attention toward *bold, definite, sharp* outlines. Our conscious attention is less likely to be attracted to the fuzzy or the vague that blends into its surroundings. We need to remember this as we communicate with others. A helpful principle to remember is that the mind commonly operates in terms of mental pictures. Creating pictures with the necessary characteristics to attract attention contributes to successful communication. These pictures can be created with words, sounds, smells, etc., as well as with physical objects. However, our learning does not depend solely on creating new pictures. We all have a "memory"—a large bank of mental pictures—and with the proper cues, "attention" can call forth pictures from this reserve.

146

What is interest? Interest is a term used to describe what takes place when we maintain our attention on one object, idea, or feeling for an extended period of time. This does not mean we are not aware of other things. We may have our mind's powers directed "here" and then, "there" by whatever attracts our attention. But if our attention keeps coming back to one specific idea or activity, we are interested in that particular thing. Our mental and perhaps our physical powers are concentrated on it more than on other ideas or activities. For example, notice what happens as you stop in front of a store to view a window display. There may be six or more items arranged to attract the customer's attention. Each of these might capture your attention momentarily, but usually you will keep coming back to one or two items. They will occupy your attention proportionately more than any of the others. This concentration of attention is termed *interest.* Teachers who learn to capture interest can help children as they learn to read, write, do arithmetic and seek other purposes of learning.

What develops interest? What is it that makes some things attract and retain attention more than others? Many terms are used to identify characteristics with the power to retain attention after it has been attracted. *Movement* or *animation* retains attention and "holds our interest." The object or the idea that catches our attention has a relationship with the fullfillment of our desires, and this has an effect on whether we will remain interested. If we feel something is vital to us, we will be interested. *Familiarity, novelty, suspense, conflict,* and *humor* are other terms that describe characteristic elements that hold a person's attention. Successful movies, television programs, advertisements, and games owe their success to the clever use of these factors. Analyze these characteristics in a television program or advertisement. You will be able to see why people are interested in them.

What is understanding? The term *understanding* as it is used here has two meanings. First, it means to recognize the context in which an idea, message, or object exists. Second, it means (a) to comprehend the meaning and function of the idea or object, and (b) to perceive its purpose, application, implications, and consequences. Seeing or recognizing the truth has to do with the first meaning; comprehending its function has to do with the second meaning. For example, a person may raise the hood of an automobile and recognize a carburator attached to the engine. He knows or "understands" what the object is in relationship to other parts of the car and may be able to explain that it prepares gasoline for consumption by the motor. This is the first type of understanding—carburators may be used to help gasoline engines function. Another person, however, may "understand" this and in addition be able to explain in detail every part within a carburator, its function, and what happens when a particular component fails to perform its proper role in relationship to the performance of the entire vehicle. This approaches the second meaning of understanding. At this level the person not only "understands" what a carburator is and does, but also the functions and consequences of each component's contribution. When you take your car to a mechanic to correct a problem, what he "understands" about your car makes a difference in his success in solving the problem.

147

What increases understanding? Some influences that contribute to increased understanding are prior personal experience, vision, or foresight (such as the logical transfer of similar experience), and the willingness to accept information from those who already possess wisdom. For example, it is easier to find your way around a new city if you have a guide who already knows the area. If you know how much salt is too much in one recipe, you can make a correct decision when no directions are given for the amount of salt in another recipe. We can increase our understanding by obeying instructions from those who know the consequences of actions beyond our own experience and expectation; this increases our wisdom or understanding. Before making your first jump from an airplane it would be wise to listen and obey those who know how to properly fold, release, and handle a parachute.

Role Definition Affects Learning

148

The roles we assume also tend to influence the learning process. The term "role" refers to how we see (a) ourselves and (b) our situation. These definitions influence how we exercise our ability to learn. To maximize learning we must see ourselves accurately and understand our roles. For example, the boss tends to speak differently to his employees than he does to his wife, and employees listen differently to the boss than they do to their children. Roles affect our learning because they influence our attention, interest, and understanding. We need to be aware of our roles and seek to overcome their limitations on our learning.

Confirming Who and What We Are

The two processes of *self-evaluation* and *self-definition* seem to confirm who and what we are. These two processes combine to structure the information we use to verify or to challenge the ideas we have about ourselves. They are like screens that influence the way we interpret information. As these screens are formed and operated according to correct principles, they reveal truth to us; when they are formed or operated by incorrect principles, they become mechanisms of self-deception. Christ taught the correct principles; rejecting these lead us to accept counterfeits.

Self-Evaluation: We evaluate ourselves by asking such questions as Am I of value? Do I count? What am I worth? Or am I worthless and expendable? In order to consistently function effectively we need to feel that we are important, that we are valuable, that we matter. The answers to these questions about our value come in the form of feelings. These feelings either confirm or deny the ideas we have about ourselves.

Self-Definition: We seek self-definition by answering such questions as—Who am I? What am I? What are my abilities? What can I do? We must each see ourselves as capable in some capacity. We must feel we are something before we can feel *worth* something. An example of the importance of self-definition can be quickly visualized in the following question: What kind of wife or mother would a woman make who never defined herself as a wife or mother? If a man does not see himself as a married man, he is not likely to behave like a married man. Would you like to be operated on for a serious heart condition by a man who defined himself as a plumber rather than a surgeon? Our reliability and our ability to accept responsibility are directly associated with what we define ourselves to be. Self-definition combined with self-evaluation determines how we see ourselves. This in turn affects how we express ourselves and how we receive expressions from others—in other words, how we learn.

149

The Worth of the Individual

Most modern educational programs emphasize the group rather than the individual. The group has primary value, even when language is used that refers to the individual. This is a natural consequence of assumptions shared by those who prefer the societal approach to understanding people and how they learn. Individual needs and goals in a societal model of learning have less priority than the needs and goals of the group. Although one may hear language that seems to emphasize individual attention and direction, the basic approach to education in most American schools is societal in structure and function. One writer expresses this philosopy in these words:

> Individual psychology is . . . wholly inadequate in its explanation of a mature human being. . . . No consideration of individual traits, however comprehensive, can explain what goes on during the educational process. That process is one of transforming individuals so that they will conform to social

institutions. Individual psychology must be supplemented by a study of the psychology of social institutions if one is to reach a truly scientific understanding of education.[19]

The foregoing view differs from the one preferred in this book. An agency approach to education and learning places a higher priority on the desires of the individual than on the group. Consequently, the individual's needs takes precedence over the systems and preferences of the social institution. Institutions are important, but they are means, not ends. In this case, the institution (the means) exists to serve the individual (the end), rather than the individual existing to satisfy the needs of the institution. John A. Widtsoe offers the following example:

> The conception of The Church [of Jesus Christ of Latter-day Saints] and its responsibilities places a high valuation upon the individual. If religion must enter every concern of every person, the value of the individual must be very great. Indeed, such high valuation is a necessary conclusion from the story of life. For each member of the human race the plan of salvation was formulated and put into operation. Within every human breast lie germs of progress which, throughout eternal existence, may transform a mortal man into an immortal being of God-like powers. In light of this conception, the individual rises to huge, universal proportions.
>
> The Church, therefore, is more concerned with individuals than groups. It is well to know the average condition of the group as a whole, but it is more important to know the condition of those of the group who are lowest in happiness. The poorest, weakest, and the most needy must ever be the direct concern of the Church. If these can be raised, the average will automatically rise. It was this principle, set forth by Jesus the Christ in the parable of the lost sheep, by which the Master left the ninety-nine secure in the fold, to find and return the one that was missing.[20]

150

Soft or Hard Systems?

When working with human beings, the organization should not take precedence over the welfare of the individual. When the process of organizing becomes an end in itself, when the organization becomes more important than what is being organized, there is a danger of violating sound principles. When an organization becomes more focused on itself than on the purpose for which it was created, it runs counter to the agency approach to education. When the preservation of the system becomes more important than rendering the service the system was orginally intended to provide, the organization becomes more important than the individual. A state educational organization bulletin stressed the importance of its teacher association in these words:

> The major purpose of our association is not the education of children, rather it is or ought to be the intention and/or preservation of our members' rights. We earnestly care about the kids and learning, but that is secondary to the other goals.[21]

Originally, teacher associations were organized to improve education for children, not to preserve teacher's rights or the existence of the association. Societal systems of education tend to foster administrative systems that place the organization's needs above the needs of the individual. I call these *hard* systems. Systems that place the needs of the individual above the needs of the organization I call *soft* systems. For me, it has become a law: *When soft systems become hard systems, their survival becomes more important than their service.* Soft educational systems, those that resist letting one person or a few persons proclaim doctrines that dictate arrangements and prescribe explanations that deny the agency of others, are much better than hard systems. The experience of pre-World War II Germany is an example of what happens when a system becomes too hard. The promise of prosperity at any cost was swallowed in the atrocities of the holocaust. Education—the learning system—convoluted into a heinous form of self-destruction. The much heralded fruits of hard systems such as predictability, demonstrable outcomes, and time-cost efficiency factors must not be procured at the expense of personal agency and human dignity.

151

Man Is Capable of Learning, and Learning Is Related to Our Knowledge of God

Some principles of learning are acceptable to the agency-oriented teacher which other educators may not subscribe to. For example, an agency teacher may acknowledge that "all the minds and spirits that God ever sent into the world are susceptible of enlargement."[22] He also may assert that "no man. . . can know himself unless he knows God, and he can not know God unless he knows himself."[23] Joseph Smith taught, "It is the first principle of the gospel to know for a certainty the character of God."[24] Therefore, as Brigham Young explained,

> The greatest lesson you can learn is to learn yourselves. When we learn ourselves, we learn our neighbors. When we know precisely how to deal with ourselves, we know how to deal with our neighbors. You have come here to learn this. You cannot learn it immediately, neither can all the philosophy of the age teach it to you: you have come here to get practical experience and to learn yourselves. You will then begin to learn more perfectly the things of God. No being can thoroughly learn himself, without understanding more or less of the things of God: neither can any being learn and understand the things of God without learning himself: he must learn himself, or he never can learn God. This is a lesson to us.[25]

Brigham Young recognized the practical implications of the Savior's injunction that for man to obtain eternal life, he must know the Father and Jesus Christ (John 17:3). From this perspective, man's learning involves a cyclical principle. As we properly study ourselves, we will come to a greater appreciation of our Father; as we come to understand the true character of God by keeping his commandments, we will learn more about our own nature. Education that does not lead us to this type of knowledge is faulty (BM, Moroni 7:15-17).

> Having a knowledge of God, we begin to know how to approach him, and how to ask so as to receive an answer. When we understand the character of God, and know how to come to him, he begins to unfold the heavens to us, and to tell

us all about it. When we are ready to come to him, he is ready
to come to us.[26]

The knowledge from God about our physical being is given
to us as if we had no physical body. It is given to our spirit being.

> All things whatsoever God in his infinite wisdom has
> seen fit and proper to reveal to us, while we are dwelling in
> mortality, in regard to our mortal bodies, are revealed to us in
> the abstract, and independent of affinity of this mortal
> tabernacle, but are revealed to our spirits precisely as though
> we had no [physical] bodies at all; and those revelations which
> will save our spirits will save our bodies. God reveals them to
> us in view of no eternal dissolution of the body, or
> tabernacle.[27]

Thus, it is shortsighted to attempt to understand people as if   153
they had no spirit dimension, capable of receiving divinely given
insight and understanding. Because of this shortsightedness, most
contemporary learning theory regarding learning is faulty; it cannot
lay the correct foundation for an agency approach to education.

The knowledge necessary to establish the most correct
foundation for agency education resides in the archives of the
ordinances of the priesthood of God. Said Joseph Smith,

> Reading the experience of others, or the revelation given
> to them [other people], can never give us a comprehensive
> view of our condition and true relation to God. Knowledge of
> these things can only be obtained by experience through the
> ordinances of God set forth for that purpose. Could you gaze
> into heaven five minutes, you would know more than you
> would by reading all that ever was written on the subject.[28]

> We are only capable of comprehending that certain
> things exist, which we may acquire by certain fixed principles.
> If men would acquire salvation, they have got to be subject,
> before they leave this world, to certain rules and principles,
> which were fixed by an unalterable decree before the world
> was.[29]

"The question is frequently asked, 'Can we not be saved without going through with all those ordinances?'" Joseph Smith answered,

> No, not the fulness of salvation. Jesus said, There are many mansions in my Father's house, and I will go and prepare a place for you. *House* here named should have been translated kingdom; and any person who is exalted to the highest mansion has to abide a celestial law, and the whole law too.
>
> But there has been a great difficulty in getting anything into the heads of this generation. It has been like splitting hemlock knots with a corn-dodger [a thin, pliable, piece of wood or metal] for a wedge, and a pumpkin for a beetle [hammer or mallet]. Even the Saints are slow to understand.[30]

The Eternal Nature of Learning

154

Isaiah poetically expressed the process of learning: "precept must be upon precept, precept upon precept; line upon line, line upon line; here a little, and there a little (Isaiah 28:10)." Joseph Smith taught that learning was like climbing a ladder, and the process extends beyond this mortal existence:

> When you climb up a ladder, you must begin at the bottom, and ascend step by step, until you arrive at the top; and so it is with the principles of the Gospel—you must begin with the first, and go on until you learn all the principles of exaltation. . . . It is not all to be comprehended in this world; it will be a great work to learn our salvation and exaltation even beyond the grave.[31]

Brigham Young also saw learning as a continuous endeavor:

> We are in the school and keep learning, and we do not expect to cease learning while we live on earth; and when we pass through the veil, we expect still to continue to learn and increase our fund of information. That may appear a strange idea to some; but it is for the plain and simple reason that we are not capacitated to receive all knowledge at once. We must

therefore receive a little here and a little there.[32]

We might study and add knowledge to knowledge, from the time that we are capable of knowing anything until we go down to the grave. If we enjoyed healthy bodies, so as not to wear upon the functions of the mind, there is no end to a man's learning. This compares precisely with our situation pertaining to heavenly things.[33]

Reason Alone Is Insufficient

Those who do not separate the physical from the spiritual, or disengage the secular from the sacred, carry the spirit of an agency approach to learning. Clearly, the responsibility for learning is on the learner, and success in learning depends on divine assistance. Reason is useful but insufficient; it can be a safeguard against blind impulse, but not a guarantee of truth. Reason can serve both as a bulldozer on the landscape of ignorance and a surgical scalpel to the body of mystery. But reason does not make us warm and accepting; it is not a reliable cosmic compass. It is faith that activates the Liahona of life;[34] it is revelation that leads us into eternity and makes known to us the directions we should travel. In limited ways we can learn on our own, but if we desire to approach our potential as learning, growing beings, we must not limit our vision to the physical world or rely solely on reason to fathom the most fundamental questions. There is a better way to teach and to learn.

155

10

Conscience, Maturation, and Agency

*Education from the Mormon point of view must be
mental, physical, moral, and spiritual. There is a
knowledge that pertains to time, which makes men
wise and capable here; and there is a knowledge that
pertains to eternity which makes men wise and
powerful there. Between them is this great difference:
The knowledge of this world does not include the
knowledge of the eternal worlds, but the knowledge of
those worlds does include the knowledge of this world;
and this is the education advocated and sought after
by the Latter-day Saints. —Orson F. Whitney*

The Whole Person

In 1919 the first Rudolph Steiner, or
Waldorf, School was established in
Europe. Today, these schools exist in
many countries, including the United
States, Canada, Mexico, and South
America. An independent school or
school system is not unique. Maria
Montessori, A. S. Neill, and hundreds of others have pioneered
educational enterprises apart from public or government sponsored
schools. Depending on one's assumptions about education these
various private school endeavors are perceived in a number of
ways—good, bad, elite, eccentric, productive, wasteful, useful, etc.
When they have succeeded, it has generally been due to an
emphasis on a legitimate human capacity that appealed to the
people who supported them. My point in mentioning the Waldorf
schools is simply to cite an example of a school program that has
thrived on emphasizing the need to educate the "whole human
being."

Those who currently support the Waldorf schools emphasize
that "no dogmas are to be introduced into the school." Yet they
recognize that

> the human being . . . not only consists of a physical body . . . but . . . also an astral body which contains what has evolved in the pre-existent life of the human being before birth, or rather, conception, and unites this [spirit being] to the bodily nature that lives on the earth between birth and death.[1]

Because instructors concede this fundamental truth, though it is not taught in the schools, sponsors maintain they are better prepared to understand those whom they teach. The important point they make is this: Anyone "who knows how to understand the human personality scientifically, not merely externally, but according to body, soul and spirit *will also understand the way the human personality of the growing individual is revealed.*"[2] For these educators the greatest teacher in the Waldorf school is the child himself; what the school instructors see in the child from week to week, from year to year, "is the expression of a divine spiritual being that descends from purely spirit-soul existence and evolves here in physical body existence, . . . uniting with the line of heredity . . . from parent and ancestors." This view of man creates a

> tremendous reverence for the growing person who, from the first day of his existence in a physical body, shows how his inner soul nature is revealed in his features, in his first movements, utterances of sound, and first beginnings of language. . . . And from the daily revelation of this mysterious spirit-soul being he [the instructor] discovers what he has to do.[3]

This view of the individual is quite different from that espoused by most popular educational psychologies. This difference has generally fueled the success of the Waldorf schools. As one of their proponents has said,

> I have not the slightest intention of saying anything against present-day experimental psychology and educational methods. I know full well what these branches of science are able to achieve, and I am also able to appreciate it. But just the fact that these branches of science exist makes it imperative that a deepening of our educational life take place.

For despite all the praiseworthy work that has been carried out experimentally in psychology and education it does in fact prove that, fundamentally, modern education has not helped us to get any closer to the real human being, but, on the contrary, it is now even further away than before.[4]

Agency education, as in the Waldorf schools, has a different educational focus than do most modern school systems. Like the Waldorf schools, the difference is not based on introducing dogma into the educational process. Rather it is based on how the assumptions people make about God, man, and nature influence the way education is perceived and carried out. This chapter examines another dimension of these assumptions that influences how we relate to those with whom we work and associate. It considers human maturation and related matters that affect the learning and teaching processes.

Four Dimensions of Human Expression

159

There appear to be four dimensions in which the human personality expresses itself: the physical, the mental, the moral, and the spiritual. Orson F. Whitney points this out:

> Education, from the Mormon point of view must be mental, physical, moral and spiritual. There is a knowledge that pertains to time, which makes men wise and capable here; and there is a knowledge that pertains to eternity which makes men wise and powerful there. Between them is this great difference: The knowledge of this world does not include the knowledge of the eternal worlds, but the knowledge of those worlds does include the knowledge of this world; and this is the education advocated and sought after by the Latter-day Saints.[5]

As we are born and develop in mortality, we experience two very powerful influences that affect our education. The human personality shows these influences through modifications in how the individual relates to life and to others. One of these influences has been called *conscience*, and the other *puberty* or concupiscence.

Conscience

Conscience is the capacity to decide for ourselves the difference between right and wrong and to be accountable for our own actions. According to the Lord's instructions, it is the duty of parents to assume the responsibility of caring for and properly teaching their children, especially before the age of accountability. Until a child, begins to "become accountable" before God, each child depends on the significant adults in his or her life to provide not only physical sustenance but also a moral system. Before this time a child's capacity is very limited in the moral domain. Therefore, parents have heavy responsibilities to teach their children carefully.

> Little children are redeemed from the foundation of the world through mine Only Begotten; wherefore they cannot sin, for power is not given unto Satan to tempt little children, *until they begin to become accountable* before me. (D&C 29:46-47)

The time of accountability is designated as eight years of age:

> Inasmuch as parents have children in Zion, or in any of her stakes which are organized, that teach them not to understand the doctrine of repentance, faith in Christ the Son of the living God, and of baptism and the gift of the Holy Ghost by the laying on of the hands, *when eight years old*, the sin be upon the heads of the parents. For this shall be a law unto the inhabitants of Zion, or in any of her stakes which are organized. (D&C 68:25-26)

This condition was intentionally established by the Lord to require great things of parents, since parenthood is a serious matter. The power of procreation carries with it significant personal responsibility (D&C 29:48).

In the traditional controversy over the nature of man, many theologians describe the human family as basically evil. In most academic circles today, scholars consider man's fundamental nature to be basically good. The agency view of this book holds that "every spirit of man was innocent in the beginning; and God having redeemed man from the fall, men became again, in their infant state, innocent before God. (D&C 93:38). The perception of man as basically innocent, rather than naturally good or inherently evil, allows a unique view of the intent and process of education. Brigham Young summarized this position as follows:

> In the first place the spirit is pure, and under the special control and influence of the Lord, but the body is of the earth, and is subject to the power of the devil, and is under the mighty influence of that fallen nature that is of the earth. If the spirit yields to the body, the devil then has power to overcome both the body and spirit of that man.[6]

The Pre-conscience Years

The advent of moral accountability in a child brings with it other significant mental and physical changes. Physiological research demonstrates children are usually seven to nine years of age before they acquire the hand-eye coordination to judge safely the speed of an object, such as a baseball, moving toward them. As a result, educators recommend that some games be excluded from physical education programs in the early elementary grades. Likewise, children should be age nine or ten before they participate in the Little League baseball program. (T-ball and coach ball are alternative programs designed to protect younger children from this physical limitation.) Some activities are simply inappropriate because of the child's physical immaturity. As children mature, their capacities expand to include more complex functions and increased independence.

A similar pattern of increased ability in children at this crucial age is apparent in the mental development of a person. Normally, four-year-old children have not developed the ability to do abstract thinking. They are involved in an intensely egocentric stage of development. They are not capable of seeing things very well, if at all, from someone else's viewpoint. Jean Piaget demonstrated this fact by a simple experiment. He developed a three-dimensional model landscape from papier-mache. Then he placed the figure of a small child somewhere in the landscape and asked a group of children of different ages to describe what that toy child could see. Children under age eight, who were still in the egocentric stage, could not take the role or see the viewpoint of another. Invariably these children described what they could see rather than what the toy child was in a position to see. Older children—nine to eleven-year-olds, for example—were able to restrict their report to the objects that were within the sight range of the toy child. These older children had the capacity to differentiate their own viewpoint from that of someone else. Parents and teachers should remember young children (pre-eight) are immune from Satan but not from other children and adults.

Recognizing that younger children are limited in their physical, mental, and moral capacities should help us relate more effectively to these children. This insight may affect a person's view of discipline, curriculum, instruction, and other aspects of education. The challenge is to help children keep spiritually aligned with the "special control and influence of the Lord." In a practical sense this is difficult, for two reasons. First, each child born into mortality is subjected to the traditions and environmental influences of others. When these traditions are false and the environment is wicked, the child fails to receive the positive developmental help he really needs. If the traditions are in accordance with God's laws and the environment is righteous, the child is more likely to choose the right and find happiness. The second reason it is difficult to stay in tune with the influence of the Lord is that as we mature, we become solely responsible for exercising our agency to choose. Our choices in mortality are made against the tension of the influence of Satan (D&C 93:39). To make correct choices consistently, after reaching the stage of accountability, demands divine help. We cannot do this alone. We must have divine assistance. We must seek this assistance.

162

This proposition is not accepted by those who adopt the exclusively naturalist position. Those who believe that there is no reality outside the bubble do not acknowledge or accept the existence of Satan, an evil personality with supernatural qualities and influences. This concept of an evil power was purged from the curricular content of modern public education when the academic establishment shifted to the exclusively naturalist position. The idea of evil influences is generally considered unscientific and therefore irrelevant. Denying the reality of this powerful influence distorts the truth about the world in which we live and changes the moral nature of educational programs. Denial does not eliminate evil. The Lord has said

The glory of God is intelligence, or, in other words, light and truth.

Light and truth forsake that evil one.

Every spirit of man was innocent in the beginning; and God having redeemed man from the fall, men became again, in their infant state, innocent before God.

And that wicked one cometh and taketh away light and truth, through disobedience, from the children of men, and because of the tradition of their fathers. (D&C 93:36-39)

Prepuberty Education—From Birth to Accountability

During the first few years of life children learn many things. Children are curious; they explore and experiment with vigor and zest. Knowledge about our own physical abilities as well as our world is nearly a constant quest. Physical appetites and motor skills, language acquisition, communication tools and strategies, the management of physical objects, and numerous other aspects of human comprehension are the focus. These opportunities, tasks, and experiences fill up a young child's life. Picking things up, pushing things around, tipping things over, and spilling things about are the marks of childhood explorations. However, certain capacities lie dormant and undeveloped during the earlier years. One of these is the capacity to distinguish between what is right and what is wrong. Everyone interested in education needs to consider carefully this fundamental issue.

163

We have discussed how children, by nature, are very wrapped up in their own pleasures and needs; they usually act on the basis of what they expect will result in pleasure for them. But at the same time, children are almost completely subject to the will of others; they are not physically free to satisfy every personal desire. Furthermore, they are not psychologically free, since it is very easy for them to interpret an adult's commands as expressions of their own will.

Because children cannot differentiate social cues, they need authoritative guidance, first from parents, then from teachers and other adults, and later from institutions their parents esteem, such as the church and school. The mother's influence is paramount, since she usually sets the standards and expectations children are most aware of. Until children approach the age of accountability, to be good is to be obedient. What the parents want is right from the children's moral perspective. The expectations of the mother, reinforced by the father, become the child's moral system. Brigham Young maintained that "if children are not taught by their mothers, in the days of their youth, to revere and follow the counsel of their fathers, it will be hard indeed for the father ever to control them." [7] Obedience, self-control, respect, curiosity, and persistent work habits nurtured in the home will show up at school.

Another example of a child's early learning relates to habits that become the foundations of self-discipline. As my wife and I struggled to help our seven children learn to eat, drink, walk, and move about the house safely, numerous challenges arose. For instance, it is impossible for a baby in its early months to eat by itself with a spoon, but as a child develops he is able to pick things up and put them in his mouth. Children seem to like this independence, so food they can pick up with their fingers becomes popular. But not all food, such as mashed potatoes and vanilla pudding, are aesthetic finger foods—at least to onlookers or to the mother or father who must clean up the mess, mop the floor, and wash the child. We discovered that in order to preserve our family culture, it was necessary to pay the price in time, patience, and firmness to insist that some foods be eaten from a spoon held by Mom or Dad or an older brother or sister. We were not impressed by those who suggested that our children's learning could be impaired or their creativity stunted if we prevented them from swimming in their food.

164

The practice of spoon-feeding not only reduced household messes and clean-up efforts, it also established an early childhood pattern of order and discipline. This order and discipline became a foundation for other teachings later on. This simple practice also meant that our children did not learn some eating behaviors they would have to unlearn later. The basis was established for acceptable table manners as the children became accustomed to taking food from a spoon instead of a fist. An acceptable habit was developed that replaced the impulsive expression of personal desires.

As young children learn a language, other ways to teach become available. In addition to personal example, stories that include the examples of other personalities can be used. Examples of parental modeling, inspirational stories, admirable figures of authority, and others expose children to moral behavior outside their own personal experience. Content like this, when endorsed by parents who demonstrate they agree with the positive models and disagree with the negative ones, assists the child in recognizing moral order. This means that if a parent expects a child to act lovingly and the parent presents a model of loving behavior, as well as stories about loving behavior, it is very easy for the child to practice acting lovingly.

Consequently, there is no better time to teach obedience than during these very early years. Children naturally want pleasure but depend on others for that pleasure; thus, they are anxious to please others if it leads to positive satisfactions. Before children can say, "I ought," they need to have the experience of responding to commands of clear, definite expectations. Every child is especially open to this training in the innocent or preconscience period of its life. Parents are held responsible for providing such training in a caring, loving, and consistent manner.

Boys and girls need to know what their parents and teachers want them to do. If parents and teachers are confused, the children will be, too.

Clearly establishing and enforcing standards for young children does not mean adults should be dictators. Neither does it make of them behaviorists in the classical sense. The parent-child or teacher-student relationship should be loving and emotionally supportive. It should be sensitive to that spirit personality within the physical bodies of children and the right of children to determine their rightful purposes here in mortality. Children are natural learners and have an inquisitive nature that leads them to ask endless numbers of questions. Parents and teachers have many opportunities to stimulate a child's learning by taking time to explain how and why things happen. Children often seem to enjoy hearing reasons and explanations. But responding to and stimulating a child's curiosity should not be interpreted as letting young children decide on their own what is right and what is wrong. Adults err when they assume that explaining the consequences of certain behavior to a five-year-old releases them from the responsibility of seeing that the child does the right thing. God has declared otherwise, and the child deserves and is prepared to receive rightous parental regulation.

In moral matters, the parent's will is the child's primary source of social order. Reasons may or may not be attached to parents' commandments for this age group. For example, a father may say to his three-year-old child, "Daddy doesn't want you to play in the road because a car may hit you." The child may or may not understand what it means to be hit by a car. And the child may not be hit by a car, but should still learn to obey because "Father said so." For the child of this age the will of the parent is usually reason enough. David O. McKay explained that

> Unhappiness in the child's life, as in the adult life, springs largely from nonconformity to natural and social laws. The home is the best place in which to develop obedience, which nature and society will later demand. *The child should learn these rules of conformity during the ages from three to five;* and if parents do not get control of the child during this period, they will find great difficulty in getting control later. [8]

166

Prepuberty Education—From the Age of Accountability to Puberty

The period immediately preceding puberty has been labeled a latency period. It is a quiet time for most youngsters who are busily putting their own view of the world together. Children become aware of their ability to do their own thinking and recognize what they think and feel is separate from what others think and feel. Children realize that even the adults they so recently viewed as all-powerful are subject to external authority. For example, during these fairly quiet years, children acquire the capacity to distinguish between their father's will and the abstract rules that govern father's behavior. Children will notice that Father slows the car down in the thirty-five mile per hour zone and speeds up in the fifty-five mile per hour zone. They question discrepancies between the speedometer and the posted speed limit.

In other words, it is natural for children in this stage of life to become preoccupied with rules and regulations. They are prone to develop an enormous respect for such regulations and are keenly sensitive to them. Any playground is arbitrated by "It's not fair" or "But those are the rules." Children during this time frame are capable of sensitivity to others' feelings, but the rules are usually more important. This may pose some challenges, but it also offers crucial opportunities. A child who has developed a feeling for duty and obligation can obey and take comfort in the rules, even when confronted by authoritative personalities or peer group pressures that would tempt a move in an unhealthy direction. These years are an ideal time to teach children to do chores, take responsibility, learn citizenship, and commit to moral principles and religious commandments.

Most important, children at this age, by their own volition develop a basic disposition and an initial attitude that will influence a number of major decisions. What kind of person will they marry? How will they feel about service to others? What kind of living do they want to make? What style of spending are they comfortable with? How much reverence will they pay to parents and God? Will they tolerate greasy hands, like those of a mechanic? Do they enjoy sewing or cooking, tidyness, physical cleanliness, or verbal expression?

The decisions themselves may be tentative, but underlying values can and ought to to be established during these quiet years. Soon will come puberty, when the latent powers of procreation will unleash their shock waves. Then intellectual doubts, peer group pressures, and social self-consciousness begin to intrude forcefully upon the individual's personality. The time before this happens is the golden period to establish anchor points for the child to hang on to. Brigham Young taught that

167

> these noble, God-like principles should be instilled in them [children] in their youthful days, that when they grow up, they may never feel a disposition to deceive, or to commit iniquity, or turn away from the holy commandments of the Lord, but have power to control and govern themselves, subduing every inclination to evil, and every ungovernable temper, that they may secure to themselves eternal life.[9]

Not only is this the ideal time of personal, conscious formulation of character, it is also the period in which the foundations for curricular subject matter should be laid. Principles related to language and arts, mathematics, science, and social studies, appropriately introduced at this time, can be grasped in ways that will sustain the students' later development—when the subject matter becomes related to personal missions in life, and before the subject matter takes second place to social relationships fostered by puberty. There is a time and season for all things; this is the time and season for exploring simple fundamentals.

Puberty and Adolescence

As the maturation process unfolds, changes associated with the reproductive system occur in the individual. Between the ages of eleven and fourteen most young people experience changes in their physical, intellectual, and moral capacities that permit both the expression and control of procreative powers. These initial changes are sometimes called puberty. Puberty marks the passageway from childhood to adulthood. This period of development called adolescence extends from puberty, when the procreative capacity begins to unfold, until it is completed. In a legal sense, this period terminates at the age of majority, when a person turns eighteen or twenty-one years old in the United States.

168

It is important for the agency oriented educator to recognize that changes related to puberty and adolescence are more than physical. There are also changes in the powers of the intellect and the moral capacity that help govern the emerging powers of procreation. David O. McKay observed,

> If you would have your child live a life of virtue, of self-control, of good report, then set him a worthy example in all these things. A child brought up under such home environment will be fortified for the doubts, questions, and yearnings that will stir his soul when the real period of religious awakening comes at 12 or 14 years of age. It is then that he needs positive teaching regarding God and truth and his relations with others. Activity in the Church is a good safeguard during youth. [10]

On another occasion he directed this instruction to the youth themselves, emphasizing they are not left at the mercy of the physiological urges they feel. God has designed human maturation so that individuals can be in control if they so choose. It does help if the control system has been properly developed in the earlier years. Nevertheless,

Young people, you can be in this world, but not of the world! You have entered into that state of life when you are driven by heavenly-bestowed passions. There are some young men who, recognizing this fact, say, "Well, having these passions, why cannot we gratify them?" And they receive justification sometimes from some modern psychologists, false teachers and leaders who say that repression is wrong; that indulgence is the natural course of life. But I say, do not be misled! I repeat, young people, you are in that period of life in which *your physical nature manifests itself, but you must also remember that God has given you, in that same period of your life, power of reasoning; he has given you the power of judgment, discretion, and self-control, and these for a divine purpose.* Let reason and judgment be your guide, your balance.[11]

Modern psychology does not emphasize that human beings, even those in adolescence, possess the capacity to properly control the physical urges associated with reproductive maturity. Instead, most school textbooks describe man as an evolving organism primarily subject to biological and environmental influences. These textbooks do not emphasize human will nor the spiritual principles that govern it. Agency educators reject this type of psychological thinking. It is contrary to an agency view of human nature.

169

The "moral" philosophy of modern society can be seen in the way its most highly trained professional investigators perceive their work and formulate their questions. For example, consider the way professional scholars viewed maturation at the beginning of what was called the "sexual revolution." A brief statement from *The Annals of the American Academy of Political and Social Science* in 1968 is typical. After raising the question of ideology (how we should think about this subject) and considering the wide range of differences that exist—extending from "religious and other antisexual prejudices" to "antireligious and antipuritancal biases"—the writer poses the following questions:

What normative frames of reference [about maturation] can be expected, believed in by large masses of people, and followed, in a society which no longer requires that people be fruitful and multiply, in which the people have adequate methods for the control of pregnancy, and in which the possibility of injury to voluntary participants in a sexual encounter (in the form of venereal disease) can be diminished to the vanishing point? Will monogamy, fidelity, and the union of sex with love become anachronisms? Will the prohibition on adult-child sexuality and on incestuous relationships be thrown overboard as part of a heritage that is no longer meaningful in a not-too-brave but very new world?

In other words, what are the philosophical, ethical, moral, psychological precepts that will emerge and be meaningful in a world that re-examines sexuality after some two thousand or more years of fears and inhibitions, of rituals and myths? Without procreation, with its fears and desires and its human and social needs, where is sex? What is it? Thus, one could continue. The problems are many, they are difficult, but they are not insoluble. [12]

170   A careful examination of these two paragraphs illustrates the mindset that now controls much of contemporary education. The significant point is not that questions are being raised, but the nature of the questions being raised and the context they create. The emphasis may be subtle, but the impact is powerful. Notice (a) the assumption that society no longer requires man to be fruitful and multiply, (b) we possess adequate methods for the control of pregnancy, (c) the negative physical results of voluntary sexual encounters can reach the vanishing point, (d) monogamy, fidelity, and sex united with love may become outdated, (e) prohibitions against incestuous and adult-child sex may be thrown overboard as a meaningless heritage, and (f) the guidelines regarding maturation of the past two thousand years are related to fears, inhibitions, rituals, and myths. These questions are now premises intertwining in everything from television soap operas to the best selling books to media talk shows. Collectively they represent an anti-agency system of thought. The fact that we feel something is now a frequently used justification for finding a way to give it expression.

The truths mingled with the foregoing questions may convey to some individuals a persuasive sense of confidence. But they may also be deceptive. Collectively these questions are simply extensions of the position expressed in the *Humanist Manifesto II* (1973 item #6), where a carefully thought out preference is expressed for tolerating individuals who "express their sexual proclivities and pursue life-styles as they desire." This position, in contrast to "orthodox religions and puritanical cultures," holds there should be no prohibition "by law or social sanction [of] sexual behavior between consenting adults." Twenty years later some problems, such as AIDS, declining birth rates, families in disarray and dissolution, and child and spouse abuse have become more evident. These trends emphasize shortcomings associated with the exclusively naturalistic position.

Agency oriented educators will help adolescents recognize the pervasive educational bias that surrounds them. So much of what youth are exposed to may be false, but it comes in a convincing context of authority. For example, a widely used college textbook on psychology discusses the changing sex roles in modern society. After stating that biology determines whether we are male or female, the text reports that society determines how we play the parts of man and woman; preference of style is simply a matter of cultural conditioning. The author cites statistics that nearly half of all married women who live with their husbands and who have children over three years of age have been employed. He then refers to a single study to answer the question: What effects did this employment have on their children?

171

> The clearest answer concerns the daughters, at least in middle-class families. Daughters of working mothers tend to be somewhat more independent, are more oriented toward achievement, and perform better at school than do daughters whose mothers are not employed. In addition, they tend to think more highly of themselves (and indeed of women generally), are more outgoing, and seem somewhat better adjusted socially. These differences suggest that the working mother may well give the child something that it might otherwise lack, especially if the child is a girl—a female model for the development of independence, personal competence and a feeling of self-esteem. [13]

The content and tone of this message is very different than that expressed by Ezra Taft Benson:

> Mothers, stay close to your daughters. Earn and deserve their love and respect. Be united with their father in the

rearing of your children. Do nothing in your life to cause your daughters to stumble because of your example. Teach your daughters to prepare for life's greatest career—that of homemaker, wife, and mother. Teach them to love home because you love home. Teach them the importance of being a full-time mother in the home. [14]

And it is different than Spencer W. Kimball's counsel that

> Women are to take care of the family—the Lord has so stated—to be an assistant to the husband, to work with him, but not to earn the living, except in unusual circumstances. Men ought to be men indeed and earn the living under normal circumstances. . . .Too many mothers work away from home to furnish sweaters and music lessons and trips and fun for their children. Too many women spend their time in socializing, in politicking, in public services when they should be home to teach and train and receive and love their children into security.[15]

> I beg of you, you who could and should be bearing and rearing a family: wives, come home from the typewriter, the laundry, the nursing, come home from the factory, the cafe. No career approaches in importance that of wife, homemaker, mother—cooking meals, washing dishes, making beds for one's precious husband and children. Come home, wives, to your husbands. Make a home a heaven for them. Come home, wives, to your children, born and unborn. Wrap the motherly cloak about you and, unembarrassed, help in a major role to create the bodies for the immortal souls who anxiously await. When you have fully complemented your husband in home life and borne the children, growing up full of faith, integrity, responsibility, and goodness, then you have saved your accomplishment supreme, without peer, and you will be the envy [of all] through time and eternity. [16]

When we carefully consider both the natural and the supernatural aspects of human maturation, we are directed toward very different conclusions.

172

The Adolescent and Authority

Before the advent of conscience, young children wanted to know, "Who tells me to do it?" Accountable children wanted to know, "What are the rules?" Teenagers want to know, "Why should I do it?" They begin searching for meanings. They want experience, discussion, and abstract thought. The quest is for principles that account for the existence of rules and the requests of personalities. Sometimes their search for meaning becomes the question "Why shouldn't I do it?" As teenagers strain relationships with adults to test the limits of their freedom, they rebel against what they interpret as injustice or hypocrisy. They are not just posing intellectual questions; they are exploring spiritual issues as children of God whose moral awareness is expanding in preparation for life as a parent, an adult, and a professional.

The adolescent becomes sensitive to people in a new way. In the later preteen years, the rules were all important, but now conflicts arise. "Should I lie if it's for my best friend?" the teenager asks. Hungry for the truth behind the rules, adolescents challenge regulations as part of the search for their own adult identities. For these reasons, children between the ages of twelve and fourteen are in a time of real religious awakening. They are ready to test the worldview they have been quietly assembling during the prepuberty years.

173

The adolescent feels different about authority than do children in the pre- and postconscience periods. The four-year-old sees authority as a personality, usually that of his parents. The ten-year-old sees authority as the rule that even his parents have to obey. The eighteen-year-old, however, is capable of perceiving principles and governing himself by those principles; the authority of a parent or teacher now becomes a testimony to the authority of the principle. But what is the principle? This is the quest. Capable of moral maturity, of voluntarily obeying the influence of eternal principles and the will of our Heavenly Father, young people innately desire to know what these principles are. They yearn for the teacher who can unveil them, who invites their examination. Early on, parents were caretakers, later rules became the schoolmaster, and now they recognize that power resides in principles.

These different attitudes toward authority can help us understand the most successful methods to use as we work with people in each of these three periods of a person's life. Four-year-old Melissa will accept direction and feel good about it if she clearly understands her father's words, "I'm your father and I want you to." Ten year-old John will feel better about obeying authority when he sees the connection between a request and the rule that transcends the person making the request. By the time John is seventeen, however, he is not satisfied with either of these reasons.

When John is challenged for parking in the faculty parking area, he will be searching for more than a statement from the principal declaring he must not park in that zone. The principal in fact faces three general options. First, he can tell John: "You cannot park in the faculty parking area *because I said so*"—which would have been sufficient if John were five years old. If the principal told John, "You cannot park in the faculty parking area *because that is a rule at our school*," this would have been appropriate for a ten-year-old. But John is not five or ten. What he wants to hear and understand is an explanation of the general principle that justifies the rule. This is how John learns at his new level of maturation. This is how he will learn the correct principles so he can govern himself.

This habit of questioning rules to find the principles is a good one. If adolescents find enough good principles behind man-made and natural rules, they develop faith that principles validate even God-given laws that transcend their present capacity to understand. This faith will guide them through the legalism of the law into the spirit of the gospel.

If we understand the nature of human readiness to learn, we will be careful not to restrict moral growth by habitually using the wrong approach at any given period of a person's life. Pressuring small children to reason things out in the moral domain is both unrealistic and frustrating if what they really need is simply, "Because Mommy wants you to." If adolescents, on the other hand, are forbidden to reason and explore, they may rebel. Or their moral development may be retarded; they may become dependent on authority figures to make and enforce their moral decisions. Hence, the motivation to engage themselves in a good cause of their own free will—making positive, creative use of the power that is in them will be lost.

Sensing the Landmarks of Human Maturation

Parents and teachers are more likely to be helpful instructors if they are aware and sensitive to the maturation process. None of us know everything necessary to fully understand another person, but there are some general landmarks that can improve our relationships. As indicated previously, the advent of conscience and puberty are significant events in each of our lives. We are different before and after these capacities are activated within us. They influence us physically, intellectually, morally, and spiritually. Making no claim for completeness, figure 10-1 illustrates the type of landmarks that can guide us in relating more effectively with those we teach. The more sensitive we are to this information, the more prepared we are to make wise decisions regarding others. Comparing the descriptive material and examples in this chapter and the chapter that follows to figure 10-1 may be helpful in organizing your perception of the maturation process and how it relates to teaching. (See also the chart in Appendix B.)

175

The Idea that Man Is an Animal

The view people take of man—his origin, nature, and destiny—seems to condition seriously the conclusions reached regarding the educational process. Some educational ideas and practices are developed by people who begin with assumptions contrary to the agency approach discussed herein. In retrospect, President Joseph F. Smith's instructions to the authorities of the Church in 1914 seem painfully prophetic. He requested that the people should be warned unceasingly against three dangers, one of which was *false educational ideas*:

> There are at least three dangers that threaten the Church within, and the authorities need to awaken to the fact that the people should be warned unceasingly against them. As I see these, they are the flattery of prominent men in the world, false educational ideas, and sexual impurity.[17]

It was during this very period of time that several of these contrary notions gained a popularity that later allowed them to dominate western philosophical thought and confuse its educational practices.

A Sense of Direction—Some Landmarks

	Birth - Age 8	Age 8 - Puberty	Puberty - Adulthood
Physically	Depend on adults for care and protection.	Rapid growth of the body and its functions.	Body reaches maturation. Increased sensitiviy to physical differences between self and others.
Intellect-ually	Focus is on the self. Curious and open.	Capacity for logic emerges. Distinguishes between self/others. Sense of ownership for own ideas.	Ability to deal with abstract ideas increases.
Morally	Innocent and susceptible. Dependent on moral order of others. Authority perceived as other people.	Conscience develops. Authority perceived as rules. as well as other people.	Authority can be viewed as principles that govern both rules and people.
Spiritually	Receptive and open.	Sense of sin develops. Capable of repentance and forgiveness.	Heightened sense of spiritual awareness as distinct from the physical.

176

The fruit of any tree is likely to carry in its seeds the limitation inherent in its rootstock (Matt. 7:16-20). Pragmatic observation may not be sufficient to test educational tools. We need to test them in terms of long-range implications and check carefully how they fit with other important and true ideas and principles. Results alone do not mean an idea or a method is appropriate for use or that it should be used at all. Oatmeal packed into a noisy transmission may quiet it down and temporarily obscure the problem, but it may not be the best treatment.

We live in a time when many people are concerned about how to produce educational tools and strategies. Caleb Gattegno, for example, makes an interesting observation in *The Adolescent and His Will.* He notes that from a scientific point of view, the almost universally accepted idea that man is an animal is merely a popularized hypothesis. Gattegno acknowledges that in one sense man can be considered an animal, but raises the question, Is he more animal than he is mineral or vegetable? The intent of his question and argument is most interesting. [18]

177

This practice of classifying man as an animal has resulted in two errors, according to Gattegno. First, man is assimilated into the animal kingdom. This is evidenced by the fact that some are still looking for the "missing link" between man and other animals. The search goes on in spite of the many religious accounts, including Genesis, that describe the creation of man as an event separate and distinct from the animal creation, just as the animal creation was separate and distinct from the creation of the vegetable. The second error, according to Gattegno, is that this assumption takes into consideration only a portion of human life—the manifest animal portion. The confusion resulting from these erroneous assumptions has sponsored investigations which study only the elements in man which relate him to the animal kingdom.

This emphasis on man as a physiological organism only is contrary to what many people know to be true. It identifies man as the product of inferior antecedents—originating from a lower life form and totally dependent on himself. The educational process can change quite drastically when the opposite assumption is used—that the human family is the offspring of superior progenitors and can and does receive their help and assistance. The agency approach to education considers man to be a spiritual as well as a physical being, subject to and the product of his spiritual nature. "When a man is full of the light of eternity, then the eye is not the only medium through which he sees, his ear is not the only medium by which he hears, nor the brain the only means by which he understands." [19]

Those who focus solely on the physical body, perceiving it as a product of organic evolution, and pursue their understanding of education through an examination of the body's properties and characteristics in this context, distort or deny the "proper foundation for all education." [20] There is no room for free agency as described in revelation in the popular modern supposition; human origin and development is solely determined by a naturalistic movement from simple to complex, from lower to higher, and from inferior to superior. The fall, atonement, and resurrection have no place in these non-redemptive theories; agency-oriented educators will resist substituting such theories as *standards* by which to determine their educational thought and practice. The truths that reside in the observations of the physical sciences, valuable as these are, should not be substituted for the standards of truth given by revelation for our salvation. For it is our spiritual being that is in the greatest jeopardy, not our physical body, which of necessity must return to the dust. Surrounded by different walls of knowledge, care must be taken to lean our intellectual ladders against the one with the sure foundation.

178

Ultimate Reality is More Accurately Seen Through Morality and Religion Than Through Science and Physical Phenomena

The closing note in this chapter on conscience, maturity, and agency is the type of priority needed to maximize individual development. Freedom is closely related to awareness. When we are aware of what is happening to us, we are in a better position to make wise choices. Ignorance is an effective prison. Developing children, from birth through adolescence, deserve to understand the type of world they live in. They have the right to be informed in a way that maximizes their opportunities to comprehend and fulfill their inherently spiritual nature. This right is taken from them when they are incorrectly nurtured or instructed. Perhaps the most important of all teachings are those that pertain to man's origin, nature and destiny.

Consequently, it is extremely important in pursuing agency education that you feel comfortable using an eternal perspective to view children's learning experiences. A popular claim reflected in modern school curriculum is that moral and religious judgments are not part of the "real world," but merely images people develop and support with private evidence, not real-world experience. This personal evidence is considered insignificant because it is beyond the realm of "objective" or "public" demonstration. Therefore, it is not essential to the "general welfare"; it cannot be as binding or as widely applied as scientific knowledge. It has authority and meaning only to the individual who discovers it. Many modern scholars have characterized the existence of moral and religious thought in this manner. [21] Religion may exist, but it is not central to the human predicament as is physical matter.

Since the turn of the century, intellectual circles have been generally dominated by nonreligious thought. (In its most extreme expression, the movement is called *logical positivism*.) Empirical science is considered the primary if not the sole arbiter of truth about the world. By its focus on the material world, scientific method lends itself to physical demonstration and examination. It fits well within the bubble discussed previously and is comfortable for those who define reality exclusively within the bubble. Those who take this view tend to claim that no conceptions of good or right are binding; they merely express an individual's personal attitude or feeling. When the collective attitude of a group is established, as confirmed by social science, this becomes the legitimate basis for determining right and wrong at that time and place among that people. This type of valuing has been called *relativism*. In this view, moral and religious considerations, like scaffolding, are temporary; they are considered incidental to the "real work" of exploring, utilizing, and physically enjoying ourselves and our environment.

It is important to be aware of this way of looking at the world, because it heavily influences the context for modern educational thought and programs. It is the context in which today's students are reared. And as later discussed, it is also the context in which laws influencing education are created. When one works and lives among people who accept, knowingly or unknowingly, only the physical aspects of life and scientific evidence as the legitimate foundations for education, there is less room for tolerating an agency approach toward human development. There is little room in such a view for agency education. What a person thinks dominates what a person does.

Not everyone, however, has been pleased with the accuracy of the prevailing philosophy. Karl Popper, Michael Polanyi, Thomas Kuhn, and others have challenged the adequacy of the strict materialistic point of view. These thinkers argue that in the final analysis imperative logical procedures do not govern the construction of scientific theory. Science is more analogous to composing a symphony or developing a plot for a novel—a kind of heuristic adventure, quite personal and private. The foundations for scientific thinking in any particular period are not arrived at scientifically; they are personal inventions or the results of a conversion of a community of scientists to a set of rules or paradigm that guides their work.

When one takes this point of view, it is possible to argue that morality and religion constitute the real world. Scientific knowledge, important as it may be for our material well-being, can be viewed as the imaginary world of personal speculation. This does not diminish the usefulness of science in exploring the physical world. But from this perspective, science becomes a tool operating on a temporary physical realm, and scientific knowledge becomes a practical collection of artificial constructs that fit into the temporary conceptual framework we call present-day science. The real world, from this perspective, can be considered the world of morality and revealed religion. It is this dimension of man's nature that should govern his valuing. Why? Because it will determine the quality of his life, long after he leaves mortality.

Knowledge of the temporary, physical world is secondary to knowledge that sustains and preserves man's moral and spiritual character. This is where the real substance and true foundations of human education reside. This is the base upon which we should build our educational enterprises. The physical world is important, but it is transitory and imperfectly understood. The moral and religious world is the world that will endure; it is linked most closely to ultimate reality. Thus one could argue that students should be grounded in and operate primarily from the moral and religious perspective rather than the temporal, scientific perspective. This requires a different approach to education.

Latter-day Saints do not need to speculate on this argument. They know that moral and spiritual knowledge is most reliable; but it is not always easy to be valiant and retain integrity to this knowledge when living and working in a world dominated by counter notions. At times it may be difficult to discern the extent of our own entrapment in these other philosophies. But difficult or not, the examination is essential to our ultimate welfare.

If we reverse the modern description of the real world, if we proclaim that we are spiritual beings, the children of Heavenly Parents who have in fact (1) provided us with moral laws that adequately protect our intended destiny and (2) warned us that what we understand about this temporal order of life is merely a "shadow as seen through a glass darkly," then we may reach different conclusions about the oughts and ought nots of living, teaching, and learning. Taking this position certainly creates a different environment, but it is an educational environment that best complements the individual's maturation process. It is a way to teach the children differently than they are now commonly being taught.

181

II

Growth, Development, and Lifestyle

Encouraging and emphasizing right actions is the most productive approach in relating to children (birth to puberty), while encouraging and emphasizing good thoughts and intentions is the most appropriate and productive approach in relating to adults (puberty through adulthood).

Defining Education

Every definition of education reflects some particular view about God, man, and nature. Most of these definitions emphasize a particular human concern such as (a) the practical side of physical experience, (b) man's mental capacity to reflect on ideas, (c) the environment as an influence on man, or (d) the independence of the person. Each dimension represents important forces that shape one's educational experience. The uniqueness of the various definitions results from emphasizing one particular aspect of our relationship to ourselves, to others, and to our world. Consequently, the different definitions can become very complex and can lead a person in very different directions.

183

An Action Definition of Agency Education

Describing the growth and development of Jesus, the gospel writer Luke said that he "increased in wisdom and stature, and in favour with God and man" (Luke 2:52). These few words encompass the aim of agency education. The emphasis in this action definition of education is on bringing together and balancing the various forces that influence our growth and development. The focus is on properly relating these forces rather than emphasizing a particular influence. When correctly balanced, the physical, intellectual, moral (social), and spiritual aspects together blend our development into a positive rather than a destructive lifestyle. Education in this sense is a matter of developing a lifestyle that permits us to fufill our earthly mission and divine destiny. It involves priorities.

Priorities and Lifestyles

Personal fulfillment comes as we successfully combine our physical, mental, moral, and spiritual capacities. Orson F. Whitney described this balanced education:

> If I were asked to define more particularly my idea of a perfect education, I would say it is the full and uniform development of the mental, the physical, the moral and the spiritual faculties. . . .The spirit and body are so intimately associated, and the various parts of human nature so mutually interwoven, that neither can be neglected without injuring the others.[1]

184

Further, David O. McKay intimated man's existence can be dominated by any one of these four capacities—the physical, the intellectual, the moral, or the spiritual.[2] Any of these areas can become our governing lifestyle. Though seldom exclusively physical, intellectual, moral, or spiritual, people's lives are often characterized by one of these approaches. Education, formal and informal, is the path that leads one to select a lifestyle.

Physical Level. Living at the physical, or animal, level makes one a prisoner of his or her physical appetites. In this lifestyle, thoughts and acts are characterized by subjection to selfish, carnal desires or impulses. Gratification is the ultimate goal. Bodily desires control the intellect, ignore morality, and blind the person to the spiritual. The physical dimension is not evil, but it requires appropriate control as we learn to prioritize. People learn to keep their appetites within the bounds the Lord has prescribed, as they subject their physical nature to reason and morality and seek their own spiritual nature. Otherwise, growth and development as a human being decrease rather than increase. The Hebrew prophets have exhorted their people to master the urges expressed at the purely physical level of life. We have a divine heritage and are capable of more than an animal existence (I Cor. 2:9-16).

Intellectual Level. The adage "mind over matter" expresses the power of the intellect over physical impulse. We can govern our physical being and direct its action to serve the powers and interests of our intellect. Weight lifters, dancers, and athletes do this all the time. This principle leads to a higher and more versatile existence than that of following the human passions, but it may occur independent of recognition of right or wrong, good or evil. The person who ignores legitimate physical needs like food, water, exercise, and rest in order to pursue obsessively some intellectual objective makes a slave of the body. This pattern can also dominate a person's life. Letting intellect alone master one's life is no guarantee of happiness. In order for us to increase rather than decrease growth and development, we must subject both mind and body to those moral principles that preserve and protect humankind.

Moral Level. Moral discipline demands a greater strength than that required to guide the body and the intellect. Mere intellectual control of the physical body is not enough. The moral life requires that both the intellectual and the physical capacities of man be subjected to principles that protect the rights and welfare of all. Moral conduct requires us to identify and choose right over wrong and good rather than evil in our actions. As we bring the body and the intellect into alignment with righteous principles, we must sometimes sacrifice our physical or intellectual desires. This moral state is a necessary requisite to spirituality.

185

The scriptures mention virtue repeatedly (D&C 4:6; 121:45; 122:2). *Virtue is the proper application of knowledge as it pertains to man's eternal well being.* Virtue may refer to the power or influence inherent in a supernatural or divine being. To acquire virtue, one must voluntarily observe moral standards of right conduct. These laws lead us to act in our best interest and in that of others. Virtue is moral excellence. When we embrace positive principles of truth, we give them life and vitality through our personality; we begin to generate virtue. As part of the growth and development process, this increases the divine nature of the human soul.

Spiritual Level. Spirituality, the highest and most refined level of life, is the awareness of victory over one's physical and intellectual self; it is the sense of being in harmony with moral law and the feeling of communion with the infinite.[3] This cannot be arrived at without divine assistance (John 6:44). The sweetness of constant spirituality, as a lifestyle, comes not only from the awareness that we are operating on true principles, but from the impact of the glorious vision that unfolds to the individual who is in communion with the infinite. Spirtuality lifts man onto the field of pure freedom.

The basic principles of morality have been placed in the custody of various cultures according to their readiness and willingness to abide by them (BM, Alma 29:8; 12:9-11). They are passed on from generation to generation through various patterns of institutionalized instruction. The full powers of spirituality are given only through priesthood ordinances. Priesthood officers are empowered to administer these ordinances—keys to spiritual understanding—in an orderly fashion only to individuals willing to comply with the requirements. These ordinances and their accompanying knowledge are frequently referred to in the records of antiquity. Often changed, distorted and lost, this knowledge is referred to as the "mysteries of God" (BM, Alma 12:9-11; D&C 42:61-65; 6:7,11; 8:11; 11:7; 76:5-10). With this knowledge man discovers the true higher education.

186

Developing Good Dispositions and Right Actions

Some have made distinctions between *rightness* and *goodness.* The word *right* is related to action, and the word *good* is associated with disposition.[4] Some people conclude that individuals can be taught to *do* the right and that in so doing they will become good. This position proceeds on the premise that eliciting "right" actions creates "good" dispositions. The expression "if you can't think yourself into a new way of acting, then act yourself into a new way of thinking" reflects this position. The emphasis is on the person's actions. The strategy is to influence the disposition by carefully stimulating and controlling the individual's actions. For example, the driver who begrudgingly maintains the established speed limit because a policeman is behind him may be doing the right thing, but he is not doing it for the right reason (out of his own goodness). The idea in this approach is that if the driver repeats the proper behavior often enough, on his own, he will eventually feel good about operating his vehicle within the prescribed limits.

An alternative approach is to assume it is disposition that determines action. The emphasis then becomes one of focusing on a person's disposition, the assumption being that when the individual seeks the "good," right actions will inevitably follow.

The focus of concern in this approach is intention. David O. McKay said, "Thought is the most real thing in existence. What a man thinks, he knows as he knows nothing else in all the world."[5] Given this premise, it is understandable why some people feel that the very best way to educate people is to educate desires rather than simply encouraging them to act in specified ways. For example, if I want my child to learn to read, I will not begin by compelling the child to demonstrate competence in word mechanics, even though I know that this is important. Rather I will strive to help the child feel a desire to read, since seeking competence in word mechanics will naturally follow.

The old saying "The road to hell is paved with good intentions" seems to contradict this second premise. At least it raises the issue of integrity. But then, integrity can also be an issue when one questions the sincerity of someone's actions. Just because a person does something doesn't mean he is sincere about it, says the critic. In either case the challenge to the agency oriented parent, teacher, and student is to encourage integrity. Hypocrisy must be overcome. But this still leaves us with the question: Which of the two approaches is the better to follow in selecting educational tools and strategies?

187

A Basic Rule

From an agency point of view, both approaches have merit in helping others move toward the spiritual lifestyle initiated by personal volition. Observation of our experience reveals a cyclical influence. Right actions do lead to good thinking, and thinking good does sponsor right actions, just as improper thoughts can produce undesirable acts. The application of one approach or the other should be based on the circumstances. If we use the principle of maturation discussed previously to guide us in making this choice, the basic rule would be this: *Encouraging and emphasizing right actions among children (birth to puberty) is the most productive, while encouraging and emphasizing good thoughts and intentions is the most appropriate and productive approach for adults (puberty through adulthood).* This rule, a guideline for balance, is not intended to be interpreted as an either/or statement. It may at times be appropriate to invert the rule, but it can be a useful principle.

Reasons for the Rule

Maturational development suggests that the time to emphasize behavioral compliance is before puberty, below ages twelve or fifteen. From an agency perspective the moral and mental processes are less in command during these early years because they are not yet fully developed. Action in response to rules and authority figures is more natural and effective. Children are more inclined to gain understanding through action during these prepuberty years than they are through abstract thought. During and following adolescence, the full power of spiritual sensitivity and moral awareness normally becomes available. The capacity for reflective learning matures; therefore, the educational approach needs to shift focus. The appeal for appropriate performance should now be made through emphasis on good thoughts, presuming that right actions will follow. At first this shift will be difficult, because it is a new realm of experience for the young person; parents and teachers may be unskilled and impatient. Shifting to this plane of control, however, marks the maturation of Christian character. Moving in this direction is an aim of agency education.

188

Letting one's actions condition one's thinking is Aaronic (preparatory) in nature, as Paul explains in chapter three of his letter to the Galatians. Moses, according to the Old Testament, was required to use this system because of the lack of development among the people he was called to lead. Emphasis on proper actions can be a schoolmaster, a pattern of learning that is preparatory. Even today, law enforcement in our society reflects this distinction. Physically mature adults who somehow failed to develop their moral nature are still dealt with at the behavioral level. Our prisons are full of individuals who seem incapable of responding to life except by our communicating with them through restrictive actions.

The second sequence of control, allowing one's thought's to create and shape one's actions, is Melchizedek in nature. Paul explains this distinction in chapter seven of the book of Hebrews. God-like independence and productive character exists only when the spirit controls the body in compliance with moral and spiritual principles. As long as our disposition is governed through controlling or dictating behavioral action, we are not fully self-reliant—we are not truly free. We are dependent on the will of others. When thinking good constantly fills the mind and right actions follow, we approach our ideal nature. We establish a moral foundation conducive to the spiritual level of living. We "increas[e] in wisdom and stature, and in favor with God and man" (Luke 2:52).

Actions vs. Behavior

At this point it is important to distinguish between action and behavior. *Action* includes the idea of intent. *Behavior* intentionally ignores intent. Generally considered from a spectator's point of view, behavior is classified, described, and otherwise viewed in terms of stimulus and response. Behavior is considered to be environmentally induced. To change behavior, one changes the environment. One then observes changes in behavior.

Action, on the other hand, is understood from the agent's point of view. Viewing others' actions means that we must comprehend their intentions as well as their behavior. It means that we must put ourselves in the others' shoes, as the saying goes. This means empathizing, using our capacity to participate in another person's feelings and ideas. We understand people as they are rather than as they appear to be from their behavior. In order to do this, we must tune in to the spiritual dimension.

189

From an instructional or learning viewpoint, this means that those students who can put themselves in the teacher's place will sense the teacher's intent and more accurately understand his or her performance. When students fail to make this effort, it is easy for belligerence, confusion, and resentment to well up within them. Some teacher actions, when viewed only as behaviors by the students, are experienced as abrasive and undesireable when they were not intended to be such. David O. McKay emphasized the need for students to develop an attitude that would enable them to respond to the teacher and the experience in a positive manner when he said:

> Another element, and more important, contributing to spiritual growth, is the mental attitude of the students themselves. It is fundamental for a student to realize that his success in the Seminary [adolescent school for religious instruction] depends upon himself. . . . But, whatever the outward influence be that led him to the Seminary, it must ever remain an exterior factor to the moral and spiritual

growth of the student himself. The source of the spring of spirituality lies in the mind, the spirit itself.

The very first step, therefore, toward the growth of spirituality in a student is the realization that the ultimate purpose of life is the perfecting of the individual; that the purpose of our Father in heaven is to make men and women like himself, and that even the Lord could not do this without making men free.[6]

Teachers who empathize with the feelings of their students can understand what would escape them were they only to rely on observations of their students' behavior. Emphasizing actions as the primary means of influencing disposition before puberty is not behavioral conditioning. Behavioral conditioning theory consciously discounts the role of intent in the learning process. Action, as defined here, presumes that a child's feelings, intents, and motives will be recognized as emphasis is placed on desired performance.

190

The Role of Caring and Loving

Joseph F. Smith explained how to respond to actions instead of behaviors. He taught that this could be accomplished by caring for and loving the other person:

> If you can only convince your children that you love them, that your soul goes out to them for their good, that you are their truest friend, they, in turn, will place confidence in you and will love you and seek to do your bidding. . . . But if you are selfish and unkindly to them, and if they are not confident that they have your entire affection, they will be selfish, and will not care whether they please you or carry out your wishes or not, and the result will be that they will grow wayward, thoughtless and careless, and although you may drill them, like a parrot, to repeat verses and to speak in concert, and all that sort of thing, they will do it mechanically, without affection, and without its having that effect upon their souls that you desire it should have.[7]

For the Learner. This distinction between action and behavior and the influence of caring and love are especially important.

When we desire to be like other people, to acquire their skills, attributes, and abilities, it is necessary to obtain their point of view. To learn ways of living, acting, and feeling, as opposed to merely learning about them or going through the motions, we must put ourselves in the position of those who practice those actions. To become a great violinist, one must acquire the perspective of a great violinist in relation to that skill and ability. This experience does not seem to depend on some particular curriculum organization, and there are probably a great variety of ways for someone to put himself in another person's frame of reference. The essential requirement is that we assume the other person's point of view, to make the admired way of life our own (BM, Alma 32:27). Actors and actresses know that it is impossible to portray convincingly a character without doing this. And theatrics is only a temporary expression of this process! A true and effective principle for educators as well as actors, the transition in education may be more real and more permanent. Students must take care to choose wisely what they want to become. The student must be seeking, and the teacher must model what the student is seeking.

191

For the Teacher. Parents and teachers who wish to communicate effectively with their children or students can also apply this principle. Caring and loving are the legitimate means for reaching out and into others' lives. In order to penetrate the barrier of behavior, we must envision the intent behind the act; we must put ourselves in the other person's place. We must see things from another's perspective. This process helps us to understand people as they are. And understanding others as they are can improve our ability to communicate with them. The following story exemplifies this idea.

A man was putting up a sign, PUPPIES FOR SALE; and before he had driven the last nail, there was a small boy standing at his side. That kind of sign seems to attract small boys. The youngster wanted to know how much the puppies were going to cost. The man told him they were very good dogs and that he did not expect to let any of them go for less thant $35 or $50. There was a look of disappointment, and then a question: "I've got $2.37. Could I look at them?"

The man whistled and called "Lady!"—and out of the kennel and down the runway came Lady, followed by four or five little balls of fur, with one lagging considerably behind. The boy spotted the laggard and, pointing, asked, "What's wrong with him?" The reply was that the veterinarian had said there was no hip socket in the right hip and that the dog would always be lame. The boy's immediate rejoinder was, "That's the one I want to buy. I'll give you $2.37 down and fifty cents a month till I get him paid for." The man smiled and shook his head. "That's not the dog you want. That dog will never be able to run and jump and play with you."

The boy very matter-of-factly pulled up his little trouser leg and revealed a brace running down both sides of his badly twisted right leg and under the foot, with a leather cap over the knee. "I don't run so well myself, " he said, "and he'll need somebody that understands him."[8]

192

The distinction between action and behavior is illustrated when one compares the ideas of certain educators and theorists with principles revealed by God. A current educator observed that "What a person *said* might be valid data but what he meant was unknowable."[9] Another modern theorist said, "the primary function of analysis is not to gain a greater understanding of the child, but to more effectively cope with the behavioral problems at hand"[10] On the other hand, Brigham Young counseled that we should never judge others until we know the intention of the action. "When you know the intention of the act performed, you will then know how to judge the act."[11] The Doctrine and Covenants emphasizes this distinction in the statement, "The Lord your God . . . is a discerner of the thoughts and intents of the heart (D&C 33:1)." And we are commanded to become like him (Matt. 5:48). Although mortal man is limited in discerning the thoughts and intents of others, it is possible for us to see beyond their behaviors. We can seek divine assistance in relating spirit to spirit.

Agency oriented parents, teachers, and students must avoid the shortsightedness of contemporary views that focus on behavior rather than action. Too often, our generation merely float their educational surfboards upon the sea of learning as they wait for the next popular fad to come along. We seem enthralled with riding each new wave until it dissipates. And frequently, the ride becomes more important and exciting than the source of the wave or its ultimate destination.

Decisions and Choices

A difference in educational strategy takes place when one shifts from emphasizing the way a person acts to focusing on the disposition of a person. As one moves *the primary concern* away from the *public expression of a choice* to the *private creation of a decision* the emphasis changes. One can think of a decision as the private expression of intent. A choice could be considered the public expression of that private decision. By observation, others may view the choices we make, but only by discernment can we learn of others' decisions prior to their expression in the form of a choice.[12] As a teacher I can look at the children in my classroom and know there are reasons these students are present before me. Choices were made, voluntarily or by compulsion, that brought each child to my room. Without seeking to know, however, I cannot discover the decisions that preceeded the choice that brought the child to my room. There is a difference in relating to this child on the basis of his choices instead of his decisions. Understood together, they may give me a better basis for establishing a proper relationship with the child.

193

When children are young, it is easier to relate with them on moral matters, for example, by focusing on their choices. As they pass puberty and move into adolescence, it is then possible to begin discussing the importance of their decisions and the processes that influence these decisions. This approach is based on the idea that influences affecting a person's decisions eventually control his choices. Young children need parents and teachers that understand their inward decisions but relate to them on the basis of their choices. Youth and adults need parents and teachers who challenge them to master their decisions and who are able to relate to them on the basis of their decisions, not solely on the basis of their choices. This is the path to reliable independence.

Example of an Application of this Principle

For example, when a nine year-old fails to do her homework and decides to run off to play with friends, a parent's response may appropriately be to reprimand the child on the basis of her choice (behavior). She was not in the right place doing the right thing at the right time. A nine year-old can readily understand and recognize that she was not doing what she was supposed to be doing when she was supposed to be doing it. She can understand there are rules and that they should be obeyed or there will be negative consequences which are in her best interest to avoid.

When a sixteen-year-old fails to do her homework and decides to run off to visit friends, however, a parent's most appropriate response, from an agency point of view, would be to focus on the *decision* she made rather than on the *choice* or *public expression of that decision* (her behavior). It is true that the sixteen-year-old was not in the right place doing the right thing at the right time, but she will be much more receptive to having her decision questioned than she will to having her action challenged. Like the nine-year-old, she understands that there are rules that should be followed to avoid negative consequences. But unlike the nine-year-old, she is equipped to challenge the rules. To challenge her action will likely create a debate over issues that may not be related to the parent's primary concern. Her attitude may be, "As long as I get my homework done, what difference does it make when I do it?" After all, she continually watches other adults express their autonomy by modifying their schedules for doing things. It is the decision, not the choice or act, that the sixteen year-old needs to have evaluated. Sixteeen-year-olds are dealing with a new awareness of the way decisionmaking fits into their lives. They have little experience and therefore less confidence in making decisions than they do in exibiting behavior. Choices or behaviors are "old hat," decisions are "new territory." Hence they are more willing and interested in discussing decisions than behaviors.

Teenagers, like adults, are quick to defend their actions. They tend to be less reactive when it is a decision that is being discussed. This is because they are now fully equipped to deal with learning at the decisionmaking level. Younger children are not as prepared to engage in this type of learning. They have a greater need to understand and address their decisions in the form of actions or choices. They like to have their intentions considered, but they can clearly understand they are accountable for their behavior. Following puberty, individuals are more inclined to feel that learning takes place in the realm of decision rather than on the field of action or behavior. It is here that they are now prepared to learn, and it is here where they are most likely to be receptive. It is here that they need to learn in order to feel the sense of growth and development.

12

Teachers And Teaching

Truth is manifest through personality, and learning is strengthened when it can be seen through the actions of others. There is a tendency for learners to withhold full commitment to righteous principles when their teachers are not moral models. Learners want and need worthy examples who are living witnesses to what they teach. The teacher is the curriculum, particularly in character education.

Teachers As Makers of Pictures

When successful, effective photographers or painters plan their pictures, they spend considerable time, effort, and talent on framing the subject in a context. The painter imagines in his mind the boundaries of the scene he wishes to capture on canvas. With an objective in mind, the photographer selects the lens that will reproduce on film the desired image of a person, place, or thing. Photographers and painters are in the business of communication; teachers face a similar task. They too establish objectives, utilize information, and seek to frame it for presentation to others. Knowingly or unknowingly teachers are makers of pictures.

The photographer's selection of an appropriate lens depends on whether he wants a microscopic view of a mosquito's leg or a wide-angle view of the city skyline. The teacher's selection of a proper approach is also determined by the kind of picture she wants to share with the student. We have probably all seen magazine pictures so magnified and out of context that we could not recognize the original object. Likewise we have each probably squinted at a panoramic view of some area, trying in vain to see in more detail some small portion of the larger scene. Similarly, it is important that students understand where the part fits into the whole, how knowing math can help them in their lives. Or how the scope of European history compares to life in their town in the 1990s.

Agency oriented teachers will benefit from carefully selecting a proper frame of reference to give meaning to the pictures they wish to share with their students. Sharing takes effort; it requires caring enough to adapt the material to the language and limitations of the learner. Otherwise, there will be little understanding. At times, teachers, like some photographers and artists, may ignore their student's needs and create paintings or produce pictures only for themselves or their peers. This may have value for the teacher, but it can be a serious disservice to students. It may leave them disinterested, confused, or content with erroneous conclusions. Learners need teachers who not only make good pictures, but who are able to connect themselves and their students with the pictures they make. Agency oriented teachers take their cues from the personal desires, interests, and goals of the learner. Under divine influence it is the student who is the pilot, not the teacher; the teacher joins the trip as an inspired navigator. In this role the teacher provides assistance to help the learner see clearly where to go and how to get there.

196

Sometimes teachers fail to deal with students sensitively. They may use their social authority to lead students into areas of personal interest that are inappropriate, or take advantage of the immature students' appetite for the unusual or sensational. Because of their own limitations, such teachers use microscopic lenses almost exclusively. With a huge magnifying glass in hand, they entice the student to examine things they are unprepared to understand. The focus presented to the students is a distorted fragment; they are pressed so close to the mural on the wall of life that they never see the complete or even a large portion of the picture in its proper context. Such students come away from their instructional experiences believing that some small part, magnified out of all proportion, constitutes the whole picture.

Curricular matters related to sexual maturation, economics, and politics, and extracurricular experiences in athletics, dance, and music are sample areas where this often occurs. This type of instruction is neither appropriate nor necessary. That we are subject to this dangerous limitation is evident in the number of aphorisms in the English language that describe it: "becoming involved in the thick of thin things," "making mountains out of molehills," and "so close to the tree that he cannot see the forest." At the other extreme are the teachers who lack preparation to do anything but sketch broad, impressionistic scenes for their students. These superficial, vague, wide-angle visions may be so lacking in detail and close-up examination that the students lose interest and wander away, unable to feel a relevant relationship with the teacher or the picture. Agency teachers will take care to avoid either type of distorted instruction.

With proper preparation, such weaknesses in picture-making on the part of the teacher can be avoided. Very young children need to see enough *simple detail* in order to understand its contribution to a bigger picture. For example, they need words, and the detail provided by a simple vocabulary, before they can make sentences, paragraphs, or stories. Lacking experience and wisdom, adolescent students need to view wide-angle presentations with only a limited amount of appropriately selected magnified close-ups. Intense analysis and examination of detail is *less important* than the *relationships* between larger aspects of the "big picture." Later in life, when they have tested a personal framework for viewing the whole picture, they are ready to take *the magnifying glass* in their own hands to examine the mysterious detail of life's distortions, dilemmas, and paradoxes. Young people should not be prematurely introduced to these quandries. As they develop they will discover these questions for themselves; then is the proper time for discussion. To do otherwise is to risk meddling with their faith. Tender youth should not bear the burden of being used by frustrated adults who are working on their own problems.

197

Agency teachers carefully allow others to create or destroy the way they resolve the quandries of life—especially the youth. They are willing, if asked, to share their own resolutions but not in a manner that *compels* others to live on "borrowed light." Agency teachers do not seek to establish a following of their own. They avoid creating their own order of disciples. They are not in the business of converting adherents who become dependent on them. They are in the business of helping others become independent, self-reliant, and strengthened in their relationship with God. Agency teachers are servants, not intellectual or physical slave masters. Students see their good works and glorify our Father in Heaven.

Being What You Want Your Students To Become

Jesus was the greatest teacher because he was most ideally what man should become. The more a teacher can be what he wants his students to become, the more effective he will be in leading them in that direction, once they decide that is what they want to become. When a person knows that what he teaches is true, there is a spirit that gives power to what he says. Jesus followed this pattern in his teaching and he taught his disciples to follow it also. He told them to be examples in righteousness and love, to accept others as he had accepted them, so they could "feel and see" the way (BM, 3 Nephi 18:25). Students, too, must "feel and see" in order to master reading, writing, art, or arithmetic as well as personal conduct.

Students learn best when they have experiences with living models with whom they can test the information they learn. Recall the premise established previously: *truth is manifest through personality.* Any self-instructional learning is augmented when that truth can be seen through others. When interaction with moral models is lacking, the tendency is for the student to withhold full commitment to the righteous principles they learn. Students want and need worthy examples who are living witnesses of what they teach. The actual number of living, positive models children are exposed to does not seem to be the critical factor; good models do not need to constitute a majority. They may not even be contemporary or contiguous with a student's learning experience. But they are necessary, even if contact with the students is brief. The memory of a positive model, teamed with current instruction, can result in deep, personalized commitments by the student. In one sense, the teacher is the curriculum, especially in character education.

198

Seeking Clarity Amidst Conflict and Confusion

Part of the mystery of how we learn and how this learning affects how we behave exists because we do not understand fully the relationship between man's thinking, feelings, or his actions. Yet teaching must occur in relationship to these dynamic aspects of the human personality. Psychologists and professional educators, as we have noted, (a) discuss the intellectual capacity as a *cognitive* process, (b) emotions and feelings as an *affective* process and (c) action as *behavior.* Many theories on cognition and affect have resulted, with a number of attempts to show how the two might be related. There is little consensus, however, and the speculation and experimentation continue. Part of this problem is caused by the fact that most research is conducted to discover clinical explanations of thinking, feeling, and acting. Clinical explanations lend themselves to manipulating the processes they explain. People want to know how we "tick" so they can control the "ticking."

The scriptures give a general explanation of the learning process which can resolve much of this confusion. For agency-oriented parents, teachers, and students who accept the assumptions of this book, this scriptural explanation clarifies why true education is self-education and suggests the importance of both thoughts and feelings to one's actions—to moral learning. This explanation is not conducive to controlling others. To the contrary, it stresses the importance of the individual controlling himself. But the insights do provide a simple and straightforward guide to effective instruction. The approach described, however, does require familiarity with some terms not commonly used in modern educational literature.

Desire, Disposition, Willpower

The terms *desire, disposition,* and *will* appear throughout the scriptures. Though these terms are not precise synonyms, they refer to the same dimension of man's being. Each of the terms is associated with man's heart or character, that is, the present condition of a person's development, his attitude or inclinations. Learning, from a scriptural point of view, is situated in this spiritual dimension of man's being; it is commonly referred to by the words *desire* or *will,* terms synonymous with life. A human being devoid of all desire or will is a nonfunctioning person. Because desire or will is rooted in life, and life is a secret, by divine decree a mystery to man (PGP, Moses 4:28-32), we do not possess a complete understanding of the way it works (I Cor. 13:12). The just must live by faith—by a partial knowledge (Romans 1:17; BM, Alma 32:21,26). Learning to the agency-oriented teacher is thus best comprehended in the form of principles based on revealed truths. Although as mortal teachers we do not fully comprehend the learning process, we can teach in a manner that complements the true nature of learning by establishing integrity in our own lives. As teachers we can honor the agency bestowed upon those we assist in the learning process. *We do not need to operate by a clinical theory which suggests that our major role is to dominate, manipulate, and control the learning process in those whom we teach.*

Desire, as used in the scriptures, is the basic directional drive in the human being. It is the willingness to invest our energy, in the form of attention and interest, in a particular situation. Desire is the most fundamental expression of personal intent. Desires form and fuel actions. That there are more than five hundred references in the scriptural standard works to the word *desire*, evidences that it is a force which sponsors human behavior. It expresses man's will; it constitutes his disposition. As described in a previous chapter, it is a manifestation of man's heart.

"Through desire a man . . . seeketh . . . wisdom" (Proverbs 18:1). The Book of Mormon makes it equally clear that desire is an expression of the will of man as allowed by the agency granted him. Man is free to act as he desires and to gain what he desires (Alma 29:4-5; 41:5). Desire is the fountainhead of action and is the most primary motivational guide (Alma 32:7). In a broad sense it is simply an expression of faith.[1] God has granted man an agency of freedom in which to express his desires, a realm in which to choose and act. Within the agency granted to him, man is free to exercise his own desire, to choose for himself, and consequently to determine the outcome of his own existence (Helaman 14:30-31).

200

Knowledge Influences Desire

Accurate or inaccurate knowledge influences the nature of desire (Helaman 14:30-31). This explains why teaching is such a powerful enterprise among the human family. It exerts great control over the quantity and quality of knowledge among the human family. When the knowledge students embrace is inadequate or inaccurate, they may desire things that are unrealistic, unlikely, or impossible. Some high school football players, for example, may be led to use steroids, cut corners in their studies, and develop unrealistic expectations of gaining large sums of money by naively anticipating a future in professional football. Careless coaches and parents can send false messages.

Enos, a Book of Mormon personality, offers an example of how knowledge infuences desire: "Now, it came to pass that when I had heard these words [of forgiveness from the Lord] I began to *feel a desire* for the welfare of my brethren, the Nephites; wherefore, I did pour out my whole soul unto God for them" (Enos 9, italics added). Desire, then, is the energy of man's soul being expressed. When we express this energy, to that extent we invest ourselves toward something. Enos indicated that "he began to feel a desire"; his desire was expressed through his feelings. This is why our feelings are so important to our learning. Our desires are expressed through our feelings, and our feelings influence our actions; hence the accuracy of the statement "For as [a man] thinketh in his heart, so is he" (Proverbs 23:7; Matt. 12:34; 15:9). The agency oriented teacher will recognize that the desires of a person's heart are a primary influence on the learning/teaching process. Any philosophy or theory of instruction, any program or administration that ignores or defies this principle, is inconsistent with the agency approach to education. Students who feel a strong desire and express that desire in feelings that lead to disciplined action are the students who will learn—letters, language, arts, numbers, or whatever.

Commitment, Values, and Responsibility

As we have experiences and open ourselves to more and more knowledge, this information can be organized and used according to our feelings—according to our desires. The acquisition of knowledge provides the opportunity for us to act upon it and to express our desire through our feelings regarding that knowledge. In this way knowledge influences our desires. If there is no knowledge, there can be no expression of desire in relationship to knowledge. Knowledge creates the opportunity for desire to be expressed and made manifest. Knowledge enables man to be led by his own desires—his own will. Knowing the truth can make us free if we act upon it properly (John 8:32). "Now, we see that man had become as God, knowing good and evil, . . . and thus we see they became subjects to follow after their own will" (BM, Alma 42:3,7).

201

Our expression of desire in response to specific knowledge or information reveals our willingness to invest our efforts in that direction. This is the key to teaching children to read, use numbers, or express themselves in writing. The investment we make toward activities or objects reveal, the *value* we attach to those activities or objects. This indication of worth or value is an expression of *commitment*. We commit our energy, attention and interest, and thereby create a value for ourselves—no commitment, no value; no value, no impact on personal development. This process functions in the subtle areas of informal socialization, such as developing habits, as well as in formal instruction.

A careful observation of any person's activities confirms this simple, powerful process at work. Wherever we choose to invest our resources, there we will discover the forces which shape and form our personalities. The more intense our application of the process, the more impact upon our development. This process is simply expressed in the words of Jesus: "For where your treasure [investment, commitment, value] is, there will be your heart [character and disposition] be also" (Matt. 6:21). If we consistently invest in kindness, caring, and consideration, we become a caring person. If we consistently invest in the study, experimentation, and use of woods for building, we become skilled craftsmen. If we consistently invest in the exploration, use, and production of music, we become musicians. If we consistently invest in lies, theft, and deception, we form a deceitful character. We become the product of our own choices, which become our own investments. Agency-oriented teachers strive to complement this process in a positive way.

202

Our efforts to protect this commitment are often referred to as *responsibility. We are responsible to the extent that we protect commitments to something we value.* For example, when others feel I am not behaving responsibly, they are, in effect, suggesting I am not protecting commitments they feel are valuable and worth protecting. We assume responsibility—and protect commitments—according to priorities. We respond to what we feel is worthwhile or valuable according to the cluster of values affecting the role or context in which we see ourselves at a given time. The general notion of this idea can be sensed in the statements of Jacob in the Book of Mormon:

> And we did magnify our office unto the Lord, taking upon us the *responsibility,* answering the sins of the people upon our own heads if we did not teach them the word of God with all diligence; wherefore, by laboring with our *might* their blood might not come upon our garments, . . . and we would not be found spotless at the last day.
>
> Now, my beloved brethren, I, Jacob, according to the *responsibility* which I am under to God, to magnify mine office with soberness, and that I might rid my garments of your sins, I come up into the temple this day that I might declare unto you the word of God.
>
> And ye yourselves know that I have hitherto been diligent in the office of my calling; but I this day am weighed

down with much more *desire* and anxiety for the welfare of your souls than I have hitherto been. (BM, Jacob 1:19; 2:2-3, italics added)

Analyzing Jacob's statement in light of the preceding discussion of teaching and learning as it relates to desire indicates that Jacob had assigned a value to the office he held and to his relationship with God. At some time in Jacob's experience he had invested enough effort to select information regarding his calling, and he felt good about it; he had confidence in his position. The text tells us that he took upon himself the responsibility of magnifying the office. *In other words, he acted to protect his commitment to that which he valued.* This action led to a further intensification of his feelings, which were then expressed in the form of even more desire—more investment of self, more expenditure of energy, attention, and interest—in this case toward the welfare of the souls of his fellowmen. The same process applies in every educational endeavor—in the sciences, mathematics, language arts, or social studies. When we choose to invest our resources and then act to protect those investments, we participate in learning.

203

This process of teaching and learning was applied to moral education by Joseph F. Smith:

> The education then of our desires is one of far-reaching importance to our happiness in life. . . . God's ways of educating our desires are, of course, always the most perfect, and if those who have it in their power to educate and direct the desires of children would imitate his prudence, the children would be much more fortunate in combatting the difficulties that beset men everywhere in the struggle for existence.[2]

Observations for Teachers

1. *Tentative thinking.* It is common for individuals to limit their self-investment, to be aware of information without acting upon it. This ability to think at a tentative level might be compared to an automobile motor idling while the clutch is depressed or when the transmission is in neutral. The motor is running, but it

does not significantly involve other dimensions of the vehicle. The drive shaft is not engaged and the wheels do not turn. As a common and probably healthy alternative to action, individuals occasionally need to think at a tentative level. Individuals need time for the heart to ponder and evaluate what it will use and what it will not. Those teachers who wish to honor individual agency must honor this process as they strive to teach others. Systems that attempt to force or impose the will of one personality upon the learning processes of other accountable personalities is antagonistic to the agency approach to education.

2. *Tentative action.* Individuals also commonly limit their inward commitment to act while they experiment with the actions, not linking the action to significant feeling. This going through the motions frequently occurs when an individual is behaving under external pressures or when he is testing some action by trial or error. Like tentative thinking, tentative action is often a fortunate characteristic in human behavior; it may preserve the health, safety, and freedom of the individual. Agency-oriented teachers will recognize and understand the value of this process. It helps explain much of the behavior one observes in the learning/ teaching process. Demands by teachers that border on violations of personal agency are usually met by tentative action by students. Students may go through the motions in response to external motivational techniques, but will lack the internal commitment. A student who does the assignment for the teacher rather than herself engages in a tentative action.

3. *Significant performance.* Investment or commitment of self becomes a significant performance when it extends beyond the tentative levels and passes over the affective (feeling) threshold—that is, when it is sponsored by real intent, with a significant degree of commitment and value to the individual (Moroni 10:4). For example, an eleven-year-old girl might be induced by her mother to wash the dishes each evening, but she may not want to do them. She functions at a below-threshold level of self-investment, and the quality of her work usually reveals it. Later in life she may meet a young man who admires a girl who willingly washes the dishes. Discovering this fact may cause the young lady to pursue her dishwashing task from an internalized, self-sponsored, above-threshold motive. This experience of washing dishes may call forth even more self-investment when she begins to take personal pride in the quality of her work as a homemaker.

4. *Commitment and responsibility.* The greater the investment of self, the higher the degree of commitment and the greater the likelihood for an increased sense of responsibility. Responsibility is acting to protect one's investments. We are responsible when we honor our own commitments. We are irresponsible when we commit and do not honor our commitment. Others perceive us as responsible persons when we honor the commitments they feel should be honored. Understandably, the mother who buys an expensive toy for her five-year-old, who upon receiving it promptly smashes the toy, will be upset with the child. He has just destroyed her investment; he has violated something she valued. Her reaction is to consider the child irresponsible. The same process operates in all our relationships with others. Think of the last conflict you may have had with another person. Most conflicts are rooted in one or both parties acting in a way that does not protect some idea, object, or procedure that the other party values, or feels ought to be protected.

5. *Predicting action.* The more intense the involvement (investment of self), the more predictable the overt performance. This intensity and consistency of involvement was perhaps the focus of the Savior's challenge to those who contemplated joining his kingdom. Jesus compared the individual's commitment to family and material possessions to their commitment to the Kingdom of God (Matt. 10:37-39; 19:21-22; Mark 10:28-31). This concept appears also in Jesus' statement, "For where your treasure is, there will be your heart be also"(Matt. 6:21). Significant investment of self is a major element of integrity and character. It is evident in the athlete on the field of performance, the musician in the studio, the scientist in the laboratory, and the student in the classroom. It is the source of success and stability in any role we choose to perform.

205

Motivational Forces That Influence Desire and Disposition

Fear is a common form of influence used by individuals to motivate others. Fear, the anticipation of discomfort, pain, embarrassment, rejection, and other undesired experience, has long been used by governments, institutions, and individuals to elicit behavior and exert control over others. John Watson, the American psychologist, argued that it was fear that sponsored and maintained the influence of religion in the lives of people. He claimed that "if the fear element were dropped out of any religion, that religion would not survive a year."[3]

Teachers have traditionally used fear to motivate learning in their students. The "hickory stick" is a symbol of traditional formal education. Although the fear of physical punishment is less prominent in modern education, fear itself is still a prominent instrument of motivation and control. The terms *compulsory* and *mandatory* are both linked to the police powers of state and federal governments that sponsor public education programs. Letter grades, examinations, failure notices, demerits, dismissals, and many other instruments associated with fear are used by teachers to pursue their teaching assignments. Many teachers say that they cannot succeed in their assignments without these fear-producing motivational tools, which do work. People learn to read, write, and do arithmetic, and many other things under the influence of fear-producing motivational techniques. But the fact that these tools work does not make them right.

Rewards are another common form of motivation to learn. The enticement and reinforcement of physical and psychological rewards controlled by others at their discretion is the other major motivational strategy. Both fear and rewards lend themselves to manipulation; one person exercises questionable dominion over another person. Admittedly, both these strategies are demonstrably effective. Most theories of instructional discipline use one or some combination of both forces. But this appeal to man's physical nature is not the only way to view motivation. There are ways to influence human action that do not address primarily the physiological motives of hunger, pain, thirst, and so forth.

Charles W. Penrose expanded the view of motivation beyond punishment and reward to include a higher law:

> There is a higher law to which we all should advance, and that is that men should learn to do right for righteousness sake; men should learn to avoid wrong because it is wrong, . . . not because there will be a penalty inflicted . . . but because it is wrong and their souls revolt against it. Men should do right for the love of it, not because there is a reward for doing right, but because right is good, and is beautiful, and is exalting. But have all mankind reached that high plane? No; very few have advanced to it. The doctrine of condemnation has to be preached to the world as well as the doctrine of

salvation. People have to be encouraged by the hope of reward, and deterred from doing wrong by fear of punishment; whereas, he that is governed by the higher law—the law that God lives, that Jesus Christ lives—says, "This is right, therefore I will do it; that is wrong, therefore I will avoid it *because* it is wrong; for if I do wrong it debases me, but if I do right it exalts me." . . . "If you will keep my commandments you will be rewarded; if you commit transgression you shall be damned." That is the word of the Lord to the world.[4]

Agency educators know they live in the world, but they do not believe they have to be of the world and subject to all its lesser regulations and conditions. They are free to strive for a lifestyle of a higher level. They are free to learn and teach a higher principle.

There is an appeal to human motives that comes from and is directed toward man's spiritual dimension. This approach is spiritual in nature. The focus as well as the origin of these influences is spiritual rather than physiological. At least seven of these spiritual forces are described in the scriptures: (1) the power of positive example, (2) faith in God, and works based on that faith, (3) the realization that all are God's children, (4) the alignment of oneself with gospel principles, (5) prayer and fasting, (6) the instructions of the Holy Ghost, and (7) the pure love of Christ. Each of these has two characteristics: (a) they are types of knowledge and awareness which stimulate and nourish our positive desires to grow, and (b) they will never generate immoral behavior.

Because children learn to read, write, and do arithmetic in the absence of these forces, many teachers find it difficult to associate them with influencing children to learn to read, use numbers, or learn the alphabet. This, however, does not diminish the value or usefulness of these influences in the educational process. In fact, agency-oriented parents, teachers, and students strive to incorporate these spirit-based motivational forces into the learning/teaching relationhip as a means of influencing the desires and dispostions of the individuals involved. They do this because the presence of these spiritually based influences introduce light as well as truth into the learning/teaching process. They contribute wisdom as well as knowledge to the individual's education. It is an added dimension that enhances both the teacher and the student.

207

This explains why Brigham Young instructed Karl Maeser "that neither the alphabet nor the multiplication tables were to be taught without the Spirit of God."5

Discipline

Perhaps more than any other single concern, the problem of discipline seems to haunt the educational environment, especially in formal settings like schools. Most classroom teachers would probably say that discipline—student control—is their single greatest challenge. Numerous interruptions are ever-present, hovering about the teacher and the learner, seeking to disrupt the task at hand. The inability to cope with these forces probably destroys more learning and discourages more teachers than any other single factor.

Hundreds of books and many theories have been created to help teachers and students cope with discipline. A universal recipe that always works has not been found. But there is a usable, effective principle for agency-oriented educators. Properly used, it provides a powerful and effective approach to discipline. The principle was expressed by the Lord to Joseph Smith in 1833. (D&C 95:1). It is a simple formula that is familiar.

208

Love Them, Correct Them, and Prepare A Way For Them

The Lord indicated that three things were necessary in order to establish and maintain an effective learning/teaching relationship. How God relates to us is a pattern we can follow in relating to those whom we serve.

First, love them. John the apostle said that God's love for us is what makes it possible for us to love God. "We love him, because he first loved us" (I John 4:19). Teachers must first love their students, parents must first love their children; and by this they make it possible for their students or their children to love them in addition to their loving God. The simple fact that we love someone does not ensure that they will love us in return, but it opens the way and makes it more likely.

Second, correct them. Mutually accepted standards must exist in a healthy relationship that communicates knowledge and wisdom. A principle useful in parent-child and teacher-student communication was revealed by the Father to his children on earth in these words: "There is a law, irrevocably decreed in heaven before the foundations of this world, upon which all blessings are predicated—And when we obtain any blessing from God, it is by obedience to that law upon which it is predicated" (D&C 130:20-21). This can be a pattern for parents and teachers. Like God's interactions with his children, a parent and teacher's instruction should be based on established standards. These basic standards have been revealed to us by God. Without righteous order (the law), there can be neither justice nor mercy. Everything becomes arbitrary and relative, impulsive and chaotic. Confusion and disorder rather than success and satisfaction are the result. (BM, 2 Nephi 2:10-13).

Third, provide a way. Children and students need help. That is why parents and teachers are needed to provide the way. They must assist the child, the student, by helping them discover or providing the right thing to do. How this is accomplished may vary from person to person, depending on the talents and readiness of the respective personalities. It need not be perfect, but it should be personal. It may not be totally adequate, but it should be appropriate. Nephi, the Book of Mormon prophet, expressed this principle: "I will go and do the things which the Lord hath commanded, for I know that the Lord giveth no commandments unto the children of men, save he shall *prepare a way* for them that they may accomplish the thing which he commandeth them" (1 Nephi 3:7, italics added). Parents and teachers may not always perfectly prepare the way for their children and students, but this principle can guide their instruction.

Elizabeth Barrett Browning, in a well-known sonnet, gives us a useful clue to implement the principle of loving, correcting, and providing a way for our children and students. She asked, "How do I love thee?" and then said, "Let me count the ways." In a direct response to the challenge, this approach can help parents and teachers both because every person is unique, and no two people love, correct, or prepare help in exactly the same way. Furthermore, because each of us is unique, no two children (or students) can be loved, corrected, and helped in exactly the same way. Our talents, gifts, resources, dispositions, and personalities are different. Both need and response are potentially different, but we must each do what we do with integrity to what we are. My muscular, masculine athletic coach did not express love, make corrections, or prepare the way the same as my diminutive, quiet,

209

feminine but very influential literature teacher did. Yet both were effective teachers.

This approach to discipline urges children and students to follow voluntarily the truths they experience. They become disciples, not of the parent or teacher, but of the principles espoused. This type of discipline can apply to a group, but ultimately it reduces itself to the individual. Discipline is a matter of one on one. I must ask myself the question: How can I express my love to John (as his father or as his teacher) so he will know that I love him? Then I must ennumerate the possible ways, trying each one until John responds. The same holds true for correction. The list must be made, explored, and tried until the solution is found; and likewise to find the best ways for John or Mary to succeed in what I am helping them accomplish. The way for one may not be the way for another. Agency-oriented parents or teachers are sensitive to this and adjust their approaches accordingly. The real answers are not in a book; they are in people themselves.

210

Blending Discipline and Agency Oriented Education

The principle of discipline as described here does not presume to impose the authority of the teacher over the student; rather it presumes a responsibility of both teacher and the student to honor a principle of order. This is not the conventional relationship experienced by most teachers and students.

Four different authority relationships have been indirectly referred to in this book. These relationships can now be summarized and compared in the following way. (see illustrations in Appendix B and figure 12-1)

Theological approach. Traditional education in western culture popularized this relationship between teacher and student. Most educational programs during the eighteenth and nineteenth centuries reflected this approach, which is actually a remnant of Greek philosophy. Simply stated, the theological approach to education is based on the assumption that God created man and the universe and has shared important knowledge with man. He expected those who understood his mind and will to use the sacred scripture and rational contemplation to instruct the rising generation in the truths he had revealed. Theology was the human science of studying the mind and will of God; reason was the instrument by which this was accomplished. Transferring this knowledge from one generation to another required strict compliance to an authority structure that empowered the older generation to deliver the information they possessed to the younger generation. This transfer was confirmed by having the learner satisfy the teacher with an oral or written demonstration to show that he had correctly grasped the message. Lessons were characterized by orderly presentation by teachers and deferential recitation by students. The catechismal approach became very popular. The teachers received their authority from God and the Church or from a divinely authorized state ruled by a king or monarch. It was the duty of the teacher to see that students became obedient and contributing members to the religious and social order. This is the structure behind the educational program described by Jennifer in Chapter Four. The hierarchal authority relationship can be illustrated as

Societal approach. The enlightenment, renaissance, and reformation movements created an atmosphere and mood that weakened the general confidence of many people in the supernatural view of the world. And when the academic intellect in western culture replaced the supernatural view of the world with an exclusively naturalistic view that ignored the supernatural, the order of authority in education changed. Modernists view man as the highest form of life in a naturalistic world. He is evolving, as is the universe, from the simple to the complex, and from a lower to a higher order. The Social Order has replaced the authority of God and the Church. Society, a natural phenomenon, was viewed as independent and autonomous. The society empowered the teacher whose job it was to see that students became useful, satisfied, and successful contributors to society. This is the structure behind the educational program described by Frank in Chapter Four. During the late nineteenth and early twentieth centuries the heirarchical relationship in education shifted to match a description that can be illustrated as

Society
↓
Teacher
↓
Student

Individualist approach. As modern educators moved to the societal approach of education, some people became critical. Although they agreed with the naturalistic worldview, they were not pleased with the way some educators wanted schools to become factories designed to produce people to be simply role players in the larger society. These critics saw man not as a blank tablet to be written upon or a piece of clay to be formed by the group, but as an autonomous individual; each has inherent capacities, will power, and purposes that are unique. The individual does not exist for society; society is simply the by-product of individuals seeking their rightful self-actualization.

212

The teacher therefore has become no more important than the student, nor has he authority to dictate what the student should become; this is the student's perogative. The teacher's role is to help the students who chart their own course through life. The teacher does not stand above the student, but at the side as a resource; the teacher cannot and should not control. The teacher supports but does not direct the student. Students determine how, what, and when to become whatever it is they choose. This is the structure behind the educational program described by Ellen in Chapter Four. The authority relationship between the teacher and student in education pursued from this point of view can be charted as

Student   ⟷   Teacher

Agency approach. The authority relationship in the agency approach to education differs from the previous three patterns. Agency education, as discussed in this book, agrees that God has created man and the universe. Institutions, including the Church, are created to help individuals fulfill their own destiny, not the reverse. David O. McKay expressed this view in these words. "The whole purpose of the Church is to bless the individual."[6] He added, "It is well ever to keep in mind the fact that the state exists for the individual, not the individual for the state. Jesus sought to perfect society by perfecting the individual, and only by the exercising of free agency can the individual even approach perfection."[7] On another occasion he summarized his position by saying, "I am one of those who believes that all institutions and organizations exist primarily for the purpose of securing to the individual his rights, his happiness and the proper development of his character. As soon as organizations fail to accomplish this purpose their usefulness ceases."[8]

Focusing on the importance of the individual does not diminish the value of society for the agency educator; society's purpose and usefulness are freely acknowledged. The issue is whether the group or the individual receives priority. In the agency approach, both the teacher and the student are subjected to their personal relationship with God (often by covenant), as well as contractual relationships with each other.

213

The teacher's role in this type of education is to relate with the student as a brother or sister who shares a personal relationship with God. The student is in charge of his or her education; the teacher is a helper. Society provides a supportive context in which this relationship can function. The needs of society should not destroy or distort the individual's quest for growth; it should enhance it. The student is responsible to principles of order which the teacher shares. These standards protect social order. This is the structure behind the educational program described by Harold in Chapter Four. The dynamics of this relationship between teacher and learner is described in the next chapter. In diagram form it can be expressed as

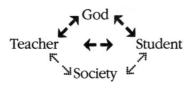

Approaches to Education

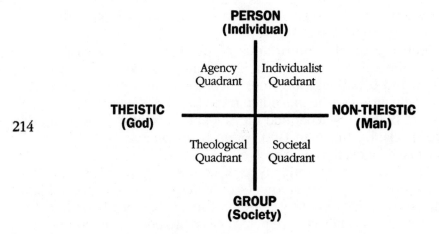

Figure 12-1

13

The Learning/Teaching Relationship

The answer to the question, Why do men love God? is because he first loved us. Students will love the teacher who first loves them. Students who express love toward their teachers may enable those teachers to rise above a number of limitations. The human disposition is a powerful and controlling influence. Prayer can change dispositions for the good. Prayer accesses both internal and external influences. It can strengthen and heal the human soul. Prayer can be a critical catalyst in the chemistry of human education.

Self-Understanding: A Key

Man's basic problem in life, from the agency point of view, is his problem of estrangement, of alienation. First, he is estranged from himself; he does not fully understand himself. Second, he is estranged from his divine origins; he does not fully understand his premortal beginnings. Third, he is estranged from his fellow men because of envy, jealousy, insecurity, selfishness, and immaturity. These are conditions that plague fallen man. The purpose of education is to help man reestablish proper relationships with himself, his origins, his fellow men, and his living God. The mission of Jesus Christ was designed to make this task possible.

Before teachers or students can improve they must either feel a need for improvement (a need to change) or possess a significant degree of commitment (or faith). For some teachers, it is easier to blame ineffective teaching experiences on the student's lack of interest than it is to face self-limitations. For some students, it is easier to blame the teacher's poor preparation or odd personality than it is to recognize their own failings. Both of these dispositions sustain estrangement and alienation. The correction for these barriers to learning is a greater degree of self-understanding: knowing the truth about God, self, and others. Self-understanding is a key to removing estrangement and alienation from one's life and hence from the learning/teaching relationship.

We must see ourselves, experience ourselves, somewhat as others see us and experience us. Perhaps this goal cannot be fully achieved, but we can at least increase our awareness. When a mutual effort is made by both student and teacher in this direction, the opportunity for potential learning is increased. It nurtures the humility that fosters effective interpersonal exchanges.

Requirements for Teaching

At least four requirements for effective teaching are evident. These four areas of potential development constitute the domain of basic educational training. A conscious effort to improve in these areas will do much to improve one's effectiveness as a learner or a teacher.

1. *Accepting others*

216

A teacher must be able to love others. The teacher's inability to communicate feeling interferes with the development of student security. The teacher's communication of love permits the student to feel the security necessary to drop his defenses against the teacher, to become involved in the learning process with the teacher. It is very difficult, if not impossible, to become *significantly* involved in mutual learning with another person on the basis of hate or fear. Love is the invitation to wholesome learning. When teachers or students feel they must defend themselves psychologically or physically, they are less able to spend that energy, attention and interest on the teaching/learning task.

In the realm of accepting others, teachers tend to be selective. Because of personality characteristics, teachers often relate to some individuals and ignore or reject others. Often this preference is not deliberate; it only reflects the teacher's own state of estrangement. The more free a teacher is from her own alienation, the less selective she will tend to be in relating to others; she may feel esteem for all, be no respecter of persons, and be able to relate to rich and poor, bond and free, male and female, regardless of race, creed or color.

Similarly, some students allow the teacher to relax, to feel free, and to express warmth, while others put teachers on guard and make them feel ill at ease. Alienated feelings between teacher and students, parents and children, make for a weak relationship. This emotional gap is causing conflict in our society as well as damaging our educational programs. For example, some parents find it easier to relate to one child than to another. Children who do not feel accepted often feel directed but not understood. This makes the learning/teaching relationship distant and cool rather than close and comfortable.

2. *Mastering self*

Teachers must strive to master themselves to the point that they are free to express themselves naturally. Without self-disclosure, interpersonal encounters can be hollow and false. In order to maximize teaching effectiveness, teachers must be capable of sharing themselves with others. Sharing oneself requires self-mastery. Individuals who lack self-control, who do not have confidence in themselves, shut themselves off from others. They are bound by their own fears. Self-mastery creates confidence, and confidence increases freedom (D&C 121:45). An authentic encounter of one person with another is usually the an effective way to teach by example as well as by precept.

217

3. *Mastering material*

Teachers must first acquire that which they wish to give to others or be willing to join in the search for what they do not possess. In teaching, legitimate ownership is a prerequisite to effective instruction. Teachers cannot properly give what they do not legitimately possess or honestly search for what they do not desire to discover. Fraudulance in teaching leads to error and confusion. Sound learning is based on integrity. Teachers should be familiar with what they give to others. They should have intimate aquaintance with their subject matter. To teach, they need to be able to *explain* as well as to *name*. True teaching is based on testifying. This requires mastery of the material; superficial preparation will not sustain inspiring instruction.

4. *Acquiring communication skills*

Teachers must master the means through which they can give to others what they possess. The communication process is a primary concern. In fact, the teacher's claim as an authority lies in communication. When teachers cannot communicate effectively, they fail to fulfill their basic role. Poor communication leads to poor teaching. The communication referred to here does not mean glib rhetoric—it means sincere, honest, and straightforward sharing of the truth. Highly articulate individuals with entertaining styles, and a polished presence at the lectern, can be poor communicators when evaluated as contributors to learning.

Students are equally responsible to be effective in communication skills. They must be able to comprehend and to respond. The students' legitimacy as learners is directly connected to their communication skills. Poor communication leads to poor learning. Perhaps this is why literacy is the foundation for the most effective and efficient forms of education. Literacy embraces fundamental skills necessary for effective communication that bridges the gap between our spirits.

A Basic Obstacle to Effective Teaching

218

A primary obstacle to effective teaching is self-understanding expressed as self-consciousness, a lack of confidence. Inexperience, unpreparedness, or immaturity can lead to self-consciousness. Almost everyone struggles to some degree with this challenge. Self-consciousness is a natural part of human growth and development. Undue self-consciousness, however, prevents healthy, successful performance in the teaching role (see stage one fig. 13-1).

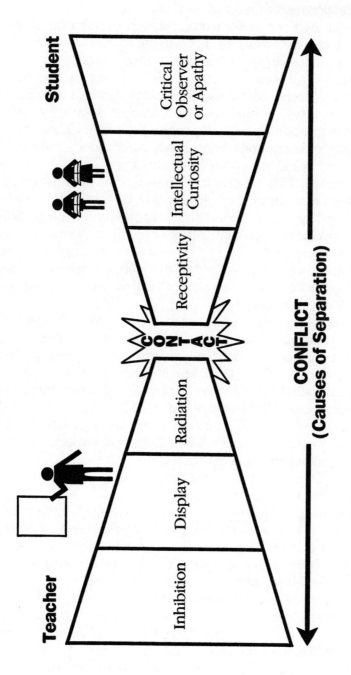

Figure 13-1

219

Personal Responses to the Teacher Role

A typical teacher's performance may reflect any one of three states. These conditions are distinct enough to be classifiable, but they are not exclusive. More accurately, they overlap, but as we analyze them we see the need for continuing personal development. A secret of successful teaching can be found in the searching and growing one does as a teacher. Nearly everyone who has attempted to teach will recognize the feelings associated with these three descriptions. They are dynamic moods and can all be experienced in a single episode of instruction.

1. *Inhibition.* This condition is characterized by inhibiting or numbing fear, evident in stage fright, lack of confidence, and a general inability to perform. Physiologically, some people experience involuntary shaking, a lack of saliva in the mouth, and moist palms. These problems may cause a person to feel less able, and sometimes unable, to perform in the role of teacher. Training and experience help people rise above this state of disabling inhibition. It can be overcome.

2. *Display.* This state finds teachers preoccupied with self-interest—focused on selling themselves. Teachers put themselves rather than their services on display—see me, see how much I know, see how colorful and likeable I am, see how much authority I have. Their teaching may be very colorful and entertaining, but its effectiveness is limited because the teacher's relationships with the students are short-circuited by the focus on the teacher's ego. This type of teaching restricts the instructional experience to a horizontal relationship between the teacher and the student; little or no room is left for inviting the Spirit of God into the learning/teaching experience.

3. *Radiation.* This condition is characterized by teachers losing their self-consiousness and their self-interest in giving themselves to others. These teachers are childlike, capable of giving without demanding any return. They serve with humility. They lose themselves, and in so doing find themselves. In that discovery each teacher reaps unexpected rewards obtainable in no other way. When in this state, teachers forget themselves and are not preoccupied with how they look or sound, or how others perceive them. The total focus is on the sharing interchange. When this giving and receiving of gifts initiated by the teacher is acknowledged and accepted by the student, there is an openness

that invites the Spirit of God into the learning/teaching relationship.

Involvement Teaching

Even though a teacher grows in proficiency, self-confidence, and capability of performing well, this growth does not guarantee his continued success. A new challenge comes with every teaching experience. Informal or formal, at home or in the classroom, each teaching experience is like each trip over a familiar golf course as we attempt to overcome anew a well-known series of barriers.

Success in teaching is reflected in the extent to which we can activate full involvement from others. But teaching and learning is not a one-way street. While teachers move toward involvement with each individual student, on any given day they may find themselves at different levels with different students. Figure 13-1 is one way to visualize the challenge teachers face who attempt to lose themselves in the process of involving students, so that students are able to realize themselves through learning.

221

Most of us preoccupy ourselves with what we are going to do during the upcoming class time. More productive is the concern with what are the students going to do. Emphasis on the latter stimulates the teacher to consider how to invite learner involvement. Students rather than the teacher or the subject matter become the focal point in planning. This is the agency oriented teacher's resolution to the question: Should the focus be on the student, the teacher, or the subject matter? Agency oriented teachers don't emphasize, What can I do in my class? This may lead to display-level instruction. Nor do they emphasize, What should my students learn today? This can lead to behavioral objectives and rigid patterns of reinforcement. Rather they emphasize, What can I share with my students that will increase their understanding, and how might I invite them into a personally meaningful experience worthy of divine approbation?

Personal Responses to the Student Role

As indicated in figure 10-1, a teacher's behavior is closely associated with the students' behavior. Students can help or retard the teacher's effectiveness to teach at the agency level. The student is in charge of the learning process. By use of authority, a teacher may exert external controls over the students' behavior, but if the objective is to assist agency learning, then students' must invite, not obstruct, instruction. Otherwise the learning/teaching process is reduced to learning patterns that operate under duress. In extreme forms this is known as brainwashing.[1] This is a form of education, but it is not the optimum form; it is not agency education. Students need to understand how they are affecting, positively or negatively, their own learning.

1. *Apathetic or critical observers.* Students in this disposition may show a lack of concern for what the teacher is doing or try to draw others' attention away from the teacher. They may whisper or even talk with associates, or they may close their eyes and sleep. Equally harmful to the learning process is the student who has a sullen, belligerent, or sarcastic attitude. What can you teach me? Who are you to be telling me? It is this state of resistance, indifference, and uninterest on the part of students that may cause teachers to assume a forceful approach to education. Teachers may feel that what they have to teach is important for students to learn, even for those unwilling students who fail to realize or appreciate it at the moment. So they feel justified exerting force, external discipline, or whatever measures seem necessary to demand the students' attention and response to the learning task. Students can and do learn under such compulsory circumstances, but it is not agency education; it is societal or theological education, as previously defined.

2. *Intellectual listener.* The student may become interested in a particular point and involved to some degree. After listening attentively or perhaps asking questions, the student may spar with the teacher with challenging comments and questions. Teachers recognize students in this stage as much by the feelings they convey as by their words. Learning at this level of involvement is generally tentative. It is mind to mind rather than heart to heart. This level of learning can be commanding and impressive, but it does not offer maximum learning. It is learning that is checked by reservations; it may block the student from obtaining what otherwise would be offered. It may also limit the function of divine influence because openness is restricted by the focus on the ego of the student. Intellectual listeners are self-limiting learners.

3. *Receptive Learner.* The term receptivity indicates an open, willing, seeking mood. Students willingly strive to understand and establish harmony with what the teacher is attempting to

222

accomplish. They voluntarily identify with the teacher's interest in them and in the importance of the ideas being discussed. Students in this state are not gullible; they retain their independence, but no longer try to protect a particular image in the eyes of others. As part of the learning experience, students find themselves communicating and being communicated with as total persons. Each accepts and feels accepted. An aura, a spirit of generative, growing, feeling envelops both student and teacher. This atmosphere invites the Spirit of the Lord to influence the instructional setting and makes it possible for the teacher to teach more than he otherwise could and for the learner to learn more than he otherwise would.

Students can help teachers move toward the radiation (giving of himself) state, if they themselves move toward the receptivity (seeking mood) state. Similarly, teachers can help students move toward receptivity if they will move toward the radiation. The accomodation is not a one-way process; it is a mutual, reciprocal endeavor. The bread the teacher casts upon the waters eventually will be the bread returned.

223

Six Snapshots of the Teacher in the Learning/Teaching Process

1. *The teacher who is primarily involved with himself.* He is concerned about his self-assurance, how he looks, and what people think about him. He is self-conscious, nervous, and inhibited. He is unable to sense the needs of his students or to concentrate on the subject matter because of his self-consciousness.

Comment on Its effect. Effectiveness of teaching is usually very limited under these conditions; when a teacher is expending his energy, attention, and interest on himself, he cannot be giving them to his students or to his topic.

2. *The teacher who is preoccupied with subject matter.* She loves the subject matter more than she loves the student. She may be eloquent and perhaps arrogant at times. She may be able to quote many passages, cite numerous sources, and give authoritative answers, or be dry and uninteresting.

Comment on Its Effect. At best such teaching may command respect or be momentarily entertaining, but it seldom has significant or lasting personal effect on the students. The students usually do not feel free to respond and interact. They often tune the teacher out, sit in silence, or talk and whisper among themselves. If they are courteous, they endure the hour, but seldom enjoy it unless the material itself draws the student.

3. *The teacher who interacts with students.* He is confident enough of himself and his preparation that he is free to sense the thoughts and feelings of his students. He is able to relate with his students and encounter their concerns and questions in a spontaneous manner.

Comment on Its Effect. Students become involved; they express themselves and their ideas. Students may challenge the teacher and his views on the subject being discussed, but they respond to the teacher's interest in them by voluntary interaction.

4. *The teacher who leads students into involvement with the subject matter.* Because of her relationship with her students, the teacher is able to interest them in a vigorous examination of the subject and an understanding of how the learning applies to the students' needs and lives.

224

Comment on Its Effect. Students question and begin to explore and study on their own. They show a hunger and thirst for more knowledge.

5. *The teacher who so structures the learning/teaching experience that he inspires his students to interact with one another on the subject and its personal implications.* The students exchange their individual feelings and views on the subject under discussion with one another. Their discussions continue after class, and they look forward to returning to the next encounter with both the teacher and their fellow students.

Comment on Its Effect. The teacher is not the continual center of attention. Important principles and the feelings and opinions of other individuals in the group share in receiving the focus of attention. Students and teacher feel truly involved.

6. *The experience in the classroom, or with the teacher, that leads the student to introspection.* This is the goal of meaningful education for older students and adults, because it leads to self-selected changes by the student. This experience usually follows meaningful involvement with others.

Comment on Its Effect. Voluntary change by students in the direction of growth and development is the ultimate aim of the conscientious teacher, and usually follows snapshots 3, 4, and 5.

Four Snapshots of the Learner In the Teaching/Learning Process

1. *The learner who enters the instructional experience under compulsion*. Under these circumstances many learners are preoccupied with escape, either physically or psychologically. The learner who is under duress, who is expected by others to learn without a personal desire to do so, seldom maintains a focused attention and interest on the task at hand. Such learners are unlikely to feel or express empathy for the teacher. They express resistance rather than receptivity.

Comment on Its Effect. Control of the learners by the teacher will probably be a central concern. Learners will often express their energy and talents in the form of a contest—learner vs. teacher. If sufficient force can be applied by the teacher on the learners, minimum standards of response by learners may be established and pursued. Stressful tension seems to be constant and deterioration of control ongoing. Communication is subject to persistant interruption as the teacher struggles to maintain control and order. Occasionally, the context will consist of sullen silence in the place of overt disorder. Students will simply ignore the instruction.

2. *The learner who is actively seeking goals that are inconsistent with or contrary to the aims and desires of the teacher*. Learners in this situation may tolerate the expectations of the teacher or the system, but expend their energy on interacting socially, writing letters, doing assignments for other classes, and seeking personal attention from peers.

Comment on Its Effect. The mood in this setting is generally overt compliance but at the minimum level of investment. The norm is to do the minimum necessary to stay out of trouble. Learners go through the motions of the required learning but only to the extent required to defend themselves. Beyond this, learners focus on goals and objectives outside the classroom. Daydreaming, doodling, and other forms of mental pursuit outside the classroom are common symptoms. Clever toleration rather than significant achievement characterizes the experience. Taking the easy way, including cheating, may be common.

3. *The learner who defines the teaching/learning experience as a means to a distant but desired end*. In this situation learners are willing to submit to the teacher's desires but find it difficult sustain

225

a high level of motivation. They accept the necessity of the experience, but the anticipated application is so far removed that an intense involvement is unlikely. Each learns because "I better learn this because someday I will probably wish I had." Learning satisfactions are sporadic.

Comment on Its Effect. A common outcome of this type of learning experience is doing the right thing for the wrong reason. Consequences bring less than maximum results. This is similar to mowing the lawn because it has been a week since the lawn was mowed rather than mowing the lawn because it beautifies the surroundings and brings personal satisfaction and pride to the home owner. Quite often such learning fails to produce the desired results or must be repeated to be useable later on. Frequently, high school coursework falls in this category; when students enter college they lack the fundamentals, even though they took the classes. And in many instances college students who complete general education requirements as freshmen and sophomores later discover that they went through General Education but General Education didn't go through them. Many people attend various types of church or civic meetings under this condition. They may be credited with training but they lack the effectiveness and vitality that could have been theirs if they had pursued the task with greater integrity.

4. *The learner who seeks out a teacher to help him pursue his chosen goals.* When this occurs teaching and learning become a joint venture. The student's desire reaches out to the teacher. The teacher follows the student's lead and comes to understand what the student wants in relation to where the student is now; mutual goals can be established. Teachers are free to offer what they have in response to what the student wants. This attitude applies to young children as well as to adults; most often first graders reflect this disposition. They want a teacher to help them learn how to read, write, and do other things they see grown-ups doing.

Comment on Its Effect. Motivation on the part of learners to engage themselves in the learning task comes from within. The application of external force such as threats, grades, and other forms of punishments are usually unnecessary. The value of external rewards is also minimized. The tendency is to do the right thing for the right reason. Challenged to provide direction rather than to provide control, teachers can adapt their approach to the

226

learning task to match those of the learner, especially for older students. Since their zeal may exceed good judgment and prudence, students may need to be assisted in exercising restraint.

Teaching with One's Whole Soul—Spirit to Spirit

In moral matters teachers are their own best teaching tool. And personal morality applies to the teaching of any subject. The effective agency teachers teach all subjects as components of character. These teachers become the most skilled in teaching with their whole soul. If we wish to become an instrument in the hands of divine influences, as Jesus was, we must teach with the total self. Our example—our positive values, commitment, and responsibility—will emanate a power and influence for good on our students. To argue that one's private life has no impact or relevance on one's professional performance is inconsistent. We cannot separate what we are from what we teach and hope to retain the integrity necessary to sustain the agency approach to education.

227

It is a magnificent experience to watch a mature mother teach her children. When she is pure, self-disciplined, and full of the Spirit, her relationship with them is a living symphony. One sees a spontaneity of precision and skill as she reveals innumerable nuances of feeling: extended freedom, tender care, soft love, playfulness, righteous indignation, disappointment, suffering, uplifting forgiveness, grief, genuine interest, satisfaction, and quick and sharp retribution. The list is almost endless; descriptive words are inadequate. Teachers can learn much from such mothers.

This is the optimum kind of teaching to influence character. As they radiate, teachers give of themselves to others without demanding any return. They lose themselves in service, and in so doing find their best self. Free from the numbing fear shown in stage fright, lack of confidence, and the inhibition of self-consciousness, teachers join the students on their side of the fence, see life through their eyes, and enjoy sharing in their experiences.

Teachers who give of themselves in this manner avoid the compulsion to sell themselves. They do not consciously put themselves on display—see me, see how much I know, see how colorful and likeable I am, see how much authority I have. They are not preoccupied with what they are going to do during the class time; their concern is with what the students are going to think, feel, and do. They are able to act and react with integrity; they are not bound in a cold, rigid plan that creates frustrating inconsistencies.

Prayer—A Tool for Teachers and for Students

The answer to the question, Why do men love God? is because he first loves us. Students will love the teacher who first loves them. The immature teacher requires students to love him before being able to love them. Prayer, for the agency oriented teacher, is one of the most effective resources to obtain the desire and ability to communicate love to others. Love can be conceived and nourished in prayer. Teachers who will talk to God about their students—about each one—can acquire the knowledge and maturity necessary to love their students first. Responsive students will love such a teacher who first loved them. And students who love their teachers tend to obey them and follow their instructions.

228

Students have access to this same power. They too can initiate love in the learning/teaching relationship by first loving their teacher. Responsive teachers will feel this caring and concern. Student love expressed toward teachers has the power to lift those teachers above their own limitations. Students who reach out and embrace the good a teacher has to offer may find that their learning will exceed the limitations of both themselves and their teacher. Personal dispositions, as previously indicated, are the powerful and controlling influence in the teaching/learning process. Prayer by the teacher and the student can change these dispositions for the good. Prayer accesses both internal and external influences. It can have both a strengthening and healing impact on man's soul. Prayer can be a critical catalyst in the chemistry of human education.

14

What Should Be Taught?

Truth is a crop worth harvesting and light makes the crop grow season after season. Literacy enables lifelong learning, and literacy develops the capacities of the intellect to comprehend through a variety of avenues—language and the expressive arts, mathematics, science, social studies, and moral and spiritual awareness. For agency educators, the goal of mastering specific content in the curriculum is a useful way to develop these basic capacities, not an end in itself.

 Education begins where creation leaves off; the infant is the product of creation, and the man the result of education. And if creation is the organization of preexisting elements, then education simply extends creation. In education, as in creation, intelligence acts upon things which are calculated to benefit the organizer. We seek education, just as we engage in creation, to obtain joy, satisfaction, and fulfillment—to make ourselves more nearly perfect, more capable, and more in harmony with our potential destiny. When this premise is applied to the practical aspects of learning or schooling, its nature becomes much more clear and simple.

Orson F. Whitney explained:

The highest idea of education is growth—self-development. The instructor does for his pupils what the husbandman does for his plants and trees—cultivates, nourishes, cares for and protects them, places them in those conditions where they can best expand according to the laws of their own being. If the tree have no life in it, if it cannot grow, what avails of all the toil of the husbandman? If the pupil will not study, will not try to learn, makes no effort to help himself, how can anyone assist him? Education is creation, but the educator does not create the faculties of the pupil any more than the gardener creates the constituents of the tree. He cannot compel the mind; he can only incite and encourage it, educating or leading out its faculties, thus converting the potential into the actual. This is the highest glory of the educator, it is the acme of his achievement. All development is the result of co-operation between the cultivator and the thing cultivated.

Since only the educated faculties are capable of "complete living," it follows that the faculties not educated are partly dead. At all events, they are asleep, and sleep is a symbol of death. This helps us to understand the significance of the spiritual death—banishment from the presence of God. To restore man to that glorious presence, to redeem him from ignorance and sin, to develop the soul in all its parts, the human tree in all its branches, awakening what is asleep, making the barren fruitful, and giving life in lieu of death, is indeed the function of education.

230

I believe faith to be the cause of all growth, as it is the mainspring of all action. Without it, there would be no education, progress would be impossible. We do nothing without first believing it can be done. The infant creeps, the man walks, by faith. Even those who scoff at faith, must exercise it in order to live, move, and have a being. God works with all men according to their faith. What if it should be found that He works with all His creations upon the same principle? "Faith as a grain of mustard seed" will "move mountains." Have you seen the root of a tree, or the bursting bulb of a plant, breaking its way through pavement of concrete or stone, rending the very rocks in order to fulfill its destiny— to respond to the call of the Creator and "Come up higher?" If man were as perfect, as obedient to law, in his sphere, as the trees and plants are in theirs, where would be the limit of his power? Earth itself keeps the law of its Maker better than mankind as a whole. Therefore shall it be sanctified, and eventually be made celestial, so that beings of a celestial order may inhabit it.

There is a spiritually scientific and philosophic reason at the bottom of the demand for faith as the first condition of salvation. Unless we believe in God, He cannot do for us all that He desires to do. He cannot give what we are not able or not willing to receive. Therefore He says, "Draw near unto Me, and I will draw near unto you." We draw near unto God by

believing in Him, and if we truly believe in Him we will obey
Him, thereby building upon the rock, and not upon the sand.[1]

Literacy that leads to lifelong learning is more than a temporal
luxury, it is an eternal necessity. Obtaining knowledge, and
understanding how to wisely use that knowledge, is fundamental
to human fulfillment. It is properly symbolic that in 1800 the
highest literacy rate in the Western Hemisphere enveloped Sharon,
Windsor County, Vermont. Here, in a remote New England valley,
frontier men and women developed learning skills equal to those
of world-renown Sweden.[2] This remarkable learning atmosphere
was not wasted on the family of the Prophet Joseph Smith. Like
other families in this unique rural environment, as circumstances
permitted they nurtured and perpetuated the value of lifelong
learning. Today's Latter-day Saint families should continue in that
worthy tradition. Literacy is the requisite to lifelong learning; truth
is a crop worth harvesting. As a wise uncle once counseled,
"Obtain as much light and knowledge as possible—it's a light load
to carry."

231

Five Fundamental Parts of the Curriculum
Language and the expressive arts (dance, painting, music,
etc.), mathematics, science, and social studies are the common
divisions of today's elementary curriculum. Until the turn of this
century a fifth aspect was a central concern—morality.[3] These five
curricular elements provide avenues for expressing fundamental
faculties of man's intellect—aesthetic judgment, deductive and
inductive logic, normative comparison, and discerning right from
wrong. Although not always recognized as such, developing these
capacities should be a primary focus of formal education.

Too often, teachers fail to help their students understand that
the school curriculum should develop particular capacities of the
intellect. Instead, they become preoccupied with the subject matter
and instructional methods and do not consciously focus on the
development of these capacities. This shows how we get too close
to the tree and obstruct our view of the forest. The reading books,
bulletin boards, flash cards, and all the paraphernalia teachers
use—including the skills that develop in the students from using
these materials such as the ability to read, manipulate numbers,
sing the musical scale and so forth—are simple means to much

more important ends. Yet all too often, these means become ends in themselves. The result is that we lose sight of the true nature and purpose of education. We become less effective teachers, and students are hampered in their quest for learning.

For more than a century, American educators have attempted to refine the objectives of the public school curriculum. To illustrate the distinction between means and ends, consider four of the five fundamental components—language (including the arts), mathematics, science, and social studies. Each of these components represents a specific type of thinking—a set of glasses, if you will—by which each person perceives different aspects of the world. We assume that all four sets of glasses are necessary if a person is to maximize his or her personal understanding, effectiveness, and satisfaction. This is the reason, for example, that the State University of New York (SUNY), Oswego experiment, focused on these four human capacities.[4] These educators recognized the importance of developing each of these capacities in each student.

232

The distinction between these respective components are readily recognized in the performance pattern of most elementary school teachers. For example, it is common practice to divide up the school day into these four areas. A teacher tells her students, "Put away your reading books and get out your math books," or announces, "Now we are going to do science." At secondary levels, although the four popular segments of the curriculum pie are subdivided into smaller slices, the desired objective remains the same: *prepare students to see the world around them by helping them develop four special capacities of the intellect.* (See fig. 14-1). The subject matter itself is simply a means of exercising a particular intellectual capacity. If any of the four sets of glasses are missing or defective, then students will be handicapped. Students will be unable to understand what otherwise might have sustained and improved their lives. The same can be said of the moral capacity. And as we shall see, it also applies to the spiritual domain. Developing these basic functions should be the focus of schooling.

Curriculum and Catagories
and
Creative Capacities

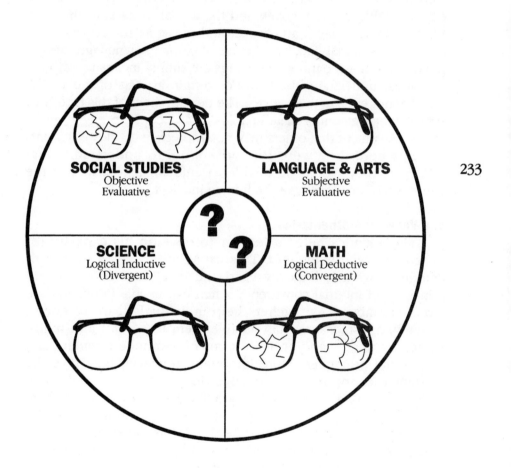

Figure 14-1

The Value of Language and the Expressive Arts

Each area of the curriculum has its own unique characteristics, its own conceptual emphasis, purpose, evaluative measure, and declaration—what it claims to contribute. The human capacity underlying language and the arts, for example, is to make quality *personal, interpretive judgments.* In other words, "properly fitted glasses" in this area help individuals evaluate what is *satisfying and dissatisfying, beautiful and ugly,* according to specified esthetic guidelines. Language and the arts are means to this end. We use prose, poetry, art, dance, and music as subject matter to develop this human faculty. The use of particular language, stories, poems, paintings, dances, and songs are simply means to help the individual understand the value of certain aspects of the world; they are not ends in themselves. The development of this faculty of subjective judgment is what enables some people to enjoy music, art, or movement that others may not appreciate. It allows students to see where they were formerly blind, to understand what otherwise they would be unable to enjoy. This constitutes the education of one faculty of the human intellect.

234

The Value of Mathematics

Mathematics helps a learner to develop his capacity for *logical, deductive thought.* This capacity enables a person to determine what is logically valid and invalid based on certain principles of internal consistency, often expressible in quantitative terms—numbers. As teachers help individuals learn to count, quantify, and measure, they enable them to control and utilize matter by understanding it in terms of symbolic numbers and conceptual principles. More important, however, they give the student the opportunity to develop the capacity of logical deductive thinking. As students learn that $3 - 2 = 1$, and then affirm the correctness, the internal consistency, of their answer by demonstrating or "proving" that $2 + 1 = 3$, they develop a capacity that is more important than the specific skill of "adding" or "subtracting." It is the difference between learning that a worm on a hook will catch a fish versus the capacity to understand that all fish must eat in order to survive; therefore all forms of fish food are potential "baits" for catching fish.

Another way to experience this deductive power is illustrated by the following problem. A person has ten United States coins;

one of the coins is a quarter, another a dime, another a nickel, and another a one-cent piece. What is the least amount of money that that person can have? In order to figure out the answer, the student must deduce (use deductive logic) and determine what could be the least total value of the six remaining coins. This capacity of man's intellect allows him to dissect the natural world with the language of numbers. This "set of eyeglasses" gives man the power to *perceive order in nature and to make greater use of this natural order.*

Teachers and students should look beyond the immediate task, such as taking algebra and passing the algebra exams, and recognize how algebra enables a person to develop the capacity for deductive thought. Confidence comes from understanding the role of balance in an equation: $2 + 4 \times 3 = 3 \times 4 + 2$ ($2X + 4Y \times 3B = 3B \times 4Y + 2X$). Similarly, our understanding is enlarged by recognizing that order sustains principles or theorems. Learning mathematics adds more to a person's life than merely being able to use a particular form to solve specific types of problems—percentages, geometry, calculus and so forth. Too often students feel they are learning a form of math that will have no application in their lives but to prepare them for higher forms of math that will also have no application in their lives. Some people may learn forms of mathematics that have no practical application in their lives. But all people can profit from the development of their ability to think deductively. Science contributes another dimension through its use of explanation, prediction, and control.

235

The Value of Science

Science develops one's capacity to use *empirical, inductive thought.* The elementary school teacher who directs her students to plant a bean in a paper cup of soil and observe the consequences of sunlight and moisture supplies these students with another "set of glasses." She is teaching them how to *confirm or disconfirm guesses about results* that may later be substantiated or denied on the basis of tangible, physical observation or demonstration. Through equipping students with a methodology of *prediction* based on manifestations of natural law, the teacher helps students develop their capacity to access their physical environment, and through this gain understanding of the harmony of a dynamic, natural order.

The Value of Social Studies

The hours spent discussing social studies is the educational optometrist's attempt to help each learner develop a fourth "set of glasses"—the capacity to *recognize and assess norms and values.* Expertise in social science allows people to understand what different peoples consider to be normal and not normal, desirable and not desirable. Mr. Rogers' invitation to "Come on over to my neighborhood," a field trip to the fire station, a study of the Civil War, or a comparison of food, housing, and clothing in different cultures are all examples of how we teach students *to exercise proficiency in normative/valuative observation.* In its mature form, as practiced in our culture, this mode of thought is buttressed by the language of statistics, an empirical technique, justified by mathematics and used for normative conclusions. Statistics allow us to communicate another form of prediction. For example, statistical tools help us predict who will win elections and calculate probabilities related to other patterns of human behavior, such as birth and death rates. Such predictions form the base for various economic enterprises such as the insurance business.

236

Assisting the Learner

Essentially, what teachers in our schools do can be reduced to this analogy of how to fit students with one or more "sets of glasses." Each of these capacities of the human intellect, when developed, reveals to the person a different dimension of life, just as cameras, X-ray machines, radar instruments, and sonar devices are each designed to capture different dimensions of existence. In this same way the "glasses" of our intellect become instruments that enable us to appreciate and participate more fully in our world. These basic capacities undergird all curricular experience, even subjects that seem more remote, such as physical education, theology, philosophy, art, shop, foreign language, and word processing.

Traditionally, elementary school teachers are expected to have some expertise in all four areas. Their task is to help the student to (1) find satisfaction through language and the expressive arts, (2) use numbers to validate deductively the internal consistency of theorems, (3) experience the inductive search for empirical confirmation of a prediction, and (4) discover values and normative behaviors through observation and statistical prediction.

Growth in the first area can be revealed when children bring home a drawing from school and proudly show their parents, or when they recognize a word on a roadsign and exclaim, "I know that word." The capacity to think with numbers is manifest by the eight-year-old who explains to her four-year-old brother that his nickel and three pennies will not buy the candy bar he wants. By virtue of his accumulated empirical experiences, a ten-year-old can predict that the fence is too high to jump over. And the teenager in junior high school who suddenly must have certain styles of clothes is revealing the capacity to discern social norms and expectations. Secondary level school teachers are usually specialists who spend all their time working with only one or two sets of these glasses.

Too often, both elementary and secondary teachers and students become lost in the curricular means and fail to recognize that it is the general capacity and not a particular application of the capacity that we need to develop. The details of school studies are soon forgotten; it is the expanded capacity that remains to enrich our lives. This is where the educational emphasis should be placed.

237

There is nothing mysterious or intimidating about these capacities when they are properly understood. As they use them parents actually initiate and develop the basic training of the child. The more effectively this is done in the home, the easier it is for children to excel when they get to school. Parents usually teach the child the rudiments of the alphabet and language use. They also help the child learn basic numbers and apply those numbers. For example, when a mother asks her four-year-old to bring both of his shoes or to indicate with his fingers how old he is, she is exercising his mathematical capacity. Whenever ingredients are combined to bake a loaf of bread or prepare other foods in the kitchen, the child is exposed to the rudiments of science. Comparison between the rules a child follows at home with the way things are done in a playmate's home is the beginning of social studies. Too often parents, teachers, and students fail to look beyond the subject matter; they do not focus on the process of developing the basic capacity (the glasses themselves). By concluding that mastery of the subject matter rather than the development of basic intellectual capacities is the primary goal, learners confuse means and ends. Our contemporary educational practice is weakened by this lack of vision. It is not the best way to teach the children.

The Missing Component

Historically (until this century), a fifth component was part of the educational curriculum of Western culture. In fact, it was the most fundamental component. This set of glasses equipped students to see and to receive the value of revealed standards of conduct and character. Despite the usefulness and pertinence of the four components we now use, many people feel the vacuum created by this missing "set of glasses." Contemporary curriculums in America are now largely devoid of any formal attempt to help students identify moral imperatives. As Irving Kristol and others have duly noted, textbooks no longer direct students in discerning right from wrong. The academic intellect in our society is in disarray; moral consensus has essentially evaporated, and the nation's vision is seriously impaired.[5]

This missing component is a critical void in the curriculum. Training in language and the arts can help a person make personal, subjective judgments about beauty and satisfaction; social studies skills equip a person to recognize social conformity according to period, place, and people; neither mathematics nor science claim their glasses are at all designed to reveal morality. In other words, *we make serious attempts to help students develop their capacities to determine what is beautiful or ugly (language and the arts), valid or invalid (mathematics), confirmable or disconfirmable (science), conforming or nonconforming (social studies); but there is little or no provision in the curriculum for developing the child's ability to choose what is right or wrong in an imperative or absolute sense (morality).* Critics of this condition frequently suggest that the perpetuation of such education may result in the demise of democratic society. Agency education places the development of personal character at the very center of the learning enterprise. It is the hub of the wheel.

Nurturing the development of strong moral capacities in students can be a major contribution of agency educators, who know that moral preparation is essential to spiritual growth. Those who are committed to the divine laws of moral order and the directives of the living God are in a unique position to assist young people. The example they provide and the insights they can offer are invaluable. I vividly remember one such instance in my own life, though it happened nearly fifty years ago. When I was a boy, I frequently went with my father to the Ogden, Utah stockyards. We lived on a farm, and the stockyard was the place we would buy and sell some of our animals. During one of these visits my father taught me a lesson that has increased in value over the years. It was a spontaneous bit of instruction and probably took less than a minute to deliver.

A Black Goat Named Judas

The holding pens for the cattle, hogs, and sheep were on the bank of the Weber river. A fenced bridge spanned the river and connected with a ramp that angled up to the top story of a meat processing plant located on the other side. Since the animals to be butchered had to be herded across the bridge and up the ramp, the men who managed this operation developed a clever solution. They trained a black goat to enter the sheep pens, mingle with the white sheep, and then lead the way across the bridge and up the ramp through the door of the processing plant. Once inside the doorway, the goat stepped aside, and the sheep pressed on to their ultimate fate.

I remember watching this scene as my father explained the operation. He paused, then added, "Let that be a lesson to you; be careful whom you follow. Make sure you know where you are being led."

I've never forgotten that experience. When I think of parents or teachers leading, teaching, and morally strengthening the rising generation, I remember how my father did it—in simple but lasting ways. The opportunities to teach important lessons are not always planned. They arise out of our day-to-day experiences—here a little and there a little, taking advantage of a teaching moment.

Children are like little mirrors toddling about, reflecting images of adult thinking, language, and mannerisms. The prayers my wife and I offer are also the prayers we hear when our children take their turns. The spiritual quality of the language in the home, the respect and consideration displayed, and the general atmosphere seem to inescapably mirror us, the parents. The way I treat my wife has an influence on how she treats our children and vice versa. If we snap or shout at our children, they're soon snapping at each other and at us. Our norms of behavior as parents seem to become the norms of behavior in our family. The same pattern extends into the schools. The moral standards of the adults we place before our children will be the moral standards that govern the communities in which our grandchildren will be reared. It is a sobering thought and a commentary on the social conditions that now surround us.

The Founding Fathers and the Separation Doctrine

In most societies, moral education has not been a legal issue. In fact, many societies have provisions not only for moral but also spiritual instruction to occur in their schools. In America a decision was reached soon after its founding to separate the spiritual education of the citizenry from the political machinery. The notion of religous liberty was a sensitive and highly valued right. It was determined, therefore, that spiritual education with its emphasis on ordinances, rituals, and worship as well as special spiritual knowledge would be reserved to the individual and the church of his or her choice. A man's religion and spiritual education was not to be dictated by the state. This became known as the separation of church and state.

The founders, however, did not intend to exclude moral education from state and community sponsored instructional programs. Most of the states now include in their state constitutions provisions for moral education. In fact, these founding documents itemize dozens of specific character traits that by law are established as educational objectives. There is a growing gap, however, between what is legislated and and what is practiced.[6] The exclusion of moral imperatives from the curriculum (teaching right from wrong) evolved as the controlling segment of society changed its perception of the universe from both a supernatural and natural view to an exclusively naturalistic view—the view from inside the bubble. The movement to this position has a long history in Western culture; it is a central storyline in our heritage.

Four Reconciliations—The Storyline of Western Culture

From a traditional point of view, Western culture was the result of the reconciliation of Hebrew-Christian teachings with classical Greek science and philosophy. Christian ideas were modified to fit the Greek metaphysics of Plato. This was the first great reconciliation. St. Augustine articulated this merger in his

240

writings, and medieval Christianity flowered.[7] The resulting church and state were brought together in a dangerous and oppressive marriage. (See chart in Appendix B.)

A second reconciliation occurred when medieval Christiantity (Augustine's Platonic Christiantity) was modified by the 12th-cenury Aristotelian views of the Scholastics. The merger is typified in the writings of Thomas Aquinas. This development set in place forces that ultimately culminated in the Enlightenment, Renaissance, and Reformation.[8]

The third reconciliation emerged when Thomistic Catholicism (Scholasticism) was displaced by the new science of Descartes, Copernicus, Galileo, Newton, etc.—the pioneers of modern science. Empirical observations buttressed by new mathematical tools replaced the pure logic of Aristotelian rationale. Each of these systems of thought, however, invoked reliance on some supernatural "force" to account for the origins of "purpose and design" and hold together man's conception of the universe.[9]

241

The fourth reconciliation was the most radical. During the late nineteenth and early twentieth centuries, a new intellectual power structure emerged. Traditional views were set aside; the idea of a deity, a first cause, and many of the sacred tenets of Hebrew-Christian religious thought (e.g., the Fall and the Atonement) were pushed aside in favor of an exclusively naturalistic and humanistic science, which admitted no need for a supernatural deity or force to justify its existence or function.[10]

In consequence, this modern reconciliation brought changes to the definition of morality. Moral relativism, in various forms such as conforming to group norms or the arbitrary desires of the individual, whatever these might be, replaced divinely instituted imperatives.[11] Now a controversial topic, morality has been increasingly ignored in the curriculum of American education. Four sources of theory on morality are described in figure 14-2.

242

Sources of Theory on Morality

	Traditional (Theistic)	Marxist (Historical)	Sociological (Scientific)	Individualist (Autonomous)
BASIC DEFINITION	Morality is doing what God requires one to do.	Morality is doing what history requires one to do in pursuit of the final end.	Morality is conforming to social mores.	Morality is doing what one thinks and feels one ought to do.
PRIMARY ASSUMPTION	God knows what is best for man and has revealed or will reveal this to him.	Within history is a "law" of progress that will lead to ultimate good.	Society knows what is best and reveals this to man.	Individuals progress by responding to their natural (physical & mental) capacities.
CONSEQUENCE	Acknowledge Deity	"Deify" History	"Deify" Society	"Deify" Individual

Figure 14-2

Spiritual Education

While traditional education in America included provisions to help children develop physically, mentally, and morally, the moral dimension of the curriculum has recently become an object of such intense controversy that it has been consciously avoided. Although nearly impossible to separate moral suppositions and their personal expression from the instructional process, there is confusion and dissent over how to do this in a pluralistic and democratic society. Moral education is one challenge that parents, teachers, and students are currently struggling to resolve. Spiritual education, however, is another aspect of learning; spiritual education extends beyond moral education and deserves a treatment of its own.

Sometimes in the preoccupation with subject matter, student needs, and the instructional process, parents and teachers may lose sight of the uniqueness associated with spiritual learning. A person may be gifted in teaching or acquire a significant ability to help others develop physical skills, conceive intellectual information, or comprehend moral precepts. When it comes to religious knowledge, however, an added dimension becomes necessary for a learner to appropriately enlarge his understanding. The Spirit of Christ is given to all men and assists them in learning and knowing (D&C 93:2). But Jesus taught that there was an aspect of understanding which was reserved to be delivered under the direction of a special instructor—the Holy Ghost (John 14:16-17, 26). No human teacher can fulfill this stewardship.

243

A Special Instructor—The Holy Ghost

The nature of subject matter associated with spiritual matters that reaches beyond the bubble combined with the uniqueness of human personality, requires a special instructor—one who is capable of teaching more accurately than mortal man, who understands the mystique of human personality and is capable of instructing without the limitations of imperfect language.[12]

This teacher doesn't serve everyone. He serves only those who prepare themselves, who qualify to be instructed by him through submitting to the principles and ordinances of the gospel of Jesus Christ. The instruction delivered by the Holy Ghost extends beyond our profane interests to spiritual matters, which men are not capable of teaching one another (D&C 76:116-117). This is an important precept for agency-oriented teachers who agree with the premises expressed in these pages. We must understand that our role is limited by the stewardship of the Holy Ghost.

Some who study spiritual knowledge may assume that because they receive spiritual enlightenment from the Holy Ghost on particular matters, they are authorized to control the spiritual instruction and mold the theological understanding of others. Those who have "been warned" (D&C 88:81) and those who have "desires to serve" (D&C 4:3). can witness to their own spiritual experiences as directed by the Spirit. But it is inappropriate for one person to impose his or her personal views on others or to unduly shape another person's thoughts and beliefs to conform to their own. Only those who hold ecclesiastical keys and proper stewardships are authorized to declare doctrines as they are directed by God. This context provides a proper check and balance system to prevent and correct abuses. We may share our beliefs when appropriate and as a witness, but we are not authorized nor is it our role to dictate the spiritual growth and development of another personality. The Holy Ghost is commissioned to govern in this domain.

244

Teachers have ample work in stimulating proper physical development, conveying accurate information, sharing moral precepts, and encouraging their students to prepare themselves to receive spiritual instruction from the Spirit by keeping the commandments and serving others. As teachers fulfill this role, they become instruments in the hands of the Lord; by the way they live they invite the Holy Ghost to perform his instructional and motivational role, regardless of the setting in which the teacher and student interact. Teachers need not assume responsibilities for instruction that lies outside their own stewardship and capabilities.

In his love, the Lord assigned a special teacher to tutor individually each of his children who comply with his ordinances. In this way we can learn at our own rate and in congruence with our personal experiences, strengths, and weaknesses. It is not for any mortal to presume arbitrarily to guide the spiritual instruction of any of his brothers or sisters. That the Holy Ghost provides spiritual understanding for one person doesn't mean that that sequence of understanding should become the pattern for anyone else. Complying with specific moral standards is a requisite to spiritual worthiness, but individualization is a characteristic of the spiritual knowledge that follows the ordinances.

An abundance of universally applicable standards in the moral realm exists to form the curriculum and challenge the teachers of any educational program. Among them are the Ten Commandments, temperance, patience, brotherly kindness, and charity. Adequate intellectual data—things both in heaven and in the earth, things which have been, things which are and things which must shortly come to pass, things at home and abroad related to nations, countries and kingdoms—also stand ready to be shared by teachers. We each need the Spirit to guide us in doing these things correctly. In fact, we should not attempt to do them without the Spirit (D&C 42:14-15). The effective fulfillment of these tasks forms the foundation upon which the Holy Ghost can build spiritual enlightenment in the lives of individuals. If we do our job effectively as parents and teachers, he will take care of his. Of this there should be no doubt. We should not infringe upon the stewardship of the Holy Ghost; our intent should be only to complement it.

245

Part III

Agency Education: In Principle And Practice

15

Organizing Yourself as a Student and a Teacher

Agency education is inseparably connected to the standards of expectation established by its participants. If God is to participate in the learning/teaching experience, his expectations must be considered as well as those of the teacher and learner. Aligning ourselves with divine expectations is liberating because they demand striving, sharing, and serving; they bring to the learning experience principles validated by the past, present, and future. Knowing and doing what is true makes us free.

Organizing and Preparing

To be effective, agency education requires organization and preparation. This organization and preparation begins with the *person*, extends to the *place*, and then to the *materials*.

Organizing ourselves. Bringing personal order, proper principles, and sensible priorities into our own lives is a first and most important step. When we are disorganized, living in violation of correct principles and without the benefit of priorities, we are not in position to learn or teach in the agency mode. Teachers who are unwilling or unable to give of themselves to their students, whose minds are primarily on other matters, who dislike what they are teaching, or whom they are teaching, and those who do not understand what they are teaching, are not organized as agency teachers. Students who do not attend class, who do assignments from some other course when they are in class, who fail to concentrate and participate while in class, who do not search out what the course offers to them personally, are not organized as agency students. Parents who do not see their children as their basic responsibility, who limit their role to providing food, shelter and clothing, who focus their interest, time and energy more on vocation and personal needs rather than on rearing their children are not organized as agency-style parents. Children who disengage themselves from family responsibilities, standards, and service functions, and who resist assuming personal responsibility to engage themselves with the family are not organized to profit from what the family has to offer. The same principles apply in a formal school.

Planning or envisioning what one intends to do is another important step toward getting ready to learn or teach. The individual who is organized well as a *person* is in the best position to organize a learning/teaching *place* and learning/teaching *materials*. However, it does not work as well the other way around; we are unlikely to succeed as an agency teacher or student if our primary focus is on organizing the place and materials, important as these may be. Teachers who spend a great deal of time preparing their room and gathering together teaching materials, for example, will still be lacking if they do not prepare themselves as well. Those who are living correct principles and pursuing proper priorities—doing the right things, at the right times, in the right places—are the individuals who are in the best position to prepare, plan, and envision the learning/teaching experience.

This chapter emphasizes the challenge to organize ourselves. Only brief treatment is given to the lesser but still important matters of organizing *places* and *materials,* or of *envisioning* and *preparing* specific learning/teaching tasks. A more extensive treatment of these items is left to others or another time. (One very useful exploration of these two areas is found in Boyd K. Packer's *Teach Ye Diligently,* Salt Lake City, Deseret Book Co., 1975.)

Purity: a Prerequisite to Learning

The Hebrew poet suggests that purity is the fundamental prerequisite to true learning—ordering one's life so as to be worthy to "stand in his holy place," having "clean hands, and a pure heart." He "who hath not lifted up his soul unto vanity, nor sworn deceitfully. He shall receive the blessing from the Lord" (Psalms 24:3-5). The person who has ordered his life in this manner is the one in the best position to learn the truth and to teach the truth in light on any subject. Obviously, it is possible to learn many things of this earth without being pure. And purity alone, devoid of effort, will not bring one to a knowledge of any truth—earthly or heavenly. Nonetheless, purity is the primary step if one wants to learn what can be learned and see it in its proper light. Impurity darkens the intellect; light is lost even when the truth remains. "Behold, here is the agency of man, and here is the condemnation of man; because that which was from the beginning is plainly manifest unto them, and they receive not the light. And every man whose spirit receiveth not the light is under condemnation" (D&C 93:31-32). Those who are impure resent this principle of learning; they strive to discount it by seeking after signs—by asking for demonstrable proof and offering contrary evidence.

Making Home a Center for Organizing Ourselves

In its finest sense, teaching probably is, as much as any vocation, a vocation of service. A cardinal requirement of the teaching role is that it be performed by a person who is free, able, and disposed to serve others. Similarly, learners who are free and are disposed to concentrate on the task at hand are the most likely to learn. The ability to step beyond our own needs and lose ourselves in meeting the needs of others is a significant prerequisite to continuing success as a teacher. The freedom to concentrate, the desire and ability to focus on the material or skill to be mastered, and the disposition to be receptive are vital to success as a student.

251

Everyone has needs, and these needs are often demanding. They can be disciplined, but they cannot be consistently ignored without effect on one's personality. People can meet their needs and have their needs met in orderly and appropriate settings. The primary setting in which we should satisfy our needs is the family. Here the optimum conditions can prevail for small groups of people to interact with others in mutual satisfaction. When conventional family circumstances associated with marriage do not prevail, a single person can join a family or create a home with friends. This can be a place above reproach where domestic and personal tasks can be properly addressed. It is not good for man, woman, or child to be alone.

Difficulties often arise when individuals look beyond these kinds of home settings to satisfy their basic needs. For example, when teachers use relationships with students primarily as an arena in which to satisfy their personal needs, they twist education to serve the teacher rather than the students. When teachers develop fulfilling and satisfying relationships at home with companions, children, or roommates, they are more free to serve others when they leave the home. Individuals who do not have this type of order in their personal lives lack a vital type of organization. Even though they may have organized the *place* and the *materials* they use in their teaching, this lack of *personal* organization appears as they teach others. Students who lack the support of a sustaining home environment are likewise handicapped in their role as learners. The support system does not have to be ideal, but it does need to exist , and the more nurturant, the better.

Stewardship

Another dimension of personal organization is stewardship—the bestowed opportunity to manage our lives and legitimate responsibilities with proper regard for the rights of others. It involves power, authority, and relationships. Sensing and honoring our own stewardships and those of others are an important aspect of organizing ourselves. Clear understanding and acceptance of our roles and our stewardships contributes to personal organization. It gives strength and resilience to our lives. For example, to the married teacher the principle of stewardship begins with self and extends to one's spouse and to children within the family. Fulfillment within these relationships helps form the foundation that supports and sustains the extension of stewardship beyond the home. For unmarried teachers, stewardship is founded in the relationships that exist between self, family, and other significant persons who share the domestic setting. For children who are students, stewardship is feeling a sense of identity and location; it involves responding to opportunities and fulfilling responsibilities that contribute to the support and fulfillment of that identity. Individuals who violate or leave unfulfilled their primary stewardships diminish their ability to learn or teach in an agency framework.

Stewardship in marriage requires that each partner teach and serve the other in a giving and receiving companionship. Comfort, security, solace, and fulfillment are created as sharing occurs between a husband and wife and their children in a spirit of unity. Within this context can be found a refuge for regeneration and a refueling of the soul for greater service, concentration, satisfaction, and consolation in suffering. Failure or disruption of this contextual support system inhibits agency education. The way we live shapes the way we teach and learn; that is unavoidable.

The Marriage Relationship: A Case in Point

When a man and woman first meet and marry, they bring with them a relatively undeveloped personality floor plan. The initial relationship reflects only a partial sharing of these rooms and plans for rooms in the floor plan of their personalities. The shortsighted and selfish nature of some marriage philosophies causes individuals to make only a one- or two-room apartment available. As soon as the excitement and curiosity of becoming acquainted in this apartment passes, the individuals become bored. Wandering about in search of the excitement of new, unfamiliar rooms of some new personality, such apartment hunters find that the result is the same. Individuals find themselves moving from one small apartment to another and then another, and so forth, in a vain quest for happiness and excitement. They have about the same experience over and over again with different partners. They live in one room, usually the bedroom, of several different partners, rather than in many rooms with one partner.

253

There is a much better way to organize ourselves for learning and teaching. If individuals are willing to make the sacrifice associated with serving and sharing, with planning and building, it is possible for a couple to construct a mansion of their own that has all the variety, comfort, and excitement necessary for full and complete joy. When we truly seek for and accept invitations, we can have the privilege of visiting and enjoying with each other many previously unexplored and undeveloped rooms. And we can plan and then create together additions that complement and fulfill our marital mansion.

This vision of marriage needs to be taught to our youth. It is best taught to them in their own home, but it can be substantially reinforced by teachers who themselves live in mansions of their own. Teachers who live in the mansions of the soul are the finest teachers. They are the teachers who can lead, guide, and direct into happiness those they are privileged to instruct. They are the teachers who strengthen and inspire individuals and consequently lift communities to higher levels of righteousness. They build a better world. We need more of these teachers.

The Vitality of Integrity

The power of integrity, the strength that comes with correct alignment, will be built into the teacher's performance as a proficiency in sharing and applying teaching and leadership talents at home increases. Like an automobile out of alignment, we too drift off the road when we lack alignment. Teachers will benefit professionally as well as domestically if they conscientiously see that their families are the primary beneficiaries of their natural and acquired talents. Too often, one sees instances in which a teacher's skills are not adequately shared with his or her own family. Like the plumber's wife who suffers through life with leaky faucets or the carpenter's wife who never gets her cabinet built, teachers' families sometimes fail to benefit from a father's or a mother's gifts and talents. It is in the primary relationships of the family that the individual is basically obligated to apply his or her talents. The home is a great laboratory. It has nice checks and balances and incredible safeguards. Sometimes professionalism may take a person's eye off the mark. The greatest growth in teaching proficiency will come to those who willingly and diligently practice their skills in their own home.

254

What is Leadership?

Effective leadership in education requires order, vision, and understanding (D&C 107:99-100). An executive is not necessarily a leader. One can execute, or put things into effect, without creating order, vision, and understanding. Effective leadership requires communication that teaches (Exodus 18:20). Without successful teaching there can be no successful delegation. Without delegation there can be no extension of leadership. Lasting leadership is the result of effectively communicated instruction.

Effective leader relationships require power and authority (D&C 132:20). This authority is manifest in three forms: the power of a personality, the influence of an office, and the support of an organization. Leadership is the result of effectively combining these three resources for some purpose. The home is the most ideal and effective setting in which to develop and practice leadership. It is in the home that personality, office, and organization can be most clearly and completely unified. A man can preside no more effectively and safely over others than he can preside in his own home. A woman can lead and influence others no more effectively and safely than she can govern in her own family. Integrity is the seal of success in these important matters. Individuals may find temporary influence and achievements without this integrity, but time has a way of laying bare the character of the human soul. Truth is hard to hide. The home is a model training ground for those attributes which contribute to effective agency education.

For example, a man can improve his ability to communicate by communicating with his wife and children. A father's communication with his family will improve as he (a) becomes more orderly in his relationships with them (i.e., doing what he ought to do when he ought to be doing it); (b) identifies goals and directions (i.e, develops with other family members a shared vision of where they are going as a family); (c) exercises understanding (i.e., responds to the needs of others as these are discerned or made manifest).

And proper delegation can be learned in the family. The head of the household will learn to delegate (share power and responsibility) as other family members are authorized and taught to do the things that need to be done in order to achieve the goals the family has set. A secret to successful and effective professional performance is to practice successful and effective principles in our own home. This prepares and preserves the power of integrity in our performance. Brigham Young expressed this principle in these words:

255

> A man should, in the first place preside over himself, his passions, his person, and bring himself into subjection to the law of God; then preside over his children and his wife in righteousness; then he will be capable of presiding over a branch of the Church. But many Elders are contending about presiding over churches, when they are not capable of presiding over themselves or the least child they have.[1]

Homes whose parents lack integrity are vulnerable to the enemies of family fidelity. Schools staffed by educators lacking integrity are vulnerable to the enemies of education. A society whose homes and schools are at risk is a society in jeopardy. Material resources and financial affluence are no defence when a lack of integrity attacks the human enterprise.

Standards of Expectation

Standards of expectation are another dimension of organizing ourselves in learning and teaching. Discipline, for instance, is an important key to personal and instructional organization. Discipline is primarily rooted in expectations. To illustrate, consider children who come from homes where parents command little in the way of respect and order. Imagine these children confronting a teacher who expects more than is required of them at home. Such children become restless and resentful under these circumstances. When the pressure builds and confrontation occurs, it is difficult to resolve problems in a positive way. Teachers who are viewed negatively are unlikely to find much support when they seek parental help. The level of our expectations sets the performance tone; when the home and the school disagree on expectations, difficulties arise.

In contrast, some children come from homes where equal or higher standards of conduct are expected than their teacher requires. In this circumstance, serious discipline problems are much less likely to occur. And when they do occur, they are more easily resolved without the children taking serious offense. If parent reinforcement is needed to correct a problem, it is usually available and effective. The standards of expectation existing in the individual and in the home, then, are a reflection of how well we have organized ourselves for the learning/teaching experience. Where this principle is not followed, optimum education cannot endure. *Agency education is inseparably connected to the standards of expectation established by its participants.* The results are related to the way we organize ourselves. People who are mutually interested in the learning/teaching process and whose stewardships overlap will do well to discuss consciously these implications with each other.

The House as a Teaching Tool

To some extent, the physical structure of the house in which one builds a home either contributes to or detracts from the quality of family life—of educational pursuits. Parents can use the house as a means to express a home-centered philosophy to their children. Joseph F. Smith observed that the nature of the physical structures selected by a people for their residences influences their entire life-style:

There is no substitute for the home. Its foundation is as ancient as the world, and its mission has been ordained of God from the earliest times. From Abraham sprang two ancient races represented in Isaac and Ishmael. The one built stable homes, and prized its land as a divine inheritance. The other became children of the desert, and as restless as its ever-shifting sands upon which their tents were pitched. From that day to the present, the home has been the chief characteristic of superior over inferior nations. The home then is more than a habitation, it is an institution, which stands for stability and love in individuals as well as in nations.[2]

Certainly the physical structure alone is not the determining factor in establishing a stable home. Extravagant and ostentatious structures can be not only immoral in themselves, they can become centers of pride and debauchery, and abuse all that is sacred about the family. Humble homes that represent the best that honest labor and personal circumstances will allow can be domestic castles that   257
will improve from generation to generation. But over time our intentions will manifest themselves in the way we house ourselves. And this intent will shape our education.

It has been observed that some houses and neighborhoods are designed and constructed as if no one were going to have any children. Likewise, some parents pursue their goals and select habitations with little regard for what this means to rearing children, who will in turn become parents. And children tend to perpetuate the patterns to which they are exposed. True, many of us live in a mobile society, and our occupational choices influence where we live. But this does not alter the fact that moral education occurs best in circumstances that contribute to rather than detract from strong family-centered homes. And moral education is the foundation for all other education. Education devoid of morality is dangerous and leads to social and personal disorders.

A popular study in the United States a few years ago typifies the evidence that we must live with the consequences of our decisions.[3] This study suggested that much of the moral decline in our society is a natural consequence of the "sense of rootlessness" created by the mobility of its families. When one considers that the average individual may move fourteen times during during his life and that one-fifth of all U.S. families (at that time) moved one or more times every year, it is understandable that this stress of relocation makes vulnerable the moral stability of the nation. It disconnects the family from community and extended family that serve to sustain values frequently lost in isolation.

In 1903 Joseph F. Smith gave council regarding the uprooting of families:

> The disposition among the Saints to be moving about ought to be discouraged. If communities must swarm let the young go, and let the old homes be transmitted from generation to generation, and let the home be erected with the thought that it is to be a family abiding place from one generation to another, that it is to be a monument to its founder and an inheritance of all that is sacred and dear in home life. Let it be the Mecca to which an ever-increasing posterity may make its pilgrimage. The home, a stable and pure home, is the highest guaranty of social stability and permanence in government. . . .

> A Latter-day Saint who has no ambition to establish a home and give it permanency has not a full conception of a sacred duty the Gospel imposes upon him. It may be necessary at times to change our abode; but a change should never be made for light or trivial reasons, nor to satisfy a restless spirit. Whenever homes are built the thought of permanency should always be present. Many of the Saints live in parts of the country that are less productive than others, that possess few natural attractions, yet they cherish their homes and their surroundings, and the more substantial men and women of such communities are the last to abandon them. There is no substitute in wealth or in ambition for the home. Its influence is a prime necessity for man's happiness and well-being.[4]

Times change and circumstances vary, but the principle remains the same, even though it may grate against a generation caught up in mobility. Our motives for moving from place to place are sometimes frivolous rather than wise.

The physical structure of the house itself influences the behavior that takes place therein, as many real estate agents attest. Lack of storage space and overcrowding contribute to clutter and confusion in the home. The utilization of space and the openness in design can either encourage or eliminate privacy. The designated use of space in relation to traffic patterns in the home can affect the housework, convenience, and a mother's feeling of control. Design and decor set a tone that either helps or hinders the parents in their educational endeavors with the family. Boyd K. Packer expressed similar thoughts in these words to university students:

> Now another word on this home. You can do a great deal to create in your home an atmosphere of peace and homeyness and reverence and tranqulitity and security. You can do this without much to live on.
>
> Or you can create something angular and cold and psychedelic and artificial. In a thousand different ways your youngsters will be influenced by the choice you make. You can set the tone. It can be quiet and peaceful where quiet and powerful strength can grow, or it can be bold and loud and turn the mainspring of tension a bit tighter in the little children as they are growing up, until at last, that mainspring breaks.[5]

259

The house we choose to live in influences the kind of home we will create. While what we are is more vital than how rich we are, we must recognize that we ought to do all we can to shape the environment to serve our needs. We have been charged to do this; it is our dominion. Many homes are less than they might be if the parents consciously used the physical environment to their advantage. Some may be overly elaborate, others lacking because resources were used elsewhere. Expenditures for housing must be made; and if we consciously make those expenditures to help us educate our children, we will find not only satisfaction, but an increasing sense of success. To create a worthy home is a challenge to both rich and poor.

The Lord has counseled the fathers of families to do their utmost to improve the comfort, convenience, and well-being of their families. We live in a time where many opportunities to do so are available to numerous parents. We need to recognize our opportunities and act upon them. We also need to educate youth to pursue the same goal when they marry and have families of their own. Insufficient effort is being extended toward this end. Much more could be done. A popular philosophy entices us in the opposite direction: the modern trend is to question traditional marriage commitments, limit the number of children in a family to one or two, become entertainment oriented, and seek personal gratifications beyond the home. Agency education runs counter to this contemporary style of life.

The purpose one feels a house should serve largely determines what is done with that house. If a house is merely a protection from the elements and place to eat and sleep, it will probably be quite different from one that is considered a place to entertain friends and demonstrate material success in life. If the vision a house is meant to fulfill is that of rearing a family with character, a disposition to serve others, and a potential for eternal success, the house will undoubtedly have some unique characteristics otherwise not considered important. Such a house will provide for an apprenticeship in the skills and attitudes necessary for success as future fathers and mothers.

260 Transforming Lifestyle into an Educational Resource

Every teacher who stands before a class reveals two preparations. The most obvious pertains to the course material—the subject matter and its aquisition by specific students. Good teachers give attention to lesson planning, supplemental materials, personal experiences, student characteristics, sequencing ideas, involvement techniques, etc. But another preparation that is more important transforms the teacher's personal commitment to the subject matter into values that are communicated to the student. This is the preparation that transposes the teacher's way of life into a philosophy of education, one that is felt by those with whom the teacher interacts.

Most of us are deadline conscious. We fulfill responsibilities according to deadlines that are imposed; we usually do those things first which must be done by a certain time. For example, the pressures created by the classroom to deal with students and lesson materials on a day-to-day or week-to-week basis often veils the tremendous importance of this other preparation. Similarly, parents in the home face pressures of providing food, shelter, and clothing. Domestic tasks are demanding. Self-organization and analysis have few if any deadlines in most educational programs, whether they be formal or informal. Consequently, these aspects of growth are very easy to neglect. Further, the pressures of the classroom or the home draw the teacher and parents into immediate tasks and overt coping strategies. The tragedy of this situation is that success in teaching is very shallow when the organization of self is inadequate. In fact, a teacher with excellent academic training, clever techniques, and flawless presentation may well become as "sounding brass." Rhetorically the teacher may roll on and on, but the true value, the lasting influence on the student, will be meager indeed. Likewise, parents who run board and room type homes characterized by sink and drainboard meals are unlikely to be effective agency educators.

A fundamental task of the teacher, then, is to reckon with this additional responsibility of preparation: Teachers must place it firmly in the light of consciousness from week to week, just as they study subject material and consider instructional methods; this preparation of self generates the teacher's greatest powers—the powers of attentive communication, consistent discipline, inspiration, vision, acceptance, and creative attention. Students and children are blessed when they live and learn within the influence of such preparation.

261

It would be presumptuous to propose that the solution of this problem could be communicated, package-like, to prospective teachers. As in many realms of life, the process is personal; it cannot be specified in detail. It cannot be transmitted by a prescription, since no prescription for it exists. Like the skills of artisans that are passed on from master to apprentice, success in this instance comes only through individual efforts of repetitious practice—through diligence and dedication.

But what must be practiced? How can we deal with something so abstract? These are justifiable questions with less than satisfactory, explicit answers. But the following suggestions can lead to personal insights of immeasurable value.

Getting in Touch

First, teachers and students need to feel a connection to the past and to the future if there is to be a dynamic and effective projection into the present. The personality that projects itself best is the personality that is most acutely aware of and in tune with life's purposes. A person with such a personality possesses a vitality that influences all with whom he or she comes in contact. To live in a rut is to quell a teacher's power and foster a stagnation that depresses rather than invigorates students. Like any good reporter, teachers must be in touch with the world if they expect to interpret it to others. A certain wholeness, a balance, must be sought. Narrowness is not and never has been conducive to effective human relations. Genuine education is liberating because it frees the student of provincial restraints, modes, or fashions; it puts each person in touch with principles that are validated by the past, present, and future. Even Jesus could have taught his disciples more had they not been so in bondage to the false traditions of the culture in which they lived.[6]

Second, it is helpful for teachers to engage in healthy self-evaluation or introspection. For example, we can ask ourselves (1) As a teacher, why do I think the way I think? (2) As a teacher, why do I feel the way I feel? (3) As a teacher, why do I do the things I do? And then we can muster the courage to discuss our answers to these questions with others. To achieve confidence, one must become familiar and then comfortable with the world within as well as the world without. The inner world must be in order if the full powers of the personality are to be developed (D&C 121:34-46). A continuous personal inventory of this type is a must for those who would be teachers in more than title. To know ourselves is a vital step toward knowing others; this is the pathway that leads to love and life eternal. We must become so familiar with ourselves that we cease to let anonymous circumstances dictate the direction of our development and begin to exercise the powers within ourselves to purposefully and consciously create the circumstances of our lives. This power of personal navigation is one of the fruits of divinely directed self-evaluation.

Third, the teacher should be an avid student of human activity. To teach, one must cultivate the attribute of empathy, sensing what others are feeling and recognizing how this influences what they do. A significant degree of sensitivity is essential in understanding and communicating with others. It is a vital element in effective communication. Listening is one thing, but being sensitive to thought and affect is quite another. The empathetic teacher can often discern the student's commitment to her teachings; she can reveal her own commitment to them as well.

Fourth, the teacher needs to engage in activities that will strengthen his or her faith in the value of personal existence. The life of the teacher needs to be filled with positive purpose. The unknown must be repeatedly encountered and explored in a healthy, successful manner. To continually probe this shore of wonder, despite the dangers, is an integral part of progression. It is an expression of personal faith. Without this foundation of personal faith, derived from knowing that he or she is a child of God, the teacher is unlikely to possess the confidence necessary to become a pillar upon which students can lean as they struggle through their conflicts. The teacher who emanates security, exemplifies that life is worth living and shows that what he is teaching matters is a powerful influence. Students respond to this type of preparation.

This other preparation demands more time and more consistent effort than the weekly or daily lesson. It also demands seeking and yielding to powers beyond the self. "And the Spirit shall be given unto you by the prayer of faith; and if ye receive not the Spirit ye shall not teach" (D&C 42:14). If one is seeking the answers, she is on the right road. Success lies in this direction. In contrast, the teacher who thinks she has found all the answers is flirting with failure. Humility is essential to enduring and meaningful education. It is a lubricant that smooths the instructional interaction between teachers and students.

The Student, the Peer Group, and the Family

If any one finding in research on human development stands out from all the rest, it is this: The home, the family as a primary group, exerts the greatest single source of influence on the development and moral growth of a child. The consensus is that no other earthly source of influence is as significant in shaping the child as is the family. Secondary groups, such as those in the church, school, and community, may exert significant influences, but they are seldom as powerful and controlling as is the family. The institution of the family must be recognized as a most basic educational force. If a general change in human perspective or character is to occur, the home is likely to be the key element in initiating and maintaining that change.

As the influence of the extended family has declined and the nuclear family weakened, the power of the adolescent and young adult peer group has increased. Social circumstances created by a nonagrarian, highly mobile, urban-centered society have given

263

undue power to youth peer groups. Large public schools, abundant leisure, economic affluence, and technological mobility have combined to create a power in youth peer groups that has in many ways made them an enemy to the family and its primary purposes. These conditions are a challenge to students as well as to parents and teachers. The student is in the best place to confront the negative influences and make decisions that will be in his or her best interest. This simply means that *organizing ourselves as students in preparation for learning means resisting the negative power of our peer groups.* Agency-oriented students will rise to this challenge. The alternative is to become a social prisoner to the peer group.

With the destructive erosion of the conventional family and the decline in family control over youth activities, a destructive liberality has been born. This condition is being steadily reinforced by the legislative mood in most democratic societies. The trend is to grant more and more license to children and youth, both formally and informally. One of the great educational needs is for peer group power to be brought back into balance; the nuclear and extended families must exert greater supportive, protecting influences upon the youth. Wise students will seek and honor these positive family influences rather than reject or rebel against them. Relinquishing one's independence in favor of peer group acceptance can, in effect, be committing educational suicide. Agency oriented students will muster the courage to stand apart from the peer group. Parents can help by establishing and maintaining family environments that entice students to choose family values over peer group values when they face the choice between the two. Too often, today's students do not have a choice because the family fails to offer a positive alternative to the peer group. Too many of our youth are sacrificed to this form of adult negligence.

Preparing a Place

Once a teacher is settled in his efforts to organize himself, he then needs to prepare a place in which to teach. This educational admonition pertains as much to the idea being taught as it does to the physical location—the facilities in which the teaching is to occur. The New Testament offers ample illustrations of this process.

When Jesus taught he frequently "prepared a place" by perceptively utilizing the setting he shared with those whom he taught. He framed his ideas in the natural, real-life experiences of his students. It may be helpful to have a classroom, chalk, and a chalkboard, but preparing a place goes beyond providing these educational amenities. Often Jesus prepared a place to teach by drawing upon the memories of his students. He would ask them to consider the lilies of the field or the traveler who was assaulted by thieves. Then within those frameworks of memory he presented his lesson.

Jesus helped one young man face a real choice of giving up his temporal wealth and becoming a true disciple or forfeiting his place in the kingdom. He helped a woman at the well admit to herself the incongruence of living out of wedlock. He prepared Peter to receive instruction by contrasting two experiences: fishing all night and catching nothing, then feeling the joy of a full net. For the most part Jesus used the natural context of his listeners to get their attention and focus their interest. Arithmetic can be taught by measuring cardboard boxes, social studies can be conducted on the playground, reading can be practiced with signs along the highway, and science can be pursued in a kitchen. The key to *preparing a place* is being able to understand the connection between the idea being taught and the *context* in which the instruction occurs.

265

Preparing Materials

Teachers who inspire come in many and varied patterns, but they share a magnetism which links itself with the motivation of their students. This magnetism transcends personality and propagates interest in the most unlikely students. A significant aspect of this magnetism seems to be related to the way such teachers prepare the materials they teach. There is a freshness in their instruction because it is relevant and vital.

In many ways the effective preparation of instructional materials is comparable to the modern, efficient, and wisely operated grocery store. In such a store the shelves are well stocked. There is a variety of well-displayed and delectable items to meet not only the ordinary customer's needs, but also the wants of the most enterprising gourmet. The successful grocer interests his customers in purchasing items they had not originally intended to buy. He does this by arranging his merchandise in an attractive and palatable manner, by asking fair prices, and by occasionally offering bargains "too good" to pass up.

Similarly, the inspiring teacher is well stocked and supplied with ideas that induce students to seek and enjoy rather than to merely endure the learning experience. Like grocers, teachers too must possess, display, and distribute their "goods." They must display and distribute them at the right time and in the proper places, amounts, and combinations. Just how this is done should be determined to some extent by the customers involved. The better grocers know their customers, the more effective they will be in serving them. Likewise, the better teachers know their students, the more effective they will be in meeting their student's needs and guiding them toward success.

Of all the points that could be considered at length in this simple analogy, one is particularly vital because it is so often neglected. This is handling the perishable product. Grocers spend considerable time, money, and effort to procure and meticulously care for great amounts of perishable produce. These items contain nourishment not available in other stocked goods. These items can be kept in marketable form for only a few days. After this, they become unappetizing or useless and must be replaced. This operation is often expensive and discouraging. When the difficulties of procuring and handling perishable products become too cumbersome, some grocers cut down or cease to stock such items altogether. When this happens customers soon notice the difference and go elsewhere to trade. A slothful grocer who chooses a poor quality of perishable produce or lets it spoil through neglect soon loses his customers.

The grocery store situation is very applicable to teaching. True, a teacher needs the dry goods, the staples of life, the seasonings, and so forth, but in order to be truly successful he also needs the perishable product. He needs to provide that timely, pertinent information that is a meaningful part of the student's interest and experience at the moment, not just past history in isolation or unfulfilled prophecy. Too often the difficulties connected with continually procuring and constantly caring for this perishable product become tiresome and discouraging. It seems like an extra mile. When this happens some teachers cease to stock the perishable items of current events. The "customers" soon notice the difference and would much prefer "shopping" elsewhere. But this freedom and the opportunity to go elsewhere are not always a possibility. Therefore, students remain in a captive state under a teacher who lacks a supply of the nourishment they need. A case of educational rickets may result. Students continue to come to class out of loyalty or law, enduring but not enjoying, coming in spite of and not because of the teacher's offerings. Yes, students have a responsibility to contribute, to bring something to class, but it is with the teacher that the opportunity and the responsibility reside to vitalize their classroom experience. This cannot be successfully accomplished if the teacher ignores the perishable product.

For learning to be stimulating and meaningful, it must be integrated with past knowledge. The past and the future are bursting with value, but they are most meaningful to the majority of students when they are integrated with the here and now. A dynamic and effective projection of the past and the future into the present is essential to good teaching. This process involves feelings, and feelings live in the present. One feels the past and the future through the present. Herein lies the value of the perishable product. It is the means whereby a teacher can link the past and the future, the concrete and the abstract, with life at the moment.

Each course in the curriculum needs to have balance, just as each individual needs a balanced diet. The difficulty is that the perishable product, the uncanned fruits and vegetables of the instructional diet, cannot be included in a printed outline—in the textbook—because they become dated and are like wilted lettuce or overripe bananas. In this condition they are unappetizing or unpalatable. Consequently, every printed outline lacks an essential component of effective instruction. It lacks the perishable product—the items that are marketable for only a few days. It is the teacher's opportunity and responsibility to obtain a supply of these items, to prepare them, and to integrate them into the subject being studied.

Striving, Sharing, and Serving

Watching the learning/teaching function in action clearly reveals three distinct qualities. Whenever good things occur in education, these qualities are apparent. *First*, there is a striving, an exertion of energy and focused effort. To obtain knowledge and the wisdom to sustain it, there must be a searching, seeing, and sifting. This striving is stimulating, electric, and invigorating. *Second*, the ownership of knowledge and wisdom is bestowed primarily, if not exclusively, on those who are willing to share what they discover. Teachers know that the more they share what they strive to acquire the more it becomes a part of them, and the more they own it. Students who truly thirst for understanding will best quench that thirst by using every opportunity to teach others what they are learning. Only by preparing knowledge so it can be given away do we come to fully appreciate it. We master what is rightfully ours, and we receive clear title to knowledge as we labor to share it with others. *Third*, without the goal of service, all our efforts to fill the reservoirs of the intellect are destined to create only stagnated pools. Like a lake without an outlet, the contents of our learning will turn to brine and be incapable of sustaining a full range of life. What comes in must be free to go out, or it will become contaminated and self-sterilizing. Service is like a purifying agent that renews and legitimizes the process of learning, knowing, and growing.

268

Agency education is sustained by these three elements. No educational enterprise can long endure, no educational endeavor can be fully effective, without *striving, sharing*, and *serving*. It is a pedagogical prophecy that is vindicated by every form of man's instructional experience. Agency educators should embrace these values and make them central to their efforts to learn and teach.

16

Counseling, Self-Image, and Creativity

Counseling, good or bad, is based on the counselors we invite into the intimacy of our lives and the privileges we grant them.

The light that shines upon our image cannot be lasting if it is self-generated. We deceive ourselves when we substitute a focus on self in the place of service to others.

Creativity is not mystical, it is simply organizing existing elements for some purpose. We are all supremely capable of some ordinary and extra-ordinary activity. We are all gifted; creativity is not a trait limited to a few special, gifted and talented people.

Counseling

People have always depended on each other for support, advice, reflection, and the release of feelings. Parents and teachers play a major role in this process. They are counselors. Their advice is sought and provided. For some people, this traditional counseling function has become confused as modern society has emphasized specialization and the certification of professional counselors. During the past half century counseling has been formalized and set in place as a vocational position. The new profession seeks to apply and coordinate medical, psychological, educational, and psychiatric techniques. Depending on the theory underlying the procedures, the objective ranges from helping individuals adjust to the social environment, to helping them develop into "fully functioning," "self-actualized" persons. There is growing acceptance of a trend that suggests: If you have a problem seek professional help. The status now given professional counseling and the volume of literature associated with it can be confusing.

Sometimes parents and teachers are intimidated by this highly visible professional presence. Just as professional theories of child rearing earlier this century resulted in many parents looking to experts for values that were subsequently repudiated, people can become overly dependent on counseling specialists. Agency-oriented persons should be wary of redefining their roles to conform to the shape of aggressively marketed professional services. Some expertise in professional counseling can be very helpful, but many ideas and values are inconsistent with agency education. Parental and teacher responsibilities should not be abandoned just because problems exist. Care must be exercised in seeking professional services so that good rather than harm results. Professional credentials do not guarantee that correct principles and values will be applied.

There are a number of counseling theories. Professionals market specialized help to others across a broad spectrum of behavior problems. Most counseling, though, focuses on educational difficulties, vocational guidance, and personal adjustment (e.g., marriage counseling). As the professional counselor has gained public acceptance and legal endorsement, many parents and teachers have questioned their own role and competence in responding to individual needs. Agency-oriented parents and teachers will seek to understand their relationship to the counseling function. Counseling can be helpful, but it may also generate false expectations and at times be harmful. The danger of becoming dependent on an emotional dole system is just as real as dependence on an economic dole system. Agency educators will work to avoid such dependencies.

Before recent specialization in the counseling function, parents played a major role in helping family members; also available was advice from ministers, medical doctors, lawyers, and teachers. The need for this traditional assistance to the individual has not diminished; the inclination to be satisfied with such sharing may be declining. There are those who champion the doctrine that the only safe course is to see a "professional." Nevertheless, lay people still need to give and receive counsel. It is part of the human enterprise. Agency-oriented parents and teachers should feel comfortable continuing to offer caring concern, a listening ear, and reminders to follow well-defined principles that foster happiness and joy. The salvation of society does not reside in professional services. The Lord and his appointed servants have given wise and proven counsel on most matters related to moral conduct and social service. Informed parents and teachers should feel free to share these teachings with those they serve. Legitimate counsel from professionals will conform to these revealed principles. Counsel that contradicts divinely revealed values should be avoided.

Basis of the Confusion

Modern psychology depends almost exclusively on the scientific method to establish its legitimacy. A popular assumption in the academic community is that spiritual or religious influences should not be acknowledged; they have no place in the traditional framework of the scientific method. This assumption is unacceptable to those who favor the agency position. God can and does intervene in the affairs of his children. Prayer, revelation, fasting, faith, and sacrifice can and do call down the powers of heaven in behalf of man. No counseling that ignores or denies these powers is complete. It may be helpful, but it may also be harmful.

271

Believers in the spiritual dimension that natural science ignores or denies are often considered psychological misfits or are classified as patients. It is understandable that naturalists would find religious phenomena confusing. First, religiosity has its origins in a dimension that naturalists do not believe exists. Second, understanding and explaining a condition is not a simple matter. Third, faulty religious traditions are guilty of condoning and administering numerous corrupting, destructive, and evil influences. There are good and bad spiritual influences; both can be manifest in our natural bodies and mental behaviors. Individuals are not simply good or bad; they are beings engaged in the process of choosing between good and evil, right and wrong, helpful and harmful. These conditions are frustrating to those whose perception is limited to only what they can see inside the bubble discussed in previous chapters. The frustration is compounded because (1) we often lack the understanding to correctly discern the patterns of these choices. (2) we may apply incorrect standards in determining what is right or wrong, helpful or harmful, good or evil.

These human limitations suggest that we should be very careful about whom we invite into the intimacy of our lives and what privileges we grant to them. Psychological counselors, like financial counselors, may increase our health and stability, or they may direct us into bankruptcy.

Some Guidelines for Agency Educators to Consider

1. An individual's privacy of thought and memory is a divinely bestowed right. The invasion of this domain by another person is a violation; entry by invitation is a sacred trust, a sobering responsibility.

2. Successful counseling is primarily instructional. The person seeking help receives help as he learns correct solutions to the problems he faces. Counselors who help clients find correct solutions are helpful; those who don't are not. There are many ways to help others seek and find solutions to the challenges they encounter.

3. As a seeker of counsel I can initially follow a scriptural pattern: Become worthy and receptive by repentance, willingly accepting correct guidance and direction when it is offered. When clinical conditions are severe and the power of agency has been restricted by physical injury, drugs, or other debilitations, the help of a sensitive, safe, professional may be necessary and useful.

4. Counseling abuse can be prevented by obeying God's commandments, enthroning work in my life, providing for my personal needs, maintaining family members within my stewardship, tithing my increase, serving others, assisting those in need, accepting help after my personal resources are depleted—from family and then from the church or society—until I can become self-reliant again.

272

Interviews

A vital element in the counseling/teaching process is the interview. Successful interviews are based on principles and procedures that honor the individual being interviewed and dignify the role of the one conducting the interview. Many elements may be included in effective interviews. Five of the most vital are prayer, appreciation, love, sharing information, and listening. When any of these vital elements are missing, an interview will be less effective than it otherwise might have been.

Three dimensions of the successful interview can be defined as (1) a good experience, (2) an acceptable priority, and (3) a worthwhile result. *First*, the quality of the experience influences not only the interview itself, but later interactions between the participants. A good experience is composed of meeting needs, generating feelings of satisfaction and fulfillment, and avoiding feelings of inferiority or failure. *Second*, acceptable priorities refers to the degree of investment that both parties put into the experience. Personal investment determines values, values determine our priorities, and priorities regulate the quality of our performance. Differing priorities will influence the interview. For example, if I do not want to conduct an interview or if I do not want to be interviewed my disposition will influence the interview. *Third*, a worthwhile result is created when the individuals involved in the interview feel a sense of accomplishment, service, and recognition. Successful interviews consistently reflect these characteristics.

Interviews that fail to meet needs, but instead create feelings of inferiority or failure, are seldom satisfying or rewarding. Likwise, if the interview has a low priority for either of the participants, the reduced level of personal investment will lower the value of the interview. For example, what is important to a leader may not be important to a follower. Worthwhile results are rare under these circumstances, and there is little likelihood of participants leaving the experience with a feeling of accomplishment, service, or recognition. It is helpful to remind ourselves periodically of these fundamentals. The chart below may be used to "quick check" how we are doing in our interviews with others.

273

Analyzing and Evaluating an Interview

	Mark Yes or No	
	You	Other Person
1. A Good Experience		
2. An Acceptable Priority		
3. A Worthwhile Result		

fig. 16-1

Pursuing Self-Image vs. Preparing to Serve Others

Should self-image, self-love, positive mental attitude (PMA), etc., become an educational goal? This is another educational question closely related to the counseling function. The basic answer to this question for the agency educator is no, because healthy feelings about the self are by-products of other activities. They are not independent ends that can be sought after for their own sake.

Latter-day Saints and other Christians are tempted by today's pop psychology to substitute a *focus on self* in place of *service to others*. A great deal is said in contemporary psychological, and educational literature regarding self-concept, self-esteem, self-acceptance, self-love, and positive mental attitude. We are encouraged to seek these as ends in themselves. As noble as these pursuits sound, they can become a counterfeit for certain characteristics that contribute to true personal development and stability in the individual.

Preparing to serve others is a legitimate educational goal. To focus on one's self-image is dangerous because it threatens the development of humility. Scriptural counsel is clear on this matter. If men come unto God he will show them their weaknesses, that they may become humble. If they become humble, he will make them strong (Ether 12:27). Whosoever will save his life, must lose his life for the Savior's sake and the gospel (Mark 8:35-38). When we are in the service of our fellow beings we are in the service of our God (Mosiah 2:17). He that trusts in his own heart is a fool (Proverbs 28:26).

At some point in our lives we may lose confidence in ourselves. If we have built our house on our own image, we face a crisis. At this point we have two options: (A) exercise faith in something beyond self, or (B) sink into despair. The scriptures teach that trusting in one's "self" is not the answer, but that exercising faith in God is. Korihor and others like him attempted to follow the faithless path. The consequences are clearly described (see Alma 30:17, 60; D&C 1:15-16).

To be overly concerned about one's own image is to have an eye on something other than the glory of God. Sometimes people interpret Leviticus 19:18, "Thou shalt love thy neighbor as thyself," to justify seeking self-esteem. The context of this statement, however, clearly refers to not avenging or bearing grudges against others and to the Golden Rule (Matt. 7:12). This counsel was not intended to tell us what to think about ourselves. It is simply observing that people generally love themselves; therefore, we should love others at least that much, instead of judging or abusing them. (cf. Lev. 19:18 vs. John 13:34).

274

Consider the following counsel that suggests we are limited without God, and that it is by seeking divine help and following correct principles that we gain lasting feelings of worth. Saving our life is a matter of losing it in service to others (Mark 8:35). The focus for those who desire to succeed in the long run is to recognize our own nothingness and God's goodness (Mosiah 4:6-11). True growth comes as we develop an eye single to his glory (D&C 4:5). Here is the foundation of lasting self-esteem.

We must seek the image of God, not simply an image of self, no matter how positive that might be. It is the image of God, not our own image, that must be engraven upon our countenances (Alma 5:14, 19; Mosiah 4:5-12). We must seek a sense of confidence in God and a sense of our own nothingness in comparison to him (Moses 1:10-14; D&C 121:45-46). We are to love one another as Christ has loved us (John 13:34). Cosmetic creations are fleeting, they wash away in the vicissitudes of life. True character develops as we become like our creator.

In light of this, how do we develop good feelings about ourselves? Personal well-being and good mental health are simple matters. We must keep the commandments, learn to earn our keep by the sweat of our brow, and tend well the stewardships assigned to us. We can (1) develop a proper *self-identity*, so we know who and what we are capable of, and are consequently capable of many things, and (2) develop a sense of *self-worth*, so we feel worth something, because we are capable of doing something and doing it very well. We cannot feel worth something if we are unable to see ourselves as something. Those individuals who live moral lives live according to principles that protect others as well as self. Caring for ourselves and serving others produces positive feelings. These positive feelings result from developing personal skills and engaging in actions that enable us to care for ourselves, our families, and others. When this is done well, we do not need a substitute system. Seeking self-esteem as a goal in itself is like trying to catch the wind. Like sails on a boat, we may feel temporary success. But in the end the wind will mysteriously disappear, and we will end up floating on a sea of despair.

275

Creativity: A Choice Between Competing Definitions

Creativity is another dimension of learning and teaching of interest. Agency-oriented parents and teachers may perceive this topic differently than it is frequently portrayed in modern society. Like the emphasis on self-esteem, some of the perceptions related to creativity appear to be misplaced. The ability to create is an important and remarkable human capacity. It deserves to be handled in a beneficial manner for each individual, not for a selected few. We should be constructive rather than destructive in both our conception and use of this power. This is not always the case.

There is strong evidence that modern education and other aspects of the society stifle individual development by communicating a restricted and mystical view of creativity (mystical meaning obscure, baffling, or inexplicable). A great deal of the literature and far too many of our young people see creativity as a trait limited to a few special, gifted, and talented individuals. I do not believe this is true. We all are supremely capable of some ordinary and extraordinary activity. "Every man is given a gift[s] by the Spirit of God. . . . And all these gifts come from God, for the benefit of the children of God" (D&C 46:11,26). We are all gifted. Moroni exhorts us to "deny not the gifts of God, for they are many; and they come from the same God. And there are different ways that these gifts are administered; but it is the same God who worketh all in all; and they are given by the manifestations of the Spirit of God unto men, to profit them" (Moroni 10:8). Good creations, therefore, are manifestations of gifts (creative powers) that people have been given by God.

276

Some gifts, apparently, can be misapplied. Because of our agency we may use some talents with which we have been blessed for evil purposes. In addition, there are evil gifts. We have been admonished to "lay hold upon every good gift, and touch not the evil gift" (Moroni 10:30). Recognizing the difference between good and evil gifts and understanding the way to properly manifest our good gifts is important. "And the way to judge is as plain, that ye may know with a perfect knowledge, as the daylight is from the dark night, . . . every thing which inviteth to do good, and to persuade to believe in Christ, is sent forth by the power and gift of Christ; wherefore ye may know with a perfect knowledge it is of God" (Moroni 7:15-16). On the other hand, "whatsoever thing persuadeth men to do evil, and believe not in Christ, and deny him, and serve not God, then ye may know with a perfect knowledge it is of the devil . . . [The devil persuades] no man to do good, . . . neither do his angels; neither do they who subject themselves unto him." (Moroni 7:17) And "the spirit of Christ is given to every man, that he may know good from evil" (Moroni 7:16).

Our contemporary society seems to have rejected an older, more broadly defined view of creativity and replaced it with a narrow part of that older definition. More than a decade ago researchers announced that none of the theoretical accounts of creativity appeared to explain adequately its nature or provide for it to be measured.[1] Our understanding of this subject has increased little since then; clarity is scarce and confusion is abundant in most educational settings.

The Ancient Meaning of Create

The ancient definition of "creating" is illustrated by the Hebrew word *barah*, as used in Genesis 1:1: "In the beginning God *created* [barah] the heavens and the earth." This commonly meant he organized existing elements for some purpose.[2] Before the 20th century, creating was generally perceived as making; common descriptors included words like *ordinary, natural, common, widely practiced, expected,* and *easily understood.* "Creating" in this sense was expected of everyone. In fact, in those prespecialization eras, if one did not develop a fairly wide repertoire of creative responses, life quickly became less enjoyable and much more insecure. A loaf of bread, a basket, a tool, a shoe, whatever, was very much an individual creation. Skills to perform these creative acts were widely dispersed and carefully perpetuated. People who could not create their own products went without or with much less than those who could.

Man was considered the offspring of God—created in his image and likeness; he was to become like his Father in heaven.[3] And in the same manner that God created by organizing things out of existing elements for some purpose, so should man form his creations. Creativity was an inherent aspect of man's very nature. This view of creativity is very broad, and it is not restricted to the mystical. Jesus, the great teacher of Israel, voiced this philosophy in his statement: "The Son can do nothing of himself, but what he seeth the Father do" (John 5:19). Following some pattern toward a predetermined end was acceptable; it was not viewed as noncreative behavior, as it is in some modern textbooks. [4]

277

This ancient notion of creativity, viewed from man's perspective, did have a mystical dimension to it. Man's ways were not God's ways. He did not understand all that God understood. Abraham, Jacob, and Moses marvelled at the power and wisdom of God. They did not always understand his mighty works or the gifts that made these works possible; such were a mystery unless God provided explanations. But in their own human stewardship, these patriarchs were very comfortable learning to become like God. Creativity for the ancients was a continuum. Creating consisted of using their God-given talents to organize existing elements for proper purposes: planting and harvesting, building and preserving, singing and dancing, adoring and reverencing. Only that which God gave to them without explanation, which they could not comprehend, was mystical. More than mystique, creativity included a common application of human capacities (see figure 16-2).

278

Creativity Continuum

_____///////////////
(common)   (mystical)

figure 16-2

A New Definition Of Creativity

A modern perception of creativity has recently come to dominate both professional education and the arts. The new definition equates creativity with the unusual; common descriptors include words like *new, novel, strange, different, spontaneous,* or even *bizarre* products and actions. As J. C. Gowan et al. observed in 1967, "Creativity is a word which has recently been taken over by science from religion [and] it is almost impossible to discover it in a dictionary or encyclopedia more than a decade old. It is a new concept, recently attributed to the personality of man, and still fraught with some mystical connotations."[5]

This new definition of creativity tends to be elitest and mystical in nature. And for that reason agency educators will avoid perpetuating this narrow view of creativity. It restricts, even debilitates, the individual, and may add confusion and inefficient complexity to the educational enterprise.

Limitations of the New Definition

I became concerned about the definition of creativity several years ago while teaching courses on the subject to prospective teachers. Frequently I began the first class period by asking students to suggest words they considered to be descriptors or indicators of creativity. Consistently, the reported list was dominated by terms such as *new, unusual, unique, strange, different,* and *novel.* After reaching a tentative agreement on the definition of creativity, I would ask the students to indicate, by an uplifted hand, how many saw themselves as creative individuals. The response was always the same: only a few (usually 10 to 20 percent) of the twenty-five to thirty-five students would respond in the affirmative. They had been taught to see themselves as noncreative persons. The idea of doing something creative was intimidating, and their confidence was low.

This response pattern enticed me to reexamine the literature related to creativity; I found the exploration fascinating. Researchers did not agree on the approaches to the comprehension of creativity, nor did these theories explain adequately its nature or provide for its measurement.[6] The more carefully I examined the record, the more apparent the confusion became.[7] I found abundant clues to why students perceived creativity as a product rooted in some mystical "twilight zone." Titles like C. A. Morizot's *Just This Side of Madness* and D. W. Fritz's *Perspectives on Creativity and the Unconscious* clearly convey a message that creativity is not to be found in the ordinary or common. Rather, it is portrayed as some type of mystical power or force beyond the immediate management of the ordinary individual. Ghiselin expressed this view in his declaration that creativity "is not to be found by scrutiny of the conscious scene, because it is never there. . . . For only on the fringes of consciousness and in the deeper backgrounds into which they fade away is freedom attainable."[8]

279

D. N. Perkins, in a recently published study, openly acknowledges that creativity is commonly perceived as a mystery.[9] Refreshingly, his overall message in this provocative report veers away from the dominant definitions in creativity literature. In his view, creating should be viewed as the application of "commonplace resources of mind,"[10] which implies the potential for creativity is more readily accessible.

Unfortunately, Perkins straddles the fence when he tries to distinguish between the verb *to create* and the adjective *creative*. He joins many others in maintaining that the verb *to create* is too general and broad in its application to be useful in defining "creativity."[11] He argues that it is necessary to use the more restrictive adjective, *creative*, to denote creativity. The distinction is important only because the operational definitions he associates with the verb and the adjective are so different. This was not the case anciently. Since World War II, entire libraries of ancient documents have been discovered—in Syria, Palestine and Egypt. The content of this vast reservoir of writings makes it clear that the ancients perceived creativity quite differently than modern man does.[12]

Early Christian apologists labored to reconcile the ancient Hebrew world view with a form of Greek (Platonic) philosophy, which held that physical matter was evil; from this a doctrinal conflict arose, adding to the confusion. In the fourth century another squabble in theology was resolved by concluding that God created things *ex nihilo*, out of nothing.[13] America's shift from a sacred to a secular society between 1880 and 1920 also contributed to the new definition. The modern belief that all knowledge originates with man made it convenient to credit those individuals who generated the latest innovations as uniquely creative. The shift seems to have set the stage for and caused much of the confusion in contemporary educational thought.

Today the literature on creativity is full of assertions, such as "In the Old Testament man was not creative,"[14] or "The faithful formalist has no chance of creating anything."[15] Such arrogant statements can be understood only as one realizes how far the pendulum has swung toward the mystic definition. Isn't it a bit humorous to imagine a modern professor, employed as a consultant to the Egyptian engineers in charge of building the pyramids, mumbling something about those people not being creative?

In a way it seems ironic that a secular world would adopt a mystical foundation for one of its most admired phenomena. Yet the evidence abounds. Some writers freely acknowledge that the "popular stereotype sometimes confuses the creative genius with the emotionally disturbed."[16] Or as the editors of the *Colorado Symposium* of 1962 argued, "The study of creativity need not limit

280

itself to the eminent, the extraordinary; [nevertheless] if we include 'everyday creativity' in our study, we may be in danger of making our conception of it meaningless."[17]

This type of thinking only perpetuates the mystical stereotype. It seems to prevail in spite of counterthrusts, such as J. P. Guilford's position that creativity can be understood and explained, and similar research findings like those of Calvin Taylor and Paul Torrance. The entanglement of creative activity with the mystical has been solidly retained in the modern definition. Focus on the exceptional has been so alluring that it has obscured the true universal distribution of the ability to create and the diverse expression of creativity in the individual.

Educators, it seems, are better served by the ancient definition which holds that *creativity is simply the act of organizing existing elements for some purpose*—a definition largely ignored and sometimes ridiculed by contemporary society. This older definition, while including the ability to originate the new and different, emphasizes the value of developing skills and products that promote the ordinary, common, and widely practiced. The older view, properly perceived, is simply an extension of the basic curriculum. Accurately envisioned, the structure and function of the general curriculum constitute a vital and exciting approach to fostering creativity as a human resource. Children who learn math are developing *divergent thinking* skills; science teaches *convergent thinking*; social studies exercise the powers of objective evaluation; language and the expressive arts provide training in the use of *subjective evaluation*. These abilities are the instruments of creative action.

281

17

Applying Agency Principles in Non-Agency Systems

The greatest barrier to agency education is inadequate personal preparation, not system restrictions. A major threat to agency education, however, is the philosophy of encroachment on the rights of the believer exhibited by modern legal theory. Legal action based on the premise that the natural world is all that is real means the only admissable evidence, the only lawful function, is temporal. Those who believe in the reality of both a spiritual and a temporal world are legally disadvantaged. The potential consequences of such law are frightening because ultimately those who believe in both a natural and a supernatural world can be considered deluded or insane. They are considered off-track because they believe in things that legally do not exist. And what must be done with such people?

Agency Principles Can Be Used In Non-agency Systems

A major challenge for those who favor an agency approach to education is to maintain personal integrity as they pursue education in a non-agency oriented system—at home or school. Many different educational programs exist in homes and schools throughout the countries and cultures of the world. Since it is impractical to discuss the specific challenges of the agency-oriented person in each of these systems, this chapter will focus on the American public school system. Using this system as a model for comparison, this chapter gives suggestions to help people remain true to an agency orientation while legitimately participating in a non-agency educational system. Obviously, restrictions to agency education exist in many systems and these circumstances do curtail the degree of opportunity, satisfaction, and success available to students and teachers. But this seldom prevents the use of agency principles where they can apply. The point to remember is that inadequate personal preparation, not system restrictions, is the greatest barrier to agency education.

I have no ulterior motive for selecting the United States public school system to illustrate how agency ideas may work within non-agency systems. The public school system is simply a well defined operation with which most readers are familiar. Other home, church, and private school approaches to education present similar challenges to agency educators. Parents in the same family, for instance, often differ on how to rear and educate their children; seldom do they begin with the same views. Imperfect people, which we all are, generate imperfect approaches to education—regardless of our preferred theory. Most of us tend to teach the way we were taught. It is often difficult to disengage ourselves from the way we were educated, even if we later discover and attempt to practice a different approach. For those who want to change, it is important to recognize that conscious personal adjustments must be made. The United States public school system provides a base for comparing differences and identifying realms of freedom.

284

This chapter describes the U. S. public school system in terms of its general assumptions and then illustrates how an agency-oriented parent, teacher, or student might use the freedom within those assumptions to practice agency principles of learning and teaching. A similar path would be followed in seeking accommodation with any other system of education—large or small, formal or informal. Analyzing home or church programs of instruction is equally enlightening. Appealing as agency education is to many people, few systems seem prepared to actually practice its principles.

At some juncture in any of these mergers, different individuals may reach a point where personal commitments and system requirements become incompatible. Then a critical choice may be necessary. A teacher may decide it is necessary to say to a school district, "I cannot teach under these circumstances; the compromise is too great, too damaging, to my personal integrity." A parent may say, " I cannot, in good conscience, subject my child to this type of experience; I must seek an alternative." For many people, however, the tolerance and space for accommodation in most school systems is seldom fully utilized. It would generally make good sense to use the opportunities we already have before deciding to reject a system in its entirety. This is generally the case for the public schools and those who work in them. Agency oriented educators will generally find many opportunities to practice principles of agency education within the public school system. To begin with, at least, the major barriers to practicing agency education principles will be found in the individual more than in a particular school system.

Original Purposes of The Modern Public School

The United States of America is a pluralistic society, composed of many different peoples and creeds; the society operates on principles of participatory citizenship; most citizens enjoy broad legal rights and opportunities. Under these circumstances the nineteenth century decision to establish state-sponsored, tax-supported schools resulted in some ideological compromises. Religious and social preferences were often set aside in order to focus on acceptable curricular goals the community held in common. The public schools were originally formed to promote moral character related to good citizenship and provide basic education in literacy and skills related to a productive life in the society. These schools did not intend to assume responsibility for sectarian religious instruction. Such purposes do not conflict with the goals of agency educators. They can still be pursued by parents, teachers, and students in today's schools.

285

There are in public schooling, however, constraints as well as flexibility. For example, the public schools now function on the assumption that the supernatural is irrelevant to the primary purposes of the school. Schools also presume to mold individuals, through applying external influences as necessary, to fit the needs of society. Consistent with this notion are the ideas of mandatory school enrollment and compulsory attendance laws. Children must enroll in school and they must attend school; it is a law in our society. These premises establish the context and underlie the curriculum for public schooling in America. People may debate nuances of these premises and quibble over intentions, but the general application is so evident that it is beyond reasonable dispute. Applying some agency principles may be constrained by these factors.

Defining the stewardship of the public school—who, what, when, why, and how to teach—has been dynamic, clearly reflecting changing values in the country, including considerable confusion. A general observation is that the public approach to education tends to "level" in its operation. In other words, it functions to serve the majority, it focuses on the average. Minority needs and desires are often avoided because accommodation to all of these demands would destroy the system itself. Everyone cannot have everything they might want. On the other hand, in some settings it may be inappropriate to have something nearly everybody wants. Tension seems unavoidable.

Agency-oriented parents, teachers, and students, therefore, should not expect to find in this type of system what they might consider ideal learning/teaching conditions. Generally, however, they will find ample opportunity to practice many of the principles they feel are appropriate. For example, the public school system usually avoids dictating the type of worldview a person must believe; it does not require teachers to define students in a particular way; it seldom restricts how the teachers view themselves or the parents of those they teach. Textbooks and curriculum materials generally reflect an exclusively naturalistic bias, but most schools allow considerable freedom for teachers and students to explore other options related to our national heritage. This gives considerable lattitude to agency-oriented teachers who are willing to do their own homework. Public schools are also tolerant of a wide variety of educational philosophies and instructional theories. Agency educators who are willing to work within existing policies are likely to discover considerable freedom to practice many of the principles they believe.

Within the current rigidity of the public school structure, there is considerable room for the agency-oriented parent, teacher, and student to function in a positive way. It requires tolerance, patience, and understanding of others; but the opportunity is there. The degrees of freedom in any given school or district may vary, depending on the people who operate the system and the community in which it is situated, but generally speaking, there is room for reasonable if not generous accommodation. The public school system still offers more freedom than is often recognized or utilized. The very breadth of the system and the local nature of its administration preserves considerable flexibility in its function. Within this context, agency oriented educators can apply many desirable principles. The primary barrier is personal unpreparedness.

286

Preparing to Work Within the System

America has a heritage that originally endorsed numerous values complementary to agency education. Many early colonial beliefs, the founding documents of this nation, and the general principles espoused by most of its founders fit well within the philosophy of a responsible, self-directed, religiously oriented, divinely sustained journey into learning. The Mayflower Compact, Declaration of Independence, U. S. Constitution and Bill of Rights, and all of the state constitutions are rich resources for agency oriented educators. Changes briefly described in this chapter have altered some of the earlier views, but if a person desires to do so, it is still possible to reconstruct and make use of the American heritage. This will require individual initiative, because the complete story is no longer included in the curriculum. Adequate resources for understanding and utilizing this heritage are readily available for those who do their homework.

With reasonable effort, supplemental materials can be collected that will enhance family instruction and enrich most state-provided curriculum guides and textbooks. For example, simply using original materials to tell the story will demonstrate that early Americans believed in both a natural and a supernatural world. They acknowledged that God existed and taught that a person's conduct in this life was significant in terms of his or her life after death. William Bradford's *Of Plimmoth Plantation*, the story of America's taproot colony written by the man who governed her for nearly 40 years, reveals the original spirit and mission that sustained many of the early colonists.[1] Public polls indicate that most Americans still acknowledge this ancient dualistic worldview as their own and most state constitutions and statutes reflect it in their language. It is not illegal in American public schools to introduce students to the worldview of the founders and inform them of how this worldview was subsequently rejected, first in academic circles at the turn of twentieth century and later in legal thought and practice. Agency educators need to be informed.

287

Understanding the Legal Context

In order to avoid unnecessary problems and at the same time preserve and make use of existing freedom, it is important to understand the legal context in which one is operating. An examination of the evidence, for example, shows that the U.S.

Supreme Court has followed the lead of academia and changed its worldview. Consequently, between 1790 and 1943, the expressed judicial assumptions of the Court changed from vertical, theistic assumptions to horizontal, agnostic assumptions. Fundamental constitutional concepts regarding the nature of man and Deity, the relationship of state and federal constititutions and governments, as well as the nature and role of education in a free society changed. This major shift in premises is changing our social structure.The changes are well documented.[2] The main ideas can be summarized in three periods of time: 1790-1868, 1868-1943, 1943-present.

Prior to the passing of the 14th Amendment to the U. S. Constitution (1868), the Court's assumptions included such ideas as (1) man has a personal relationship with a Divine Creator, (2) this Creator is the source of man's inalienable rights, and (3) man possesses a divinely bestowed conscience that enables him to recognize the higher natural law to which societal law and personal conduct are to be reconciled. During this early period, Supreme Court jurists expressed in their decisions a personal accountability to God, their individual consciences, and to the country. It was reasonable under these assumptions for the Court to give equal deference to decisions of other governmental entities (the States), because they presupposed those agencies were governed by that same theistically based supernatural law and national allegience recognized by the Court.

Previous to the 14th Amendment, under the theory of states' rights, the citizen was not in direct contact with the national government. He owed allegiance to his state, and the state dealt with the nation. That theory was set aside under the 14th Amendment. People were now considered to have a direct relationship with both their state and the national government. In addition to specific rights granted by the state, each citizen could now expect protection of certain fundamental rights by the national government. This action authorized federal intervention in areas previously ignored at the national level. Hence, as the Supreme Court modified its assumptions about God, man, and nature, there was significant impact in areas formerly governed by the states—particularly in eduction.

Between 1868 and 1943 the Supreme Court gradually abandoned its reliance on premises that acknowledged supernatural and higher natural law influences. These original premises were replaced by legal thought anchored in (1) social consensus and (2) "science" acceptable to the Court. A clear illustration of this break with the past is the Court's transformation in thought and act cited in two cases heard during the decade of the 1940s. In 1940, the Court rendered a decision regarding *Minersville School District v. Gobitis* and in 1943 it reversed itself in *West Virginia Board of Education v. Barnette.* This dramatic reversal can be easily understood by recognizing that the Court shifted from one set of assumptions to another in rendering its contradictory decisions.

In the *Gobitis* case (310 U.S. 586 1940), the Court reviewed a challenge to a compulsory flag salute requirement in a school district in Pennsylvania. The father of a family of the Jehovah's Witness denomination maintained that requiring the pledge of allegience violated their faith's interpretation of the command in Exodus 20:12 to serve no graven images. He further claimed that he should be reimbursed for tuition which he had to pay to send his child to a private school, since the child was ejected from the public school for violating its pledge of allegiance policy. A majority opinion joined by seven members of the Court found that the school's practice of pledging the flag was constitutional. They explained that the student was free to continue attending a private school at the parent's expense, if he didn't want to participate in the public school's flag salute ceremony—that the school district was not liable to pay for the student's private education.

289

Three years later in *Barnette (319 U.S. 624 1943),* six members of the Court joined in a majority opinion which found the identical practice unconstitutional. In this case the circumstances applied to members of a family of the same faith living in a school district that had adopted a State Board of Education policy established on the basis of the *Gobitis* decision. An obvious question is, What permitted the Court to change its position? The answer to this question is simple. The Court based the second decision on a different set of assumptions than those used in the first decision. The facts were the same. The conflicting outcomes of the decision-making processes applied in these two cases highlight the significance of adopting a new worldview. Changing premises may lead to diametrically different conclusions. In each case the decision is understandable if one understands the assumptions implicit in the Court. Again, the facts did not change. The assumptions used to interpret the facts did change. The subtlety lies in the fact that the Court does not explicitly acknowledge its rejection of the old premises and adoption of the new. The consequences of *Barnette* are further amplified by the fact the Supreme Court, under auspices of the 14th and 1st amendments, was using constitutional law to determine educational philosophy—an area in which it had no prior direct involvement.

Specific Aspects of the Court's Changing Assumptions

The *Barnette* decision reveals four significant consequences of adopting a new worldview. In this decision the Court

1. rejected the *stare decisis* relevance of prior precedent, which was grounded in natural law and theistic assumptions **(meaning the Court no longer considered its prior decisions as binding upon its present decisions)**;
2. rejected the role of legislative judgment in areas that could affect an individual's exercise of a right enumerated by the Bill of Rights **(meaning the Court's view of an individual's exercise of his rights was more fundamental than the laws passed by state legislatures)**;
3. adopted a requirement of "scientific" proof from the field of education to establish the parameters of state action that would be considered constitutional **(meaning that the state, if challenged, was obligated to provide "scientific" proof acceptable to the Court to demonstrate that its educational programs did not violate the individual's rights)**; and
4. changed its assumptions regarding the process by which individual internalization of societal values and cohesion occurs **(meaning that the Court assumed that personal values are established by presenting information to an individual, rather than that personal values are the result of the individual making a choice in relation to that information, based on free will and a divinely bestowed conscience)**.

What Major Changes Did This Introduce Into Legal Thought and Practice ?

A number of changes in legal thought emerged during the period between 1868-1943. Two examples are (1) the source of

290

individual rights and (2) the nature of judicial review.

The Source of Rights. The second period of 1868-1943 is a period of conflict and confusion. The Court gradually abandoned the idea of a constitutional recognition of a Deity that bestowed upon man inalienable rights as expressed in the Declaration of Independence. This change resulted from the advancement of four interrelated doctrines: *first,* the gradual abandonment of the idea that man has a personal relationship with Deity; *second,* the gradual abandonment of the idea that man's inalienable rights were granted by God; *third,* the redefinition of equality (from the idea that all men are of equal value in the eyes of God to the idea that equality shall be defined in terms of tangible possessions or government granted privileges); *fourth,* the Court began to remove from the states and assign to itself the constitutionally based duty of ensuring the citizen's protection of his inalienable rights. In other words, man's inalienable rights are to be perceived as based in government, not God, and hence subject to the Court's interpretive protection.

291

The Nature of Judicial Review. During the 1868-1943 period the Court adopted philosophies consistent within its own rulings and began to change its position on when to review state action in the moral police-power area. Also, having abandoned the theistic assumptions implicit in the nature of rights and evidence, the Court's opinions reveal the creation of new and different standards. These new standards were consistent with the Court's efforts to establish a nontheistic basis for legal continuity and consensus. This occurred in two ways. First, the Court modified the contextual framework in which it applied standards called "conscience," "natural law," "morality" and "equality"—terms now given new and drastically different definitions. The new contextual framework was more in harmony with the horizontal assumptions and new definitions being used in its analysis. Second, the Court changed what it would accept as permissible evidence: It thus moved from general principles rooted in a supernatural (vertical) world-view and toward only that which can be manifest in a naturalistic (horizontal) worldview. Reality was limited to what was inside the bubble. (See chapter 5) .

Three examples of changes in the Court's actions:

1. The role and definition of "conscience" as a connection of obligation between man (including the Court) and Higher Law changed. Earlier (1844), the Court had determined that innate "conscience" could even supersede *stare decises*—rational argument based on prior precedent. In the third period (1943-present), conscience is more frequently considered simply the individual's reflection of social consensus. The Court no longer maintains that it is subject to a divinely connected "conscience" that transcends reason.

2. In jury instruction, the phrase "moral certainty" was replaced by the phrase "reasonable doubt." Jurists are now presumed to possess a rational capacity but not a moral capacity that can be applied in the legal process.

3. The idea that "eternal justice . . . comes from intelligence and truth"[3] to guide the conscience of the Court was abandoned during this period of time. "Natural law" is no longer defined as allegiance to a higher, theistically based set of principles or laws; natural law is now considered compliance with social consent, existing law, or custom.

292

It is clear the mechanism used by the Court for defining right and wrong changed. It shifted from what the individual should do because of a relationship to Deity and divinely established natural law, to what legal institutions (i.e., the Court, Legislature) defined or required as necessary. A man's spoken word was no longer considered his bond (moral obligation); man was held to his written and attested word (legal responsibility). During this second period, the Court also established the concept of "legal science." This entailed more than accepting evidence that could be defined as "scientific"; the issue was what scientific evidence would the Court accept as "established." Though the Court at this time did not obligate state legislatures to follow its lead in establishing and conforming to the principle of legal science, the process was initiated and continued to develop. The requirements to supply physically demonstrable (acceptable scientific) evidence eventually displaced the appeal to traditional or theistically endorsed norms and principles. Evidence from expert witnesses became more significant in shaping decisions than compliance or noncompliance to moral imperatives based on Higher Law.

What Do These Changes Mean?

As the U.S. Supreme Court abandoned its theistic frame of reference regarding the nature of man, government, and education, the confusion regarding legal decisions related to education increased. Well known cases dealing with praying in school, reading the Bible, posting the Ten Commandments, providing secular teachers in parochial schools, and teaching evolution are only tips of an emerging iceberg. By its action the Court thrust itself into the formation of educational policy and philosophy, giving itself a power previously invested in local and state agencies. The Court now makes decisions that it is not at present authorized or empowered to implement. This bold intervention disturbs the conventional United States definition of *education* as *a local responsibility, a state function, and simply a federal interest.*4 More important, perhaps, is the notion that this federal intervention is now operating upon assumptions that are not the same as those held by many at state and local levels. By careful examination it can be shown that the Court now operates in conflict with the underlying premises and explicit language expressed in most state constitutions. Part of an agency educator's freedom lies in understanding and perhaps working to protect his or her own state statutes.

293

An examination of the texts of all fifty state constitutions during each of the three periods reveals that in varying degrees, all fifty states recognize Deity; 45 of the 50 preambles to the state constitutions refer to Deity. In other words, although the Supreme Court has changed the framework it uses to make decisions from that used by the founders of this nation, state constitutions still reflect the language and ideas of a supernatural worldview. This sets the stage for a divisive and conflicting power struggle in public education during the next decade and possibly into the twenty-first century. This conflict may redefine the practice of education in the public school system. The Court's constitutional authority to make legal decisions need not be challenged, but the assumptions it uses certainly can and ought to be made explicit and carefully examined by the citizenry—especially by educators. The inconsistency reflected in recent decisions by the Court are caused by its inconsistent use of assumptions and its failure to make public the assumptions it uses. This demands public attention if fundamental freedoms are to be preserved.

When people understand both a correct principle and the error in the alternative to that principle, they are prepared to exercise their agency in choosing between right and wrong. If people understand only a single proposition, their choice is limited—like voting in an election where only one name appears on the ballot. If two propostions are understood but we are unable to see a damaging difference, the tendency is to accept both propositions, even though they may be contradictory. Accepting contradictory propositions leads to doublemindedness (hypocrisy) and unstable character. These weaknesses are fundamental enemies of freedom and will destroy our liberty. The corruptness from within that flows from such forces constitutes our greatest enemy (see 2 Ne. 28:5-9; Alma 8:5-7; 10:27; Hel. 16:15-22; 3 Ne. 1:9; 7:2).

Our society is ripe with examples of doubleminded behavior. "Watergate" and "Irangate" are household terms. Wallstreet, Congress, government agencies, electronic evangelism, professional and collegiate sports, and many other segments of society are affected. Our communities are fractured by moral and legal scandals that focus on individuals who portray themselves as morally upright but who behave without integrity. The same problem is apparent throughout the world—in China, Japan, Russia, England, and other countries. Human value structures are undermined by doublemindedness; embracing contradicting standards is fatal to self-government.

Examples of Inconsistent Decisions by the Court
Consider the following examples of inconsistency in decisions reached by the Court. Notice particularly that those who hold to vertical view values are at a disadvantage when subjected to the Court's horizontal perspective. For example,

1. When the Court considers claims that the "establishment of religion" clause is being violated, it assumes that anyone exposed to the idea or actions in question is being coerced. Those who believe in Higher Law values must demonstrate by scientific evidence acceptable to the Court that their ideas and actions are not coercing others. This is nearly impossible, because they are placed in a position of proving a negative—that something does not exist. Hence, when people have included prayers, Bible reading, and posting of the Ten Commandments in public schools, these actions have been ruled illegal, despite uncontroverted affidavits that deny the existence of coercion. Such affidavits are considered

294

insufficient evidence, while no explicit evidence of coercion is required beyond establishing the presence of possible religious influences. On the other hand, when a legal challenge concerns the "free exercise" clause (such as free speech), the Court assumes there is no coercion on anyone exposed to the ideas or actions in question, unless it can be proved by scientifically acceptable evidence. The burden of proof is now shifted to those who feel they are being coerced to their detriment. Hence the Court has protected the use of profane and vulgar language in school textbooks and the presentation of agnostic or atheistic philosophies that deny the existence of Deity, in spite of parental objection. The presence of a printed list of the Ten Commandments is assumed to be infringement, while the presence of a list of profane and vulgar terms is not. This inconsistency in the Court's assumptions regarding coercion is biased against those who believe in traditional "higher law" values and religious premises. The religious believer is placed in a disadvantaged position, and the nonbeliever is given the legal advantage.

295

2. In 1968 the Court recognized that "religious schools pursue two goals, religious instruction and secular education" (*Board of Education v. Allen*, 392 U. S. 236, 245. 1968). Notwithstanding this statement, the Court has subsequently ruled that private, religious schools confer no secular benefit on their students (*Grand Rapids School District v. Ball*, 473 U. S. 373, 384-387, 1985). For the Court to deny that any secular purpose or benefit can come from a student learning gymnastics, Spanish, geography, or mathematics in a religious school seems strangely biased. Because of this view, however, the Court is able to deny the religious segment of society benefits that are freely bestowed on the nonreligious sector. The Court does this despite the fact that the religious school is providing services that under all other settings are considered nonreligious. The bias of the assumptions of the Court against the believer and in favor of the nonbeliever is again manifest.

3. The bias apparent in the foregoing examples is further manifest when one recognizes the Court's earlier holding that "because our institutions presuppose the existence of a Supreme Being," our national and state traditions justify giving greater deferential treatment to practices or policies which

favor religion (*Zorach v. Clauson*, 343 U. S. 306, 313, 1952). The Court also states, "Our history is replete with official references to the value and invocation of Divine guidance in the deliberations and pronouncements of the Founding Fathers and contemporary leaders" (*Lynch v. Donnley*, 465 U. S. 668, 672, 1984). Why, then, is it unacceptable to allow in the public schoolroom as a matter of constitutional law to (1) recognize the historic belief in Deity, or (2) present scientific evidence or belief of the possibility that there was a nonevolutionary creation of man or the Universe? The answer, of course, is that these contradictions are produced by the new horizontal assumptions of the Court, which now favors the unbeliever over the believer in vertical "Higher Law" traditions. Greater legal freedom and power is given to one than to the other.

4. The Court has ruled that schools can legally stand in the place of the parents (a *loco parentis* relationship) in a First Amendment Speech setting, but they cannot legally stand in the place of parents in a First Amendment religion or a Fourth Amendment search and seizure setting. In other words, school personnel can decide if material that might be considered pornographic is detrimental to a student, but they cannot decide if information regarding religion or Higher Law values is detrimental to a student. Again, the same legal bias against the believer is apparent.

5. The Court has also determined that "mature" public education students have a constitutional right to (1) express in a school setting their sentiments regarding matters related to divisive national warfare (e.g., feelings about Viet Nam policies) and (2) decide, without assistance of parents or government, the religiously and morally "complex" issue of seeking an abortion. On the other hand, the Court assumes (1) that the same student is not capable of deciding when a schoolroom discussion is promoting specific sectarian doctrine, and (2) that "coercion" exists when the discussion is presented as accepting Higher Law assumptions as a matter of law or history. From the believer's point of view this inconsistency establishes as a matter of law a protection for the student to do what may be wrong, but to make it illegal for the student to hear a discussion of something that may be right. These

inconsistencies are sobering warnings to those who value religious freedom.

A Summary of the Legal Confusion

Since World War II, the U. S. Supreme Court has changed its standards of judicial review regarding matters of educational curriculum from favoring the supernatural, vertical tradition to the exclusively naturalist, horizontal tradition. This change occurred independently of legal or philosophical justification and without public acknowledgment. A clear reflection of the growing secularization of the academic mindset in western culture, this change has resulted in some conflicting, and possibly unsettling, decisions by the Court. Some of the decisions are these:

a. Parochial schools appear unable to qualify their secular purpose.

b. Public schools may teach the Declaration of Independence, but they may not have authorization to teach it as truth. (In fact, the Declaration of Independence itself, because of its assumptions, may be considered unconstitutional as a segment of public school curriculum, just as the Ten Commandments have been.)

c. Mature minors have the capacity and the right to decide whether or not to have an abortion; however, they are not able to discern between a class lecture giving historical or social information and a prosyliting presentation of religious doctrine.

d. The teaching of morality in public schools, if it is based on Higher Law values, may be interpreted to be unconstitutional.

e. States are expected to educate their citizens, but they may not be totally free to educate them according to their own constitutions and statutory provisions.

In the face of this social and legal confusion created by a Court that has substituted modern assumptions for traditional ones, parents and teachers need to understand their options. One of these options is to tie educational curriculum to the state constitution and its Higher Law assumptions. At present, informed parents, teachers, and students are free to act under state documents until they are legally disestablished. In this way individuals are seeking to preserve the heritage of the Founders as

297

the foundation for their schools. This strategy also pushes changes into the light of public discussion. If school-related lawsuits challenge state constitutions as well as local school districts, the public is much more likely to become informed and concerned. Another option is to do nothing. The future freedom and morality in the public schools and in the society at large appear to hinge on our response to this window of opportunity.

A Positive Approach

In spite of what may be an alarming situation to agency educators, there is room for positive action. First, the agency-oriented teacher can apply all those principles and practices that do not conflict with established legal restraints. Second, informed parents, teachers, and students can act in conformance with state constitutions and legislative enactments until they are specifically rescinded by the higher Court. Third, events that have happened, as outlined in this chapter, can be made part of the school curriculum; more people will then become aware. Agency educators do not have to be proponents or opponents; they do have to be presenters. Truth can fight its own battles if the people have access to it. Fourth, agency principles can be vigorously applied in all settings that do not fall under the present jurisdiction of the Court. The public schools may have suffered from restrictions placed on them, but we can practice agency principles in all unrestricted areas. We can teach a correct principle, compare it to a counterfeit, and explain the weakness in the counterfeit.

298

Seven Principles of Agency Education Acceptable In the Public Schools

The United States Constitution was fashioned to maximize the opportunity to exercise individual freedom within the bounds of moral order. Regardless of changes that have occurred thus far in this country, each person can still be encouraged to

1. *Accept the freedom to act.* Choose to respond to opportunities that exist.
2. *Pursue self-identity.* Discover who one is, where one came from, and what one's destiny might be.
3. *Exert self-discipline.* Achieve mastery of one's appetites, passions, and desires.

4. *Give and receive respect.* Share in the atmosphere of honoring others and being honored by others.

5. *Assume personal responsibility.* Make a contribution, and by doing so, become part of human sociability.

6. *Experience self-development.* Feel the rewards of growth and achievement.

7. *Exhibit self-reliance.* Create and provide for oneself and one's dependents.[5]

Each of these universal principles, which are in full harmony with the Abrahamic Covenant, the Decalogue, and the American heritage, can be formulated into educational objectives that can be pursued in the public school system. See figure 17-1 for a comparative illustration of how these principles correspond with values held in different cultural contexts.

Face Realistically the Primary Cause of School Failure

Amid all the attention given public education and its problems, seldom do people admit or discuss the primary cause of classroom failures—the "mood" in the classroom. American public schools are funded, we understand, to teach our children the three R's. Many of us experienced the basic public school curriculum of language and arts, mathamatics, science, and social studies. Teachers and administrators in the schools strive to blend teaching methods with their knowledge of these subjects. But subject matter, methods, and the money to provide them are not the fundamental challenges in today's schools; they are just the safest to talk about. In spite of the emphasis which recent national and state studies have placed on these elements, the teacher and the student in the classroom knows they are not the true foundation of successful education—important as they may be. Teachers and students both know that teaching and learning ultimately depend on personal freedom and moral order. If the *mood* in the classroom is not constructive, no amount of methods, money, or mental brilliance will produce effective learning. Personal duress, moral disorder, fear, rebellion, confusion, and chaos do not nurture optimum learning or teaching. Moral order and personal freedom sustain the fundamental desire to learn and teach.

When student peer groups establish a mood of apathy, defiance, or disorder, effective educational processes are destroyed.

299

Elements and Principles that Foster a Moral Society

Universal Elements	Covenant Version	Mosaic Version	Americanized Expression	Political Tenent Governments Should:	Educational Expression Students Need To:
Action	Accept the freedom to act	Acknowledge a divine creation	Freedom to act	Provide mankind an environment of freedom in which to act	Affirm the feeling of agency by experiencing the opportunity to make choices
Identity	Pursue self-identity	Honor one's parents	Self-identity	Allow mankind the opportunity to pursue self-identity	Acquire a positive confirmation of who they are, what they are capable of doing and becoming
Discipline	Exert self-discipline	Do not kill	Self-discipline	Encourage mankind to exercise self-discipline by establishing just laws and administering them in equity	Be exposed to people, rules, and principles that elicit self-control and individual governance
Respect	Give and receive self-respect	Do not commit adultery	Mutual respect	Encourage mankind to treat others as they would like to be treated	Promote the disposition of treating others like they want to be treated
Responsibility	Assume personal responsibility	Do not steal	Personal Responsibility	Encourage mankind to assume personal responsibility	Preserve and protect the rights, properties, and privileges of all individuals
Development	Experience self-development	Do not lie	Self-development	Allow mankind the opportunity to pursue self-development	Acquire and demonstrate knowledge and skills that contribute to personal and social satisfaction
Reliance	Exhibit self-reliance	Do not covet	Self-reliance	Allow mankind the opportunity to experience self-reliance	Create sufficient labor and frugality to sustain one's self and legitimate dependents

Figure 17.1

And when teachers and administrators create and nurture moods of cynicism, the learner/teacher relationship is squelched. Public education is now victimized by the destructive influences of negative moods as never before. We have drifted from the Golden Age when American public education was admired worldwide. The magnetic influence of a positive context for schooling has largely evaporated. The educational atmosphere of the past—simply portrayed in the television series *The Waltons*—does not prevail. As one school leader observed, "We are continually hiring additional administrators to help us cope with poor behavior [students and teachers] that flows from a lack of values and moral education."

After World War II, public schools across the nation, following the pattern set in higher education, radically scaled down their involvement in character formation and the teaching of our nation's most important values. The power structure in our society, led by the new philosophy of the universities, moved America away from the heritage established by the founding fathers. The stabilizing influence, expressed in the statement "Frequent recurrance to fundamental principles is essential to the security of individual rights and perpetuity of free government,"6 was ignored. Parents and teachers in America became confused regarding whose responsibility it was to educate the children. Situational ethics replaced divinely given moral standards; social ethics that emphasized group concerns like foreign policy and civil rights overshadowed individual ethics that emphasized individual responsibility and accountability to God.

Individual rights were determined by the Court, not, as expressed in the Declaration of Independence, given to man by God. In our legal system, the notion of "reasonable doubt" took the place of "moral certainty." References to religion and morality based on religion disappeared from school textbooks. History texts were rewritten as if Sunday did not exist as a day of the week in American history. The context for making decisions in the U. S. Supreme Court and in State Departments of Education followed the trends in higher education. The language and the assumptions in our state constitutions, which retained the decision-making framework of the Founding Fathers, were ignored.

We will not solve the problems of the public schools without addressing these more fundamental issues of freedom. Successful public education flows from human hearts, not legislative budgets.

301

Money cannot redeem man from his sins; only repentance can do that. Affluence cannot sustain increased levels of achievement; only humility, gratitude and a spirit of service can.

18

Scholarship

Scholarship is an ill-defined term; it means different things to different people. In academia, slices of scholarly meaning have become rigorously applied scepters of authority. Agency educators shy away from such narrow restrictive views because they curtail freedom and confuse ends and means in the search for truth. There are three general patterns of scholarship, none of which should say to the other, "We have no need of thee." These patterns seek to understand (1) man's relationship to God, (2) man's relationship to man, and (3) man's relationship to things.

Context for Understanding Scholarship

 Creating and receiving messages through speech, writing, or signal is a characteristic of human consciousness. The notion of *message* gives meaning to nearly every facet of life—language, intention, action, and interaction. Whatever else active human life may entail, nothing appears quite as fundamental as our ability to give and receive messages. For example, in many prison systems the punishment deemed most severe, short of removing life itself, is solitary confinement—the absolute curtailment of human communication and interaction with others. If you remove from life all that fits under the term *message*, very little remains.

Opposite to this curtailment is education, the conscious and intentional interaction with the messages of others. The very existence of education as an enterprise depends on the creation, delivery and reception of messages. If there are no messages, there can be no education, regardless of how one chooses to define education. If messages exist, then one not only has the possibility of education, but also the challenge of dealing with the messages. The combination of these factors inevitably defines education and the form it takes. All other educational concerns build from this foundation.

Communication is the substance of human interaction. When this interaction is formalized for whatever purposes, one is engaging in a form of education. In western culture, the intentional involvement in this process has been called schooling. The history of schooling reveals an ongoing struggle by individuals to understand and control the process of dealing with messages and the skills that create them. Personal motives vary but the task remains essentially the same—*how to govern the process of schooling by connecting some purpose to the messages.* The conscious struggle to put purpose into the schooling process has been called scholarship. Effectively connecting messages and purposes is the trademark of good scholarship. Scholarship is not a single or stable activity. It has taken on a variety of patterns. Over time, however, various traditions of scholarship have been manifest.

304

Three Types of Scholarship

Differing themes have produced three general varieties of scholarly tradition. One pattern of scholarship is formed by individuals who place a central emphasis on understanding *man's relationship to God.* The study of messages that relate God to man and man to God is the central focus of this type of scholarship. It became manifest in Western culture through the early Hebrews and is exemplified in Moses' Pentateuch, the first five books of the Bible. A second pattern of scholarship emerges from a focus on *man's relationship to man* as revealed through the recorded experiences of his human ancestry. This pattern was popularized for Western culture in ancient Greece. It grew out of efforts to purify, preserve, and transmit the messages of the poets of antiquity, for example, Homer's *Iliad* and *Odyssey.* A third pattern of scholarship issues forth from efforts of the human family to understand and communicate *man's relationship to nature* and man's strivings to make use of natural resources. Western culture also attributes this tradition to Greek origins and the work of such individuals as Anaximander, Anaxamenes, and Aristotle.

In modern western culture it is easy to identify these three rather distinct traditions of scholarship as *formal attempts to understand and control the schooling or message-sending process.*

From an agency point of view, all three of these traditions are valid in the sense that each one represents a legitimate area of exploration. A full and complete education must embrace all three, recognizing each approach has its limitations. This book is not the place for an extensive and detailed treatment of the topic,[1] but it is important to point out that human traditions, scholarly traditions included, can only be manifest through personality; they have no life of their own and are therefore subject to the limitations of human personality. The agency-oriented educator will recognize conflicting claims have become part of the histories in each of these traditions. Unnecessary confusion can be avoided if these claims are carefully evaluated against the standards provided in the most basic premises of agency education.

For example, agency educators will be wary of elitest claims made under the banner of scholarship. Various forms of intellectual "gnosticism"—the notion that certain people possess special knowledge which others cannot acquire—is apparent in all three traditions. True scholarship is characterized by humility, not pride. True scholarship is open, inviting participation from all who are willing and interested. Psuedoscholarship is characterized by efforts to hide weaknesses, gratify pride, pursue vain ambitions, and exercise control, dominion, and compulsion upon others. It appears that we humans, "scholars" included, tend to suffer greatly from these temptations. It may be particularly difficult for people with learning not to esteem themselves above their fellowmen (BM, 2 Nephi 9:28-29,42; 26:20; 27:15-26; 28:5). In this world the reservoirs of pure knowledge are seldom isolated from thickets of guile. The presence of truth seems to attract both counterfeits and vanity.

305

Simple Scholarship

In very simple terms, these scholarly traditions are usually introduced to children in the form of (a) learning about language: how to speak, read, and write; (b) learning about objects: their number (math) and nature (science); and (c) learning about religion: man's divine origin, purpose, and destiny. Modern schools often separate the *humanities* (man to man relationships) and the *sciences* (man to things relationships) from *religion* (man to God relationships). Thus there is little or no formal training in many schools—in other words, little or no scholarship—having to do with understanding man's relationship to God. This matter is left to the family and the church. The other two traditions are well represented and often compete with one another for attention and for the budget.

In recent years the humanities (*the humane lettres*), that area of scholarship which explores man's relationship to man in the classic sense, has been less popular in the budget than scholarship that focuses on man's relationship to things. Modern society has become fascinated, even captivated, by the exploration of man's relationship to things (*science and technology*). This accounts for the observation that we have become a materialistic society. It is also apparent that most of those who promote, as well as those who want to change contemporary education, make proposals designed to improve the scholarship related to *man's study of man* or *man's study of things*. Less attention, in the public and private sectors, is given to improving education by enthroning the scholarship of faith—emphasizing the study of *man's relationship to God* (*the sacred lettres*).

306

A Practical Definition of Scholarship

If we accept the premise that scholarship is simply an intentional effort to understand and communicate something about the relationships that exist between man and God, man and man, or man and things, we will have common ground to stand upon. This makes it reasonable to understand why people have applied the term "scholar" to little children in Sunday School, elementary schools, and college prep schools. "See the teacher with her little scholars gathered round." For the agency educator, this is a legitimate use of the term. Anyone who engages in the process of exchanging messages that clarify or enrich man's relationship to God, to man, or to things is participating in the scholarly process as agency educators could define it. Encouraging the development of voluntary servants rather than selected *savants* is the goal of scholarly pursuit for agency-oriented educators (Matt. 20:27; BM, Mosiah 4:15). To do this successfully requires the development of a disposition to search, the acquisition of effective skills, and the expansion of one's understanding. In this sense little children, as well as learned professionals, may qualify as prepared and productive scholars.

Avoiding the Pitfalls of Scholarship in the Intellectual Community

At a more *sophisticated* level (though not necessarily more true or correct), it has become popular to reserve the term "scholar" for those who meet more narrow and selected criteria. Note that the word "sophisticated" comes from the term sophist, which may denote clever but unsound and pretentious reasoning. Refining the definition and restricting the use of the term *scholarship* has led to controversy in the academic world. For example, in the early 1800s, a new definition of scholarship, following the pattern of the modern scientific method used in the physical sciences, took form in Germany among scholars of the oratorical tradition. In this scholarship, man's relationship to man as seen through the classic literature was the focus. In America, Christianity was coming under serious attack by scholars representing the naturalistic worldview of modernism—those who study man's relationship to things. A number of conservative American university people went to Germany to further their education during this period. They became enthusiastic over the new form of German scholarship and saw it as a way to defend Christianity from the scholarly critics of their day. A cluster of these individuals at Yale University became known as the New Haven Scholars (in Connecticut.).[2]

Noah Porter, one of these individuals, described this new and tightly structured definition of the scholarly approach as

> the presentation of findings and conclusions "in the form of exact observation, precise definition, fixed terminology, classified arrangement, and rational explanation." This definition had four corollaries. First, scholars belonged to recognizable disciplines that were defined by their subject matter and certain guiding principles and methods. . . . Second, the scholar belonged to a community of scholars and built upon its work. . . . Third, the scholar consulted facts . . . historical facts . . . [though] Porter's facts were those that "the soul" could discover "concerning itself" . . . Fourth, scholarly argument followed certain rules of style.[3]

Ralph Waldo Emerson, a contemporary of Porter's, rejected this format for qualifying as a scholar. He did not feel the scientific method was the crucial ingredient of scholarship. Nor did he consider prescribed relationships with an elite group the key to obtaining useful knowledge. He felt the most fruitful path to truth was an honest and intuitive scrutiny of life itself. Simply observing facts, arranging them into an argument to be set forth in an "unbiased" and candid spirit, and presenting them for a disputational review by peers was not the only (or best) form of scholarship. Emerson felt this so-called "objective" approach could only lead to "appearances," not to the true and important facts of life. In his 1837 Harvard Phi Beta Kappa address, "The American Scholar," Emerson explained that the true scholar's methodology is to follow a path that will reveal "in the secrets of his own mind" those truths which are "in the secrets of all minds." Emerson did not think it was necessary to cloister in the confines of a college or university in order to discover and disseminate truth. He chose to secede from the traditional institutions and to carry his message to the people through lyceums (public lectures).

308

These two subsets of the oratorical tradition, one similar to the methodology of the natural sciences and the other reminiscent of the days of Cicero, are examples of the range of difference that can exist within a given tradition of scholarship. The explicit rigor in the New Haven version of scholarship was certainly fashionable for that day. It came at the dawning of an era that was to give birth to a *positivistic* spirit (restricting truth to that which could be viewed as logical and empirical) that would help stimulate the industrial revolution and create the social sciences.

The differences and confusion generated by such a multitude of conflicting views is very apparent in today's education. At this very writing the American Medical Association is struggling with the widespread practice of paying doctors to appear in the courts as "expert witnesses" to provide testimony in medical malpractice suits. This has resulted in the medical profession narcissistically attacking itself, doctor against doctor, with contradictory "scholarly evidence." One is left to ask the question, What is the source of arrogance on the one hand, and naivete on the other, that would lead a person to deny Emerson the title of scholar while expecting a judge or jury, untrained in medicine, to decide which of two or more contradicting scholarly testimonies is true?

A More Clear Path

The agency-oriented educator is one who accepts the supernatural as well as the natural components of existence, who pursues light as well as truth, who desires to serve more than be served, who recognizes that the temporal is an extension of the spiritual and that man is indebted to God for his knowledge. This type of educator is capable of defining and pursuing scholarship in a unique way. Given freedom to examine all three areas of scholarly exploration—God, man, and nature—all useful methods are available. But these educators are careful that the method always remains a *means*. It must not become an *end* in itself. There is the temptation to become so enamoured with the tool that the tool becomes more important than the purpose it was designed to fulfill.

The agency-oriented person recognizes that the basic responsibility for validating scholarly claims rests upon those who hear the report. Creators of reports have their own sets of integrity-related responsibilities, and these do not include compelling others to accept their witness or punishing them when it is rejected. Scholarly reports may be persuasive but they should not be coercive. Just as the teacher's role is to be a witness to the student who chooses to accept or reject, so the scholar becomes a witness to his audience. The major purpose of scholars discussing scholarly reports of any kind is to encourage personal clarification, not public ratification; the objective is to invite other interested parties to engage in the task of investigating the report for themselves, not to engage in a rhetorical dispute over doubts or criticisms. True scholars create, report, explain, and clarify; they listen, comprehend, confirm, correct, and reject. To engage in debate, disputation, argument, contention, self-serving salesmanship, and other forms of intellectual compulsion is not scholarship—it is rhetoric.

Hugh Nibley answers the question

309

> What was rhetoric? Aristotle defines it as the "art of persuasion," the technical skill by which one convinces people—convinces, that is, everybody of anything for a fee, to follow Clement of Alexandria. It is the training and skill by which one can make unimportant things seem important, according to Plato, or, to quote Clement again, "make false opinions seem true by means of words."[4]

In this classical sense, rhetoric is not scholarship;[5] honestly revealing information that may be personally validated or invalidated by others is scholarship. The best scholars, like the best teachers, are willing to assist those who seek their help in validating or invalidating their reports. In this type of environment positive relationships rather than adversarial relationships are fostered.

But cooperative effort is not possible when the participants have exclusionary commitment to a single tradition or method of scholarly pursuit and seek to impose it on others. True scholarship cannot thrive if people are unable or unwilling to accept help when it is offered. Galileo experienced this when he tried to share his discovery of the telescope with the people of his day. Many people refused to look through the telescope "to see for themselves"; they were unwilling to assume the responsibility to validate Galileo's testimony. He had searched, found, and reported. They refused to shoulder their responsibility as it is defined in this view of scholarship.

310

After properly acknowledging the source of our premises, the methods we used, and the way we arrived at our conclusions, we should present our message as clearly and honestly as possible, clarifying where necessary. Then, the audience can determine for themselves the validity of the message. It is not necessary in this view of scholarship to submit to a process of public disputation until one wins the approval of a selection of peers. Jesus advised the students of his day that if they wanted to know the truth of a proposition, once they understood it, they should test it for themselves (John 7:15). Moroni uses the same instruction to those who desire to know the truthfulness of the message in the Book of Mormon (BM, Moroni 10:3-5). Personal examination of any claim seems to be a mark of true scholarship. A student who wants to test the validity of the times tables can know for himself if he is willing to perform his own tests. The listener's path to pure scholarship is first to hear, second to understand, and then to do. Anything less is a movement away from scholarship towards some other form of response. The scholarly response to this book, for example, is to read it, understand it, and then to act upon it. In this way readers can determine for themselves whether or not they should accept the writer's message.

At some point the faithful realize that all truth comes from God. We may use a variety of methods to confirm and clarify the applications of truth, but the source is singular. David Allan's story of his role in developing the standard by which all atomic clocks in the world are governed is one example of how temporal truth comes from God to man. In part he says:

> Academically, my credentials are limited. It's almost as if you're down here with your finite wisdom bouncing around and taking the hard knocks; every once in a while, by hard work and persistence, you feel that spirit of enlightenment that has divine origin. Then you say, 'Eureka!' and you run with it. . . . If you are a humble follower of He who knows all truth, the doors are wide open. The Lord will help us use our talents to inspire one another in all kinds of things.[6]

Russell M. Nelson, a pioneer in the field of heart surgery, also describes the reality of divine assistance in the acquisition of temporal knowledge. "You should know that it was through the understanding of the scriptures, and 'likening' them to this area of interest, that the great field of heart surgery as we know it today was facilitated for me."[7] Many individuals have recognized and acknowledged divine influences in their attainment of understanding; more of us should do likewise.

311

The following three examples will help clarify the nature of scholarship in its holistic sense. Each of these personal narratives depicts scholarship in action, although in very different settings—at home, at school, and in the laboratory. The first account comes from a young mother, the second from a new teacher, and the third from a searching scientist.

A Mother's Search for an Answer

When our first baby was born I wanted to be the best mother I could. I nursed her for several months and then began feeding her with a bottle. By the time she reached her first birthday, I had heard many ideas on the best time to wean her from the bottle. Some people said as soon as she could drink from a cup she didn't need her bottle. Others said babies should have a bottle until they were two years old. I was confused and concerned, because I did not have a clear answer. I decided to make the problem a matter of prayer. I wanted to know what was best for my baby.

After praying, I pondered and analyzed the situation for about a week, trying to understand how well she would do without the bottle. I noticed, too, that she liked to play with her toys and books in the crib before she took her nap. One day a little after her first birthday the thought came strong to me that I shouldn't give her the bottle, and I shouldn't let her cry for more than ten minutes.

On that day, after giving her a hug and telling her it was nap time, I gave her a big cup of milk and let her play with her toys in her crib. She fussed for just a few minutes and fell asleep. I knew that was an answer to my prayer. She could do just fine without her bottle, so I never gave it to her again. Heavenly Father answers our prayers when we are sincere and seek his help, even in things as small as taking a bottle from a baby.[8]

312

A Student Teacher's Search for an Answer

In my first class for elementary education major[s] we were assigned to do ten hours of service working with handicapped or learning disabled children. It was through this project that I met Daniel, an energetic five year-old with shining eyes, smiling freckled face, and ragged clothes. Daniel's situation was quite sad—at home and at school. October had come and gone and Daniel still had not learned to write his name; a skill that others in his class had mastered weeks before. This was my assignment, to teach him to write his name.

Having had no training in the methods classes, I really didn't know any special way to help the learning disabled child. I was on my own to do as I thought best. First, I tried to have Daniel trace his name. I soon found he had very little hand coordination, so for the first three or four classes we just practiced forming letters.

Weeks went by and Daniel's name was still unreadable. Not only were the letters poorly formed, but no matter what I tried, Daniel could not get all the letters in their proper order. I would even write his name for him and have him try to copy it, but it seemed like the task was impossible.

After six weeks had passed, Daniel was able to form somewhat readable letters, but he could never place them in the proper order. I had exhausted my limited resources as a tutor, and I knew there was nothing more that I could do. The night before I was to teach Daniel for the last time, I knelt beside my bed to say my evening prayers. I asked my Heavenly Father to bless me with the wisdom to know how to help Daniel. As I was praying, a picture of Choo Choo Train popped into my mind. The impression was so strong that I stopped praying and wondered where that thought had come from. I resumed my prayers, and the impression came again. I thought, "Okay, I think that is an answer. I'll give it a try."

The next day at school, Daniel and I went over all we had studied and practiced during the past weeks—which amounted to a few letters in the wrong order. Then the Choo Choo Train came to my mind again *with an additional thought*—a train has to go in order. I immediately drew a picture of a train for Daniel: an engine, a coal car, a passenger car, and a caboose. I asked Daniel, "What makes a train go?"

"The engine," he said.

I asked, "What happens if the caboose is in the front?"

"It won't work" he replied.

We played with the order of the cars a little longer, then I asked, "Why won't the train go if the engine is not in front?"

He said, "'Cause the cars are out of order, it won't work."

"Daniel," I said, "that's just like your name—all the letters have to be in the right order or it won't work. The 'D' is like the engine, it starts things going; all the middle letters must follow in their proper order, and the caboose is the 'L.'"

Daniel's eyes lit up, "Oh, I get it now," he shouted. He grabbed the pencil from my hand and for the first time in his life, he wrote his name correctly.[9]

A Geologist's Search for an Answer

My master's thesis dealt with the crystal chemistry of a mineral called staurolite, and, like most academic investigations, it answered a number of questions but left some other important ones either unaddressed or unsolved. This mineral is characterized in nature by the presence of iron and magnesium, and I realized that a couple of the significant questions could be answered if I could synthesize a zinc variety that had not been found in nature. We had equipment of the sort typically used for the synthesis of minerals, and I knew the conditions of pressure and temperature that had been used in synthesizing other staurolites, because the iron and magnesium varieties had been made at other laboratories.

313

Optimistically, I set out to make zinc staurolite, but the attempt failed. After a few more failures, I pushed zinc staurolite to the back of my mind and went on to my doctoral research, hoping that I would one day have a chance to reopen the investigation.

A few years later, that chance came at BYU. A different sort of apparatus than I had had in graduate school, the tetrahedral press, was available here. Again, my attempts met with failure; each experimental run resulted in a combination of compounds, but zinc staurolite was not among them. I felt strongly that if iron staurolite and magnesium staurolite could be synthesized, then zinc staurolite could too, but all attempts to do so at pressures and temperatures near those appropriate for the two former varieties were unsuccessful.

I have always felt that if what I was doing was worthwhile and was important to me, then it was in some measure important to the Lord also. This conviction led me to make the synthesis of zinc staurolite a matter of prayer. I told the Lord that I had done everything I knew how to do and had still been unsuccessful in an effort that I was sure had the potential for success. I explained (unnecessarily, I am sure) what I had done, and then asked what I should do. As clear as I have ever heard anything, I heard a voice say, "Run your experiment at 30 kilobars and 750 degrees Celsius." I was astounded, because not only was the temperature higher by a substantial margin than I had tried, but the pressure was a full 50% higher than any pressure I had thought remotely reasonable. Nonetheless, that is what I had been told, so the next morning I went straight to the laboratory and put in a run at 30 kilobars and 750 degrees Celsius. The result was pure zinc staurolite with not so much as a trace of anything else.

I proceeded with the research and found that I could synthesize not only zinc staurolite, but also the iron, mangnesium, cobalt and all intermediate varieties under the same conditions. When the work on zinc staurolite was complete and it was time to publish the results, I struggled with the issue of acknowledgement. How should I say that I had determined the correct conditions under which to accomplish the synthesis? Under the circumstances it seemed not just presumptuous but blasphemous to take credit myself. On the other hand, acknowledgement of the Lord in a professional journal, if by some oversight it was not declared "out of bounds" by an editor, was sure to bring ridicule from

314

the general scientific community, and that seemed like an undesireable result for both the university and myself. After prayerful consideration, it seemed appropriate to simply state the conditions under which the synthesis was accomplished, without acknowledging either how it had been determined or that there had been any unsuccessful tries at other conditions. I am not sure that that would always be the correct action, but in this case the Spirit confirmed to me that it was.

One might wonder why the Lord had enough interest in zinc staurolite to tell me how to make it. I believe the answer is that He didn't. He was interested in me (as He is in all of his children), but more important, I had to know, then and forever, that He is omniscient. If God knows how to make an obscure chemical compound never before made by either nature or man, then there is no doubt in my mind that he knows everything. Before this experience I would certainly have acknowledged my faith in the omniscience of God. Now I can testify with more than faith that He knows all things. And though I do not yet know why my faith was insufficient and had to be replaced by knowledge (if indeed that was the case), I am very grateful for the experience. Further, it strengthened my conviction that the Lord stands ready to assist in the work that goes on to further the mission of this university; I am not sure that that statement can be generalized to other universities, but I know that it is true here.[10]

315

Some Solutions Lie Outside the Realm of Scholarship

It is well to remember that personal scholarship is not the only or even the best solution to all of man's quandaries. It is unnecessary and unwise to put every claim to a personal scholarly test. Many satisfactory conclusions can be reached without engaging directly in the scholarly process. For example, a man may report that cigarettes contain nicotine and that nicotine tars will often cause cancer in human tissue. It would be unwise to begin smoking cigarettes in an effort to validate or invalidate the man's report. Trustworthy witnesses can be valid substitues for personal scholarship.

Likewise, youth who are advised to avoid premarital sex could apply the principle of obedience to God's commandments in the place of scholarship and save themselves great heartache. They do not need to affirm that the promiscuous lifestyle leads to health hazards and is spiritually injurious. Every lesson in life does not need to be learned as a result of direct personal experience. Common sense and faith are just as important to human happiness as scholarly sense.

19

Lesson Preparation

Laws or principles govern in the moral and spiritual domain as well as the temporal domain. Just as (a) showing, (b) telling, and (c) doing apply in the temporal domain, teaching (a) according to the covenants, (b) by the spirit, and (c) as a witness prevail in the moral and spiritual domain. We will seek, prepare, and deliver more successful instruction if we comply with these principles. Temporal and spiritual principles are often interdependent; used together they constitute a fulness.

Two Basic Approaches to Preparing Lessons

Agency educators believe in a universe of law and order. They also believe there are two dimensions of existence: the temporal and the spiritual. Certain laws govern the physical dimension; other laws govern the spiritual dimension. These two separate dimensions are designed to complement each other. The mortal domain is temporary; the spirit domain is eternal. What we experience as temporal or physical reality symbolizes the spiritual or eternal reality. This creates two challenges for educators.

On the one hand, teachers are challenged to move from the "real" (experiencing the laws of the physical life) to the "ideal" (experiencing the laws of the spiritual life), to move from what is to what ought to be, from the temporary to the permanent. This is the foundation of moral and spiritual instruction, leading others from the physical to the spiritual. When Jesus taught with parables he was making this transition since a parable is an earthly story with a heavenly meaning; he was leading people from the physical to the spiritual. On the other hand, teachers need to understand that when they teach about temporal or physical things, it is often necessary to use simulation (see figure 19-1). To proximate the "real"—the temporal or physical—is to simulate it. Simulation is imitation, an approximation of something. In our instruction about physical things, we cannot always deal directly with the "real" thing. When an architect uses a model of a building to explain the nature of the planned structure to interested clients, he is using a simulation to help them understand the "real" thing. In order to understand the temporal or physical world we often move from a simulation to the real physical thing or experience. This is the foundation of temporal or physical instruction. Agency-oriented educators should not confuse the two; they need to understand and use both approaches.

Two Dimensions of Instruction

Temporal Dimension	Moral and Spiritual Dimension
Simulated_____Real_____Ideal	
1. Show	1. According to the covenants
2. Tell	2. By the Spirit
3. Do	3. As a witness

Figure 19-1

To understand the difference between the temporal and spiritual provides us with a key to preparing effective lessons. If we want to teach about the physical or temporal aspects of the world in which we live, we should understand and comply with the principles that govern temporal properties and operations. For example, there are laws that influence human sight. The human eye cannot see physical objects without the assistance of light waves. No teacher, therefore, would expect to be successful teaching lessons that depend on eyesight in conditions of total darkness. Our physical senses are closely associated with physical laws, many of which we can describe and apply. Light, heat, odor, texture, taste, and other physical properties illustrate this association.

Laws or principles prevail and maintain order in the moral and spiritual domain as well. In order to successfully teach moral or spiritual lessons, we need to understand and comply with the laws or principles that govern this dimension of existence. For example, the statement "wickedness never was happiness" is a spiritual law. So are such statements as "Without faith it is impossible to please God"; "Except a man be born again, he cannot see the kingdom of God"; "Where there is no vision, the people perish"; "I, the Lord, am bound when ye do what I say; but when ye do not what I say, ye have no promise." Successful teachers of moral and spiritual lessons understand and honor the spiritual regulations related to those lessons. Jesus' disciples were taught this lesson when they failed in their efforts to heal a boy possessed of a foul spirit. When the boy was brought to Jesus, he freed him of the malady. The disciples then asked "Why could not we cast him out?" Jesus explained to them that "this kind can come forth by nothing, but by prayer and fasting" (Mark 9:17-29). We must comply with the laws if we are to deal successfully with moral and spiritual matters as well as temporal concerns.

Although the physical and the spiritual dimensions are distinct, they are also interdependent. Therefore, much of what we seek to learn and teach relates to both domains. We must take care not to lose touch with this reality. The emphasis may be on the physical or the spiritual, but the two are seldom totally separate. Together they constitute a fulness and this is true as it applies to the learning/teaching process. This chapter focuses on moral and spiritual lessons; many helps for temporal lessons are readily available in other sources.

319

Preparing and Teaching Moral or Spiritual Lessons

In the moral and spiritual dimension three general principles have been made very plain. First, man has been instructed to *teach according to the covenants* (D&C 107:89). Second, he has been admonished to *teach by the Spirit* (D&C 42:13-14). Third, he has been told to *teach as a witness* (BM, Mosiah 18:8-10). The promise is that if we follow these principles or laws we learn and teach more effectively. What remains is to transform these principles into practice. One way to do this is illustrated in the following steps:

1. *Read the resource material prayerfully.* Most teaching is improved as the teacher spends adequate time seriously reviewing the topic to be taught. If prescribed resource materials are not available, the teacher may need to investigate other sources for review. If divine help is expected, teachers should seek and allow time for it to be received. Preparation must precede presentation.

2. *Identify three to five of the most significant ideas that come to you as you study and ponder the material.* Most subjects far transcend the ability of learners or teachers to deal with them in their entirety. Instruction is almost always a partial examination. Deciding what part to teach to a particular audience at a particular time is an educational responsibility. Worthy teachers can receive divine help in determining what should be taught if they are receptive to spiritual guidance. Don't try to teach too much at once.

3. *Prioritize these ideas one through five.* Seldom is time for instruction unlimited. All that could be discussed invariably exceeds the time available for instruction. This necessitates choices in what to include and what to exclude. When teachers prioritize the ideas to be taught and begin by teaching the most important ideas first, then moving to the next most important, and so on, they will always have taught the highest priorities within the available time period.

4. *Relate each idea to a gospel principle(s) that supports it; if you cannot relate the idea to a gospel principle, do not teach it.* Making the effort to relate each idea taught to a supporting gospel principle is a protection against getting off track or mired down in nonrelevant and speculative instruction. Some subjects are not directly related to moral and spiritual objectives. Propriety and relevance are important ingredients in quality instruction. Sometimes teachers are ineffective or stumble because they spend their time and energy on subject matter of questionable value. Spiritual nourishment comes from the basic doctrines. It is wisdom to keep instruction connected to these basic principles.

5. *Identify personal experiences you have had with the idea(s) you have selected, and prepare to share these with those whom you teach.* Teachers teach best those things which they are qualified to bear witness. Testimony is probably the most powerful technique a teacher possesses. Students are most responsive when there is a foundation of authenticity for the instruction. Jesus "taught as one having authority" because he was a legitimate witness to the truths he shared. Good

teachers, like good athletes, "play within themselves"; they convey integrity by teaching what they understand, that to which they can bear witness.

6. Identify personal experiences from the standard works and lesson manual and prepare to share these with those whom you teach. There is a law of witnesses associated with moral and spiritual matters. By the mouth of two or three witnesses shall all things be established (D&C 6:28). Reaching beyond yourself for "a second witness" creates convincing instruction. When this law is honored, moral and spiritual instruction becomes much more effective. Complying with this law invites confirmation of the Spirit.

7. Invite those whom you teach to share personal or scriptural experiences which they feel are related to the idea being discussed. No single teacher is likely to serve every need of every student in the instructional process. Frequently, the experience of others in the class will be the most useful to some students. The principle "let one speak at a time and let all listen unto his sayings, that when all have spoken that all may be edified" (D&C 88:112) makes education effective and economical. It has a powerful positive influence on the participants. Sometimes teachers end lessons before they allow the students to witness to their own insights. An invaluable resource is lost when this happens.

321

The worksheet which follows (see figure 19-2) is an example of one way for a teacher to apply the foregoing principles in the preparation of a lesson. First, select a topic. Next, identify and rank three or more declarative statements related to the topic. Connect each item with a gospel principle or ordinance. After listing some personal experience, feeling, or observation for each item, note a corroborating witness from the scriptures or study guide. As you present the material, invite class members to share their experience with the subject.

Preparing a Lesson—Worksheet

List 3 ideas related to _____ and relate each of these to a gospel principle or ordinance.

Idea (declarative statement)   Gospel Principle/Ordinance

1.   1.

2.   2.

3.   3.

322

Your Personal Witness (each item)
1.

2.

3.

Witness from Scripture/Study Guide
1.

2.

3.

Witness from Class Members
1.

2.

3.

Figure 19-2

Preparing and Teaching Temporal or Physical Lessons

The elementary teacher frequently speaks of *show, tell*, and *do*. The physical world is comprehended best when it is *encountered directly, explained simply*, and *experienced personally*. Most mothers understand that these procedures are the key to a child's learning. It is by following these steps that children learn how to feed themselves, tie shoelaces, clean up toys and perform a myriad of other tasks common to the physical world. In order to show, tell, and do, it is often necessary to use simulations, facsimiles, models, or some other variation of the real thing. But when possible, beginning with the real object or activity is usually the best approach.

Principles that Apply to Both Temporal and Spiritual Instruction

Three guidelines, not necessarily in this order, can help teachers prepare and deliver effective instruction. *First*, start with the concrete and move to the abstract. *Second*, begin with the simple and move to the complex. *Third*, let the learner confirm the lesson. Instructors often violate these guidelines, but the practice is common among successful parents and teachers. The principles are equally useful in both temporal and spiritual instruction.

The first principle can be illustrated with the observation of a child learning to recognize and understand what a dog is. First, the child needs to see a dog (or a picture of a dog—a simulation); then he must be told that what he sees is a dog. Last, he must have some personal experience with a dog to validate for himself the nature of his observations. It is not uncommon for children in the initial stages of the learning process to call a cat a "dog." The two animals have similar enough characteristics to confuse a young child. Only after repeated and cumulative experiences will the child develop the abstract concept to classify which animals are in fact dogs. Likewise, it is only after many *concrete* perceptual experiences with heat, wind, cold, ice, and rain that a child obtains the *abstract* concept of *weather*. Learning about the physical world moves most naturally from the concrete to the abstract. This principle also applies to moral and spiritual matters. For example, teaching a person to become service oriented follows a similar track. Lessons should be planned and delivered accordingly.

The second principle is illustrated in a simple story concerning food and its relationship to sustaining our physical bodies. Some people spend many years studying this relationship.

323

They take chemistry classes, learn difficult vocabularies, engage in complex experiments, and study economics. Our nation's economy is inextricably related to food. Production, marketing, sales, and transportation are involved. But the most successful teachers will remember to follow this guideline: Let simple explanations be the foundation for understanding more complex ideas. Too often, teachers begin in the middle or at the wrong end. The mother in the following story did not make this mistake.

Food for Pat and Patty

Pat and Patty were twins. They lived on a big farm fifteen miles from town. One winter they were snowbound for two months. It was impossible to get to town.

"Mother, we'll starve!" exclaimed Pat.

"No, we'll just use the food the Lord has provided," mother answered.

"What food?" asked Patty.

"We have some seeds," said Mother.

"Seeds?" questioned Pat and Patty.

"Yes, we have some wheat we can grind into cereal and flour. We have lots of dried beans to cook. We have dried corn and canned peas. We also have roots."

"Roots?" questioned Pat and Patty.

Mother answered, "Last summer and fall we stored beets, carrots, and potatoes. Besides, we also have some leaves."

"Leaves?" exclaimed Pat and Patty.

"Yes, vegetable leaves, we canned some spinach and stored some cabbage in the sand. We also have fruit."

"I know," said Patty. "Apples and canned peaches."

"And we have meat," said Pat, "from our pigs, cows, sheep, and chickens."[1]

Too many of us are not taught that the food necessary for human survival is initially provided as seeds, roots, leaves, fruits, and animals. Milk comes from cows, not bottles or cartons. Further, we often lack the personal knowledge and skills to successfully produce and transform these natural elements into palatable foods that will sustain life. We have not been properly taught. We have skipped beyond some of the most basic lessons in our journey into the complexities of modern knowledge.

This condition became apparent to me when, as the bishop of a number of families in need of food, a farmer offered me a generous amount of poultry. Excited to share this donation with those in need, I set about contacting the families in an effort to divide up the contribution. But a problem developed. Yes, all those I contacted were thrilled at the prospect of receiving a chicken dinner—until they discovered the chickens were still alive, fully feathered, and in a coop at the farm. In the end, no one took the chickens because no one knew how to transform a live chicken into table food. In this case our modern training seems to have played a tragic trick on us.

Moving from the simple to the complex is equally important in teaching moral and spiritual matters. Learning to obey in little things, for example, prepared Abraham to be obedient when his supreme test came—the command to offer his own son as a sacrifice (Genesis 22:1-19). Likewise, Nephi, the son of Helaman, was so diligent and faithful that he perfected himself to the point that the Lord said he would grant unto him whatsoever he asked, for he knew, "Thou shalt not ask that which is contrary to my will" (BM, Helaman 10:5). Each of us can grow in this way, from the simple to the complex, until we have been fully tried and tested.

325

The third principle is closely associated with the first two. Showing and telling, seeing and hearing, are not sufficient. As we move from the concrete to the abstract and the simple to the complex we must have personal confirmations of what we learn. If we are to understand the physical world or the spiritual world, we must have something to *do* with them. We must become our own witness, confirming for ourselves those things which we need to master and pass on to our posterity. The teachers who help us the most will be those who assist us in our journey into learning, by not only showing and telling, but by providing a way that we can do something with what we see and hear. The student who only sees and hears the bell never quite gains the same understanding as the student who rings the bell. Mortal life was intended to be an experience, not merely an observation. Seeing the flowers and being told about the flowers is not the same as smelling the flowers. Education that limits itself to show and tell is suspect, its constituents are in jeopardy. Agency educators will strive to make sure that the instructional water gets to the end of the learner's row—doing will be emphasized as well as tell and show.

Seeking Both Skill and Ideas

As in spiritual matters, doing in the temporal domain does not mean that everyone or anyone must experience everything; it does mean that everyone should experience something vital to them. And, while it is important to be concerned about doing things right, we should first be concerned about discovering the right things to do. It is possible to do something right only to find out it was the wrong thing to do.

Modern society, however, has become a society of specialists. Most of us are chicken eaters but few of us are chicken fixers. Over the past few centuries, the advent of technology has triggered a proliferation of knowledge. From the days of Leonardo da Vinci when it was fashionable for at least a few people to strive to learn everything, we have moved to a day when the goal is for most people to learn everything about something. The rest of us are encouraged to learn at least something about many things. In the transition, however, we may have lost a needed balance. Increasingly, we seek to qualify for a vocation that depends either on our hands or on our heads—seldom do we seek both. Ironically, specialization has put us in prison at the same time it has set us free. We often have more, but are frequently capable of doing less.

Consistent with agency education, a general rule is that each family would desire to rear children that are qualified to earn a living with their hands and also with their heads. To focus on one or the other is shortsighted, unless circumstances peculiar to the individual prohibit seeking both. Like the switch-hitter in baseball, there is a personal as well as a social advantage to acquiring the balance and appreciation that comes when one can do both. Brigham Young said,

326

> I delight to see the mother teach her daughters to be housekeepers; to be particular, clean, and neat; to sew, spin, and weave; to make butter and cheese; and I have no objection to their learning to cultivate flowers, herbs, and useful shrubs in the gardens. It is good for their health to rise early in the morning and work in the soil an hour or two before breakfast. . . . I would not have them neglect to learn music and would encourage them to read history and the Scriptures, to take up a newspaper, geography, and other

publications, and make themselves acquainted with the manners and customs of distant kingdoms and nations, with their laws, religion, geographical location on the face of the world, their climate, natural productions, the extent of their commerce, and the nature of their political organization; in fine, let our boys and girls be thoroughly instructed in every useful branch of physical and mental education. . . .Teach the little boys to lay away the garden hoe, the spade, etc., where they will not be destroyed by rust; and let them have access to tools that they may learn their use, and develop mechanical skill while young; and see that they gather up the tools when they have done with them, and deposit them in the proper place. Let both males and females encourage within them mechanical ingenuity, and seek constantly to understand the world they are in, and what use to make of their existence.[2]

Despite cultural and demographic changes that may have occurred in the past century, the general philosophy in this counsel remains valid for us all. As we seek vocational preparation, it makes sense for young people to prepare themselves to earn their living two ways—with their hands as well as their heads. Narrowing our choices to one or the other limits our choices.

327

Applying Methods to Instruction

Principles of instruction, to be effective, must relate to methods of instruction. This chapter would be incomplete without a note on this relationship. The focus in this book is more obviously on the theory and principles of learning and teaching than on techniques and methods of instruction. This is intentional, since methods are generic; they apply to all the theories of education. They may be applied differently, but they should not determine educational theory; they should simply be extensions of it. Methods are also seemingly infinite in their variety and readily available. Though very important, they are not primary; they are secondary to the theory and principles they support. Similar comments apply to technology. We live in a day when the potential for communications technology to contribute to teaching is mind-boggling. Technological hardware, however, is a tool and its value to agency educators depends on our preparation to use it in the right way for the right purposes. At present we have more technological capacity than educational competence; like an ill-prepared hunter armed with the finest guns going into the field with a sack full of unidentified ammunition. Three illustrations should suffice to emphasize the importance of selecting appropriate methods to facilitate effective and inspiring instruction.

First, methodology gives identity to what is being taught. In order to teach a principle effectively to others, the teacher needs the assistance of a method, technique, or device. For example, in this chapter three basic elements of successful lesson preparation are identified for moral and spiritual instruction: *teach according to the covenants, by the spirit, and with the law of witnesses;* three others are used for temporal or physical instruction—*show, tell,* and *do.* These elements constitute a framework, a skeletal structure that supports effective instruction. But the skeleton alone, like the human skeleton, is incomplete; it needs to be fleshed out in order to take on identity and life.

This principle—that methods help give identity to what is being taught—can be illustrated for potential teachers by showing them a skeleton, or a picture of a skeleton, and asking them to imagine what the person might have looked like who originally used the skeleton. They may be able determine some characteristics, such as height, gender, etc., but at best a full identity will remain a mystery. After showing the picture of a skeleton, show a picture of a person. Point out to the students how much more identity a body has—how much more interesting and complete the body is—than the skeleton alone. Then explain that the relationship of the body to the skeleton is similar to the relationship of methods to principles of instruction. They need each other. Without the skeleton, the body would become devoid of identity. Likewise, methods without instructional principles to sustain them become misshapen masses with unclear meanings; instructional principles without methods are sterile and lifeless, like a skeleton without a body.

Second, preparation is necessary to make instruction palatable. In order to teach this principle effectively, a method or way of illustrating the idea so it can be appreciated and understood is needed. One way to illustrate this principle would be to give students a tablespoon of unpopped popcorn kernels. Invite them to enjoy their popcorn. Notice how many eat it and how much they enjoy it. It is edible but it is not very palatable.

328

Now, either pop some of the kernels or give to students prepopped salted and buttered or candied popcorn. Invite them to eat it and notice the difference. Then explain that proper preparation of lesson materials is just as important as proper preparation of food items, if we expect them to be palatable to people.

Third, spiritual messages may need earthly carriages in order to arrive at their destination. Methods are available in infinite variety. Temporal or physical images can convey moral and spiritual ideas. Parables are examples of applying this method to instruction. A parable is an earthly story with a spiritual meaning. The method or technique is to provide, or call attention to, some common concrete experience that is very familiar to people and then attach to the experience a spiritual or abstract idea. This is what Jesus did in the parable of the sower. One advantage of this method of instruction is that it reveals information to those who have eyes to see and ears to hear, while it conceals information from those who, seeing, see not, and hearing, hear not. Those of us who miss the spiritual message are those who have not subjected the natural man to the spirit. We cannot see the spiritual kingdom of God, though it is all around us (John 3:3-5). We do not understand, because of unbelief (BM, Mosiah 26:3). We do not open our eyes to see it and our ears to hear it (BM, 3 Nephi 11:5). We must become humble and seek divine assistance in order to tune in, to become aware (D&C 136:32). If we do this, then we can know (Luke 24:32). Otherwise, we are locked into a horizontal perspective and do not see or feel what the vertical view offers us. We forfeit our vision and perish as to things of the spirit, seeing only that which is in the bubble.

329

Whenever teachers use the the words "*is like*" in a sentence, they attempt to use the transfer technique or method in their instruction, whether they are applying it in the spiritual or the physical domain. Comparison and contrast are important and powerful methods of making instruction more effective. But they must be sustained by correct principles. The successful agency teacher will begin with correct principles and let them guide him into complementary methods. It does not work the the other way around; methods do not come before principles in agency education.

Teaching Values in Today's World

Consider how the foregoing information applies to a specific application. The Church has developed a values based program for young women (girls age 12 through 18). The curriculum of this program is based on seven specific values. The teacher's task is to help the young women incorporate these seven values into their character. This is a challenging assignment and it is made more difficult because of the confusion that has been introduced by the competing world view we have discussed in this book. For example, in the past when a person was taught what was right, society usually reinforced that teaching by making clear what was wrong and why it was wrong. Today, this is not always true. Depending on the setting, both "right" and "wrong" are approved, and confusion results. This new condition is apparent in the government, workplace, school, church, neighborhood, and family. People may cue their behavior on one value in a particular setting and on an opposite value in another setting. Observing the language used by young people in a Latter-day Saint seminary and comparing it to the language used by the same individuals on the high school campus is just one example. Thus it is not uncommon for people today to operate their lives on more than one value system.

330

A New Challenge for Parents and Teachers

A new instructional challenge is created by this presence of two (or more) conflicting value structures within the same individual—especially when these value structures are isolated or insulated from each other, and each is socially endorsed as "acceptable." Today, in order to effectively teach a person to embrace a single value structure that sustains integrity, the parent or teacher must assume a greater role in the teaching process. In addition to carefully teaching what is right, we must also clearly explain how the opposite of that teaching is wrong and why it is wrong. Then, and only then, can we be confident that the individual has enough information to make an effective choice based on his or her own agency.

When this type of confrontive and contrasting instruction is missing, the individual tends simply to compartmentalize contradictory teachings into different value structures. These differing values are then used to cue the person's actions, depending on the setting. We may act from one set of values in Church settings and then act according to a contradictory set of values at home, school, or work. To illustrate the practical consequences, consider the challenge of teaching the specific values outlined in the Young Women's program.

Values In the Young Women's Program

Teaching youth and adults values differs from teaching young children values. In this example the focus is on youth and adults. Teaching values to younger children requires another discussion. An example of the difference, however, is expressed in the general observation *Encouraging and emphasizing right actions among children (birth to puberty) is usually most productive, while encouraging and emphasizing good thoughts and correct intentions is the most appropriate and productive approach with adults (puberty through adulthood).*

The foregoing observation underlies a challenge facing those who teach young women the seven values of **Faith, Divine Nature, Individual Worth, Knowledge, Choice and Accountability, Good Works,** and **Integrity**: How do we help these young women obtain and maintain the thoughts and intentions that lead to right actions? The values are certainly consistent with the blessings promised through our Hebraic heritage. *Faith* helps us desire the blessings. Our *Divine Nature* attracts us to the blessings. *Individual Worth* qualifies us to receive the blessings. *Knowledge* makes us aware of the blessings. *Choice and Accountability* lead us to the blessings. *Good Works* enable us to receive the blessings. *Integrity* allows us to retain the blessings. But the practical issues are first, How does a young woman *define the meaning* of each of these values and second, What are her *intentions* regarding each particular value—"at all times and in all things, and in all places?" (BM Mosiah 18:9). Is it to stand as a witness of God? Or, do other meanings govern her relationship to these terms?

331

At the outset, these two concerns may not seem significant. After all, definitions for each value are clearly given in the *Young Women's Handbook*, and the young woman's intentions become explicit when she selects her goals and pursues activities in support of those goals. While this is true, what is frequently overlooked is that this same young woman is being carefully taught different and conflicting definitions for each of these values by other teachers in other settings. She is also being enticed to establish personal goals and engage in selected activities to fulfill these goals in support of the alternative definition for each of the values. The options are real; the counterfeits are clever and deceptively enticing (see figure 19-3).

Young Women's Program
Lifestyle Value Conflicts

Value	Celestial Expression	Terrestrial Expression	Telestial Expression
FAITH	Embracing the atonement of Christ	Hopeful expectations	Being lucky
DIVINE NATURE	Developing God-given qualities and talents	Deserving of admiration by others	The right to control others
INDIVIDUAL WORTH	Using talents to fulfill divine mission	Experiencing popularity, feeling important	Believing I am better than others
KNOWLEDGE	Seeking knowledge by faith and by study	Achieving in school or at work	Acquiring information that generates wealth, power, and control
CHOICE AND ACCOUNTABILITY	Doing what God wants, accepting consequences	Doing what I want and accepting consequences	Doing what I want and not getting caught
GOOD WORKS	Building the Kingdom by nurturing service	Doing things that bring personal rewards	Experiencing power and personal gratification
INTEGRITY	Acting consistently with right not wrong as revealed by God	Acting consistently with right and wrong as determined by some group	Acting consistently with personal desires

Figure 19-3

332

For example, imagine a young lady named Jennifer. Jennifer's teacher in the Young Women's program may have successfully introduced and reinforced the idea that to possess the value of *Faith* means to feel the need to embrace the atonement of Christ. This definition is made plain in the *Young Women's Handbook*. Jennifer may also have established appropriate personal goals, such as "I will work to strengthen my testimony." And she may plan and carry out activities in support of that goal, such as (a) "I will say my prayers every day," (b) "I will memorize the words of a hymn and repeat them when I have bad thoughts," and (c) "I will bear my testimony twice in the next three months." Jennifer's teacher may monitor this program and encourage her in personal progress interviews.

The teaching problem becomes more clear, however, as we realize that although Jennifer may do many good things and demonstrate commendable success in her values program in church, she may act quite differently at school or in her personal social life. In these settings she is being taught a different definition of *Faith*, establishing different goals in support of that definition, and engaging in different activities to achieve those goals.

In the secular setting, *Faith* is usually defined as *hopeful expectations*. It has nothing to do with the atonement of Christ. Jennifer will be setting different goals to fulfill this alternative definition. And she will plan and carry out alternative kinds of activities to achieve those goals. For example, she may aspire to be the Junior Prom Queen. In her mind this may entail a special wardrobe. Positive relationships with particular people will be critical. And involvement in certain activities may appear requisite. This values program also receives positive endorsement, and Jennifer will be evaluated (if not personally interviewed) by significant persons in her social circle to determine her degree of success.

A powerful social reinforcement, with its own rewards and punishments, urges the internalization of this alternative value system. The system is solidly entrenched and may take on such forms as cheerleaders, athletes, cowboys, rockers, or any other subset in the teenager's peer group. The presence of such alternative value structures sets the stage for Jennifer to exhibit behaviors that could be contrary to the plan she is pursuing in her Young Women's Program. She may be quite comfortable with these

333

conflicting behaviors, without feeling significant dissonance, because conscience is a spiritual attribute subject to social conditioning. This is why teaching is so critically important.

Similar comparisons could be made of each of the seven values. Consider just one more extension. In the Young Women's Program the definition of *Individual Worth* means using divinely bestowed talents to fulfill one's personal mission in life. Goals like sharing talents with others may be set; and activities such as playing the piano, baking cookies, and sewing—all for good causes—may be carried out. At school, however, *Individual Worth* is not commonly perceived in spiritual terms. Rather, it *is defined as experiencing popularity and feeling important.* The goals are different, and so are the activities. Under these circumstances, Jennifer may use questionable language, engage in undesirable activities, and identify with those who do not support Church standards in order to experience the feeling of importance and popularity. Which definition of *Individual Worth* is going to cue Jennifer's choices—the school definition or the Church definition? They both seem to work, used in the right places.

334

Types of Values

The entire dilemma facing Jennifer and her teachers is more extensive than the partial illustration provided but the basic problem is the same. The description of lifestyles described in the Doctrine and Covenants (Section 76) provides a helpful way to understand the issue. In this revelation, the Lord describes individuals whose lifestyles are built on three major value structures: first, those striving valiantly for a celestial order in which men and women seek to become like God; second, those who are blinded by the craftiness of men but still seek to live by moral principles characteristic of a terrestrial order; third, those who would constitute a telestial order, who seek gratification, whatever the cost—lying, adultery, and other activities pleasing to the devil.

Each of these categories is based on different assumptions about everyday decisions; each fashions its own definitions for terms related to values (see figure 19-3). Nephi saw our day and wrote extensively of these conflicts (see 2 Nephi 25-33). He observed that some individuals would strive to live in harmony with celestial goals; others would turn aside. One group would content itself in the values of a hedonistic philosophy—eat, drink, and be merry, for tomorrow we die; another group would proceed with a little more caution, but the result would leave them short of their potential as children of God. He noted that Satan would seek to confuse our values and choices through apathy, rebellion, and intellectual pride in an effort to claim our souls.

The conditions described by Nephi form the context in which values are taught today. Some voices caution us to seek righteousness and avoid the very appearance of evil, while others teach that a little bad language, a few bad scenes, an R rating is nothing to be concerned about; just focus on the "redeeming social value." All will be well with us. The competition between these value structures is intense. At Church we hear that *the greatest love is service to others.* In schools our children sing that *love of self is the greatest love of all,* while on the radio we are admonished not to care what's right or wrong—just so we help each other *make it through the night.* The prophets counsel us not to lay up treasures that moth and rust can destroy, but glittering advertisements proclaim that possessions are the great source of enjoyment and happiness. We are advised by our spiritual leaders to exercise self-denial and by promoters of pleasure to go with all the gusto we can, because we only go around once.

335

The Teacher's Task

Helping youth and adults acquire values that will protect and strengthen them in this kind of environment demands more than simply pointing out what is right. It requires the identification of counterfeit values and an explanation of why they will cause us to fall short in our efforts to develop the characteristics necessary to qualify for life in the celestial kingdom. Long ago the Lord warned us that doublemindedness—following contradictory value systems—makes a person unstable in "all his ways" (James 1:8). Properly exercising our power of choice can free us of this instability, but the power of agency cannot be exercised in ignorance (D&C 93:31). The Spirit can guide us in making the correct choice, but we need to see the necessity of the choice before we will choose between one thing and another. The ancient lie is that we do not need to choose; we can have our cake and eat it too.

When we are encumbered by compartmentalized value structures, we are often blind to the choices that need to be made.

It is as if there was no choice. We are captured by relativism, that is, "When in Rome do what the Romans do." Anything is okay if you are in a place and among those who endorse it. Under these conditions, as Lehi told his sons, all things become "a compound in one"; everything becomes relative with no distinguished differences (2 Nephi 2:11). When opposites or differences are not distinguished, it is difficult to discern between good and evil. We must be able to see the differences between right and wrong before we can effectively choose between them. Therefore, the teacher who helps her young women confront the differences in value definitions also helps them to be better able to exercise their agency to choose.

What enables a teacher to do this? A basic answer to this question is in the counsel on preparation the Lord gave to early Church leaders (D&C 88:78-80 and 93:53.). We must gain a knowledge of those systems which generate the alternatives being offered to us. We must understand how they function and the nature of their shortcomings. The more we comply with this counsel, the more the Lord will help us see and understand what is necessary to fulfill our callings. The more prepared we will be to "magnify the calling whereunto I have called you, and the mission with which I have commissioned you" (D&C 88:80).

336

The task is not as monumental as it may seem, because we are not working alone. We have our own faculties and facilities, but we also have the counsel and assistance provided in the scriptures and by living prophets. We have each other, and we have the Spirit of the Lord to assist us. And we know that "the Lord giveth no commandments unto the children of men, save he shall prepare a way for them that they may accomplish the thing which he commandeth them" (I Nephi 3:7). Part of this *way* is bringing to bear the power of many witnesses as outlined in the lesson preparation sheet at the beginning of this chapter. There is no effective substitute for teaching according to the covenants, teaching by the spirit, and teaching with the power of the law of witnesses. This must be kept clearly in focus when we are engaging in activities and instruction that involves showing, telling, and doing. The *showing* that occurs must be directly related to the *covenants*, the telling must be in harmony with the Spirit, and the *doing* must improve each girl's capacity to act as a witness of God. This will result in effective moral and spiritual instruction.

20

Evaluation, Tests, and Grading

Evaluation that grows out of self-assessment is consistent with agency education. While standards, which others may help provide, are important, human volition should be placed at the center of educational evaluation. But self-assessment and observations by others is not enough, we also need to know how we stand with God.

It is inconsistent with the agency view of education to develop and administer instructional programs based solely on externally imposed systems of evaluation. A fundamental weakness in popular approaches to evaluation is the emphasis placed on the measurement of overt expression; the act is separated from the intent and the information behind the act.

Current Practices

Agency-oriented educators view evaluation, tests, and grading procedures in a different light than do most conventional educators. The popular societal approach to education trains students to fit into society. As Edward L. Thorndike wrote many years ago, "The aim of the teacher is to produce desirable and prevent undesirable changes in human beings by producing and preventing certain responses. The means at the disposal of the teacher are the stimuli which can be brought to bear upon the pupil."[1] Though seldom expressed in words, the practical emphasis of most modern education clearly supports the assumption that the individual exists for society more than society exists for the individual. Man is considered a very pliable animal, to be shaped into whatever society wants or needs. Human behavior can be determined by conditioning us to respond to the stimuli of the environment. We begin as a "blank slate" on which society writes. John B. Watson, a famous psychologist, expressed this view in 1924:

> Why don't we make what we can *observe* the real field of psychology? Let us limit ourselves to things that can be observed, and formulate laws concerning only those things. Now what can we observe? . . . The rule, or measuring rod, which the behaviorist puts in front of him always is: Can I describe this bit of behavior I see in terms of "stimulus and response"?[2]

In this approach to education, the ultimate goal of schooling is to help socialize individuals to be contributing role-players in the society. Skill training, scientific evaluation, standard competencies, behavioral objectives, and standards for certification are all greatly valued, stressed, and rewarded. Recent emphasis on cognitive training has not altered the role of competitive evaluation, tests, and grades in schooling. Educational purposes and curriculum are designed and instruction is delivered with the intent of rating students. In a formal role, the teacher tests students and assigns grades. Methods that produce as quickly as possible the desired competency are valued, and measures are developed to validate these methods. In other words, the primary educational goal is to demonstrate to society that schools are succeeding in shaping the students to fit social roles. Reading, writing, arithmetic, and other aspects of the basic curriculum are viewed as criteria to determine which students will become doctors, lawyers, engineers, scientists, etc. Parents trained in these settings usually reinforce both the assumptions and the methods. The disposition underlying the societal approach is inconsistent with agency education, in which the learner, not the teacher or the system, assumes the greater responsibility for evaluation.

Evaluations administered by the school in societal systems are generally designed for school personnel to demonstrate to others where their students stand in the *shaping* process. The presumption is that what is being measured is what ought to be measured and learned. Further, it is assumed that testing devices are *reliable* (they consistently measure what they claim to measure) and *valid* (they accurately measure what they claim to measure). On the basis of these premises, students are evaluated and assigned grades arbitrarily by comparison with each other (e.g., graded on the curve, using the highest student score as the optimum standard) or arbitrarily by some other standard (e.g., grading by percentage, using 100% as the standard).

A popular assumption in our society is that we can measure both a person's *intelligence* and *achievement*. This can be deceptive and may lead to false conclusions. For example, we do not know what intelligence is, at least "educators and psychologists have never been able to come to complete agreement on the term or on the concepts it involves. . . . Actually, our definition of intelligence is circular, since we are in effect saying that intelligence is what intelligence tests measure."[3] This puts us in an awkward position. As one observer points out, "They don't know what it is, but they're getting better and better at measuring it."[4]

The problem is similar in measuring achievement. Conventional multiple-choice tests such as those employed in standardized testing depends on the perception that it is scientifically neutral and objective; there are "right" and "wrong" answers to the questions being asked. A number of problems accompany this perception. Consider three. First, the scholarly community itself does not agree on how to define "scientific," "neutral," or "objective." Philosophical journals contain many articles that pose different perceptions of these terms. Second, even if one overlooks the difficulty with this basic presumption, the problem of successfully communicating with the student remains. Cultures create variables that tests often ignore. Third, assumptions associated with ideas such as the "normal curve" may become part of our thinking and shape our educational practice. For example, a school may presume some form of talent distribution such as a few bright, a large number of average, and a few dull. When conventional grading procedures fall under this spell teachers and students are trapped. If a teacher succeeds in helping all her students earn A's she is charged with grade inflation. Hence, the most successful teacher can be viewed as a failure by the system notwithstanding the actual performance of herself or her students.

Representatives of cultural minorities have amassed abundant evidence of the bias that occurs in testing due to the assumptions inherent in the use of language. Much serious criticism has been written in recent decades that challenges the use of achievement tests to compare, rate, and rank people. David Owen's *None of the*

Above: Behind the Myth of Scholastic Aptitude is a readable, forthright introduction to the problems of comparative testing.

Nevertheless, by the use of sophisticated statistical systems to create standardized tests (such as the SAT, ACT, GRE, etc.), students are assigned percentile ratings which show their standing in comparison to other students in the nation. These test scores, combined with grades generated within the local systems, are used to sustain and defend the educational enterprise. Individuals are given honors, granted financial rewards, admitted or denied admission to higher schooling, and in other ways classified by these procedures in the schools and for society. This type of educational system establishes a false sense of confidence among those who use it. It becomes easy to think we know more about people and processes than we really do. It may be argued that quantitative measures may be harmful as well as helpful. They may lead to false expectations or injustices. For example, the highest rated students are not always hired, or they may fail to perform when they are hired. This is evidenced by the difficulty researchers have in establishing consistent correlations between school test scores and "success" as determined in the marketplace. At best, school achievement scores seem to predict school achievement as long as the school system remains constant, but predicts little else.

340

One way to gain a feeling for the limitations of present school evaluation practices is to consider recommendations for changing them. Ernest L. Boyer, for example, suggests, "There is an urgent need for new and better ways to assess students as they move from school to higher education." Specifically, what he and his colleagues propose is "a new assessment program, one that would evaluate not only the *academic* achievement of the student . . . but would evaluate other areas of talent, too. The assessment program we need is not to screen students out of options, but help them move on with confidence to college and to jobs."[5] Boyer's statement represents the gentle kinds of changes being recommended. Others, more harshly challenge the entire structure of the American school system.

Marxist Criticism of American Schools

Marxist critics of American education, for example, maintain that the current evaluation system is structured to convince Americans their education is based on individual merits—we get what we earn. They argue that this claim is false and point to government statistics which reveal that those who have the money, power, and influence before they enter the school system retain the money, power, and influence after they leave the school system—regardless of how they performed. "Every society," they say, "will reward some individual excellences, . . .[but] the predatory, competitive, and personally destructive way in which achievement is rewarded in U.S. schools and colleges is a monument not to creative rationality, but to the need of a privileged class to justify an irrational, exploitive, and undemocratic system."[6] These critics claim that "great efforts are made—through testing and counseling—to convince students that their lack of success is objectively attributable to their own inadequacies."[7] The disturbing evidence used to support these claims would probably be taken more seriously if the program these critics offered as a substitute did not suffer the same potential weaknesses they criticize.

341

One alternative proposed by these particular socialist critics is to use the schools to pursue a thinly veiled doctrine of subversive political revolution. This position is fueled by a motive that is in conflict with our American heritage and the values of our own founders who conducted a revolution of their own. Following the plan proposed by these Marxist educators simply leads to another societal school system under a different political system that offers less personal freedom.

There is no room in their program for divine purpose. The strategy to bring about the change they desire includes guidelines such as, "revolutionary educators must be in the forefront of the movement to create a unified class consciousness. Socialist teachers must not only demand control over their activities; we must also extend this control to students and the broader community." And "socialist educators should take seriously the need to combine a long-range vision with (winning) victories here and now. . . . [in support of] revolutionary reforms built around such issues as democracy, free classrooms, open enrollment, adequate financial aid for needy students, and development of critical antidiscriminatory and socialist content of education."[8] While these strategies may sound positive, agency educators should not be deceived as to their ultimate outcomes. One value of understanding such critics is that it sharpens our recognition that similar positive sounding educational reform proposals may lead in radically different directions .

Apparent Limitations

Although the type of evaluation system now used to govern most schools is widely accepted, it is not the only way to think about assessment in education. Agency educators will avoid imposing externally based, other-directed, judgmental forms of classifying human beings as the major form of evaluation. Although some laws are necessary to protect human rights and sustain social order, learning/teaching relationships can function quite safely and productively without imposing external coercion in the form of a grading system. Higher order standards can be emphasized. Students can be helped to rely on internal motives that free them from the terrible waste of fighting the system, or worse, cheating to beat the system. Trust and responsibility can replace the adversarial mechanisms common in most classrooms if we are willing to change our views about education and those we teach. Competition and comparison among students are not requisite to the most effective teaching. They often foster a destructive pride that inhibits the best education.

342

As most readers recognize, academic grades in societal education programs inevitably become a component among the various instruments of control; they serve the interests of the system more than the interests of the student. Grades derived from calculations based on external observations determined and applied by representatives of the system, as most are, have proven a useful shield for representatives of the system. They can be understood and defended as long as one holds to the assumptions underlying the societal approach to education. In fact, once they become entrenched, the system may become very dependent on them. These practices, however, are not harmonious with the premises of agency education.

When educators transfer into numerical or letter symbols their judgments about how much students have learned (1, 2, 3, or A, B, C), the difficulty is laid bare. The evidence used by those who claim that tests accurately measure what people know, or what they can accomplish with what they know, is flawed. The agency educator asks, How can we justify a procedure that allows one-tenth or one-hundredth of a single point to separate an A grade from a B grade or a C grade from a D grade? And beyond the limitations of the internal rationale in the grading system, there is the larger and more important question regarding the propriety of imposing external, empirical, "objective" systems upon learners. Too often, the claims of those who espouse these procedures have proven to be unfounded.

For example, during the 1960s, enthusiastic researchers, educators, and social workers lobbied effectively with government agencies and private philanthropic sources for money to conduct experimental and evaluative research in education. They promised demonstrable results and cited various adaptations of the "scientific" approach (the systems described above) as the means for producing and demonstrating these results. Their proposals were compelling, but ironically, the very systems used to justify the expenditures of millions of dollars during the 1960s were unable to produce sufficient evidence to justify their original claims. Advocates found themselves incapable of either demonstrating persuasive, positive results or convincing those who provided the money why the programs didn't work. This condition in education led to a withdrawal of many federal funds during the early 1970s and a serious questioning of the actual impact of different programs on the schooling process. Several efforts were initiated to analyze the results of educational research.

343

An editorial in the *Educational Researcher* summarized the results of some of these efforts to measure programmatic experiments. Three of the most probing reviews of educational research were reported to have reached the same conclusions:

1. The impact of schooling on children is far less than we thought it to be.
2. We are unable to measure the long-range outcomes of schooling on a child with the tools available to us.
3. Schooling may be only as effective as the quality of the entrants.[9]

Later research efforts then shifted away from trying to measure general program claims toward an examination of the specifics of what is and is not happening in education.[10] This emphasis stimulated a myriad of national and state studies describing the conditions of American education, headed by the famous document *A Nation at Risk*. It has also refocused research on teacher preparation and the instructional strategies that have been so prominent in educational literature during the 1980s. The saga continues about what is happening in education, what should be happening in education, and how this can be determined.

Means versus Ends in Education

While American education borrowed heavily from corporate thinking and behavior during this century, the emphasis on (quantitative) measures, money, and balance sheets increased. One result has been a de-emphasis on "weightier matters." When leaders are obsessed with results and the demonstration of those results, little room remains for patience, long-suffering, kindness, gentleness, meekness, and love. When the focus switches to applying these nonquantifiable principles to support effectiveness and perfection, there is less reason to be preoccupied with comparative test scores and academic grades. Unlike big business, the *means* is the *end* in agency education. The "bottom line" is not some quantifiable measure of outcome; it is the quality and character of relationships—man to God, man to man, and man to things. Measures can be helpful, but they cannot be central in agency education, as they often are in other approaches.

Although modern administrative theory and practice did not begin with the idea of separating moral purpose and instruction, it has made it convenient to ignore traditional moral values. For example, Paul Hanus helped pioneer the adaptation of modern corporate management theory to education, just as Frederick W. Taylor popularized it in business. At the turn of the century, Hanus stated a noble intent for moving in this direction:

> [The aim of education] is to arouse and develop all the worthy interests and corresponding powers of each individual . . . in order that his life as an individual may be as full and rich as possible, and that no artificial obstacles may stand in the way of his spiritual and material advancement.[11]

The intended fusion of moral and material objectives did not develop. Rather, a gradual separation occurred. As the foregoing paragraph illustrates, when a strong unity of purpose prevails, a

344

clear distinction can be made between *means* and *ends*. Hanus does this in his statement. The first half of the statement indicates what has to be done (the means) "in order that" the ultimate goals (the ends) can be achieved. The traditional objectives of education are stated after the "in order that" clause. One of the difficulties in contemporary education is that we no longer have a strong consensus on these traditional purposes. Consequently, we have shifted our focus to the *means* of education and made them the *ends* of education. This shift has contributed to an increased emphasis on external measurements. For example, consider how the following means have become educational *ends*. And notice how we face a vacuum where once there was a consensus regarding the ultimate ends of education. Students should

think for themselves *in order that* _____
acquire a love of learning *in order that* _____
seek excellence *in order that* _____
be able to read *in order that* _____
write and do arithmetic *in order that* _____
attain high achievement scores *in order that* _____
acquire demonstrable skills *in order that* _____
exibit classroom courtesy *in order that* _____

Traditionally, the ultimate ends of education have been moral and spiritual in nature. Modern educators, however, have been increasingly satisfied to use the *means* of the educational equation as the end of education—its ultimate purpose. One advantage of this shift is that *means* are generally more identifiable, concrete, and empirical or measurable than are *ends*. This fits nicely with modern administrative theory. For example, it is one thing for people to reach agreement on means, such as students should *think for themselves*, or *acquire a love for learning*, or *seek for excellence*, or *be able to read, write and do arithmetic*. Disagreement arises quickly, however, on the long-term values. This becomes apparent as soon as one adds an "in order that" to some practical declaration and then seeks to complete the second half of the equation by indicating the ultimate purpose. This is illustrated in the simple statement: Children should learn to read *in order that* _____ . It is convenient for administrators to avoid disagreements over what might be written in the blank space, such as "they can read the Bible," or "they can read the great books," or "they can be informed citizens," by letting the means become the ends. This appears to be what has happened in many aspects of American education; most recently it can be seen occurring in elementary and secondary schools. The pattern follows the changes that took place in our universities several decades ago, when character education was dropped as an educational aim.

A century ago, William H. McGuffy's eclectic readers were used in nearly every school. They promoted the mastery of both reading and self. Noah Webster's Spelling Book ("blueback speller"), another instructional mainstay, was replete with traditional values related to character formation, such as "Refrain from all evil; keep no company with immoral men," "Whatever is wrong is a deviation from right, or from the just laws of God or man," and "How happy men would be if they would always love what is right and hate what is wrong." Learning to read or spell was a means to a greater end, and that end was clearly manifest in the curricular materials as well as the instructional process. Adminstration defined its purpose as providing educational resources *in order that* students might be able to achieve moral and spiritual ends. This is no longer the case. We may not need McGuffy's readers today, but we do need the moral emphasis they brought to society.

Although Paul Hanus enthusiastically promoted a scientific approach to administration founded on efficiency principles (such as reducing education to budgetary line items), he did not intend that we set aside moral concerns, any more than did Horace Mann. Their intentions were quite the contrary. But complex and formal budget-based administration tends to make the means (the quantifiable and dollar cost items) become the ends. These tangible items get talked about most. One seldom finds moral objectives reduced to budgetary line items opposite their respective dollar costs. Day-by-day administrative practices tend to focus on the tangibles more than the intangibles. This leads to nonquantifiable dimensions of education receiving less and less agenda time. Anyone with experience in contemporary administration knows this is true. The very jargon we use attests to this. Terms such as, *input/output, cost-effective, performance standards, criterion referenced, bottom line, our "product,"* etc., mirror this condition. These terms have replaced the moral language used by past educators. This significant change may lead to the destruction of our traditional educational system. Agency educators will guard against this happening in their educational endeavors.

Recently I listened to a three-hour, statewide televised conference on educational policy. The various studio centers were filled with dozens of people, among them most of the important personalities in the state's power structure—from the governor to classroom teachers, parents, and students. Not once in all the dialogue did I hear a serious expression about the "why" or ultimate purposes of education. The focus was exclusively on "how" and "for how much"

Just as quantifiable elements have become the standards for recognition and reward in general administration, they have also come to dominate classroom management. For example, *means*—such as high achievement scores, demonstrable vocational skills, and minimal classroom courtesy for example, being quiet—are most often perceived as ends in classroom management. Former *means*, such as "excellence" and "productivity," are now considered worthy goals in and of themselves. They are no longer considered means to higher ends, they are the ends. The goals that used to explain *why* we educate, such as honesty, compassion, citizenship, integrity, and moral character, are largely ignored by current policy-makers and reformers, who usually only address issues related to *how* we educate and for *how much*.

347

Official documents associated with educational administration also provide anecdotal illustrations of the shift in emphasis. For example, a certificate issued in 1917 by the State of Idaho to teach in the public schools reads: "This certifies that Harold B. Lee *is a person of good moral character* and has passed an examination in all branches required by law." The certificate continues with a list of the subjects in which the holder is qualified to teach and his test scores in each of these areas as measured by a state examination. A similar certificate was issued by the State of Utah in 1900. It verified that the recipient, George H. Brimhall, was *"a person of good moral character."* At mid-century, Utah still tied certification to the code of ethics espoused by national, state, and local educational associations. But what contemporary educator now receives state certification to teach or administer "on the condition of" individual moral character or the requirement of adherence to an ethical code? The "licensing" documents themselves mirror the changes that are occurring.

It appears that the application of corporate management philosophy, which arose from man's experience with utilizing and controlling things, seriously jeopardizes traditional values when it is applied to the educational process. Applied to people, these principles of utilization and control that work so well on things seem to distort if not destroy an important component of personal education. Teachers tend to emphasize external rather than internal motivational techniques. Students concentrate more on grades and "beating the system" than they do on learning and defining their personal mission in life. People are held accountable for what can be objectively measured; the "weightier matters," which cannot be effectively measured, tend to be ignored. One questions whether these overt practices, when applied to people in a grading system, can be defended on the basis of Christian principles. Some people believe they cannot.

348

Teacher Preparation and Evaluation

Lack of moral concern is conspicuously evident in teacher preparation and training. While more and more is being required of prospective educators in professional programs, less and less of this additional requirement deals with the teacher's character.

One simple but significant illustration of the moral void is reflected in teacher evaluation instruments. These instruments are both numerous and varied. But they seem to have two things in common: (1) emphasis is placed on observable, quantifiable performance criteria, and (2) items related to personal or professional morality are absent. If one uses preservice and inservice evaluation instruments as the primary guide, it is easy to conclude that moral or character education is not a high priority (or a priority at all) in contemporary American education.

The specific content of teacher evaluation instruments also reflects an important philosophical bias. Although I know of no formal study on this particular observation, the examination of a number of schemes, lists, instruments, etc., used to evaluate student and full-time teacher instruction show they are based on the quantifiable elements discussed previously. It seems somewhat ironic that when these teaching evaluation devices are applied to what is known of the instructional patterns of Jesus of Nazareth and Adolf Hitler, Hitler usually scores higher than Jesus. This raises a serious question for agency-oriented educators: Are we measuring the teaching characteristics of greatest importance? Apparently the measures we are using do not emphasize the characteristics that made Jesus a master teacher.

Another View

A fundamental weakness in the popular approach to evaluation is its emphasis and reliance on the measurement of overt behavior. The act is separated from the intent behind the act. Agency education favors keeping the two together and emphasizing the role of the individual in initiating, determining, and reporting achievement. The emphasis in evaluation is placed as much or more on what cannot be measured as it is on what can be measureed. Brigham Young said:

349

> There is one principle I wish to urge upon the Saints in a way that it may remain with them—that is, to understand men and women as they are, and not understand them as you are. You see the variety of mind, disposition, judgment, and talent, and variety in explaining and communicating thoughts. There is an endless variety, and I wish you to understand men and women as they are, and not to judge your brother, your sister, your family, or any one, only from the intention. When you know the intention of the act performed, you will then know how to judge the act.[12]

Strictly "objective" measures of educational achievement seldom, if ever, account for the intention behind the behaviors they assess or measure.

It is inconsistent with the agency view of education to develop and administer instructional programs based on externally imposed systems of evaluation. A worthy principle is implicit in the observation that men are "to act for themselves and not to be acted upon, save it be by the punishment of the law at the great and last day, according to the commandments which God hath given (BM, 2 Nephi 2:26)." Human volition should be placed at the center of educational evaluation. The person is at the center, and he or she uses standards (which others may help provide) to guide the assessments that are made. Teachers may share their observations and judgments, but these should not supplant the individual's own evaluation. The principle and spirit of this approach to assessment is illustrated in John's account of the "woman taken in adultery." The scribes and pharisees brought the woman to Jesus in hopes to entice him into a legal entrapment. Jesus ignored their attempt to make him judge the woman and turned their attention to the responsibility of evaluating their own actions (John 8:3-11).

Evaluation that grows out of self-assessment is the most consistent with agency education. Conventional report cards based on external judgments and comparisons between students are inconsistent with agency education. Grades, as applied in competitive education, are viewed as arbitrary symbols determined by others and for others. They are created primarily from fragments of presumably measurable external evidence. Generally devoid of personal intentions, these widely used "objective" measurements seek to classify and control human beings for social purposes. In this sense they violate the very premises of agency education.[13] To understand the negative influence comparative grading can have on a relationship, simply shift the focus from teacher/student to husband/wife. Evaluation is important to a healthy growing marriage. But imagine what would happen to a relationship if one spouse began giving letter grades to the other based on how he or she compared with other individuals. The outcome is fairly predictable, and it applies as well to the relationship between a student and teacher.

But self-assessment and observations by others is not enough. We also need to know how we stand with God. We are promised divine assistance to help us understand our weakness and our strengths. "And if men come unto me I will show unto them their weakness . . . for if they humble themselves before me, and have faith in me, then will I make weak things become strong unto them" (BM, Ether 12:37). We can also know when the Lord is pleased with our performance.

350

Proceeding with Faith

The idea that man is limited in his ability to comprehend reality is consistent with the gospel of Jesus Christ. The definition of faith, the first principle of the Gospel of Christ, as a partial knowledge supports this proposition (BM, Alma 32:21). Apparently it is not necessary and perhaps not possible for man to develop a system that allows him to objectively see things as they really are, have been, or will be. Paul the apostle quoted the Old Testament prophet Habukkuk to make this point: "the just shall live by faith" (Habukkuk 2:4; Romans 1:17). In other words, even those who are most "on target" in mortality will be conducting their affairs without the assistance of instruments, systems, or devices that permit them a perfect knowledge. This proposition has special relevance for agency-oriented educators, because their stewardship is to help others understand mortal life as it relates to their origin and potential destiny. What we can and do know in mortality is limited. This limitation should not disturb us; we can function within this framework and lose nothing of importance if we exercise our faith.

In his discourse on faith, Paul shared his view on man's limited ability to comprehend reality. He taught that faith is knowing a few important things which serve as evidence that a more expansive reality exists beyond man's temporal comprehension. This "evidence of things not seen" is a tiny shadow of the reality that transcends mortal man's normal capacity to comprehend (Hebrews 11:1). Paul lived with a partial knowledge and ascribed greater value to that which is not seen than to that which is seen. His view of education enveloped both the seen and unseen.

351

When one begins to think of education from this platform and remains true to it, the role of evaluation, tests, and grades takes on new perspective. The positive contributions these tools can make become more clear. People cease to be objects to be rated and engineered; rather they become partners in a common quest. Evaluation is sustained as a vital dimension in the learning process. Inquiry into proficiency, however, comes primarily from the student rather than the teacher. Tests are requested rather than required, and they are used in a supportive rather than a judgmental context. A personal emphasis on acquiring the ability to serve others successfully, replaces the system's emphasis on competitively acquiring symbols that set one above or below others. Confirmation of competency is provided by the teacher as a qualified and respected witness, but not in the form of judgments symbolized by an A, B, C, or F. Personal recommendations from those who know and can vouch for competency are respected, just as newcomers accept recommendations from natives regarding a restaurant, a good auto mechanic, or travel conditions.

Competence in the marketplace is subject to the respective stewardships of the marketplace. Stewards (employers) over these various stewardships who seek others (employees) to assist them in their work are the authorized judges; perceptions of others are merely supplemental. Ultimately there can be no substitute for true apprenticeship. And in the schools, comparative grade point averages (GPA) are essentially meaningless because they lack a significant relationship to whether the students are successfully discovering and fulfilling their personal missions in life.

Accurate Records More Basic Than Experimental Research

The agency mode accepts the premise that education is basically a matter of responsible people sharing their own choices rather than a system in which certain individuals seek to shape and fit human subjects (or "objects") into social roles. Accepting this premise changes our educational priorities, including data collection. For example, keeping accurate records becomes more fundamental than pursuing experimental research. The better the records are kept, the less the need for expensive research and evaluation procedures. Likewise, the better the records, the less expensive and the more likely the success when refined methods of evaluation are appropriately applied to assist in the assessment processes.

Ample counsel in the scriptures emphasizes the need for meticulous records. A support system called the *law of witnesses* is provided to qualify the records and ensure their reliability. Without question we should keep the very best records. They are essential to effective administration. But the scriptures do not emphasize the type of research and evaluation currently used to control and reward people in business, government, and education. As described in the scriptures, evaluation is cooperative and unifying, not competitive and divisive. It involves factual records, judgment, discernment, and interview exchange, not "objective," depersonalized, disengaged projection. An extensive system of interviews honors the line of authority and links the respective stewardships. Highly sophisticated (and usually very expensive) experimental type research, which can be helpful in some cases, does not seem to be very practical or useful unless it comes after

352

and is based on a solid foundation of reliable records. The issue is one of perspective and order.

Abuse of Research

Evaluative research, with its fetish for "objectivity," has come to play a problematic role in the management structure of modern society. People in weak positions have used research as a weapon to compete with people who occupy strong positions. When a person occupies an office that grants him control over others, he has a low need for research to pursue his goals. His opinion or judgment is power, and he can act solely on that basis. In order for those in weaker-status positions to challenge higher-status officers, they must use some type of leverage to strengthen the authority of their lesser position. It is common to use "research findings" as the leverage. At times the striving becomes a contest for power and influence more than a search for truth and improvement. The true value of research and its great potential for good is compromised.

353

Because research has become a very effective political tool in our society for exerting influence, one might consider that research and evaluation can become tools for power as much as they are instruments for collecting evidence. Quite often, when a person who occupies a position of status in an organization meets with his superiors, he will resort to so-called evaluative research or hard data to protect his position or exert influence. Typically he has obtained this data by requesting his subordinates, if he has any, to select and prepare evidence. This trains them to use the same scheme in their relationships with others in the organization, including the boss himself. The outcome of this type of structural relationship is a plethora of conflicting data. Light and truth are often displaced as the primary intent and the quest for power and influence takes their place. Competition and pride are fostered. Wholesome consensus is rare in this type of environment.

Comparing Approaches to Teacher Evaluation

A common approach to helping teachers understand their performance is to invite students to give them feedback. This feedback is generally obtained by having students answer a number of questions prepared by a researcher or group of researchers about how these students perceive their teacher. There is a major difficulty with this type of teacher evaluation: the questions asked are a reflection of the biases inherent in the assumptions the writer of the questions makes about the educational process. In other words, questions can be formulated that reflect an approach to education that conflicts with the views and intentions of the teacher. Thus the teacher may rate very poorly because the researcher structured the evaluation instrument according to educational assumptions different from those used by the teacher. Or the questions are so vague as to represent little more than "how much did you like or dislike the teacher and your experience with him?" This is a common problem faced by agency oriented educators. It is very important, therefore, to make sure that the biases of the evaluation instruments and procedures are in harmony with correct assumptions we should be using about the learning/teaching process. Otherwise it is fair to ask, Why use them at all?

To illustrate possible differences, compare the following four sets of propositions. First, notice the differences in emphasis. Some of the statements are nearly opposites. The first set favors the assumptions that underlie the agency approach to education, the second a societal approach to education, the third an individualist approach, and the fourth a theological approach. (These examples are intended as representative samples, not complete descriptions.) Ask yourself which of the four sets you would prefer to use as a teacher. Which of the four sets would you prefer to use as a student? Why? This exercise may reveal to the reader some of his or her own commitments or preferences. You may imagine a rating scale of some sort in front of each of these propositions to indicate different degrees, such as Yes, Usually, Unclear, Somewhat, No.

Agency Education Oriented Propositions (Compare Howard's story in Chapter Four)

1. Teacher shares personal aims of the course and invites students to identify their personal objectives within the context of the course.
2. The focus of instruction evokes a sense of personal mission in both teacher and student.
3. Curriculum is sufficiently ambiguous, flexible, and incomplete to sustain a personal spiritual search.
4. Discipleship to a human teacher is discouraged.
5. Personal integrity is emphasized.

6. Teacher respects each person's divine mission above and beyond the particular school curriculum.
7. Teacher is deeply committed to own perspective but acknowledges it may be incomplete.
8. Teacher exhibits an unconditional love for the students.
9. Teacher formulates the course to be taught from subject matter of which he or she is a competent witness.
10. Students personally evaluate the ideas encountered in the course and measure them against divine standards.
11. Students demonstrate that they are accountable to divinity, apart from any teacher feedback.
12. Students seek divine assistance, knowing that what they want is not always what they should do.
13. Students feel and display a responsibility for one another's success as part of their own stewardship.
14. Students, in consultation with their teacher, evaluate their own personal progress in the course.

355

Societal Education Oriented Propositions (Compare with Frank's story in Chapter Four)

1. Prescribed objectives are clearly stated and disclosed to the students at the beginning of the course.
2. Focus of instruction prepares students to contribute effectively to society in a chosen career.
3. Student responsibilities are clearly defined by the teacher, and due dates on assignments are specified in advance to accommodate the system.
4. Assigned workload is appropriate for credit hours given.
5. Assignments are clearly tied to course objectives set by the teacher.
6. Teacher enthusiastically holds the student's attention and interest.
7. Teacher has a thorough knowledge of the subject matter.
8. Teacher motivates each student to accomplish the prescribed objectives.
9. Teacher maintains classroom control.
10. Classroom is neat and orderly.
11. Teacher places students in groups according to abilities when necessary in order to maximize achievement.
12. Exams accurately measure achievement of course objectives.

13. Exams equitably compare individual achievement with academically accepted standards.

14. Grading procedures fairly reflect student effort and ability.

15. Curriculum appropriately separates church and state.

Individualist Education Oriented Propositions (Compare with Ellen's story in Chapter Four)

1. Teacher encourages all students to establish their own objectives.

2. Focus of instruction facilitates individual growth, development, and self-actualization.

3. At any given time, students may be engaged in a variety of activities, thus making the classroom a hub of activity.

4. Adequate resources are made available to ensure a rich and stimulating learning environment.

5. Sufficient time is provided each student to personally explore the material according to his or her interest.

6. Teacher is approachable at any time.

7. Teacher is secure in ambiguous situations and does not feel threatened by student challenges or questions.

8. The teacher frequently gives non-judgmental feedback to each student.

9. Feedback given to students is specific, genuine, and honest.

10. Students learn what they want to learn without becoming dependent on the teacher.

11. Students evaluate their own progress without regard to comparison with others.

12. Comparison of students is effectively avoided.

13. Classroom is free from indoctrination and the imposition of social or religious dogma.

14. Intellectual restraint is avoided; tolerance of individual beliefs and practices is encouraged.

Theological Education Oriented propositions (Compare with Jennifer's story in Chapter Four)

1. Course objectives provided for the students are obviously grounded in absolutes (for example, the scriptures).

2. Focus of instruction stresses compliance with prescribed standards.

3. Teacher guides students to correct answers through carefully worded questions.
4. The authority of the teacher is respected by students at all times.
5. Each student is expected to be prepared to respond or participate at any given time.
6. Faster students are patient with slower students.
7. Each subject discussion is appropriately related to absolute principles (scriptural doctrine).
8. Major ideas, rules, and laws are reviewed sufficiently to ensure attention.
9. Teacher is an example of virtue, mental discipline, and integrity.
10. Teacher radiates love and concern for each student.
11. The teacher devotedly sets high expectations and academic goals for each student who is rewarded according to his performance.
12. Shoddy performance is not tolerated.
13. Students comply with rigorous standards of intellect and morality.
14. Opportunities are provided to contemplate and meditate on the value of divine influences.

357

Assisting Students with Personal Evaluation

Six guidelines may assist the agency teacher in helping the students evaluate their learning:

1. Provide standards for the student to use in assessing his or her own work.
2. Help the student use those standards in assessing his or her work.
3. Share with the student your perception of his or her work.
4. Keep accurate and appropriate records of the student's work.
5. Help the student apply his or her work so that legitimate feedback is generated on its quality and effectiveness.
6. Encourage others to appropriately share with the student their perception of the work.

21

Teacher Training—the Original Pattern (or, Grandparents are Also Important)

No educational program will rise above the strength of the family units it serves. The family is the primary school for all other schooling—in language, numbers, history, music, and the arts. The family is the first and foremost site of teacher-training. Hence, every idea or act that seeks to disorganize, weaken, or destroy the family is an enemy to education. True education is character education; true teacher-training includes mastering the processes that contribute to the development of character.

359

Education is more than teaching, and teaching is more than classroom activity. Education is fulfilling one's potential, and teaching is sharing what one is in a way that helps others fulfill their potential. Teacher education, therefore, requires more than that one develop the ability to share information about reading, writing, arithmetic, and other subject matter areas. These instructional skills are important, but teacher training in the fullest sense also means developing the ability and skills necessary to contribute to another person's quest for positive character, which includes, but is not limited to, the knowledge and skills normally associated with schooling. Any conception of teacher training that ignores the primary role of character development is flawed. True education is character education; true teacher training is mastering the processes that foster the development of character. All other aspects of teaching training are secondary to this fundamental purpose. Studies show that this dimension is essentially ignored in today's formal teacher training programs. What does it profit a man if he gain the whole world and lose his own life? We may have lost sight of this significant question in today's world of specialization and technological efficiency. This chapter emphasizes a way to correct this problem by beginning in the home.

As discussed in an earlier chapter, education is an extension of creation. It begins where creation ends (see figure 21-1). Like two pieces of the same stick, these fundamental functions of life join together. The simplicity of this process shadows its eternal nature. This principle becomes increasingly clear as I experience the unfolding of my own life. As parents, my wife and I have experienced both dimensions—creating and educating. Like others, we are personal witnesses of this earthly partnership in a heavenly plan. We have observed, firsthand, the process initiated in our behalf years before by our parents.

Education an Extension of Creation

Creation   **Education**

360

Figure 21-1

The creation of each child's body, formed miraculously by the powers of life within the mother, is an undeniable reality. The culmination of this creative process in a living birth thrusts upon us an unavoidable call for learning and teaching—that we all be educators. The question is, What will be the quality of this education? We know the purpose is to foster joy, satisfaction, and fulfillment. The destiny of the human personality is to become more nearly perfect, capable, and complete. And how do we fulfill these purposes? Probably in several ways, but teaching certainly plays a vital role. Nature has its influences, but nurturing the body and spirit by teaching is the process over which we have the greatest control. What we experience in these relationships with others is a primary source of training for future teachers. By divine design this training is positive; loving is as natural as living, unless we choose to make it otherwise by violating the guidelines we have been given by our Heavenly Father. The spirit of God is given to every individual, and God's eternal power is manifest through his creations; the pattern is in place, and as the apostle Paul observed we are left without excuse (Romans 1:20).

As parents, we discovered a uniqueness in each child's faculties. We did not arbitrarily determine the gender or the shape of our children's bodies. This was not our stewardship. We cannot compel our children's minds, only incite, encourage, and draw out the development of their fascinating powers. We could nourish and protect, but each of these children is an independent being. Our challenge is to aid and assist as they convert their potential into an actuality. And in this process we face an unavoidable temporal test: What kind of parent, what kind of teacher am I? What can I do to improve? The answers will be unconventional if we measure them by most teacher training programs.

Teacher Training—A Basic Course

A moment's reflection may reveal that teacher training begins with our own creation and subsequent education. This is where the foundation is laid. Our practice teaching begins when we use what we have become (with the help of others) in the service of someone else. The family is the first and foremost site for training in language, numbers, history, music and the arts; it is the primary school for all other schooling. This is why every idea or act that seeks to disorganize, weaken, or destroy the family is an enemy of man's eternal welfare and why it is written "wo, wo, wo," unto those who seek to obstruct the work of bringing to pass "the immortality and eternal life of man." All teacher training begins with the family. Important learning can occur in other settings, but the foundations are laid in the family.

361

The family is the most singular and extensive of all teacher training programs. The intent of the divine plan is that each individual personally participate in this training experience. And this is what happens insofar as the plan is not corrupted or disorganized. The design is for each individual to experience birth, loving nurture, and assistance from others in every needful thing. The command is for us to subdue the earth, to use our knowledge in self-support. The pattern from the beginning was to be lawfully joined in companionship roles as husband and wife, to earn our bread by the sweat of our brow, and to multiply and replenish the earth. The plan is accomplished as we leave father and mother, enter the covenant of marriage, conceive children, and rear them to maturity. The basic nature of the male and female roles is clear and distinct. The female is to prepare the physical bodies, give birth to, and nurture infant children. The husband and father is to support and provide for his wife and children in this family circle. The wife and children have a divine claim upon him; it was the plan from the beginning. But because of our agency, the plan can be distorted, even rejected.

Since the beginning, this plan was resisted; some sought to destroy it then, and many fight against it today. Consequently, the human family is disorganized. Some individuals turn against the plan consciously, while others innocently suffer the consequences initiated by previous generations who deviated. The results are confusing and destructive. Optimum teacher training occurs in the midst of family organization; it does not flourish in family disorganization. There is a vision to which we can aspire that will kindle our instructional capacities and root them in love. The motivation to master reading, writing, mathematics, science, etc., is a natural part of the family experience. The intangibles of education, the hidden curriculum, live in the hearts of the teachers. These hearts are created and initially shaped in the family—in heaven and on earth.

362

Training in teaching techniques, helpful as these can be, are secondary and not primary considerations in teacher preparation. What we need first is to recognize the importance of the proper foundations. And we are promised the fruits of these vital foundations when the hearts of the fathers are turned to the children and the hearts of the children are turned to the fathers (Malachi 4:5-6; D&C 2:1-3; 27:9-10). Anything less than this spiritual connection is a substitute for true teacher training. Tools and techniques of teaching lack impact if they are not grounded in spiritual connections; we are strangers and foreigners, separated from true teaching, until we come together in love and friendship. No teacher training program that ignores this fundamental truth will ever rise to its full potential. Can any be found today who employ this vision and power in practice?

Original Organization of the Human Family

When Elijah restored the sealing keys to the Prophet Joseph, he set in motion the great work of reorganizing the human family through the power of the priesthood. Brigham Young mentioned a vision he had at Winter Quarters on this subject. The Prophet

Joseph appeared and gave him instructions. Among other things the Prophet told President Young to

> Be sure and tell the people to keep the Spirit of the Lord; and if they will, they will find themselves just as they were organized by our Father in Heaven before they came into the world. Our Father in Heaven organized the human family, but they are all disorganized and in great confusion.

Brigham Young then added that "Joseph then showed me the pattern, how they were in the beginning"[1] Years later, President Young spoke of this revelation in these words:

> I will now say to my brethren and sisters, that while we were in Winter Quarters, the Lord gave to me a revelation just as much as he ever gave one to anybody. He opened my mind, and showed me the organization of the Kingdom of God in a family capacity. I talked it to my brethren; I would throw out a few words here, and a few words there, to my first counselor, to my second counselor and to the Twelve Apostles, but with the exception of one or two of the Twelve, it would not touch a man.[2]

363

The ease of overlooking the power in an organized family is evidenced by the failure of President Young's associates to grasp its significance.

Obviously, this reorganization process involves the family "circle within circle" or "wheel within wheel," as the Prophet Joseph described it.[3] It means work for the living as well as those who have passed beyond the grave, culminating in a "complete and perfect union, and welding together of dispensations" (D&C 128:18). As indicated, perfection and exaltation cannot occur outside this sealing work. Genealogical labor is essential, but genealogical labor begins on earth with those who learn to love their own progenitors and their own posterity. Work for the dead depends on righteous relationships among the living—relationships that are strengthened and sustained by personal and family histories, by family group sheets and patriarchal family organizations. It was no accident that Moses used this type of evidence to support his arguments in the Pentateuch. These human responsibilities are the foundation of successful family education. They are the ingredients of successful personal and proxy temple work. They are the primary elements of true religious instruction and safe temporal training. Substitute systems and approaches will prove insufficient because they ignore vital spiritual realities.

Micah (7:5-7) describes the consequences of a disorganized human family. Selfishness reigns under such conditions, trust vanishes, and hate ultimately rules over love. Husbands and wives cannot trust each other, sons dishonor their fathers, daughters fight with their mothers and mothers-in-law. There is no real peace without organized families bound together in love (D&C 98:16-17). And without the positive support of stable families, all teacher training will be less than what it otherwise might be. Those who are in a state of disorganization may not like to hear the prophets on these matters—it has always been so and has often cost the prophets their lives. But that does not make less true what the prophets say.

364

The organized family in mortality, bound by love, respect, and service, is multigeneration. It usually consists of parents, children, and grandchildren. The instruction generated in this extended familial atmosphere is powerful in providing "double-indemnity" teaching. The curriculum is broad, wide, and deep. It has the strength of intimate reality and personal commitment. Watch any grandchild extend itself into the lives and hearts of its grandparents. Notice the simplicity of the teaching and the quality of the learning that occurs. Observe the impact on the grandparents.

Socially manufactured education, such as that provided in conventional schools, can be very helpful; it has its place and importance. But learning in these socially constructed environments cannot replace or compete with the richness and flavor of ideal education. Education in any subject that can be provided by parents, grandparents, brothers and sisters, aunts and uncles, and other members of the extended family has a power that is unmatched in socially engineered schooling. Education flowing from the family is potentially the best; all other education is supplementary. Sometimes this supplementary schooling is all we have at our disposal. But that was not the plan or the practice of schooling in the beginning of the human family. We have a direction in which to move. Public school teachers are among the first and best witnesses to the importance of the family on the disposition and learning of the child. Why then does the curriculum for the training of public teachers say so little about what is so vitally important? Where could we establish a better setting for advocacy in our communities? Why doesn't this happen? Why is the silence so deafening?

The Ideal Teacher

The ideal teacher described in the scriptures possesses many characteristics that are readily available to everyone but seemingly difficult to acquire. Ideal teachers need to possess faith, virtue, knowledge, temperance, patience, brotherly kindness, godliness, charity, humility, and diligence (D&C 4:5-6). They are to teach by persuasion, not force; be longsuffering, not impatient, gentle rather than rough; kind instead of cruel; teachable, obedient, and motivated by unfeigned love. They are to be virtuous and magnanimous, and are to operate under the influence of the Holy Spirit in administering reproof and correction (D&C 121:40-46). Such development is not acquired in a moment, a day, or a year. It takes many years.

365

It is significant that commitment to the profession of parenting (a word that encompasses teaching) is to be established by covenant. Participants will be held responsible for their performance; they will be evaluated by divine standards. Perhaps this is why the Lord provided a long training experience. He did not intend that parents cease teaching after they completed the first 20- or 30-year basic course that began with their first child. Our opportunities and responsibilities as teachers do not cease when our children leave home to establish families of their own. The teaching arena merely broadens, and the context for influence is enhanced. Patriarchal families are extended, multigeneration families wherein the curriculum is unbounded—from agriculture to zoology, carpentry to calculus—with character as the core value.

New Opportunities to Exercise Old Responsibilities

After a quarter century of study—of teaching and being taught—in the family circle, *commencement* exercises begin. One's children grow up and enroll in their own introductory teacher-training class. The graduates of the old course of instruction find themselves becoming grandparents. The time for a polished application of their skills has arrived. This new context for teaching is somewhat different than it was in the training class setting. Many of the old pressures are gone. There are fewer dirty diapers to change—except by invitation; fewer financial problems to resolve; less pressure to continuously regulate, control and cope with daily routines. Some of the mundane and troublesome assignments are gone. Ignorance has largely been replaced with knowledge, priorities about what is most important are much more clear, and the teaching moments are less likely to be routine or structured.

Agency education in this setting, however, is no less strict. Free expression is still subject to correct principles. By now experience has clarified and confirmed many of these principles. The new learners—those grandchildren—are eager to ask questions and hear answers. Surprisingly, their parents may even request counsel and instruction that not so long ago was ignored or endured. The grandparent role is different, but enjoyably so. Grandparents are in a position to be of significant help if a family environment exists that allows their help to be sought and accepted.

366

There are, however, challenges. Sometimes, for example, the urge to speak out must be curbed. And not infrequently some of our previous shortcomings in the basic course show up as glaring weaknesses in the lives of our children as they become parents. This pain is gradually eased with the liniment of time, but it is not pleasant. If we can overcome pride we now have an opportunity to make corrections. With repentance, life can become self-correcting.

Modern mobility can also be an enemy as well as a friend, by separating grandparents from their offspring; distance and time may make personal contact with one's first and second generations infrequent. Modern technology can shorten distances and provide some compensation for separation. It all depends on how we use it. Notwithstanding these challenges, the value of multigeneration teaching is worth pursuing because it provides double indemnity instruction.

Double Indemnity Instruction

Indemnity means security against hurt, loss, or damage. When the Lord organized the human family, he provided for a generational reinforcement of instruction—a patriarchal order. First-generation parents were laden with heavy and basic responsibilities, but they were not left alone to carry out their task. The patriarchal priesthood is a perfect order for family-centered education. Everyone continues to learn and to teach in this order where progress is accelerated.

Sin and Satan, however, were successful in disorganizing the human family and separating the offspring of God from pure knowledge and true principles. The gospel—the power to reorganize mankind—has been repeatedly made available for the purpose of reconciling the disorganization and replacing it with order and power. The battle continues; good and evil are still at war. Insecurity, hurt, loss, and damage are not uncommon in our own dispensation of time. The need for protection and insurance is evident. In these last days double indemnity instruction is not a luxury; it is a necessity. Father and mother are responsible to teach *their* children. But their effectiveness is enhanced when grandfathers and grandmothers effectively play their important roles. Grandparents are also parents to these children. The grandchild is also *their* child. The relationship of responsibility is one generation removed, but it is not totally removed. This is an important lesson to learn if the hearts of the fathers are to be turned to the children and the hearts of the children turned to the fathers (Mal. 4:6).

367

Wherever there are sons or daughters, they are sons or daughters of somebody. The father and mother of such offspring are potential perpetual and eternal parents. It is the mutual recognition of this relationship by children and parents that sets the stage for hearts to be turned toward one another. This is the key to developing a pattern of reinforced instruction that will strengthen families and eventually qualify them to embrace the Patriarchal Order of the Priesthood in its fullness.

Technology, affluence and mobility tend to disrupt many family relationships, bonds, and ties. The more technologically advanced a nation becomes, the weaker its family structure seems to be. The discipline that leads to prosperity is often consumed by the very affluence it creates. Abundance becomes a fuel for impulsive living, corruption, and decay. Old values get discarded and moral principles are commonly rejected in such environments. Sin is prevalent; self-gratification prevails. Maintaining righteous commitment in the face of forces that weaken and destroy family values is a challenge. Positive and powerful teaching within the family structure is the most effective protection against the negative influences of a decadent social order.

There are principles that can protect us from destructive influences, but they must be properly applied. This requires effective instruction, and the most effective instruction is multi-generational. Grandparents are capable of exerting a powerful reinforcement for parental instructions that establish protective influences in the lives of individuals, families, neighborhoods, and communities. Just as double walls protect against fire and provide insulation from cold, multigenerational instruction can help protect against the damaging influences that inflict moral and spiritual injury.

A Simple, Powerful Curriculum

What should grandparents teach? Grandparents should help teach what parents are expected to teach. They should teach what they have, or should have, recorded in their personal books of remembrance—the inspirational events and observations of their lives. Moses tells us that after Adam and Eve left the Garden of Eden and assumed their family responsibilities, they kept a record. This book of remembrance was prepared according "to the pattern given by the finger of God" (Moses 6:46). In it was kept those things of importance that men were impressed to write according to the spirit of inspiration (Moses 6:5). This is the basic curriculum that should be prepared and used for instructional purposes in our families. Much of what we have in the Holy Scriptures is taken from such records as they were kept by individuals whom God had called to represent Him on earth. These personal and precious lessons of life not only feed the spirit of man, they also activate motives for literacy and learning. Children are great imitators; they soon learn to mimic what their loved ones do and say.

Spencer W. Kimball, speaking as a prophet to today's youth, emphasized the importance of the preparation of such a record:

> You are unique, and there may be incidents in your experience that are more noble and praiseworthy in their way than those recorded in any other life. . . .What could you do better for your children and your children's children than to record the story of your life, your triumphs over adversity, your recovery after a fall, your progress when all seemed

black, your rejoicing when you had finally achieved? Some of what you write may be humdrum dates and places, but there will also be rich passages that will be quoted by your posterity. Get a notebook, my young folks, a journal that will last through all time, and maybe the angels may quote from it for eternity.[4]

Stories written and told by grandparents about their own personal lives and the lives of their own children are possibly the finest vehicles for carrying lessons into the hearts of children—young and old. Records of such incidents and episodes are priceless.

Grandparents can also share the practical lessons they have learned from life in their particular culture. Even when some may not agree with all their ideas, it is a powerful form of instruction to teach personally, as living witnesses, principles that have served to bond family relationships. One such list, for example, included the following beliefs which were handed out to children and grandchildren, along with explanations and illustrations.

369

We believe:

1. In the importance of the father and mother agreeing on fundamentals.
2. In the family being our primary focus.
3. Our house being designed for family life.
4. Our house being formally dedicated to the Lord for family purposes.
5. The husband living in such a way that a righteous wife can follow him.
6. The mother being in the home while her children are young.
7. In having prayer with our children night and morning.
8. In having regular family meetings and instruction.
9. In regular scripture reading with our family.
10. In holding periodic interviews with each child.
11. In eating together as a family.
12. In setting serious standards of personal discipline and hard work.
13. In using clean language and conduct.
14. In the power of proper example.
15. In using the Church to help us with our family.

16. In using the school to help us with our family.
17. In making identification with the family stronger than with the peer group.
18. In discouraging high school age teenagers from "pairing off" in serious romantic relationships.
19. In helping our children in their personal search to understand their mission in life.
20. In harmony, and not arguments, in the home.
21. In letting family standards prevail over friendships that challenge them.

Discussions involving grandparents, parents, and children on such value-laden statements as these form a rich and vital type of instruction. These discussions act as girders that strengthen the bridges between generations.

How Should Grandparents Teach?

370   Successful teaching by grandparents is similar to successful home teaching (priesthood visitors assigned by a bishop) as endorsed by the Church. As a bishop I often pondered the question, What makes an ideal home teacher? Among other things, it was clear that the effective home teacher must be concerned and feel an interest in his families. He must look to their needs, be available, make appropriate suggestions, contribute the right help, exert a positive influence, and do all this without meddling and getting in the road. He must be willing to sacrifice for his families, perhaps more than anyone might suspect. His interest must never fail, decade after decade.

I've known a few home teachers who came close to these ideals. But I have never met a home teacher who fulfilled all of these criteria as easily or as naturally as my father fulfills them with the families of his own children. And he does this willingly, without a formal appointment. Wouldn't it be wonderful if every family could enjoy the care that could come from having a worthy grandfather, with grandmother as a companion, assigned as their home teachers. Idyllic, perhaps, but imagine how children love their own grandparents and how much those families could profit from such an ideal instructional setting. And isn't this what the Lord had in mind? Grandparents should teach, it seems, just as ideal home teachers would teach. There are many who do teach this way.

Family Organization

The revealed mechanism for properly instituting multigenerational instruction among Latter-day Saints is correct family organization. This family organization begins with a father, mother, and their children—then later extends to grandchildren. In 1882 President John Taylor received a revelation explaining the need for and blessings of having our families properly organized. Among other things the Lord said:

> I call upon the heads of families to put their houses in order according to the law of God, and attend to the various duties and responsibilities associated therewith, and to purify themselves before me, and to purge out iniquity from their households.[5]

President Ezra Taft Benson in the October conference of 1978 encouraged all Church members to "organize your immediate and grandparent families and prepare your individual and family histories."[6] In this address, President Benson carefully reviewed five specific responsibilities related to this organization and offered additional counsel on implementing these responsibilities in one's family. The benefits of double indemnity teaching—that is, multigenerational instruction—cannot occur as effectively as it should without proper family organization.

In 1964 the Church distributed a booklet entitled *Instructions to Stake Presidents on the Implementation of the Family Home Evening Program.*[7] In this booklet church members were urged to reemphasize the home, the first and most effective place for teaching the values and virtues and lessons of life. We have been taught, "The home is the basis of a righteous life and no other instrumentality can take its place nor fulfill its essential functions."[8] The phrase "No other success can compensate for failure in the home" has become a Church motto. Equally familiar is the statement that "the greatest of the Lord's work you brethren will ever do as fathers will be within the walls of your own home."[9] And the promise has been given that if as mothers and fathers we would "rise to the responsibility of teaching [our] children in the home—priesthood quorums preparing the fathers, and Relief Society the mothers—the day will dawn when the whole world will come to our doors and say, 'Show us your way, that we may walk in your path'."[10]

Forceful instruction has been focused on helping us understand "that the whole effort of correlation is to strengthen the home and to give aid to the home in its problems, giving it special aid and succor as needed."[11] Special emphasis has been focused on the importance of letting the home do what *the home should do*. For example, Elder Theodore Tuttle in October conference of 1969 said,

> The home is the teaching unit of the Church. The parents are the teachers. The course is more extensive than a university curriculum. Always parents are venturing through it for the first time. The classes start at birth and never terminate. There are some graduations, but the schooling continues.[12]

And Elder Boyd K. Packer, in an address to Regional Representatives in June of 1974, observed:

372

> In a sense we said, now everybody get out of the way: Sunday School, Relief Society, M.I. A., Primary, Seminary, Priesthood agencies, and all; we're going to make room in the Church program for a father to preside over his family so that there are interviews, in an organized way, and opportunities for a father to meet his family.[13]

Four years later in the April conference of 1978, this family-centered emphasis was still evident in his counsel to bishops:

> Bishops, keep constantly in mind that fathers are responsible to preside over their families. Sometimes, with all good intentions, we require so much of both the children and the father that he is not able to do so. If my boy needs counseling, bishop, it should be my responsibility first, and yours second. If my boy needs recreation, bishop, I should provide it first, and you second. If my boy needs correction, that should be my responsibility first, and yours second. If I am failing as a father, help me first, and my children second. Do not be too quick to take over from me the job of raising my children. Do not be too quick to counsel them and solve all of the problems. Get me involved. It is my ministry.[14]

The mood surrounding the recent correlation movement is not unique. The same spirit attended earlier efforts to direct parents' attention to their role as teachers. Near the turn of this century Elder Stephen L. Richards said:

> I have for a considerable number of years had the opportunity of engaging in the work of the various organizations of the Church. I know something of the great accomplishments of the auxiliary organizations which devote themselves, in large measure, to the care and culture of the young. I know what great effort is put forth by them to teach the principles of the gospel, to stimulate righteousness in the hearts of the youth of Israel. It is my observation [that these great institutions of the church, however] much of the good they may accomplish, can in no sense take the place of the home. They cannot be proxy for parents. Men and women to whom have been given the most priceless heritage given of God to man—children—can in no wise escape the great responsibility devolving upon them—to rear their children in the fear and admonition of the Lord.[15]

373

Church leaders have consistently encouraged parents to assume a greater role in teaching their children throughout the century. President George Albert Smith in 1926 said:

> It is not sufficient that my children are taught faith, repentance, and baptism, and the laying on of hands for the gift of the holy Ghost in the auxiliary organizations, My Father in heaven has commanded that I should do that myself.[16]

President David O. McKay followed a similar theme in his observation that,

> Church schools, Sunday Schools, Mutual Improvement Associations, Primary organizations are all helps in government established here to assist in the upbuilding and guidance of the youth, but none of these—great and important factors as they are in the lives of our youth—can supplant the permanence and the influence of the parents in the home.[17]

The focus on family instruction sustains the vision of President Joseph F. Smith who declared in 1906 that

> When every council of the Priesthood . . . will understand its duty, will assume its own responsibility, will magnify its calling . . . there will not be so much necessity for work . . . by the auxiliary organizations, because it will be done by the regular quorums of the priesthood.[18]

This, he said, was the way the Lord designed and comprehended it from the beginning. It was the Lord's intent that we function this way, "and He has made provision in the Church whereby every need may be met and satisfied through the regular organizations of the priesthood."[19] It is imperative that parents catch the vision and assume the responsibility the Lord has laid upon them. "All our basic duties can be carried out as individuals and families if we are sufficiently determined."[20]

Families to be Tested

Repeatedly the saints have been warned that we will not always be able to do everything on the same scale we have gotten used to doing things in the affluent decades of the twentieth century. We may not always enjoy peaceful communities, fine schools, and sympathetic governance; necessities such as food, shelter, and clothing may be difficult to obtain. Under these circumstances the value of an organized and powerful family will become evident. President Kimball emphatically supported Church members rising to the full level of these responsibilities.

He describes this position eloquently:

> The mission of the Church to its members is to make available the principles, programs and priesthood by which they can prepare themselves for exaltation. *Our success, individually and as a Church, will largely be determined by how faithfully we focus on living the gospel in the home.* Only as we see clearly the responsibilities of each individual and the role of families and home can we properly understand that priesthood quorums and auxiliary organizations, even wards and stakes, exist primarily to help members live the gospel in the home. Then we can understand that people are more

important than programs, and that Church programs should always support and never detract from *gospel-centered family* activities. . . Our commitment to *home-centered gospel living should become the clear message of every priesthood and auxiliary program,* reducing, where necessary, some of the optional activities that may detract from proper focus on the family and the home. . . I repeat that our success, individually and as a church, will largely be determined by how faithfully we focus on living the gospel in the home.[21]

When we have this foundation in place—children realizing who they are, parents teaching what they should, and grandparents providing reinforcement—individuals will be in a position to become mighty builders of the Kingdom. These circumstances open wide the gates and set free the heavenly gifts of each individual. All aspects of the conventional curriculum will be enriched—reading, writing, arithmetic, music, art, poetry, science, etc. An uplifting quality of meaning and a pointedness of purpose in application will be manifest in all aspects of our education. When this foundation, framed in the family, is missing, chaotic, confused, and meaningless activity results; reading, writing, arithmetic, music, art, poetry, science, and other facets of the curriculum become ends in themselves, distorting the subjects to which they are applied. Literacy turns to depravity instead of edification, art depicts ugliness rather than beauty, music speaks to the body instead of the spirit. An example of this contrast in the area of music is illustrated in the following figure:

375

Millennial Music and Messages

emphasize

Who I am	more than	What I am

explain

Where I came from	more than	Where I am

influence

My Spirit	more than	My body

seek to

Lift me up	more than	Turn me on

describe

Solutions	more than	Problems

stress

Serving others	more than	Satisfying Self

communicate

Light	more than	Dark

express

Hope	more than	Despair

376

Figure 21-2

Fundamental education in the future is destined to shift toward home-centered, parent-directed and priesthood-assisted education among Zion-oriented communities. In these communities, the chapel-centered, auxiliary-directed, priesthood-supported programs of the Church, and the school-centered, professionally directed, and public-supported systems in the community will increasingly be viewed as supplementary sources of education. These changes may increase anxiety among some observers, but the positive results will be a light to the world.

The anxiety could arise for a number of reasons. In some cases, for example, it will mean letting go of old assignments and assumptions and assuming new ones. For others it may mean confronting the fears of letting go of one thing without the full assurance and security that there is something else reliable to hold onto. Others may feel distress in exchanging a role of public power, control, and prestige for the relative anonymity and at times drudgery of laboring in the obscurity of one's own family.

As the old wood is gradually pruned to make room for the new growth, or because it is no longer productive, some people may raise warnings or express dismay. Others may become excited, anxious and perhaps overly zealous, desiring to run faster than they are able.

Whatever the response to these developments, one can be reasonably sure the changes will be accompanied by some discomfort or distress. Progress and perfection are like that—they create leftovers and discardable refuse. Few things of real value or quality are created without requiring a cleanup of some sort. Whether it be tasty, kitchen-baked goodies, fine cabinet shop furniture, or perfected personalities, some dross, some ingredients, shavings, or imperfections will be discarded. The fears of discomfort associated with such change and resistance to the task of cleaning-up after we have done a good thing, may be the only forces that can paralyze our faith in establishing a better way to teach the children. But if we overcome these barriers our children who are taught in this way will become powerful and effective teachers.

A millennial society will emerge in our future; we can either resist or contribute to its development. The basic stewardships that will push this movement into the future reside in each family. Our society will change as our education changes. In the educational contexts of the twenty-first century, individuals from many families must do the creative work. They will need to organize existing resources into the forms, processes, and endeavors that will move society into a millennial posture. A generation will be prepared capable of preparing their children to hear and accept Christ at his coming. As this education is firmly established, temporal excellence in learning will blossom and Zion will increase in beauty and in holiness; her borders will be enlarged, her stakes strengthened, and she will put on her beautiful garments (D&C 82:14). And the children will be taught through an agency approach to education.

377

Postscript

As I concluded this manuscript, it became apparent that in writing a nonconventional book about education I had created a new dartboard—one with an alternative image to the popular models now in use. Some people will hail its appearance as useful and challenging—a new look at an old subject, worth a try. These people may develop an affinity if not a passion for the opportunities it affords. They may even invite their friends to join them in mastering the challenges it provides. These will be proponents.

On the other hand, there will opponents—especially in the academic community—those who will feel uncomfortable with the ideas and images. After all, this new model challenges the currently accepted patterns to which most of the reward systems are attached. "A dartboard! A dartboard!" they will murmur, "we have a dartboard and we don't need another dartboard." The response may be, "Just ignore it. In fact, ignore anyone who wants to play with it." But one may say, "We cannot do that; it has the bullseye in the wrong place, it must be destroyed. If that thing is allowed to hang around it's going to create confusion." But comes the question: "What can you do about it?" Followed by a predictable answer, "Well, for one thing we can make it very clear that dartboards like this one violate the rules of the game. We must remember that our professional friends will never come to our town to play if they think this is the kind of dartboard we use. And if that happens we won't be able to report our scores in the *Dartboard Journal.* We'll probably lose our accreditation and all chances of hosting the national tournament. We may even be disqualified from participating in any of the leagues. Do you want that to happen?"

Why write a book to comfort those who are disturbed and disturb those who are comfortable? President Lorenzo Snow once answered,

> It's like the schoolboy when he commences to learn the alphabet. The letter A is pointed out to him by the teacher, and she tells him what it is and asks him to please remember it. The next letter, B, is pointed out, and the boy is asked to remember that. The teacher then returns to A. What letter is that? The boy has forgotten and it has to be repeated by the

teacher. Will you please remember it now? The boy says, "O yes, I'll remember it." He feels sure that he can remember it now. But when the teacher returns to the letter once more, the boy has forgotten it again. So they go through the alphabet, having to repeat each letter over and over again. It is the same with the Latter-day Saints. We have to talk to them, and keep talking to them.[1]

And President John Taylor said,

> There is not a position that we can occupy in life, either as fathers, mothers, children, masters, servants, or as Elders of Israel holding the holy Priesthood in all its ramifications, but what we need continually wisdom flowing from the Lord and intelligence communicated by him, that we may know how to perform correctly the various duties and avocations of life, and to fulfill the various responsibilities that rest upon us.
>
> And hence the necessity all the day long, and every day and every week, month, and year, and under all circumstances, of men leaning upon the Lord and being guided by that Spirit that flows from him, that we may not fall into error—that we may neither do anything wrong, say anything wrong, nor think anything wrong, and all the time retain that Spirit, which can only be kept by observing purity, holiness, and virtue, and living continually in obedience to the laws and commandments of God.[2]

380

These are solemn commentaries on where we should be, and as educators we are quite a distance from the goal. The cares of everyday life and the constant press of cultural influences, physical and social, create challenging barriers to overcome. But our conditions are little different from those of our pioneer forefathers when it comes to keeping a strong vertical relationship—an eye single to the glory of God—and not succumbing to the shortened horizontal vision of everyday life. George Q. Cannon told the people of his day,

> When the cares of everyday life increase upon us, in the business of forming settlements, pioneering and performing our labors from day to day, we are too apt to forget that we

should constantly seek to God with the same fervor and diligence for his aid as we do for spiritual blessings.

I find that I have to be careful while engaged in business, for I know that the tendency of my mind is to devote all my thoughts and all my time and attention to the business that is in hand—that happens to occupy my attention at the time. This is the tendency of people generally, and we have to guard against it, and for which we have to be reproved, that we may not yield to it to so great an extent as to drive the Spirit of God from us. There is no necessity for this.

If we grieve the Spirit of God when we are performing our temporal duties, it is because we allow the one idea to absorb our attention too much. While we are engaged in these duties we should have the Spirit of God resting upon us, as if we are engaged in preaching the Gospel. . . .

I know it requires a struggle to concentrate our thoughts on the things of the Kingdom of God, while we are engaged in business; but this is one of the things which we have to train ourselves to and to overcome.[3]

381

The way to put ourselves in a position to accomplish what is being advised has been explained in a simple and congenial way by Amasa M. Lyman:

It is with the Holy Spirit as it is with us. When we seek to gratify ourselves in the associations around us, for whom do we seek at such a time? We seek individuals whose tastes and feelings are congenial to our own, whose 'Mormonism' is like our own. Then what do we enjoy? A free, frank, unrestrained feeling and sentiment: we pour out the feelings of our souls; there is a principle of reciprocity existing between the parties.

So it is with the Holy Spirit of truth. Where it finds a mind so regulated that there is an affinity and congeniality between that mind and itself, there is the place where it will dwell; and when that mind becomes so trained in the truth as to be completely and perfectly subject to its influence, it will remain there constantly and unceasingly; it will not pay a casual visit, but take up its constant abode with that individual, and then its light is there, revelation is there, inspiration is there; it is there to increase in intensity, extent, and in power; it is there to continually pour out upon that soul the unceasing, unbroken tide of life.

Then the fountain of life becomes established in the soul; that fountain is flowing continually and unceasingly. Even as the blood passes through the heart to the extremities of our physical system at every pulsation, so also the Spirit of truth pervades our being.[4]

The foregoing thoughts expose the limitations of conventional education. (1) When our energies and attention in education are preoccupied to the point that we fail to retain the Spirit of God in our work, we diminish the positive results. When we attempt to learn or teach without a correct, conscious, spiritual motive we move off the most desired course. "The laborer in Zion shall labor for Zion" (2 Nephi 26:31). There is no alternative policy regardless of our discipline or vocation. If we labor for money, for recognition, or for any other purpose we shift our employ to another and dilute the outcome. (2) If we want the constant companionship of the Spirit of God we must have the disposition, aims, and attitudes that will attract and retain an affinity for that Spirit. Too often our thoughts and behaviors are set to attract the approval of prominent men in the world, enhance our selfish interests, or perpetuate false traditions rather than engage us to the Spirit of God. Consider, for example, what we espouse to be our highest form of education, the modern university. Discomforting as it seems for those of us who constitute this enterprise, we must begin with an observational view that is honest and accurate.

Today's higher education in Western culture has Greek design, a medieval Christian body, and a modern high-powered corporate secular engine. It is driven and serviced by members of a number of ancient and some more recent guilds. Each of these guilds is dedicated first to self-preservation and second to some form of provisional service to the university. Membership in each guild is carefully governed by induction processes, performance ceremonies, and an elaborate network of tradition that connects each university to every other university. There are established pecking orders between the guilds and a carefully orchestrated set of policies governing the acquisition and treatment of a continual stream of students. This flow of students fuels the higher education system—both during and after their matriculation. The sustaining traditions of higher education are powerful and socially pervasive. The power structure of the society at large is carefully and continuously replenished by the many useful and requested contributions generated by this educational enterprise. Those involved in the university processes seldom make this description a conscious focus. Their interactions usually function at less macroscopic levels.

The foregoing description, however, raises serious questions for agency educators. Foremost among these are, What would a private university be like if it was truly independent of this western world system? Would there be new found freedoms that could revolutionize the efficiency and effectiveness of education? If a restorationist curriculum were invoked, would it consist of a more truth and less error than conventional curriculum? Would the nature of scholarship be redefined? Would the application of agency oriented principles significantly shrink the amount of time and expense required to assist Zion oriented individuals in their preparation to "labor in Zion"? Could 75,000 students or more be served in the same facilities and in the same time span now required by conventional education to serve 25,000? And could these students complete their preparations at equal or higher levels of competence in one-half the school time now required? Could costs be dramatically reduced? Would admissions be free from elitism? Could a generation of faculty be found that was as prepared to teach, as the generation of students were prepared to learn, who would come to such an institution? Would there be administrative courage and leadership sufficient to support such an independent venture? These are probing questions that seem worthy of serious attention.

383

It is possible to become better than we are by changing how we think and act, and as we improve personally we can improve our learning and our teaching. We do not have to be satisfied with the limitations associated with contemporary education. For the restorationist, one thing is quite evident: Human potential will not thrive in behavioristic basements or the huts of humanism; it requires roots of spiritual morality. The difference between what is and what might be is touchingly expressed in a poetic little parody called "The Lesson" (source unknown). The piece is humorous because the responses attributed to Jesus' apostles are obviously uncharacteristic, yet they typify so well where we are in our current efforts to teach the children.

THE LESSON

Then Jesus took his disciples up the mountain
and gathering them around him he taught them saying:

Blessed are the poor in spirit, for theirs is the kingdom of
heaven,
Blessed are the meek,
Blessed are they that mourn,
Blessed are the merciful,
Blessed are they that thirst for justice,
Blessed are you when persecuted,
Blessed are you when you suffer,
Be glad and rejoice for your reward is great in heaven.

Then Simon Peter said, "Are we supposed to know this?"
And Andrew said, "Do we have to write this down?"
And James said, "I don't have any paper."
And Bartholomew said, "Do we have to turn this in?"
And John said, "The other disciples didn't have to learn this."
And Matthew said, "May I go to the bathroom?"
And Judas said, "What does this have to do with real life?"

Then one of the Pharisees, who was present, asked to see
Jesus' lesson plan and inquired of Jesus, "Where are your
anticipatory sets and your objectives in the cognitive
domain?"

And Jesus wept.

384

Appendix A

Educational Choices

THEISTIC   NON-THEISTIC

385

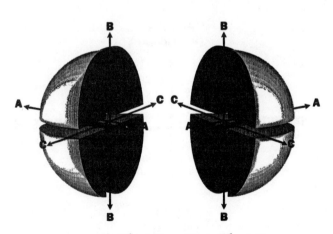

A. Theistic—Non-Theistic
B. Person—Group
C. Nature—Nurture

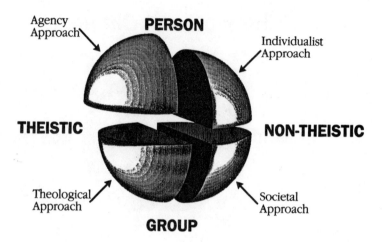

386

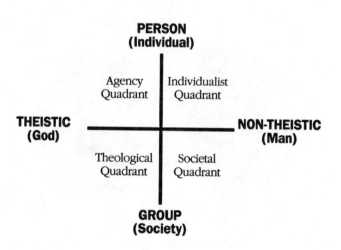

Appendix B

The Storyline of Education in Western Society

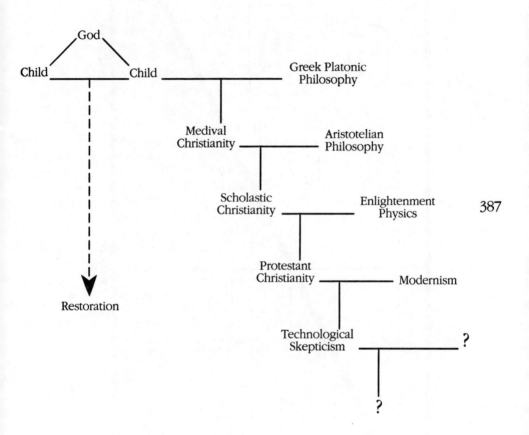

387

Maturation and Education

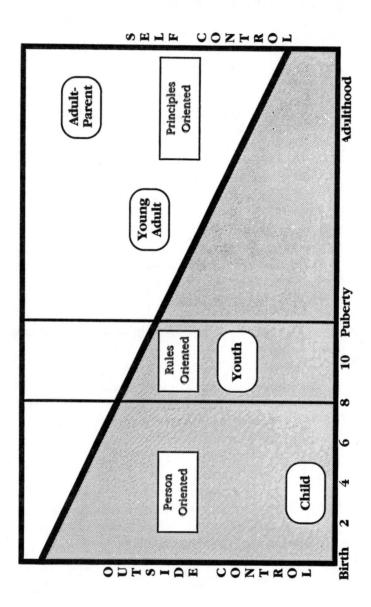

Endnotes

Preface

1. Bertha A. Kleinman, *Through the Year: A Collection of Poetical Sentiment for All Occasions* (N.P.: Published by the author, 1957), pp. 172-73.
2. Hugh Nibley, *Approaching Zion* (Salt Lake City: Deseret Book; Provo, Utah: Foundations for Ancient Research, 1989).

Chapter 2

1. Charles S. Aaronson, ed., *The Production Code*, 1930, in *International Motion Picture Almanac* (New York: Quigley Publication Co., 1966), pp. 786-793.
2. Ibid., p. 786.
3. Ibid., pp. 788-789.
4. *Rules and Regulations of the Classification and Rating Administration*, in *International Motion Picture Almanac* (New York: Quigley Publication Co., 1982).
5. John R. Howe, *The Changing Political Thought of John Adams* (Princeton: Princeton University Press, 1966), p. 189.
6. John Dewey, *Experience and Education* (New York: Macmillan Co., 1938), p. 108.
7. Robert E. Mason, *Educational Ideals in American Society* (Boston: Allyn and Bacon, 1960), p. 59.
8. Ibid., p. 60.
9. Brigham Young, *Journal of Discourses*, 3:191-192. Hereafter cited *JD*.
10. Ezra Taft Benson, *A Witness and A Warning* (Salt Lake City: Deseret Book Co., 1988), pp. vii-viii.
11. Heber C. Kimball, *JD*, 4:136.
12. Ezra T. Benson, *The Teachings of Ezra Taft Benson* (Salt Lake City: Bookcraft, 1988).
13. John Taylor, *The Gospel Kingdom* (Salt Lake City: Bookcraft, 1943), p. 277.
14. John Taylor, *JD*, 21:100.

Chapter 3

1. Matthew 5:48; 3 Nephi 12:48. The term *perfect* in this context is a translation of the Greek term *teleios*, which means "complete." The connotation of the word *perfect* can be applied in both a provisional and an ultimate sense. For

example, Job is referred to as being perfect—completely in harmony with God's way, which is the way to become ultimately complete or perfect as God is. The distance we perceive between where we are and where we might be, ultimately, should not dissuade us from seeking a completeness (perfection) in our circumstances of the moment.

2. "Give me a log hut, with only a simple bench, Mark Hopkins at one end and I on the other, and you may have all the buildings, apparatus and libraries without him"—General James A. Garfield, at a dinner for Williams College alumni, 28 December 1871, quoted in Houston Peterson's *Great Teachers* (New Brunswick: Rutgers University Press, 1946), p. 75.
3. *The Salt Lake Tribune* (Salt Lake City, Utah), Friday, 15 April 1988, pp. M1, M3.
4. Orson F. Whitney, "The School of Life," *Millennial Star* 67, no. 32 (10 August 1905): 499.
5. Orson F. Whitney, "What Is Education?" *Contributor* 6 (June 1885): 345, 349-50.
6. John Taylor, *JD*, 10:51.
7. Ibid., 10:53; italics mine.
8. Jose Ortega y Gasset, *Man and Crises*, quoted in George Charles Roche III, *The Bewildered Society* (New York: Arlington House, 1972), p. 11.
9. Barbara Walters, "America's Kids: Why They Flunk," American Broadcasting Company, shown 9 October 1988.
10. Parley P. Pratt, *JD*, 20:151.

Chapter 4

1. Richard Mitchell, *The Graves of Academe* (Boston: Little, Brown and Company, 1981), pp. 39-40.
2. Boyd K. Packer, "The Country with a Conscience," address delivered at the American Freedom Festival, Provo, Utah, 25 June 1989, p. 9.
3. A. M. Hunter, *The Message of the New Testament* (Philadelphia: Westminster Press, 1944; *Webster's New Collegiate Dictionary*.
4. Sources that discuss the hero journey are Mircea Eliade, *The Myth of the Eternal Return* (Princeton: Princeton University Press, 1954); Joseph Campbell, *The Hero with a Thousand Faces* (Princeton: Princeton University Press, 1949); Arnold

Van Genner, *The Rites of Passage* (London: Routledge & Paul, 1960); Rex Wadham, "The Hero Journey Pattern: A Cosmic Journey," unpublished Seminar Paper CIS-HJ #401, Brigham Young University, 9 August 1985.

5. Viktor Frankl, in his widely read *Man's Search for Meaning* (New York: Washington Square Press, 1963), makes the point clear that man always retains his power to choose until he chooses to give it up. "In spite of all the enforced physical and mental primitiveness of the life in a concentration camp, it was possible for spiritual life to deepen" (p. 56). "We who lived in concentration camps can remember the men who walked through the huts comforting others, giving away their last piece of bread. They may have been few in number, but they offer sufficient proof that everything can be taken from a man but one thing: the last of the human freedoms—to choose one's attitude in any given set of circumstances, to choose one's own way" (p. 104).

     In the book *Talks to Teachers on Psychology* (Cambridge, Mass.: Harvard University Press, 1983), William James makes the same point in a different way. In answer to the question, What makes a life significant? he answers: "Culture and refinement all alone are not enough to do so. Ideal aspirations are not enough, when uncombined with pluck and will. But neither are pluck and will, dogged endurance and insensibility to danger enough, when taken all alone. There must be some sort of fusion, some chemical combination among these principles, for a life objectively and thoroughly significant to result. . . . The solid meaning of life is always the same eternal thing—the marriage, namely, of some unhabitual ideal, however special, with some fidelity, courage, and endurance; with some man's or woman's pains. And whatever or wherever life may be, there will always be the chance for that marriage to take place" (pp. 165-166).

391

6. *Current Contents* 21 (27 May 1985): 22.

Chapter 5

1. Joseph Fielding Smith, *Gospel Doctrine* (Salt Lake City: Deseret Book Co., 1966), p. 21; *History of The Church of Jesus Christ of Latter-day Saints* (Salt Lake City: Deseret Book Co., 1965) 6:476, hereafter cited as *HC*; Moses 6:63; Abraham 3:16.

2. Orson F. Whitney, "Latter-day Saint Ideals and Institutions," *Improvement Era*, August 1927, p. 851.
3. Hugh Nibley, *Three Shrines: Mantic, Sophic and Sophistic* (ms. in process by F.A.R.M.S., Brigham Young University, 1987); Dio Chrysostom, *Orations* 12:15; William Whiston, *The Life and Works of Flavius Josephus* Apion I, 26 (Philadelphia: John C. Winston Co., 1936).
4. E. R. Goodenough, *Jewish Symbols in the Greco-Roman Period*, vol. 1, chaps. 1, 4, 13; see also vol. 1, pp. 1, 6, 12; vol. 2, pp. 4-6; vol. 12, pp. 74-77.
5. Walter Lippmann, *A Preface to Morals* (New York: Macmillan Co., 1929); John Herman Randall, *The Making of the Modern Mind* (Chicago: Houghton Mifflin, 1926); J. Gresham Machen, *Christianity and Liberalism* (Grand Rapids, Mich.: Eerdmans, 1923); F. L. Baumer, *Religion and the Rise of Skepticism* (New York: Harcourt, Brace, 1960); J. Turner, *Without God, Without Creed* (Baltimore: Johns Hopkins University Press, 1985_. 1986). See also H. Curtis Wright, "The Central Problem of Intellectual History," *Scholar and Educator* 12, no. 1 (Fall 1988): 52-68.
6. James E. Talmage, *The Articles of Faith* (Salt Lake City: Deseret Press, 1979), pp. 29-39.
7. Gabrial Vahanian, *The Death of God* (New York: G. Braziller, 1957), p. xiii.
8. Lippmann, *Preface to Morals*, p. 143. See Yervant H. Krikorian, ed., *Naturalism and the Human Spirit* (New York: Columbia University Press, 1959) for a definitive introduction to the study of naturalism.
9. Ibid.
10. Albert Einstein, *Out of My Later Years* (New York: Philosophical Library, 1950), pp. 29-33.
11. Ibid.
12. B. F. Skinner, *About Behaviorism* (New York: Alfred A. Knopf, 1974), p. 225.
13. Gordon R. Taylor, *The Natural History of the Mind* (New York: Penguin Books, 1981), p. 297.
14. Peter Angeles, *Critiques of God* (Buffalo: Prometheus Books, 1976). Quoted from the dust cover as excerpted from the introduction.
15. John Dewey, *A Common Faith* (New Haven, Conn.: Yale University Press, 1934), pp. 48, 51.

16. Huston Smith, "Beyond the Modern Western Mindset" in Douglass Sloan, ed., *Toward the Recovery of Wholeness* (New York: Teachers College, Columbia University, 1984), pp. 62-85.
17. Paul Kurtz, ed., *Humanist Manifestos I and II* (Buffalo: Prometheus Books, 1973), p. 16.
18. Winfried Boehm, "Is Christian Education Possible in a Secular World," forum address delivered at Brigham Young University, 8 January 1985.
19. Skinner, *About Behaviorism,* pp. 72-73; italics mine.
20. B. F. Skinner, *Beyond Freedom and Dignity* (New York: Bantam Books, Vintage, 1971), p. 202.

Chapter 6

1. The Shabako Stone, named after the King who authorized its creation, is housed in the British Museum (since 1805). According to Hugh Nibley it was first translated by James Henry Breasted (University of Chicago) in 1901 and later by the scholar K. Sethe. It is believed that the stone was engraved in the twenty-fifth Dynasty. It appears to be a faithful copy of the story recorded in the First Dynasty in Egypt ca. 3100 to 3200 B.C. See Hugh Nibley, *Old Testament and Related Studies* (Salt Lake City: Deseret Book Co.; Provo, Utah: Foundation for Ancient Research and Mormon Studies, 1986), p. 176; Hugh Nibley "The Pearl of Great Price" (unpublished ms. belonging to Brigham Young University, Department of Continuing Education), 1987; K. Sethe, *Das Denkmal Memphitischer Theologie der Schabakostein des Britischen Museums* (Leipzig, 1928), 1:64-65.
2. See Note 1 above Hugh Nibley, "The Pearl of Great Price" (unpublished ms., Lecture 21); R. Graves and R. Patai, *Hebrew Myths: The Book of Genesis* (New York: McGraw Hill, 1964), pp. 100-103 for examples of these fragmented accounts.
3. Hugh Nibley, "The Pearl of Great Price," Lecture 21.
4. Lewis Bastian, "The Intents of Schooling in Western Culture and Its Primary Antecedents: An Annotated Bibliograpy with Findings." (Ph.D. Dissertation, Brigham Young University, 1987), p. 14.
5. Nibley, *The Temple in Antiquity: Ancient Records and Modern Perspectives,* ed. Truman Madsen (Provo, Utah: Brigham Young University Press, 1984), pp. 22-23, 49.
6. Bastian, "Intents of Schooling," pp. 13-14

Chapter 7

1. See J. L. Barker, *Apostacy from the Divine Church* (Salt Lake City: Deseret News Press, 1960), pp. 468-485, or W. H. C. Frend, *The Rise of Christianity* (Philadelphia: Fortress Press, 1984), pp. 673-683.
2. Martin Luther, *The Bondage of the Will*, trans. J. I. Packer and O. R. Johnson (Westwood, N.J.: Fleming H. Revell Co., 1957), pp. 47-48. The validity of Luther's argument—that following Erasmus' thinking to its conclusion would lead to the idea that man could save himself and would have no need for God—seems to be supported by propositions contained in the *Humanist Manifesto I* and *II*.
3. For further development of the modern conflict, see Jean Jacques Rousseau's *Emile*, trans. Wm. H. Payne (New York: D. Appleton and Co., 1892); A. S. Neill's *Summerhill: A Radical Approach to Child Rearing* (New York: Hunt Publishing Co., 1964); John Watson's *Behaviorism* (New York: W. W. Norton and Co., 1924); and Skinner's *Beyond Freedom and Dignity*.
4. *Humanist Manifesto* I and II, 1933, 1973 respectively.
5. Neill, *Summerhill*, pp. 4-5, 12.
6. Talmage, *Articles of Faith*
7. See all of Werner Jaeger's *Early Christianity and Greek Paideia* (Cambridge, Mass.: Harvard University Press, 1961), but particularly pp. 30, 90.
8. Cited from a personal statement by Naomi Randall in the writer's file.
9. Pope Pius XI, "Encyclical Letter Divini Illus Magestri of His Holiness Pope Pius XI," 1936, as cited in *Selected Readings in the Philosophy of Education*, ed. Joe Park (New York: Macmillan Co., 1963), pp. 377-378, 397-398, 404.
10. Rousseau, *Emile*, pp. 8-9.
11. Neill, *Summerhill*, p. 12.
12. Emile Durkheim, *Education and Sociology* (New York: Free Press, 1956).
13. Daniel Kulp II, *Educational Sociology* (New York: Longman Greens & Co., 1932), pp. 26-27.
14. Louise Stevenson, *Scholarly Means to Evangelical Ends: The New Haven Scholars and the Transformation of Higher Learning in America, 1830-1890* (New Haven, Conn.: Yale University Press, 1986).

15. Orson F. Whitney, in *Conference Report,* April 1915. Hereafter cited as *CR.*
16. Joseph F. Smith, "A Prize beyond Computation," address delivered before the Mutual Improvement Normal class at the Brigham Young Academy, Saturday, 30 January 1892.
17. From an address delivered at the dedication of the Brigham Young Academy Education Building, 2 January 1892.

Chapter 8
1. Alan Bullock and Oliver Stalleybrass, *The Harper Dictionary of Modern Thought* (New York: Harper & Rowe, 1977), pp. 508-509.
2. Isaac Newton, *The Chronology of Ancient Kingdoms Amended* (London, 1728), pp. vii-1x, 188-190.
3. Randall, *The Making of the Modern Mind*; Lippmann, *A Preface to Morals*; Turner, *Without God, Without Creed*; evidence for the shift in specific disciplines, for example, can be seen by comparing Francis Bacon's *Novum Organum* (1620) and Paul Dietrich d'Holbach's *Systeme de la Nature* (1770) in science, or Isaac Newton's *Mathematical Principles of Natural Philosophy* (1686) and Pierre Simon Laplace's *Celestial Mechanics* (1829) in astronomy, or James Hutton's *Theory of the Earth* (1788) and Charles Lyell's *Principles of Geology: An Attempt to Explain the Former Changes of the Earth's Surface by Reference to Causes Now in Operation* (1830) in geology.
4. Robert M. W. Travers, *Essentials of Learning,* 5th ed. (New York: Macmillan Co., 1982), pp. 17-23.
5. Gordon R. Taylor, *The Natural History of the Mind,* p. 297.
6. Dalbir Bindra, *The Brain's Mind: A Neuroscience Perspective on the Mind-Body Problem* (New York: Gardner Press, 1980), pp. 1-4.
7. Michael E. Hyland, "Do Person Variables Exist in Different Ways?" *American Psychologist,* September 1985, pp. 1003-1010.
8. Arthur L. Blumenthal, *The Process of Cognition* (Englewood Cliffs, N.J.: Prentice-Hall, 1977), p. 188.
9. Edwin G. Boring, *A History of Experimental Psychology* (New York: Century Co., 1929), p. 1.
10. Modern scripture refers to The Book of Mormon: Another Testament of Jesus Christ, The Doctrine and Covenants of The

Church of Jesus Christ of Latter-day Saints, and The Pearl of Great Price as published by The Church of Jesus Christ of Latter-day Saints.

11. Neil J. Flinders and Paul Wangemann, "A Systematic Examination of the Terms, Heart, Mind, Might, and Strength As Used in the Standard Works of The Church of Jesus Christ of Latter-day Saints," unpublished paper, Brigham Young University, December 1985.

12. A more detailed discussion of these motivational influences mentioned in the scriptures can be found in Neil J. Flinders, "Principles of Parenting" (Part II), *Ensign*, April 1975, pp. 51-55.

Chapter 9

1. R. F. Biehler and J. Snowman, *Psychology Applied to Teaching* (New York: Houghton Mifflin Co., 1982), p. 138.

2. Ibid., p. 195.

3. See Benjamin S. Bloom, *Taxonomy of Educational Objectives: The Classification of Educational Goals. Handbook I: Cognitive Domain* (New York: David McKay Company, 1956); David R. Krathwohl et al., *Taxonomy of Educational Objectives: The Classification of Educational Goals. Handbook II: Affective Domain* (New York: David McKay Company, 1964). These educators classified learning in three domains: psychomotor, cognitive, and affective.

4. B. Berelson and G. A. Steiner, *Human Behavior: An Inventory of Scientific Findings* (New York: Harcourt, Brace and World, 1964), pp. 140-165.

5. Joseph Fielding Smith, *Teachings of the Prophet Joseph Smith* (Salt Lake City: Deseret News Press, 1938), pp. 94-95. Hereafter cited as *TPJS*.

6. *The Words of Joseph Smith,* comp. Andy F. Ehat and Lyndon W. Cook (Provo, Utah: Religious Studies Center, Brigham Young University, 1980), p. 204; see also Acts 17:30; Romans 2:12; D&C 45:43; 76:72; 88:99.

7. *TPJS*, pp. 94-95.

8. John Taylor, *Gospel Kingdom*, pp. 46-47.

9. Ibid., p. 47.

10. David O. McKay, *Pathways to Happiness* (Salt Lake City: Bookcraft, 1957), p. 338.

11. Orson F. Whitney, in *CR*, April 1915, p. 100; italics mine.
12. *Time Magazine*, 4 November 1985, p. 98.
13. Orson Pratt, *JD*, 2:237.
14. Brigham Young, *JD*, 1:70.
15 You will see the day "that Zion will be as far ahead of the outside world in everything pertaining to learning of every kind as we are today in regard to religious matters. . . . Let us live so we can keep that up, so that angels can minister to us and the Holy Spirit dwell with us. . . . It is for us to now to go on from truth to truth, from intelligence to intelligence and from wisdom to wisdom."— John Taylor, *JD*, 21:100; "rise to the responsibility of teaching [our] children in the home— priesthood quorums preparing fathers, and Relief Society the mothers—the day will dawn when the whole world will come to our doors and say, 'Show us your way, that we may walk in your path.'"—Harold B. Lee, *Improvement Era*, January 1967, p. 23.
16. Spencer W. Kimball, *Speeches of the Year*, "Education for Eternity," 12 September 1967, pp. 1, 5.
17. Boyd K. Packer, in *CR*, April 1983, pp. 89-92.
18. Boyd K. Packer, *Teach Ye Diligently* (Salt Lake City: Deseret Book Co., 1975), pp. 109-116.
19. Charles Hubbard Judd, *The Psychology of Social Institutions* (New York: The Macmillan Company, 1926), pp. 326-328, 340.
20. John A. Widtsoe, *Priesthood and Church Government in The Church of Jesus Christ of Latter-day Saints* (Salt Lake City: Deseret Book Co., 1954), pp. 146-147.
21. From an OEA-NEA Bulletin issued by the Oregon Education Association as quoted in *RECAPS: Concerned Educators against Forced Unionism*, 6, no. 2 (Winter 1982): p. 4.
22. *TPJS*, p. 354.
23. Brigham Young, *JD*, 16:75.
24. *HC*, 6:305.
25. Brigham Young, *JD*, 8:334-335; see also *HC*, 6:303, for Joseph Smith's thoughts on the subject.
26. *TPJS*, p. 350.
27. Ibid., p. 355.
28. Ibid., p. 324.
29. Ibid.
30. Ibid., p. 331.

31. Ibid., p. 348.
32. Brigham Young, *JD.* 6:286.
33. Ibid., 6:283-284.
34. See 1 Nephi 16 and Alma 37:37-47 for description of "Liahona."

Chapter 10

1. Rudolph Steiner et al., *Education As an Art* (New York: Multimedia Publishing Company, 1970), p. 22.
2. Ibid.; italics mine.
3. Ibid., p. 23.
4. Ibid., p. 24-25.
5. Orson F. Whitney, "Joseph Smith and Education," *Liahona, the Elders Journal* 9 (19 December 1911)405-406.
6. Brigham Young, *JD,* 2:256.
7. Ibid., 1:66-71
8. David O. McKay, "Reaching Youth . . . A great Obligation," *Instructor* 101 (June 1966): 205-207.
9. Brigham Young, *JD,* 10:368.
10. David O. McKay, *Man May Know for Himself* (Salt Lake City: Deseret Book Co., 1967), p. 296.
11. Ibid., p. 257.
12. Edward Sagarin, "Taking Stock of Studies of Sex," *The Annals of the American Academy of Political and Social Science 376* (March 1968):5.
13. Henry Gleitman, *Psychology* (New York: W. W. Norton Company, 1981), pp. 3-4.
14. Ezra Taft Benson, *To the Young Women of the Church* (Salt Lake City: The Church of Jesus Christ of Latter-day Saints, 1986), p. 12, a pamphlet.
15. Ezra Taft Benson, *To the Mothers in Zion* (Salt Lake City:The Church of Jesus Christ of Latter-day Saints, 1987), pp. 6-7, a pamphlet.
16. Ibid., pp. 7-8.
17. Joseph F. Smith, "Editor's Notes," *Improvement Era*, May 1914, p. 476.
18. Caleb Gattegno, *The Adolescent and His Will* (New York: Outerbridge & Dienstfrey, 1972), pp. 1-13.
19. Brigham Young, *JD,* 1:70.

20. Ibid.
21. Henry B. Veatch, "Religion, Morality, and Natural Law," *Listening: Journal of Religion and Culture* 8, nos. 1, 2, 3 (1973): 95-115.

Chapter 11

1. Orson F. Whitney, "What Is Education?" *Contributor* 6 (May 1885): 343-353.
2. McKay, *Pathways to Happiness,* pp. 152, 163.
3. Ibid., p. 246.
4. Thomas E. Wren, *Agency and Urgency: The Origin of Moral Obligation* (New York: Precedent Publishing, 1974), p. 84.
5. McKay, *Pathways to Happiness,* p. 155.
6. Ibid., pp. 277-278.
7. Joseph F. Smith, in *CR,* April 1902, p. 98.
8. Cited in Neil J. Flinders, "Do You Give Your Students Vision?" *Instructor,* February 1962, p. 60.
9. J. L. Kueth, *The Teaching Learning Process* (Glenview, Ill.: Scott, Foresman & Co., 1968), p. 12.
10. R. T. Utz and L. D. Leonard, *A Competency Based Curriculum* (Dubuque, Iowa: Kendall Hunt, 1971), p. 12.
11. Brigham Young, *JD,* 8:37
12. McKay, *Pathways to Happiness,* p. 310.

Chapter 12

1. Joseph Smith, *Lectures on Faith,* 1:13-24, 2:8-12, 7:3-5.
2. Joseph F. Smith, *Gospel Doctrine,* pp. 297-298.
3. John B. Watson and William MacDougall, *The Battle of Behaviorism* (New York: W. W. Norton and Co., 1929), p. 11.
4. Charles W. Penrose. Address delivered in the Twelfth Ward Assembly Hall, Salt Lake City, 12 October 1884. Published by Deseret News, 1916.
5. Ernest L. Wilkinson and W. Cleon Skousen, *Brigham Young University: A School of Destiny* (Provo, Utah: Brigham Young University Press, 1976), p. 67.
6. McKay, *Pathways to Happiness,* p. 96.
7. David O. McKay, *Gospel Ideals* (Salt Lake City: Deseret News Press, 1953), p. 312.
8. McKay, *Pathways to Happiness,* p. 126.

Chapter 13

1. William F. O'Neill and George D. Demos, *Education under Duress* (Los Angeles: LDI Books, 1971).

Chapter 14

1. Orson F. Whitney, "The School of Life," *Millennial Star*, 67 (1905): 497-501.
2. William J. Gilmore, *Reading Becomes a Necessity of Life* (Knoxville: University of Tennessee Press, 1989), pp. 20-21, 276.
3. E. B. Castle, *Educating the Good Man: Moral Education in Christian Times* (New York: Collier Books, 1962); Paul C. Vitz, *Censorship: Evidence of Bias in Our Children's Textbooks* (Ann Arbor: Servant Books, 1986).
4. A report on the experiment at State University of New York (SUNY) to incorporate a type of "structures of knowledge" emphasis related to teacher training and the four components of the curriculum is found in William E. Doll, "Preparing for the Post-Industrial Society: Oswego's New Direction in Teacher Education" (a paper presented at the AACTE meeting in Detroit, Mich., 23 February 1983).
5. Numerous recent studies address this vacuum. For example, Robert N. Bellah, *Habits of the Heart: Individualism and Commitment in American Life* (Los Angeles: University of California Press, 1985); A. James Reichley, *Religion in American Public Life* (Washington, D. C.: The Brookings Institution, 1985); Richard Vetterli and Gary Bryner, *In Search of the Republic: Public Virtue and the Roots of American Government* (Totowa, Ill.: Rowman and Littlefield, 1987); Neil J. Flinders, "Public School Textbooks: Reflections of a Shift in the Philosophical Foundations of American Education," *Proceedings of the Far Western Philosophy of Education Society*, 1986; Vitz, *Censorship: Evidence of Bias in Our Children's Textbooks*; Peter D. Hall, *The Organization of American Culture, 1700-1900* (New York: New York University Press, 1982).
6. Gregg R. Johnson, "A Comparison of the State Curriculum Objectives of Those States That Mandate Moral Education with Those States That Do Not," Ph.D. Dissertation, Brigham Young University, Provo, Utah, 1990.

7. Augustine's *Confessions* and *On Christian Doctrine*. Available in Robert M. Hutchins, *Great Books of the Western World*, vol. 18, 1952, as well as in many other editions. For additional evidence and discussions, see P. E. More, *Hellenistic Philosophies* (Princeton: Princeton University Press, 1923); *The Anti-Nicene Fathers* (9 vols.), American reprint of the Edinburgh edition (Grand Rapids, Mich.: Eerdmans, 1953), especially Clement and Origen; the Post-Nicene Fathers, especially Basil, Ambrose, and Augustine; W. H. C. Frend, *The Rise of Christianity* (Philadelphia: Fortress Press, 1984); J. L. Barker, *Apostasy from the Divine Church* (Salt Lake City: Deseret News Press, 1960); Edwin Hatch, *The Influence of Greek Ideas on Christianity* (New York: Harper & Row, Torchbooks, 1957), chaps. 2, 3, 5, 7, 9, 11; Hugh Nibley, *The World and the Prophets*, enl. ed. (Salt Lake City: Deseret Book Co., 1960), chaps. 4, 5, 9, 10, 11, 15, 31.

8. Thomas Aquinas, *Summa Theologica* (many editions available). A. C. Crombie, *Medieval and Early Modern Science* 2 vols. (Garden City, N. Y.: Doubleday Anchor Books, 1959), 1:33-97, 2:1-46; G. De Santillana, *The Crime of Galileo* (Chicago: University of Chicago Press, 1955); E. Gilson, *Reason and Revelation in the Middle Ages* (New York: Charles Scribners, 1938).

9. René Descartes, *Le Monde*, in R. Eaton, *Descartes Selections* (New York: Scribner, 1927); Isaac Newton Selections in H. S. Thayer, *Newton's Philosophy of Nature* (New York: Hafner Publishing Company, 1953), pp. i-xvi, 1-27, 41-67, 116-134, 141-145, 150-160, 168-179; W. Paley, *Natural Theology, Or, Evidences of the Existence and Attributes of The Deity* (London: Richardson and Co., 1821); D. J. Hutton, *Theory of the Earth* (1788).

10. A. Pierre Simon LaPlace, *Celestial Mechanics*, 1829; Charles Lyell, *Principles of Geology*, 1830; Karl Marx, *The Communist Manifesto*, 1847; Charles Darwin, *Origin of the Species*, 1859; Machen, *Christianity and Liberalism*, 1923; Randall, *The Making of the Modern Mind*, 1926; Lippmann, *A Preface to Morals*, 1929; Dewey, *A Common Faith*, 1934; E. A. Burtt, *The Metaphysical Foundations of Modern Physical Science* (Garden City, N.Y.: Doubleday and Co., 1954); Robert Jastrow, *Red Giants and White Dwarfs* (New York: Harper & Row, 1969); Kurtz, *Humanist Manifesto I* and *II*, 1973.

11. Kulp, *Educational Sociology* , pp. 26-27.
12. *HC,* 1:229.

Chapter 15
1. *HC,* 5:521.
2. Joseph Fielding Smith, *Gospel Doctrine,* p. 300.
3. Vance Packard, *A Nation of Strangers* (New York: David McKay Co., 1972).
4 Joseph F. Smith, "Home Life," *Juvenile Instructor 38* (March 1903):144-46.
5. Boyd K. Packer, "Eternal Marriage," *Speeches of the Year 1969-1970,* (Provo, Utah:Brigham Young University Press), p. 8.
6. Heber C. Kimball, *JD,* 3:105.

Chapter 16
1. William E. Roweton, *Creativity: A Review of Theory and Research* (Wisconsin Research and Development Center, University of Wisconsin, Madison, 1970), p. 15.

2. An ongoing debate has existed between scholars who favor the early Greek philosophies that held creation to be the product of forming from existing matter and those who prefer the doctrine of creation *ex nihilo*—making things out of nothing. However, even those who argue the necessity of the latter position because of certain Christian doctrines, such as the Resurrection, acknowledge that anciently the common belief was that existing materials are required in order to create. For example, see Jonathan Goldstein, "The Origins of the Doctrine of Creation Ex Nihilo," *Journal of Jewish Studies,* 35, no. 2 (Autumn 1984): 127-135, who states, "Believing Jews and Christians have long been convinced that their religion teaches that God created the world ex nihilo, from absolutely nothing. Yet medieval Jewish thinkers still held that the account of creation in Genesis could be interpreted to mean that God created from pre-existing formless matter, and ancient Jewish texts state that he did so" (p. 127). In a response to Goldstein's article, published in the same journal under the title "Creation Ex Nihilo Revisited: A Reply to Jonathan Goldstein, 37, no. 1 (Spring 1986): 88-91, David Winston notes that "there is no evidence that the rabbis were especially attached to a doctrine of creation *ex nihilo.* Indeed,

there is prima facie evidence that such a doctrine was far from being commonly accepted by them" (p. 91).

3. Genesis 1:26-27; Matthew 5:48 (KJV).

4. See also R. F. Biehler and J. Snowman, *Psychology Applied to Teaching*, 4th ed. (Boston: Houghton Mifflin Co., 1982). This text exhorts teachers to recognize that creative "activities should center on originality and creativity. Copying, assembling, prefabricated kits, filling in sections on paint-by-number pictures, and similar activities are less desirable" (p. 99).

5. J. C. Gowan, G. D. Demos, and E. P. Torrance, *Creativity: Its Educational Implications* (New York: John Wiley and Sons, 1967), p. 1.

6. Rowerton, *Creativity: A Review of Theory and Practice*, p. 15.

7. Textbooks of educational psychology offer an insight into this confusion. See, for example, David Ausubel, Joseph Novak, and Helen Hanesian, *Educational Psychology: A Cognitive View* (New York: Holt, Rinehart and Winston, 1978). This text claims *creativity* is one of the most vague, ambiguous and confused terms in psychology and education. Hershel Thornburg, *Introduction to Educational Psychology* (New York: West Publishing Co., 1984), doesn't even address the topic of *creativity*. Steven V. Owen et al., *Educational Psychology*, 2nd ed. (Boston: Little, Brown and Co., 1981), acknowledges that *creativity* remains as yet an elusive term and precise measurement is thus far impossible. Herbert J. Klausmeier, *Educational Psychology*, 5th ed. (New York: Harper & Row, 1985), leaves the impression that a sound body of knowledge regarding *creativity* exists and it is basically a matter of becoming informed.

8. Brewster Ghisein, ed., *The Creative Process* (Los Angeles: University of California Press, 1952), p. 11.

9. D. N. Perkins, *The Mind's Best Work* (Cambridge, Mass.: Harvard University Press, 1981), p. 2.

10. Ibid., p. 5.

11. Ibid., p. 245. See also H. E. Gruber, G. Terrel, and M. Wertheim, *Contemporary Approaches to Creative Thinking* (New York: Atherton Press, 1963), p. x.

12. *The Nag-Hammadi*, ed. James M. Robinson (New York: Harper & Row, 1977); Edgar Hennecke and Wilhelm

403

Schneemelcher, eds., *New Testament Apocrypha*, trans. A. J. B. Higgins et al., ed. R. McL. Wilson (Philadelphia: Westminster Press, 1963-66); James H. Charlesworth, ed., *The Old Testament Pseudepigrapha*, 2 vols. (Garden City, N.Y.: Doubleday and Company, 1983 and 1985); Hugh Nibley, "Apocryphal Writings," tape transcript edited by F.A.R.M.S., address given at a BYU Seminar held in Long Beach, California, 1968.
13. St. Augustine, *Concerning the Nature of God,* chap. XXVI.
14. H. H. Anderson, ed., *Creativity and Its Cultivation* (New York: Harper & Row, 1959), p. 1.
15. Ghiselin, *The Creative Process,* p. 9.
16. Gowan et al., *Creativity,* p. 2.
17. Gruber et al., *Contemporary Approaches,* p. x.

Chapter 17

404

1. See also P. D. Westbrook, *William Bradford* (Boston: Twayne Publishers, 1978).
2. Matthew M. F. Hilton "*The Contextual Framework of Opinions,* of the United States Supreme Court (1790-1987) and Its Relevance in the Evaluation of the Constitutionality of State Mandated Requirements for Moral Education," Ph.D. Dissertation, Brigham Young University, Provo, Utah, 1988 [A brief, yet fundamental overview of the legal context that confronts contemporary Americans, including participants in the public school, is outlined in the foregoing study of U.S. Supreme Court opinions (1790-1987). A computer-facilitated key-word search identified more than 14,000 contextual references in court opinions of words such as *education, morality, Deity,* and *religion.* These references were examined and reduced to a relevant collection. Subsequent analysis indicated that the Court has changed the presumptions it used in reaching decisions regarding the nature of rights and judicial review. The evidence documents the Court's twentieth-century shift from assumptions that sustained both a natural and a supernatural world view to an exclusively naturalistic perspective. These changes are reflected in three distinct periods—1790-1868; 1868-1943; 1943-present.] Note· The summaries of information used herein are by written permission and only for this publication. They are not to be

reproduced in any manner by any person or persons.

3. Ibid., p. 28.

4. Stephen J. Knezevich, *Administration of Public Education* (New York: Harper & Brothers, 1962), pp. 30-31.

5. Neil J. Flinders, *My Decision: An Act of Faith or a Piece of Cowardice* (Provo, Utah: MC Printing, 1984), p. 87.

6. This principle is found in many early documents. See, for example, Massachusetts Bill of Rights; Virginia Declaration of Rights; Utah Constitution (Declaration of Rights), Art. 1, Sec. 27.

Chapter 18

1. See Bruce Kimball, *Orators and Philosophers, a History of the Idea of Liberal Education* (New York: Teachers College, Columbia University, 1986); Nibley, *The World and the Prophets* (1954); Genevieve DeHoyos and Arturo DeHoyos, "The Search for Virtus et Veritas through an Inspired Scientific Method," *BYU Studies* 27, no. 4 (Fall 1987): 39-53; Neil J. Flinders, "Varieties of Scholarship," Brigham Young University, College of Education, unpublished ms., 1988, for a more detailed discussion of the idea of scholarship. Kimball's book offers a careful description of the two basic scholarly traditions most common to Western culture. Joseph L. Featherstone in the Foreword to Kimball's study briefly distinguishes between the two traditions by pointing out that

> The tradition of the philosophers holds that the pursuit of knowledge is the highest good: this is the line from Socrates and Plato and Aristotle to Boethius, the brilliant schoolmen of medieval Paris, the philosophies of the Enlightenment, T. H. Huxley, modern science, and the great research universities of the present. Its glory is the freedom of the intellect; its puzzle, as an educational philosophy, is what else to teach besides this freedom. (p. ix)

Featherstone then contrasts this philosophical tradition with the oratorical tradition.

> The tradition of the orators, on the other hand,

emphasizes the public expression of what is known, the crucial importance of language texts and tradition—linking to and building up a community of learning and knowledge. This is the line of Isocrates, Cicero, Isidore, the artes liberales of the Middle Ages and the Renaissance humanists, the vision of Matthew Arnold, of some teachers of the liberal arts today, especially humanities teachers, and, of course, of many religious colleges. The glory of the orator's line is its links with the texts of the past and its focus on recreating learning communities as the central business of education; its problem, as an educational philosophy, is its dogmatic and anti-intellectual idolatry of the past and its frequent assumption that virtue resides in the texts, not in what we the living make of them. (p. x)

Hugh Nibley identifies a third scholarly tradition and compares it with the premises of preachers, scholars, philosophers, gnostics, mystics, and reformers who have championed the other two traditions. The introductory paragraph to Nibley's study notes:

> In the realm of the mind, in letters, the arts, and in most of the sciences, it was the ancient Greeks, most educated people will concede, who walked off with nearly all the first prizes. It is hard to say anything on any but the most specialized and technical matters that some Greek many centuries ago did not say better. If any people ever knew and lived life well and fully, it was the chosen spirits among the Greeks. They explored every avenue of human experience; they sought truth as persistently and as honestly as men can ever be expected to seek; and, sounding the depths and skirting the outmost bounds of man's wisdom, came to the unanimous conclusion that the wisdom of man is nothing. (p. 1)

Nibley goes on to point out that Justin Martyr described for the Greeks of his day the fundamental difference between the revelatory or faithful tradition of scholarship and that of the orators and the philosophers. Referring to the most important inquiries of life he said:

"Neither by nature nor by human skill," wrote Justin Martyr, ". . . is it possible for men to know such high and holy things; but only by a gift that descends from above upon holy men from time to time." Justin explains elsewhere that these men are called prophets and are a type of human entirely unknown to the heathen world. "They do not need training in speech or skill in controversy and argument, . . . but only to keep themselves pure to receive the power of the Spirit of God, so that the divine plectrum can express itself through them as on the strings of a lyre, making use of righteous men and revealing to them the knowledge of sacred and heavenly things. Wherefore they all speak as with a single mouth and single tongue . . . concerning all things which is needful for us to know. . . . The fact that they all agree, though speaking at widely separated times and places, is the proof of their divinity. . . ." God can play on them as a plectrum plucks the strings of a lyre because they are prepared to vibrate to his touch—not by virtue of any special training, and not whenever *they* choose to respond, but whenever it pleases God "from time to time. . . ." Thus when Justin wishes to prove to a Jewish friend that the truth has now passed from the Jewish to the Christian community, his one argument is that the gift of prophecy, once enjoyed by the Jews, has now been transferred to his own people the proof of which, he says, is "that prophetic gifts are to be found among us to the present day, such as were anciently shared among you." (p. 3)

407

The articles by the DeHoyos and Flinders indicate that this faithful approach to scholarship can extend beyond the role of receiving revelation regarding "sacred and heavenly things" as described by Justin Martyr. This tradition also embraces the primary objectives of the other two traditions described above—namely, searching the records of past human experience and examining the order of nature. The primary rule of this tradition seems to be that man is obligated to do all that he can with the truth and light that is already available to him (to be "anxiously engaged in a good cause" of his own volition and not wait to be "compelled in all things" D&C 58:26-29). He is to seek learning by "study and also by faith" (D&C 88:118). Joseph Smith combined these methods in preparing the Joseph Smith Translation of the Bible, and the Brother of Jared used multiple techniques in solving the physical problem of lighting the barges which carried his party to the Western hemisphere (Ether 3:1-6). The tradition of faithful scholarship is not reserved for an academic elite, for God is no respecter of persons, but is available to all at their level of development. The requirement to continue in it, however, is dependent on the willingness of participants to acknowledge the partnership it entails with divine influences (D&C 59:21).

The faithful tradition constitutes the framework for Moses' Pentateuch, Lehi's rational treatise to his son, Jacob, Joseph Smith's report of his experience with the First Vision, William Bradford's penning *Of Plimmoth Plantation*, and George Washington's expressed assessment of his role in the American Revolution (see Matthew M. F. Hilton, "Freedom For All," unpublished paper based on Washington's correspondence, Draper, Utah, copyright 1986, 1987).

2. Louise L. Stevenson in her *Scholarly Means to Evangelical Ends* (Baltimore: Johns Hopkins University Press, 1986) documents in detail the story of the New Haven scholars.
3. Ibid., pp. 38-39.
4. Nibley, *The World and the Prophets*, p. 98.
5. Ibid., pp. 98-99.
6. Daryl Gibson, "David Allan: Out of This World," *This People* 8 (May/June 1987): 57-58.
7. Russell M. Nelson, *The Power within Us* (Salt Lake City: Deseret Book Co., 1988), p. 31.
8. A personal account by Joan Flinders, used by permission.
9. A personal account by Ann Miner, used by permission.
10. A personal account by Dana T. Griffen, used by permission.

Chapter 19

1. *Family Home Evening Manual*, 1981, The Church of Jesus Christ of Latter-day Saints, p. 20.
2. Brigham Young, *JD*, 9:188-189.

Chapter 20

1. Edward L. Thorndike, *The Principles of Teaching: Based on Psychology* (New York: A. G. Seiler, 1906), p. 8.
2. Watson, *Behaviorism*, p. 6.
3. Victor H. Noll, Dale P. Scannell, Robert C. Craig, eds., *Introduction to Educational Measurement*, 4th ed. (Boston: Houghton Mifflin, 1979), p. 271.
4. David Owen, *None of the Above: Behind the Myth of Scholastic Aptitude* (Boston: Houghton Mifflin Co., 1985), p. xvi.
5. Ernest L. Boyer, *College: The Undergraduate Experience in America* (New York: Harper & Row, 1987), pp. 35-36.
6. Samuel Bowles and Herbert Gintis, *Schooling in Capitalist America* (New York: Basic Books, 1976), p. 108.
7. Ibid., p. 211.
8. Ibid., pp. 287-288.
9. *How Effective Is Schooling? A Critical Review of Synthesis of Research Findings,* R-965-PCSF (Santa Monica: Rand Corporation, March 1972), reprinted as Averch, Harvey et al., *How Effective Is Schooling? A Critical Review of Research* (Englewood Cliffs, N.J.: Educational Technology Publications, 1974); *Are America's High Schools Effective?* Institute for Social Research Newsletter, Autumn 1972 (Ann Arbor: University of Michigan); Christopher Jencks et al., *Inequality, A Reassessment of the Effect of Family and Schooling in America* (New York: Basic Books, 1972).
10. For example, see United States Department of Education, *What Works: Research about Teaching and Learning* (Washington, D.C.: Government Printing Office, 1986); John Goodlad, *A Place Called School* (New York: McGraw Hill Publishing Co., 1984).
11. Paul Hanus, "Improving School Systems by Scientific Management," *National Education Association Journal of Proceedings and Addresses* 1913, p. 250; italics mine.
12. Brigham Young, *JD*, 8:37.
13. See Paul L. Dressel's *Handbook of Academic Evaluation* (San Francisco: Jossey-Bass Publishers, 1976), pp. 265-279, for a discussion of the strengths and weaknesses of grades in the societal model.

Chapter 21

1. Ms. History of Brigham Young, 1846-47, located in Historical Department, Library-Archives, of The Church of Jesus Christ of Latter-day Saints, Salt Lake City, Utah.
2. Brigham Young, *JD*, 18:244.
3. John Taylor, *JD*, 26:114.
4. Spencer W. Kimball, "The Angels May Quote from It," *New Era*, October 1975, p. 5.
5. *Messages of the First Presidency,* vol. II (Salt Lake City: Bookcraft, 1965), p. 349.
6. Ezra Taft Benson, in *CR*, October 1978, p. 43.
7. *Instructions to Stake Presidents on the Implementation of the Family Home Evening Program* (Salt Lake City: First Presidency of The Church of Jesus Christ of Later-day Saints, 1964).
8. Harold B. Lee, in *CR*, 1963, p. 82.
9. Ibid., April 1973, p. 130.
10. Harold B. Lee, "The Home Evening," *Improvement Era*, January 1967, pp. 22-23.
11. Harold B. Lee, in *CR*, October 1964, p. 80.
12. A. Theodore Tuttle, "The Home Is to Teach," *Improvement Era*, December 1969, pp. 107-108.
13. Boyd K. Packer's address at the Regional Representatives Conference, 27 June 1974.
14. Boyd K. Packer, in *CR*, p. 139.
15. Stephen L. Richards, in *CR*, October 1921, pp. 197-198.
16. George Albert Smith, in *CR*, April 1926, p. 145.
17. McKay, *Pathways to Happiness*, p. 118.
18. Joseph F. Smith, in *CR*, April 1906, p. 3.
19. Ibid.
20. President Spencer W. Kimball's address to Regional Representatives, 30 March 1979.
21. President Spencer W. Kimball's address to Regional Representatives, 31 March 1978, pp. 3-4.

Postscript

1. Lorenzo Snow, in *CR*, October 1899, p. 27.
2. John Taylor, *JD*, 6 (November 1964): 106.
3. George Q. Cannon, ibid., 11:33-34.
4. Amasa M. Lyman, ibid., 3:191-192.

Index

413

414

415